Erotic Journeys

Erotic Journeys

Mexican Immigrants and Their Sex Lives

Gloria González-López

UNIVERSITY OF CALIFORNIA PRESS

Berkeley / Los Angeles / London

University of California Press
Berkeley and Los Angeles, California

University of California Press, Ltd.
London, England

© 2005 by The Regents of the University of California

Library of Congress Cataloging-in-Publication Data

González-López, Gloria, 1960–
    Erotic journeys : Mexican immigrants and their sex lives / Gloria
González-López.
        p.   cm.
    Includes bibliographical references and index.
    ISBN 0-520-23083-3 (cloth : alk. paper) — ISBN 0-520-23139-2
(pbk. : alk. paper)
    1. Mexican Americans — California — Los Angeles — Sexual behavior.
2. Immigrants — California — Los Angeles — Sexual behavior.
3. Mexican Americans — California — Los Angeles — Social conditions.
4. Immigrants — California — Los Angeles — Social conditions.
5. Sex — Social aspects — California — Los Angeles.   6. Los Angeles
(Calif.) — Social conditions.   7. Los Angeles (Calif.) — Ethnic relations.
I. Title.

F869.L89M5175   2005
306.7'089'68720794 — dc22   2004062036

Manufactured in the United States of America

13   12   11   10   09   08   07   06   05
10   9   8   7   6   5   4   3   2   1

Printed on Ecobook 50 containing a minimum 50% post-consumer waste,
processed chlorine free. The balance contains virgin pulp, including 25%
Forest Stewardship Council Certified for no old growth tree cutting,
processed either TCF or ECF. The sheet is acid-free and meets the minimum
requirements of ANSI/NISO Z39.48–1992 (R 1997) (Permanence of Paper).♾

Para ti, mamá,
por tu amor desmedido e incondicional
y por enseñarme a volar y a soñar
y por acariciar siempre
mis alas y mis sueños.

En su memoria,
con cariño, gratitud y admiración
Gloria E. Anzaldúa (1942–2004)
Lionel Cantú Jr. (1965–2002)

Contents

Acknowledgments

Many generous people have made this book possible. First, I want to express my heartfelt gratitude to the sixty immigrant women and men who opened their hearts and souls and trusted me with their personal life and sexual stories. I have done everything possible to make sure this book is an honest and genuine reflection of their accounts. And second, I am grateful to those who helped me to immerse myself in their stories in order to give life to this study.

With profound *cariño*, respect, and admiration I acknowledge Pierrette Hondagneu-Sotelo for being an enthusiastic and encouraging mentor and friend for more than ten years. Without her academic guidance, unconditional encouragement, and critical revisions of different drafts, this book would have not been conceived. *Pierrette querida, de todo corazón mil gracias por siempre.* María Patricia Fernández-Kelly and Barrie Thorne stimulated my intellectual curiosity and growth and helped me with valuable and insightful comments at different stages of this project. I feel profoundly indebted, humbled, and honored for the time, energy, and dedication both of them invested to help nurture my work.

I also appreciate the many supportive professionals, activists, community organizers, friends, *compañeras* and *compañeros* who cooperated during the sampling process. I want to thank Antonio Bernabé, Francisco Cacho, Reyna Campos, Natividad Encarnación, Alice Heidy, Walter Iglesias, Irma Radillo, María Eugenia Sotelo Regil, María E. Zepeda, and all the volunteers and professionals, who along the way, unconditionally helped me identify study participants at many supportive institutions in Los Angeles. I thank these community-based organizations and schools for helping me recruit study participants and for their priceless support during the research process. My special gratitude goes to the Mexican Consulate for offering me the *Nuestra Familia* book and other didactic materials, which I used as an incentive for my informants.

Many mentors, colleagues, and friends have stimulated my feminist thinking and my intellectual curiosity in the field of gender and sexuality studies. Thank you for your support at different stages of this project: Tomás Almaguer, Constance R. Ahrons, Ernestine Avila, Lionel Cantú, Héctor Carrillo, Wendy Chapkis, Robert W. Connell, Diane di Mauro, Rafael M. Díaz, Manuel Fernández Alemany, Judith Grant, Matthew C. Gutmann, Gilbert Herdt, Michael A. Messner, Sharmila Rudrappa, Denise A. Segura, Jodi O'Brien, and Patricia Zavella. All of you are an inspiration; you have a special place in my heart.

Those who kindly edited parts or entire versions of the book manuscript include my good friends Patricia Emerson and William Rodarmor. They contributed their generous support as I struggled to find my voice in English without getting lost in translation. My gratitude goes to Naomi Schneider for encouraging and supporting this project as I went through that experience.

I acknowledge the generous financial support I received from different institutions: the Social Science Research Council for the dissertation fellowship I received through its Sexuality Research Fellowship Program; the University of California for the President's Postdoctoral Fellowship at the University of California at Berkeley; the Ford Foundation for a faculty award through the "Sexuality, Inequality, and Health: Practitioner Training Initiative" at San Francisco State University, Project Director, Gilbert Herdt; and a University Cooperative Society Subvention Grant awarded by the University of Texas at Austin. The latter provided funding for artistic and photographic work and editing. I have been fortunate to have had the support of José E. Limón, Director of the Center for Mexican American Studies, and Debra Umberson, Chair of the Department of Sociology at the University of Texas at Austin, to finish this project while a novice assistant professor. I want to express my gratitude to Victoria E. Rodríguez and Peter M. Ward for their encouragement, guidance, and support while I worked on the book. I want to thank Christine L. Williams for her insightful comments as I struggled with the final version of this manuscript — thanks for being such a terrific and supportive mentor, colleague, and friend. Lastly, I express my appreciation to Carol A. Chavez for being a patient and helpful research assistant who kindly helped me in various tasks in the completion of the manuscript.

I would never have written this book without the support of those who love me the most. Yo no hubiera podido escribir este libro sin el apoyo de quienes me aman más. Dedicar este libro a mi familia es un gesto tan modesto ante la inmensa gratitud que siento hacia mi madre por sus cuidados, dedicación y entrega amorosa de toda una vida, hacia mi padre por sus incontables enseñanzas y su valiosa presencia, y hacia mis hermanas y hermanos por su fraternal cariño y apoyo. Deseo también expresar mi profundo agradecimiento a mis entrañables amistades, a mi solidario amigo de más de una década y compañero de amor durante una etapa muy especial en este lado de la frontera, y a un hombre de sabiduría y bondad que me ha ayudado a transformar mi vida en este país. Por acompañarme en mis emocionales travesías desde que llegué a Estados Unidos, a todas y todos gracias por siempre, de todo corazón.

Austin, Texas
Fall 2004

Introduction

Me enseñaron a ser discreta, correcta y callada. Así que con toda corrección discreta me he metido contigo en la cama y como parte de lo bien educada, nada voy a decir. Así todos quedamos conformes.

I was taught to be discreet, proper, and silent. So with all appropriate discretion, I have jumped into bed with you, and since I am well brought up, I won't tell anyone about it. That way, everybody is happy.

María Elena Olivera, Revista Fem, 1995

In the fall of 1995, I started a Latina women's support group at a Los Angeles inner-city elementary school, consisting of eight adult women, mostly from Mexico. They were all mothers, and all said they were heterosexual. They all were or had been in a relationship with a man. I led the women in discussions about many of their personal concerns, including issues such as self-esteem, domestic violence, drug abuse, family life, and parenting skills. Group members met every week for a total of ten months, but during the first weeks, they didn't talk about their sex lives. After I questioned them about their silence on that topic, the women asked whether it was permissible to discuss sex-related themes. As they developed relationships with each other, the women finally began to explore their sexual concerns, fantasies, and fears. Participating in this collective experience drew me to what would become the topic of my doctoral dissertation as a sociologist: Mexican immigrant women and their sex lives.

Women undergo erotic transformations as part of their immigrant experience — that was one of the lessons I learned from my women's group. The sexual journeys that take place in the apparent isolation and privacy of their bedrooms are not divorced from their social contexts and circumstances. Instead, they are linked to the women's experiences as immigrants. Their interactions within their communities, schools, and support networks shape their behaviors and thoughts during sexual encounters with their partners.

The women's group experience led me to pursue three research questions: (1) How does immigration and life in the United States affect the sex lives of heterosexual Mexican immigrant women? (2) What sexual beliefs and practices do Mexican immigrant women bring to the United States, and how do these change in the new social context? (3) How do various dimensions of migration, such as social networks and the changing experiences of work, media, motherhood, and religion, reshape sexual ideologies and practices? To answer these questions, I approached various inner-city, community-based agencies and elementary schools serving Latino families in the city of Los Angeles to recruit and interview forty Mexican immigrant, mostly Catholic, women.

These forty Mexicanas defined sex as a fluid construct and not necessarily dangerous. This was true even among incest and rape survivors who had developed non-abusive, loving relationships with other partners. In those cases, the women reported experiences of love and erotic intimacy with men with whom they explored sexuality in safe, pleasurable ways. The diverse sexual stories of those who had never been abused also stimulated my intellectual curiosity. As I heard all the women's stories, I realized that gender and sexual identity can be nuanced and complex concepts, bringing both pain and bliss. The notion of gender as a relational category — as well as all the theorizing of multiple expressions of feminine and masculine identities — kept coming to my mind. Eventually, my work forced me to revisit my own family life. I thought of my younger brother, cleaning my apartment, cooking, and washing the dishes while I worked on my dissertation; of my older brother, ironing his own shirts while getting ready for his busy job as a manager in my highly industrialized Mexican hometown of Monterrey; and of my father, fixing mole and rice for me during my Christmas visits to Mexico. Thinking about the men in my family helped me realize that I needed to learn about the social, economic, historical, cultural, and psychological complexities linked to the construction of Mexican masculinities and sexualities, and their nuanced connections with the various expressions of women's sexualities.

As I prepared for my examinations with professors Pierrette

Hondagneu-Sotelo (my dissertation chair), and later with Patricia Fernández-Kelly and Barrie Thorne, I reflected on their observations. Many questions emerged: How are men's heterosexual identities socially constructed by Mexican society? What would Mexican men have to say about the ways the same society constructs women's heterosexual identities? What are the personal, emotional, and sexual costs Mexican men pay because of these social prescriptions? What are heterosexual men's vulnerabilities in a patriarchal society? Is sex only about power? What promotes heterosexual women's subordination and what does not? Why, how, and under what conditions do Mexican masculinities condition (or not) heterosexual women's identities? What can we learn from Mexican masculinities that can help us understand women's heterosexual experiences within a relational context and without neglecting the subordinated position of some men, such as the case of immigrant men? In short, what could I learn about heterosexual Mexican immigrant men? My motivation to begin exploring these questions was powerful, as was the encouragement I received from my mentors to build on my original project by incorporating additional, complementary interviews with a group of twenty Mexican immigrant men.

By bringing in men's personal experiences and voices, I have built on the narratives obtained from my earlier interviews with women on heterosexual relationships within both couple and family relationship contexts. The present study is also motivated by my own journey. I was born and educated, through undergraduate years, in Mexico, before immigrating to the United States, so my own experiences as a woman migrant make me an insider. I share the same social and cultural complexities with regard to sex and the erotic that my female and male informants brought to the United States. After migrating, I too experienced many of the challenges, adventures, and disenchantments discussed in this book.

Purpose of the Study

"So why do you want to interview men if you're just going to say that we're a bunch of machos?" That was Marcos's first response when I phoned to invite him to participate in this study. The narratives of my Mexican women informants had led me to reexamine my academic training, which had been dominated by Western theories of feminism and gender. Yet, it was the perspectives of Mexican men that ultimately invited me to challenge the Western feminist ideologies and theories I had been exposed to in graduate school. After examining both women's and men's narratives, I gradually became more analytical and less ideological. As Chandra Talpade Mohanty said about feminism: "Men exploit, women are exploited. Such simplistic formulations are historically reductive; they are also ineffectual in designing strategies to combat oppressions. All they do is reinforce binary divisions between men and women" (1991, 64).

This book blurs those separations: it complicates the dominant feminist scholarship that polarizes women against men and that excludes women and men of color and their experiences of heterosexual love and sex. To accomplish that goal, I situate both Mexican women's and men's histories of their sex lives at the center of my analysis. And by concentrating on their pre- and post-migration sex stories, I claim that heterosexual experiences of gender and sexuality cannot be understood in isolation but from a relational perspective. In doing so, this sociological study explores research questions about both women and men designed to accomplish four objectives: (1) examine the social, cultural, and historical contexts shaping my respondents' sex lives as they evolved in Mexico and during and after migration to and settlement in the United States; (2) explore the nuances and complexities of their erotic experiences as they simultaneously embraced a dominant sexual identity (i.e., heterosexuality) and marginalized social identities, such as being Mexican, monolingual, second-class citizens, and socioeconomically segregated; (3) study their heterosexual experiences as relational processes that are fluid, nuanced, changing, contextual, and contested; and (4) incorporate Mexican men's experiences of heterosexual sex, love, and relationships in order to study the demands and sacrifices patriarchal contexts impose upon them.

Migrant Sexualities: Conceptual and Theoretical Contributions

The sex lives of the people in this study are revealing. First, the majority of the married women (70 percent) were not virgins when they married. I explore the disjuncture between the first sexual encounters of my women respondents and a generalized belief that Mexican Catholic women value virginity. The women's narratives, for instance, suggest the existence of multiple femininities and heterosexualities within the context of Mexican society. These experiences of femininity reveal tensions, contradictions, and fluidity that allow women to have sexual agency and pleasure but also to be exposed to forms of control and danger. As they migrate, women continue reinventing these gendered and sexualized processes in flux. Second, I argue that it is not just Catholicism but an entire social system that teaches women and men to value virginity as a form of social capital. Women's perceptions of their sexualized bodies explain why and how they may use virginity — represented by an intact hymen — as a commodity they may exchange to improve their living conditions and their socioeconomic future. I introduce the concept of *capital femenino* to explain how women and men assign a higher or lower value to a woman's premarital virginity depending on the socioeconomic context in which they grow to maturity. As a social construction, virginity is expressed through public symbols. A woman's emblematic virtue is not private; it becomes a family and a community asset. Third, men's recollections of their sexual experiences confirm women's perceptions of virginity, and they also uncover the gender inequalities men are exposed to in patriarchal societies. Men's expressions of masculinities are situated within and shaped by regionally defined socioeconomic forces. I introduce the concept of regional patriarchies to argue that patriarchy is not uniform or monolithic, and also to explain how local expressions of hegemony affect not only women but men's lives as well. The men I interviewed were exposed to social expectations and exigencies including but not limited to forced sexual initiation and coercive marriage as expressions of manhood and masculinity. And fourth, these dynamics are exposed to the paradoxical challenges immigrants face. The United States — once the promised land for all of these informants — poses sexual threats for many of them. Immigrants experience an imaginary transition from tradition to modernity, from rigidity to flexibility, but newcomers' dreams may become American nightmares, fueled by the social fears that permeate immigrants' sex lives. A culture of sexual fear is present in both Mexico and the United States, and is aggravated among immigrants to Los Angeles by HIV/AIDS, the sexual abuse and kidnapping of children, promiscuity, the dangers associated with drug and alcohol use, and gang violence. But fear and apprehension are only one force transforming immigrants' perceptions of sexuality in the United States. Their erotic journeys are also shaped by social networks, women's paid employment, demanding schedules, and a fast-paced routine, among other social factors invading the most private moments of their personal lives.

In Los Angeles, my Mexican respondents revisited and reconstituted sexual beliefs and practices through community networks, work, media,

religion, casual and formal romantic relationships, and family life, including the experience of motherhood and fatherhood. And as a result of
migration, they were able to transform their multiple experiences of femininity and masculinity. Before migrating, these women and men were
exposed to various regional patriarchies, which in turn reproduced
regional femininities and masculinities. The local hegemonies in Mexico
were constructed through regional and cultural differentiation — the axis
of state-building processes in Mexican society. As Jeffrey W. Rubin
argues: "The Mexican state and regime should be perceived as parts of a
complex and changing center that coexists with and is constituted and
embedded in the diversity of regional and cultural constructions evolving
throughout Mexico since the 1930s" (1996, 86).

Rubin identifies the center as Mexico City, "an institutional apparatus
of power and decision making, and a set of 'national' cultural discourses"
(86). His examinations of the Mexican state reflect celebrated Foucauldian
notions of power as a decentralized social force embracing fluidity in its
essence, emanating from different directions, and creating resistance as it
is exercised through social interactions (Foucault 1979). Even though
Foucault has been criticized for not including gender in his theorizing,
this particular conceptualization of power informs the regional patriarchal
processes underlying the multiple sexualities existing in Mexican society.

The men's heterosexual narratives I discuss in this book expand on
state-of-the-art research on Latino men, masculinities, and sexualities.
While Mexican men and gay and bisexual experiences have received special attention across disciplines in both nations, heterosexual love and sex
have remained practically unexamined.[1] Research by Gutmann (1996),
Amuchástegui (2001), Carrillo (2002), and Hirsch (2003) has gradually
begun to close this gap. This book expands on Gutmann's 1996 study and
similarly demonstrates that there is not one but multiple masculinities in
Mexican society. By proposing the term *regional patriarchies* I seek to
explain how women and men are exposed to diverse, fluid, and malleable
but regionally uniform and locally defined expressions of hegemony and
their corresponding sexual moralities. While shaped by the socioeconomics of a local region, each one of these patriarchies takes myriad forms
and promotes various levels of gender inequality. The notion of regional
patriarchies identifies gender patterns in Mexican society based on Belinda
Bozzoli's examinations of "The 'Patchwork Quilt' of Patriarchies" in
South Africa (Bozzoli 1983, 149) and R. W. Connell's analyses of gender
and multiple masculinities as social constructions (Connell 1987, 1995).
Gender relations and diverse representations of masculinity are not the

same across historical, social, and cultural contexts. They are fluid and reproduced in social interaction, through social practice, and in particular social and geographical situations (Connell 1987). "Masculinities are configurations of practice within gender relations, a structure that includes large-scale institutions and economic relations as well as face-to-face relationships and sexuality" (Connell 2000, 29).

The terms *macho* and *machismo* have a sophisticated history and different shades of meaning in Mexico and Latin America. I deliberately did not use these terms in my interviews, and I discussed them only to probe after my informants used them. Interestingly, as I interviewed women and men, these concepts began to emerge with a consistent meaning. Several of my informants systematically brought up and freely used *macho, machismo,* and *machista* in order to describe sexist beliefs and practices in their life narratives. In their stories, however, sexism was neither a uniform nor a unidirectional force; it was flexible and alternatively reinforced, reproduced, and contested by both women and men. Accordingly, men embraced regional expressions of multiple masculinities which were not necessarily hegemonic.[2] These social dynamics either promote or challenge gender inequities, and as a consequence socially reproduce the existence of numerous and contrasting meanings and patterns of both women's and men's sexual identities. The notion of manifold sexualities and gender identities in Mexico supports Gutmann — along with other social scientists across disciplines — as he issues a warning against making sweeping generalizations and promoting stereotypes or traditional representations of Mexican women and men (see Baca Zinn 1982).

Why Mexican Immigrants? Why Heterosexuality?

This present study is innovative for three reasons. First, the sociology of immigration has remained "desexualized" — it has overlooked immigrants' sex lives. Extensive research has examined many aspects of immigrant men's (and more recently women's) lives, with a special interest in labor markets, economics, and political activism, and, more recently, family life, gender relations, and religion, among others.[3] A special concern about social and cultural change among immigrants has placed gender at the center of Mexican immigration analyses. For instance, Hondagneu-Sotelo's *Gendered Transitions* (1994) both inspires and informs this study. Just as with the women and men Hondagneu-Sotelo studied in Northern California, the immigrants who gave life to the present work redefined gender and power relations within migration and settlement contexts as they engaged in sexualized feelings, attitudes, and acts. The present study is also innovative because it focuses on the creation of heterosexual norms. The sociology of sexualities has examined the experiences of gays and lesbians since the mid-1970s. A long history of homophobia, marginality, segregation, along with the HIV/AIDS epidemic, has resulted in extensive sociological research that studies down on sex. That is, gay and lesbian experiences are examined within the social structure of power and control wherein the privileged group (i.e., heterosexuals) determines what is normative as socially accepted, appropriate, and "normal" in terms of human sexuality. In contrast, studying up on sex, that is, examining heterosexuality as the norm, has rarely been investigated. The third reason this study is innovative is that Latina and Latino sexuality research in the United States has remained confined within the behavioral, public health, and epidemiological sciences. This voluminous research literature — prompted by HIV/AIDS concerns — has been dominated by acculturation and assimilation models. Here, I attempt to fill in a gap in the migration and gender and sexualities subdisciplines within sociology by challenging the assumptions and theoretical models explaining Latina and Latino sexualities. This study offers an alternative sociological perspective that explores the intimate intricacies of Mexican migrants' eroticism, not in a social vacuum but within migration contexts vulnerable to redefined definitions of gender relations, socioeconomic segregation, and inequality.

Methods

The women and men presented in this book narrated their sex histories through open-ended interviews that lasted three hours, on average. The informants had migrated to the United States when they were at least twenty years old, and they were between the ages of twenty-five and forty-five at the time of our interviews. All of them had lived in the United States between five and fifteen years. Half of the sample (20 women, 10 men) was born and raised in the state of Jalisco; the other half included individuals born and raised in Mexico City. Although some of the study participants reported same-sex fantasies and practices, they all identified themselves as heterosexual during our interviews. I use pseudonyms in order to protect the confidentiality and privacy of my respondents. Appendix A offers the demographic characteristics of study informants.

Jalisco and Mexico City represent two of the main locations sending Mexican immigrant women coming to the United States through Tijuana. California is the destination of immigrants from Jalisco, the state that sends the highest number of immigrant workers to the United States and the state with the highest incidence of AIDS cases related to migration (Salgado de Snyder, Díaz-Pérez, and Maldonado 1996). Similarly, Mexico City has the largest proportion of ill individuals who have lived in the United States (Bronfman, Camposortega, and Medina 1989). Conservative and traditional sexual attitudes have been associated with the sexuality of Mexican adolescent women living in Guadalajara, the capital of Jalisco and the second-largest city in Mexico (Baird 1993). Jalisco also encompasses pre- and semi-industrialized rural areas. This western state is the birthplace of tequila, mariachi music, and a *charro* culture, all dominant folklore images central to the creation of masculinist identities. Jalisco lies adjacent to the state of Michoacán, where *el rapto* or *el robo* (literally, the "kidnap-ping" or "stealing" of a woman) and rape prevailed in the 1950s and 1960s (Wilson 1990; Hirsch 2003). The urban sophistication of Mexico City has been associated with increased employment and education opportunities for women, which in turn may promote more egalitarian sexual views among both genders. Based on my clinical experience with Mexican immigrant women — I have a background in couple and family psycho-therapy — it takes at least five years of permanent residence in the United States for them to establish a relatively stable personal life.

I interviewed the women in my sample during the 1997–98 academic year, after approaching three elementary schools and four community-based clinics located in inner-city Latino immigrant barrios. One of the immigrant women in the support group I conducted at the school agreed to participate in the study; I identified the rest of the participants by using a snowball sampling technique at the seven research sites. None of these additional thirty-nine women had participated in any type of women's support group at those locations, and none had been a former client of mine. A few had attended HIV/AIDS-related talks, or *pláticas,* at some of the agencies. I attended meetings at the parents' centers of the schools (e.g., ESL classes for parents, parenting classes, PTA meetings, etc.) to identify potential participants. I also located potential candidates for the project by visiting the crowded reception rooms of the various clinics where large groups of Latina immigrant women were waiting to be called for their doctor appointments.

I identified and interviewed the men after calling and visiting profes-sionals at the same agencies and schools where I had located the women

who participated in this project. In addition, I took part in meetings at
the Mexican consulate in Los Angeles and established contact with rep-
resentatives of hometown associations, community organizers, and leaders of employment centers for *jornaleros* — day laborers. After I described
my dissertation research project with the women and my desire to expand
the project by interviewing men in order to write a book, many of these
leaders invited me to meetings at their centers and organizations.

My professional identity as *la doctora* — as many men began to call
me — inspired respect and curiosity in the men. Some asked me questions
about my project or insisted that I listen to their stories about sex workers and women being raped in their small towns. Other men asked me if
I could provide professional counseling with respect to their relationships
with their partners, daughters, or wives. Because of the dual relationship
that could potentially emerge, I did not give them a consultation and
referred them to a professional in the Los Angeles area. A snowball sampling technique helped me to recruit all of my informants at these community organizations and employment centers. I interviewed the men
between fall 2000 and summer 2001 as a postdoctoral fellow in the
Department of Sociology at the University of California at Berkeley.
These male informants were not related to or acquainted with any of the
forty women interviewed during the 1997–98 academic year.

I personally conducted all of the women's interviews at the informants'
homes or at a private office at the school or clinic. Similarly, I conducted
all of my interviews with the men mainly at agencies, schools, employment centers, or in their homes. At their request, I interviewed all of the
women and men in Spanish. As an expression of personal appreciation for
participating, I gave each participant books on literature, mathematics,
and geography that I requested and received free of charge from the
Mexican consulate.

I conducted informal participant observations during the Latina
women's support group meetings I led for ten months at the elementary
school. I obtained authorization from the group members to use this
material for research purposes, and it helped me to design the open-ended
question guide I used during my subsequent interviews. In my interviews, I explored the following subjects: sexuality: general concepts; religion and sexuality; sex education in the home; puberty and adolescence;
sexuality and media; sexuality, AIDS, and sexually transmitted diseases;
sexuality, immigration, and cultural differences; sexuality and social institutions, contexts, and networks in the United States; sex education: current beliefs and attitudes as a mother; personal reactions to real-life situ-

ations (vignettes); interviewees' personal information; and interviewees' personal reactions to the interview.[4] My interviews with the men were similar and explored many of the topics I discussed with the women, including questions aimed at exploring the men's reactions to my findings with the women.

In my in-depth, open-ended question interview guide, I incorporated recollections of past experiences of what I identify as storytelling and personal reactions to vignettes. Storytelling triggers past life events recollected in the present. In Ken Plummer's *Telling Sexual Stories* (1995), he collected the coming-out stories of homosexuals and the recovery tales of women rape survivors. He demonstrates how reconstructing past stories through storytelling becomes a sociological phenomenon: stories help organize the flow of interaction, binding together or disrupting the relation of self to other and community. In his study, rape stories (recovery stories) feed upon and into community. That is, they connect the spheres of what is public and private, secret or known about. In his words: "Sexual stories lay down routes to a coherent past, mark off boundaries and contrasts in the present, and provide both a channel and a shelter for the future" (172). Plummer urges sociologists to see and analyze grounded storytelling activities and their links to social structures.

In a related way, Marta Rivas (1996) did research in Mexico that demonstrates the value of articulating sexual narratives as the best way for Mexican women to organize personal sex histories. Rivas cites Jerome Bruner (1990) to argue that narrative is one of the most common everyday life ways to express and organize language and an ideal vehicle to express and give shape to one's personal experiences. Similarly, Oliva M. Espín (1999) uses narrative techniques in her psychological research of women's sex lives as part of their migration experiences from different countries to the United States.

"Personal reactions to vignettes" consist of the researcher reading a passage to the informant and inviting her/him to verbally articulate ideas, thoughts, and feelings in response. The purpose of this technique, particularly in this study, was to gather from my informants a self-built ideology about sexual morality and controversial issues and dilemmas. I read texts (including a passage from *La Carta al Papa*, which I discuss in the last chapter) describing specific cases where the central character (or characters) is a Mexican woman exhibiting particular behaviors and/or attitudes in regard to sexuality and religion.[5]

After collecting the data, I typed verbatim transcripts of my interviews. I read and examined the interview transcripts to identify significant and recurrent themes. On the basis of those themes I categorized and coded my data in order to develop theoretical analyses (see Appendix B for a discussion of the methodological considerations involved in this project). All translations of quotations from works originally published in Spanish are mine.

I am not offering concrete, linear analyses of women's sexual practices "before" and "after" migration. My work is based on the conceptualization of sexuality as a malleable process in constant flux. Thus, I look at how pre- and post-migration social and economic complexities shape my informants' experiences of sexuality in both countries. I look at how sexualized bodies engage with each other as part of the pre- and post-migration experience. The changes women and men experience in their sex lives after migrating flow throughout my examinations of the meanings and interpretations underlying their narratives. My sample of sixty informants does not represent the totality of Mexican immigrants, and my conclusions are not aimed at drawing generalizations about the lives of other Mexican or Latina women and Latino men living in the United States. Given the sensitive nature of my interviews, I am aware of the extent to which the study participants were self-selected. Nevertheless, I greatly benefited from that process, since the self-selection process helped me to interview only women and men who were interested and candid about revealing their intimate lives to me. I have attempted to portray their sex lives in this book with the same frankness and honesty.

Mexicans Talking about Their Sex Lives?

"How did you get Mexican women to talk about sex?" "Aren't Mexican women kind of closed-minded and conservative in talking about sex?" Those are questions that colleagues in both the United States and Mexico have asked many times, even as they were intrigued by my research with Mexican women. Others have similarly inquired about my "courage as a Mexican woman" to conduct sexuality research with Mexican men.

I felt inspired to become a sociologist after reading Lillian Rubin's book, *Worlds of Pain,* in a Master's program in Psychology in the late 1980s. I switched disciplines as I became interested in learning her secret of harmonizing professional careers as both a psychotherapist and sociologist. She has also been an inspiration with regard to the ways in which she has used her clinical skills as sociological research tools. Oliva M. Espín's psychological research on the sex lives of women who migrated from different countries to the United States (1999) has similarly validated the ways in which a researcher can use previous clinical training in data collection and analysis. As a novice following their example, I have used my clinical skills to conduct sociological research. My training in couple and family therapy, and in sex therapy, provided me with the in-depth interviewing skills to approach and pursue my sociological curiosity with respect and kindness. As I noticed that most women and men were enthusiastically willing to open up about their sex lives, I let myself go while paying close attention to my interview schedule. Developing intimate dialogues with immigrants became an act of expressing care and concern for them.

My own personal history has been written in the context of heterosexual, loving experiences, and it also helped me conduct this study. I used myself as a source to answer many of the personal questions my interviewees asked. At the end of the interviews, my interlocutors surprised me with countless questions and reactions. I was asked many times whether I was a virgin, had children, was married or divorced, believed in oral or anal sex, or masturbation; whether I thought that homosexuality was sinful or not; whether I had an opinion about abortion, condom, and contraceptive use; whether I was a Mexican or a Chicana; Catholic or not; whether I had ever cohabited with or was presently cohabiting with a gringo; and whether I was satisfied with my sex life. After we finished up our interview, one of the women, Tomasita, looked at me closely and exclaimed, "Gee whiz, Gloria! You must have a fucking good sex life. Look, you don't even have acne or wrinkles!" Salomé asked me if I had a secret formula to share with her so that she would have sexual fantasies, or at least one sexual dream, about Jorge Rivero, a Mexican sex symbol. "I try, and try, but I can't. How do I do it? Tell me how, young lady!" Salomé shared with me some of the sexual frustrations and feelings of sexual deprivation she had experienced after her divorce many years earlier. After a deep sigh and a long pause, she asked, "Do I have to masturbate?" Other women, especially those raising adolescent daughters, asked me for my mother's secret in making me stay in high school and go to college. Some women expressed concerns about their children and asked me to give them basic advice to make sure the sex education they were providing for them was appropriate and well informed. I answered each of their questions unhesitatingly and with complete honesty. Interestingly, when I would carefully and gradually begin to open up about my personal life, many of my informants wouldn't even let me finish my first sentence. Instead, they would interrupt me to continue on with confessions of their own sexual experiences, fantasies, dreams, and fears. The interviewing experience became a seductive and engaging process of sexual exploration on both sides. Once these women started telling their sex stories, I couldn't stop them. Sharing sexual memories became a journey of self-discovery and reaffirmation. Twelve of the forty women reported some type of sexual violence, including sexual abuse as a child or adolescent, incest, date rape, sexual assault by a stranger, and marital rape. Only one man reported an incident of sexual abuse as a child, by an older man within his family. For those women survivors, the process gave them the hope that they could find professional help and heal their emotional wounds.

Men reported they felt similarly comfortable opening up about their sex lives during the interviews. In general, the men were more formal, reserved, and distant than the women, and fewer of them asked me about my sex, marriage, and family life. The few men who inquired about my sex life were from Mexico City, whose modernity and urban sophistication made the topic easier to raise. At the end of our interview, Diego asked if I had real-life experience with the topic of my research or whether I was a like a priest — a "voyeur" who knows about everybody's sex life but who may have little personal exposure to erotic pleasure and sex. Raúl, who was also from Mexico City, told me more than once that I reminded him of an ex-girlfriend he loved deeply who he had left behind in Mexico after he migrated. He blushed and acted in a respectful manner as I firmly redirected him to my questions and explained the ethics involved in a research project.

Conducting sex research raises controversial issues, especially when the interview is conducted in the relative privacy of an informant's home. For some of the women, being interviewed about sex in their homes represented a challenge to be honest while being cautious and discreet, especially when family members were present. I interviewed some of these women in their kitchens or their living rooms when their relatives were not at home. However, when that was not the case, many of them identified their bedrooms as the safest place to be interviewed about their sex lives.

When I went to interview Yadira at her home, I was greeted by her children and her husband. She introduced me to them as a counselor at the clinic while showing me her many lithographs of the Virgin of Guadalupe and other images of Virgins hanging on the wall. Then, she gradually led me to a bedroom while telling me in a whispering tone of voice, "If we are going to talk about sex, well . . . we need to go to the bedroom." She opened the door to a small, crowded space decorated with more religious images, at least one crucifix, and many stuffed animals. Then she lay down on the floor while complaining about the hot summer, invited me to sit next to her, and asked me to start the interview. Shortly after, she said she felt tired and jumped onto a twin-size bed, where she lay down. I remained seated on the floor, stretching my weary back many times against her bed in a scene that made me feel like a Freudian psycho-analyst interviewing her patient during a free-association session. I experienced a similar scenario with other women. Graciela complained about her lack of privacy at home and invited me to meet her at a friend's house. As with Yadira, Graciela did not wait long to take me to her friend's bedroom. "Right on! The bedroom is the ideal place to talk about sex," she stated as she lay down while patting the queen-size bed and inviting me to sit down next to her. As with Yadira, I remained seated next to Graciela during the entire interview, and again felt like an analyst in search of her innermost fears and fantasies. I experienced similar circumstances with Rosalía, Romelia, and Fernanda, who all identified their bedrooms as the ideal place to be interviewed.

I also conducted some of my interviews with the men at their homes, mainly in the living room or on the porch. In only one case did I interview a man in the master bedroom of his house, at his wife's request. Both the man and his wife were from Mexico City, and I had met her through a community organizer. She had asked me about my professional training and interests, said she believed in the importance of my project, and suggested that I interview her husband. After she talked to him, he agreed to participate in the study. When I arrived at their home, she asked me to interview him in their bedroom while she stayed outside and next to the door to be sure their children didn't disturb us. Later, the couple fixed me a cup of tea and drew me into a conversation, that included their adolescent daughter and son, about teenage pregnancy, HIV/AIDS, and gang violence in Los Angeles. In contrast to its loaded meaning in other contexts, for my research purposes, the bedroom offered my informants privacy, safety, and a sense of protection. It also provided symbolic freedom and a censure-free environment in which to talk about their sex lives.

Finally, I listened to these women and men and/or analyzed their stories in the midst of a number of sexually charged episodes in the history of the United States. The Monica Lewinsky–Bill Clinton sex scandal, the introduction of the Viagra pill, and the revelations of pedophile priests within the Catholic Church confirmed the centrality of sex in the nation's social life, even as I worked on different aspects of my own study. While

I do not discuss any of these topics here, the disjunctures and contradictions that emerged in mainstream society with regard to sexuality and sexual morality fed my motivation to write a sociological book about Mexican immigrants and their sex lives.

Organization of the Book

This book is divided into eight chapters. Chapter 1 lays out a theoretical framework that focuses on Mexican women's and men's experiences of sex and the erotic in the social sciences, including immigration studies and scholarship on gender and sexuality. Chapter 2 offers my central argument about Mexican women's need to preserve premarital virginity: far beyond religious obedience and the cult of virginity historically promoted by the Catholic Church, Mexican women socially construct virginity as a resource to improve their living conditions. I examine the ways in which both women and men build virginity as the *capital femenino* which possesses a social exchange value. Mexican women, as a subordinate social group struggling to improve their living conditions and opportunities in a patriarchal society, use *capital femenino* vis-à-vis men in order to enhance their life opportunities. In addition, a need to preserve premarital virginity interacts with gender dynamics in two ways: (1) a woman's need to preserve her virginity until marriage is deeply rooted in an ethic of family honor and respect, and (2) a woman's need to preserve her virginity is linked to a socially learned fear of sexism and men's expectation of marrying virgin women. In addition to revealing both of these dynamics, the women's testimonies unmask, first, the moral contradictions and social mechanisms of the gender inequality that heterosexual women experience while being educated in a patriarchal society. And second, their testimonies offer the possibility for women to explore sexual agency, pleasure, and autonomy in such social contexts. Chapter 3 reveals the experiences of sexual initiation among men. The men's narratives show the ways in which patriarchal prescriptions of masculinity shape both men's sexual vulnerabilities as well as women's beliefs and practices of sexuality. Their testimonies illustrate how regional patriarchies shape the lives of women and men educated in social contexts characterized by an emphasis on gender inequalities and rigid sexual moralities (e.g., in *pueblos,* or small towns). Such small-town patriarchies are more likely to assign a higher value to virginity as *capital femenino* than is the case for individuals educated in a social context where sexism is disguised or less intense (e.g., in urban contexts or large cities). Regardless of their places of origin, how-ever, a common emotion enveloped the first sexual experience of both my women and men informants: fear. Reported feelings of apprehension and concern by both women and men suggest the existence of a culture of sexual fear in Mexican society. These feelings seem to originate and be reproduced through one of the institutions shaping my informants' experiences of sexuality: the family. Chapter 4 explains how families — via maternal authority — become an important institution establishing and shaping beliefs and practices with regard to femininity and masculinity, courtship, heterosexual love, and sexuality. Finally, both the preservation and the loss of virginity, as displayed through socially constructed sym-bols (e.g., the white dress), transfigure a woman's virginity from an inti-mate and private rite of passage into one that is a public, family, and social affair.

Chapters 5, 6, and 7 examine the changing experiences of sexuality related to migration and settlement in the United States. Chapter 5 looks at how these Mexicans' sex lives are transformed by their social and eco-nomic conditions in the new country, including sexual dangers (e.g., sex-ual abuse of children, HIV/AIDS, drugs and alcohol use, and gang activ-ity) and the fast-paced economy and lifestyle migrants encounter in the United States. Chapter 6 discusses Mexican women's and men's views and experiences of the erotic in the context of their conversations with one another and within the immigrant women's community. The chapter also discusses the culture of sexuality the women actively create while estab-lishing new social metrics with regard to sexual morality and sexuality. Chapter 7 puts the female silhouette at the center of my examinations of migration and sexuality by examining how and why women reshape their sex lives (and how men perceive these changes) as part of their everyday life experiences within new socioeconomic contexts characterized by anonymity, geographical distance, softened family control, social net-working, and laws protecting women such as regulations against domes-tic violence. I also examine men's sexual transformations in the United States. Finally, chapter 8 discusses the ways in which mothers and fathers redefine their own meanings of virginity as they educate a new generation in the United States. The chapter also includes my final reflections with regard to this study's implications for reproductive health, as well as the additional research challenges for me and others to follow in the virgin field of Mexican migrant sexualities.

CHAPTER I

Twice Forgotten

*The Sex Lives of Heterosexual Mexicans
in the United States*

"I work and support myself so I don't have to have sex with my husband if I don't feel like it," Azalea says assertively. Then she adds with a chuckle, "In Mexico, I worked in a factory, but here I became an apartment manager. Before, he used to do whatever he wanted to. If he wanted to have sex, I had to go right there and do it, day or night. I had no choice. But now that's all over! That's history!"

Joaquín relates the stimulating talks he has with his friends: "Do you know what an orgasm is? Do you know what that is?" "An orgasm? Well, it's when I come." "No, you're wrong! That just shows how little you know about sex." Joaquín is describing the engaging and confrontational conversations he has had with his day-laborer friends about drug and alcohol use and sex; condom use and HIV/AIDS; virginity, women, the G-spot and sexual response; impotence and premature ejaculation; and emotional intimacy and lovemaking. He is explaining how his views of sexuality and his sexual behavior have changed, and how he has influenced his friends through the intimate conversations they have while waiting for day jobs at an employment center for *jornaleros*.

The accounts of Mexicans like Azalea and Joaquín challenge common understandings about the sexuality of Latino groups that are based on acculturation paradigms. Research informed by acculturation and assimilationist perspectives assumes that Latinas and Latinos adapt or acculturate into mainstream society's values and attitudes, that is, the modern, liberal North American white dominant culture (see, e.g., Guerrero Pavich 1986; Marín, Gómez, and Hearst 1993; and Fraser et al. 1998). Nevertheless, for the women and men in this study, exposure to U.S. mainstream culture and society is neither a direct nor an immediate stimulus responsible for transformations in their sex lives. Instead, as illustrated by Azalea, a Mexican immigrant's sexuality may be shaped by full-time paid employment, enhanced financial status, and a changed power relationship with her partner. For men like Joaquín, sexuality is affected by the social interactions taking place within immigrant communities, where conversations with sex-related themes become part of everyday life. For the Mexicans in this study, women's and men's sexualities echo transformed social and economic practices and altered expressions of gender and power relations within the context of migration.

This chapter analyzes some uncritically accepted assumptions and offers an alternative sociological perspective on the impact of immigration and life on the sexualities of heterosexual Mexicans. The framework I have developed draws theoretical connections between gender and sexuality and immigration studies. This model examines Mexican heterosexualities as processes that are interwoven with social, economic, and everyday life contexts. These informants actively construct and reconstruct their lives as they unpack their "sexuality luggage," which has been partly formed by gendered sexual ideologies and practices previously established in Mexico.

Migrant Sexualities, Gendered Relationships, and Everyday Life

For the women and men I interviewed, sexuality refers to the attitudes and behaviors, beliefs and practices, emotions and feelings, and fantasies and acts they engage in as they experience the erotic. Their narratives contribute to a better understanding of the sociology of gender and sexuality in a number of ways.

Sexuality is part of immigrants' gendered everyday life experiences. Mexican women's and men's sexualities are socially constructed as they navigate the gendered everyday social practices in which they participate. As indicated by researchers who have studied Mexican migration, gender, and cultural change (Hondagneu-Sotelo 1994; Woo Morales 1997; Hirsch 2003), any transformation in heterosexual experience is better understood when it is examined within the context of the reorganized social prescriptions of gender relations of power and control that take place in the United States. Regardless of which side of the border Mexicans are on, their erotic journeys are subject to the yearnings and fears associated with sex.

Sexuality is embedded in pleasure–danger paradoxes and contradictions. Diverse forms of female sexuality emerge as women and men socially exchange their sexual desires and fears along a pleasure-versus-danger continuum (Vance 1984). In this way, Mexican expressions of eroticism are examined within a feminist paradigm that explores women's sexuality as "simultaneously a domain of restriction, repression, and danger as well as a domain of exploration, pleasure, and agency. To focus only on pleasure and gratification ignores the patriarchal structure in which women act, yet to speak only of sexual violence and oppression ignores women's experience with sexual agency" (Vance 1984, 1).

In the case of men, different expressions of pleasure versus danger may also influence their experiences of sexuality before and after migrating. Men, for instance, may pay a high price for complying with hegemonic expressions of masculinity (Connell 2000, 11), especially in the realm of sexual initiation. Their sexualities expose heterosexuality as a fertile terrain for change and contestation. Sex, distinctively dangerous and pleasurable for both women and men, begins to be shaped by a central social institution: the family.

Sexuality is created and reproduced through and within family life. Even though there is wide diversity of family arrangements and expressions in Mexican society, the family is the primary and original locus of social control, redefining and ordering the politics of gender relations linked to women's and men's experiences of heterosexual sex and loving relationships. The families of the immigrants I interviewed created and reproduced what R. W. Connell (2002) identifies as the gender regime. That is, families create and reproduce "a set of arrangements about gender" in order to regulate the meanings of sexuality and heterosexual relations for their children. In the process, double standards of morality and gender inequality are enforced yet are flexible and contested. Migration and generation reshape them. For example, after migration, a mother may redefine her views of virginity and premarital sex, as she educates a daughter in a different socioeconomic context in the United States. And a father's concern about protecting his daughter from sexual involvement with an "undesirable" man (e.g., a gang member) living in the immigrant barrio becomes more of a priority than his "old" wish that she remain a virgin until marriage.

The family processes involved in the social reproduction of normative heterosexualities do not exist in isolation but within socioeconomic contexts. As Dennis Altman suggests, "Gender and sexuality come together through the family, and family structures themselves, far from being fixed or 'natural' as moral conservatives insist, are ultimately dependent on social and economic structures" (2001, 43).

Sexuality is shaped by social, cultural, political, and economic forces. Mexican immigrants' experiences of sex within heterosexual relationships are extremely complex. Those experiences are linked before and after migration to gender politics resulting from social and economic forces that are culturally influenced and historically determined. Prior to migration, their sexualities are created and reproduced within a larger "sex/gender system" (Rubin 1976) that is shaped by regional economies, multiple patriarchal processes, and a culture of sexual fear that permeates the sex lives of both women and men. After migration, sexualities are vulnerable to new, and often perplexing, political, social, and economic forces (see di Leonardo and Lancaster 1997; Ross and Rapp 1997; Hennessy 2000; and Altman 2001). In the case of Mexicans migrating to highly industrialized, capitalistic U.S. metropolises, these include socioeconomic segregation and its risks and dangers; patterns of labor and work within a fast-paced routine of everyday survival; and immigrant cultures of sexuality created within contexts of urban anonymity and isolation. These immigrants redefine their experiences and the meanings of the erotic within contexts of racial, socioeconomic, and gender inequality.

Sexuality is a relational and contextualized process of "doing" gender. On both sides of the border, Mexican heterosexual eroticism is relational. That is, as we zoom our analytical lens, Mexican narratives of heterosexual sex reveal how women and men "do gender" as part of everyday life (West and Zimmerman 1987). Their sex narratives reveal the nuanced tensions, complexities, contradictions, and paradoxes surrounding their erotic experiences. For instance, looking at the relational dimensions of gender, we can identify when, how, and why women may exercise agency and sexual power in various sex/gender arrangements. In that regard, these Mexican sexual narratives also confirm my modest understanding of Judith Butler's (1990) celebrated theorizing of gender as a *performance:* gender is fluid and relational because individuals "do" it, and they "do" it differently as they engage in social relations with each other within specific and changing contexts.

Sexuality, a gendered process, is thus shaped by the same traits of gender. "In talking about 'gender,' we are not talking about simple differences or fixed categories," writes Connell. "We are talking about relationships, boundaries, practices, identities and images that are actively created in social processes, come into existence in specific historical circumstances, shape the lives of people in profound and often contradictory ways, and are subject to historical struggle and change" (2002, 27). Being such a nuanced and fluid process, sexuality has a delicate yet powerful connection with the most vulnerable part of an individual — their feelings and emotions.

Sexuality is emotional and individual. Emotions and feelings attached to the changing cultural meanings of what is sexual emerge *collectively* as part of immigrants' heterosexual intimacies but also *individually* as part of their unique personal sex histories. For my informants, fear, pleasure, apprehension, tension, anxiety, frustration, sadness, desire, concern, happiness, confusion, joy, bliss, excitement, pain, and yearning, among others, become part of a colorful rainbow of contrasting collective yet subjectively experienced emotions and feelings embracing fantasized and actual erotic experiences. These emotional expressions of sexuality are shared collectively as they are shaped by society. For example, some rural women develop a socially defined collective fear of sexism for not having been virgins at marriage. But emotions are individually experienced as well, so a rural woman may experience the same fear differently, based on her personal history, such as her involvement with an abusive partner. Sexuality, as a gendered process, is social and cultural, but it is also subjective and personal (Chodorow 1995).

Such emotions also coincide with Connell's (1987, 2000) notion of *cathexis* — emotional energy. In my study, this psychic energy may be attached to an idea (e.g., the importance given to virginity) or may be part of my respondents' emotional reactions to the erotic. Women and men emotionally construct their meanings and interpretations of sexuality. In this way, sexuality becomes the terrain wherein both the social and cultural and the subjective and personal embrace one another. As Connell writes, "Sexuality is the realm of intimate contact where particularly strong emotional bonds are forged" (2002, 91).

The dimensions of migrant sexualities delineated above are mutually dependent and reinforcing. Each dimension shapes the others as immigrants' sexualities flow and change. As part of this process, immigrants embody sexual desire and the erotic as they experience, redefine, and reorganize their sex lives. This sequence can be best understood in a metaphorical way. As Ellen Ross and Rayna Rapp (1997) suggest: "In sexuality as in culture, as we peel off each layer (economies, politics, families, etc.), we may think that we are approaching the kernel, but we eventually discover that the whole is the only 'essence' there is. Sexuality cannot be abstracted from its surrounding social layers" (155). And for a more comprehensive examination of these interdependent "social layers" that both embrace and become the "whole," I situate my study within the sociology of gender and sexualities, migration research, and Latina and Latino sexualities scholarship.

Gender and Sexuality Studies: "Studying Up" on Mexican Sexualities

> As a pervasive institution within other institutions (state, education, church, media), heterosexuality helps guarantee patriarchal regulation of women's bodies, labor, and desires.
>
> Rosemary Hennessy, *Profit and Pleasure*

Studying up on sex, that is, examining heterosexuality, has been addressed with the purpose of "revealing and demystifying the mechanisms of power, identifying their internal contradictions and cleavages, so as to inform movements for change" (Messner 1996). Similarly, Adrienne Rich (1980) and Evelyne Accad (1991) have examined the possibilities for social change by incorporating heterosexuality and sexual politics into women's struggle for social justice. Scholars such as Janet Halley (1993), Chrys Ingraham (1994, 1999), Lynne Segal (1994), Jonathan N. Katz (1995), and Michael Messner (1996) also advocate the critical examination of heterosexuality in the power structure. For example, Katz explains how the term *heterosexuality* was created and established in the late nineteenth and early twentieth centuries to define a privileged and normal sex category. As a consequence, socially organized practices of unequal power have been established in which men dominate women and heterosexuality dominates homosexuality. Katz also uncovers the dynamics by which heterosexuality has been established by scientists throughout history as normative and non-problematic. His analysis offers some explanation for why social scientists have not viewed heterosexuality as a "problem" to be studied or analyzed.

"Studying up" on sex reformulates the sociological study of Mexican sexualities from both a theoretical and methodological perspective: theoretically, because Mexicans' sexual transformations are better understood when they are examined within the power structure of society from within the "matrix of domination" perspective, that is, the socially organized interlocking system between race, class, gender, and geographic location (Collins 1991); and methodologically, because "studying up" integrates theory and social practice.

Mexicans, Migration, and Sexuality

Despite the desexualized nature of existing immigration studies of Mexican women and men, there has been interdisciplinary research on the sexual experiences of immigrants, based on two specific paradigms: transnationalism and assimilation.

TRANSNATIONAL MODELS: SEXUALITIES IN CIRCULAR FLUX ACROSS BORDERS

Recent interdisciplinary studies on Latina and Latino sexuality incorporate immigration from a transnational perspective as an important context in which sexualities are organized. Lourdes Argüelles and Anne Rivero (1993) illustrate how some Latina immigrants use transnational migration, both into the United States and returning to Mexico, as a way to cope with or escape from gender and sexual inequalities. In their study, one woman fled from Guatemala to the United States in order to avoid her husband's sexual and physical abuse. A second Latina went back to Mexico City after her brother — who sexually molested her as a child — migrated to the United States and tried to resume the same abusive behavior. After being reunited with her alcoholic and abusive father in Mexico City, however, the woman decided to return to the United States, but this time to a big city (Los Angeles) where she could "get lost" and thus avoid her abusive brother. The experiences of other women have also shown how their sex lives have been transformed after migration to the United States (Espín 1999).

Studies of gay men, health-related issues including HIV/AIDS, and migrants' concerns about marital intimacy, and reproductive health similarly point up the multiple connections between sexuality, gender, and immigration. A pioneer in Mexican gay men's studies, Carrier (1995) has shown how homosexual men involved in transnational migrations renegotiate their sexual positioning (the *activo/pasivo* dichotomy critiqued by some for promoting static ideas about sexual practices) to create a third category: *internacionales*. *Internacionales* have no sexual role preference and may play both the anal insertive and receptive role. Bronfman and López Moreno (1996) found that migrants from Michoacán (homosexual men and heterosexual men and women) learned a diversity of sexual practices during migration. And Cantú (1999, 2000, 2002) has examined the ways in which sexuality organizes immigrant gay Mexicanos' identity formation, migration processes, and incorporation experiences.

The women and men I interviewed illustrate parallel processes. For some of the Mexicanas participating in this study, "transnational migrant circuits" (Rouse 1996, 254) help structure their sexualities. Having been exposed to HIV/AIDS literature in their immigrant communities, some women shared this information with their relatives during their trips back to Mexico. The reactions of relatives to these conversations further reshaped their views of sex. Other migrants reconsidered their views of marital love and fidelity when they were confronted during their return visits to Mexico by the conflicted conjugal lives of their relatives. In a third instance, some women redefined their sexual beliefs and practices as they made reproductive decisions with the help of relatives or close friends who live in Mexico who gave them advice on contraceptive methods.

Thus, a transnational perspective can explain the central aspects of the fluidity of some Mexican women's sexualities and the continuing, circular, and interminable nature of their transformations beyond borders. Although this study deals only with immigrants who currently live in the United States, my informants' stories often sound exactly like the narratives Hirsch reported in her transnational studies of the heterosexual marital intimacies of Mexicans living in El Fuerte (in the state of Michoacán), Degollado (in Jalisco), and Atlanta, Georgia.

ASSIMILATION MODELS: "SEXUAL ACCULTURATION" WITHIN MAINSTREAM SOCIETY

Pioneering research on the sexuality and sex lives of U.S. Latinas and Latinos is found primarily in psychology and the behavioral sciences. Mostly informed by the acculturation model established in the early 1980s (Padilla 1980), this sexuality research associates changes in Latina women's sexuality (behavior and attitudes) with acculturation.[1] Sex research based on the acculturation model perceives the sexuality of Latinas and Latinos as a unidimensional entity that is transformed along a continuum between both a Hispanic, or Latin American, sexuality (traditional and conservative) and a North American sexuality (modern and liberal). Using this analytical framework, researchers have argued that "as they acculturate, Hispanic men and women apparently begin to take on the attitudes and behaviors of sexuality that are part of mainstream U.S. culture, which differs from traditional Hispanic culture" (Marín, Gómez, and Hearst 1993, 173).

As a point of departure, the acculturation perspective established a landmark in multidisciplinary research into Latino and Latina sexualities, including groundbreaking research on HIV/AIDS and reproductive health.[2] Consequently, in the early stages of my dissertation work I was influenced by this popular model. But as I continued with my fieldwork, completed my interviews, and finished my data analysis on women's sexual histories, I became disenchanted with this theoretical framework. Having immersed myself in the social and cultural worlds of my informants, I learned about the complexities of their daily lives within their immigrant communities, and I saw the need for a sociological perspective that would incorporate their experiences of gender, socioeconomics, and ethnic segregation.

In the first stage of this project, and as I listened to the women's sexual stories, I discovered that the sexual transformations of my respondents in the United States were complex, nonlinear, and diverse. Their sexuality transitions involved social processes that had nothing to do with becoming sexually acculturated. Instead, due to socioeconomic and racial segregation, a transformation in a Mexican woman's sexuality might be deeply connected to the social dynamics and processes taking place within her own immigrant community. Even though these women were exposed to U.S. mainstream society, I learned that many of their liberating sexuality transformations were not necessarily associated with the acculturation process. Instead, Mexican women actively engaged in practices that alternatively promoted emancipation and constraint as they experienced sexuality transformations in the new country. And they did this while exchanging information and sharing information about their sex lives as part of their everyday life interactions with other immigrant women. The women I interviewed described their conversations about sex with their acquaintances, friends, neighbors, and relatives as part of a mutual effort to help one another cope with sexual difficulties and concerns. Some of them talked about sex during their informal, day-to-day interactions with one another, some reserved such talk for more private conversations, and others conversed about sex as a part of their normal routine at their jobs, as was the case for Hirsch's immigrants in Atlanta, who related their coworkers' conversations about women and orgasms (2003, 228). Through these conversations, some women reported, they became sexually literate or discovered some type of emancipation, while others recalled being stigmatized. A woman from a small town in Jalisco now living in an immigrant community in Los Angeles might be introduced to someone who had been raised in a sexually more progressive urban setting, like Guadalajara or Mexico City. That interaction might, in turn, have helped her to become more open with regard to her own sexuality. Thus, women who became more liberated in their sexual behavior were not necessarily responding to a process of "sexual assimilation." Instead, they were responding to more situated and contextualized social circumstances within their U.S. social and cultural worlds. As was the case for the immigrants Hondagneu-Sotelo (1994) interviewed, these women were being sexually transformed within and by their own immigrant communities, not by the dominant culture. Their sexuality transitions were thus more sophisticated, as they did not automatically become more "Americanized," sexually speaking.

The women and men in this study challenge the acculturation and assimilation paradigms. Their sex lives are surrounded and imprinted by social dimensions that include gender processes and socioeconomic segregation, race, and citizenship; their everyday life experience of surviving in a complex capitalistic society; and their residence in immigrant communities, where women and men actively participate and create cultures of sexuality. The people I interviewed created and promoted sexuality discourses through their daily life conversations and dialogues with other Spanish-speaking immigrants, and these sexual discourses ultimately became an important part of their life and survival as immigrants.

From them, I also learned how and why their sexualities reflect a continuity between the present and the past in Mexican society. In the next section, I offer a general outline of the historical forces that have defined normative paradigms of heterosexuality, as well as some of the popular culture expressions of female sexualities, in Mexican society.

Historical Overview of Mexican Women and Heterosexuality

> *Es indispensable que la autoridad del hombre continúe tanto como la inferioridad respectiva de la mujer, la cual debe ser eterna como la naturaleza.*
>
> It is essential for the man's authority to continue, as well as the respective inferiority of the woman, which should be as eternal as nature.
>
> J. M. Rivero, "El destino de la mujer" (1846)

Mexico was a very different society at the end of the twentieth century than it was at the beginning of the century. The revolutionary movement, which started in 1910, is identified with a transition that led to equal rights for women (Canak and Swanson 1998). The first two feminist conferences in Mexican history took place in Mérida, Yucatán, both in 1916 (Rocha 1991, 257–58). The feminist agenda of these meetings addressed such women's issues and concerns as sexual health and education, the right to vote, divorce, and equal rights within the marital context (Amuchástegui 2001, 81). Mexican women finally received the vote in 1953. In the 1960s, after the establishment in 1959 of one of the first family planning clinics in Latin America (Rodríguez, Corona, and Pick 1996), oral contraceptives entered the Mexican market for the first time (McCoy 1974, 379). The birth control issue deserves special attention, given the decrease in birth rates that occurred in Mexico during the last decades of the twentieth century. According to the Consejo Nacional de Población, fertility rates decreased from an average 7.3 births per woman in 1960 to 2.4 births in the year 2000 (CONAPO 2003).[3] Studies conducted in rural areas experiencing gradual industrialization, such as Michoacán, show that during this period of time women's exposure to both contraceptive and family planning professional services since the 1980s, as well as pressure from national economic recession, were influential on a their decisions to have only three or four children in recent years (Mummert 1992). Also, the numbers of women of reproductive age using contraceptives increased from 30.2 percent in 1976, to 44.7 percent in 1982 (LeVine 1993, 152). In the 1970s, the Mexican government played a role in this phenomenon, investing in a major national family planning program whose television theme song was "La familia pequeña vive mejor" ("The Small Family Lives Better"). All these changes took place as women's participation in the formal economy gradually increased from the 1930s throughout the 1970s, within a system whose laws prohibit discrimination against women but whose practices restrict the kinds of occupations women can enter (see González Salazar 1980). In response to the restructuring of international and global economies within the last decades, young women living near the U.S.–Mexico border began to be concentrated in specific sectors of the economy, such as assembly plants or *maquiladoras* (Fernández-Kelly 1983). While the economic participation of women has increased 67 percent within the last two decades, and middle-class women have benefited from college and professional employment opportunities, most women remain in low-paying jobs, and one study found that women make 86 percent as much as men (Canak and Swanson 1998).

Feminist academics, activists, and socially progressive women's organizations have passionately defended women's rights and concerns since the 1970s (Lagarde 1997; Lamas 1998, 2001). But traditions and social norms regulating women's sexuality in contemporary society still reflect their precolonial, colonial, and pre-industrial origins, in spite of modernization attempts, globalization, neoliberalism, and the spread of computers and the Internet throughout Mexican territory.

The social control of women's sexuality in Mexico goes back to pre-Columbian times. In Spain, Christians, Muslims, and Jews promoted patriarchal ideologies during the seven centuries preceding Columbus's expeditions to America (Mirrer 1996). But pre-Hispanic Mesoamerican groups also embraced values and social practices that favored men over women (J. Tuñón Pablos 2000). Thus, doctrines promoting such belief systems have their origins in both the Iberian peninsula and in pre-Columbian Mexico.

Although there is continuity and change throughout history, and although regional variations exist, academics frequently associate the history of Mexican female sexuality with the Spanish values of power and control that have been carried down and socially reproduced since the colonial period (Lavrin 1989). Through a predominantly patriarchal authority, state politics and gender relations became and remain interdependent phenomena (Dore and Molyneux 2000). In that regard, some scholars have examined how women's subordination became part of colonial state-building and central to the nuanced expressions of everyday life in a new, mestizo Mexican society (e.g., Tostado Gutiérrez 1991). At the core of these interconnected processes, the original social mechanism controlling women's sex lives in colonial society was established through a system that interconnected race, class, and gender. In that regard, Elizabeth Dore offers an example of how gender politics and female subordination became central for the Spanish colonial state as it attempted to cope with its anticipated collapse:

> Rich *mestizos* and *mulatos* often purchased racial mobility, or "whitening." These changes tended to blur race- and gender-based social distinctions. In their efforts to shore up the old social order, the Portuguese and Spanish colonial governments enacted laws in the late 1770s that strengthened parents' rights to veto their children's choice of marriage partner. Although at first glance these laws might seem of marginal significance, they were important signals of the states' attempts to reinforce more absolutist understanding of patriarchal authority in the home and in the body politic, as a number of historians have argued. (Dore 2000, 12–13)

Colonial society strategically situated the family as an institution in order to reinforce its political power. But the state and its complicit families did not act alone: the Catholic Church promoted these civil laws through its sermons and spiritual counseling (Tostado Gutiérrez 1991, 119–20). This and earlier paradigms of social regulation established by the colonial elite were frequently bolstered by Catholic ideals of sexual morality. Canonical documents, theological treatises, confession guides for priests, and other official documents prepared, approved, and promoted by the Church reinforced these early regulatory codes of sexual conduct (Lavrin 1989; Marcos 1989; Amuchástegui 2001).

In the early nineteenth century, the independence and secularization of the former colonial society did not improve women's social status. "Governments appropriated for themselves powers previously wielded by the Catholic Church — the regulation of marriage, annulment, sexuality, and legitimacy of birth" (Dore 2000, 21). In the first Mexican constitutions, for example, men would be granted their citizenship status at a younger age if they were married than if they were single (16). This is only one of the ways in which the gender–state mutual interaction contributed to the consolidation of the state: heterosexual love authenticated the formation of the patriarchal family, which ultimately reified the creation of a coherent and unified national identity (Varley 2000).

These beliefs and practices gradually were extended to and adopted by subordinate social classes and colonized indigenous groups. And even though these early state formations evolved throughout the years and decades to come (e.g., in divorce laws, women's right to vote, legislation against rape, etc.), mainstream Mexican society has systematically accepted the multiple expressions of these very early underlying social processes for controlling female heterosexuality. Throughout history, the social and geographical contexts of the Spanish conquest have socially reproduced this paradigm through a multitude of social mechanisms. Historian Ann Twinam has examined the state of female heterosexual affairs in colonial Latin American to explain what many Mexicanas experience in a contemporary Mexico that still ascribes to many colonial social norms, especially as they apply to women who live in small rural towns: "Questions of honor, female sexuality, and illegitimacy thus become inextricably linked. Women who engaged in premarital or extramarital sexual relations not only lost personal reputation and honor, but could beget additional family members whose illegitimacy excluded them from family honor. The double standard characteristic of colonial society meant that similar sexual activity did not as certainly threaten the personal honor of the elite male as that of the female" (Twinam 1989, 124). Other researchers have also pointed to historical evidence of these same patterns that associate women's sexuality, virginity, and family honor within the context of Mexican colonial societies (D'Emilio and Freedman 1988; Gutiérrez 1991; Tostado Gutiérrez 1991; Stern 1995). These and other intricate connections between the family (represented by parental authority) and the sexualities of women, and men, have survived the test of time. This centrality of *la familia* in the sex lives of women and men of Mexican origin has been consistently identified by sexuality research with both homosexual and heterosexual populations (see, e.g., Almaguer 1993; Zavella 1997; Rivas Zivy 1998; Díaz 1998; Prieur 1998; Cantú 1999; Amuchástegui 2001; Rafaelli and Ontai 2001; Carrillo 2002; Castañeda and Zavella 2003; Hirsch 2003; and Hurtado 2003).

Even though both traditional and contemporary literature may emphasize the importance of the Catholic Church as a determinant source of domination on Mexican women's sexuality (e.g., Guerrero Pavich 1986; Espín 1986; Amuchástegui 1994; Zavella 1997), in secularized contemporary Mexican society, at a macro level, it is the state that has alternatively reinforced or "dismantled some of the legal and institutional foundations of patriarchal authority" (Dore 2000, 25). At a micro level, the family as an institution (and as the original accomplice of the patriarchal state) becomes the social channel through which Mexican women's experiences of heterosexual relations and love have been socially controlled and governed in everyday interactions. Beyond Catholic moral ethics, gender dynamics linked to crucial aspects of a woman's heterosexuality (e.g., virginity, pregnancy out of wedlock, etc.) are defined through many socially constructed family politics. I am not suggesting that Catholic religious guilt and punishment and state and family control are exclusive of each other. In fact, they reinforce each other as they mutually interact. What I am arguing is that the Catholic Church may promote, in theory, ideologies that restrain Mexican women. However, the family, one of the original vehicles of social reproduction serving the patriarchal state, is the institution that in fact enforces and reformulates gender politics linked to female heterosexuality and ultimately puts them into practice.

This book hopes to establish a dialogue with the academic work currently being conducted on sexuality in Mexico. I frequently refer, for example, to the book *Virginidad e iniciación sexual en México*, written by the Mexican social psychologist Ana Amuchástegui (2001), who also examines the connection between sexuality and Catholicism. Her studies are based on social and cultural discourse analyses of subjective sexual meanings and moral theoretical paradigms, and she offers comparable findings with regard to the subjective meanings that rural and urban women and men attach to virginity and their first sexual experiences. While my research findings frequently coincide with Amuchástegui's, I offer a different analytical dimension that incorporates a sociological perspective of gender relations, power, and inequality within regional socioeconomic contexts.

Normative Female Heterosexuality in Modern Mexican Society

In contemporary Mexican society, traditions and social norms regulating heterosexual women's behavior identify a young woman's sexuality as family property. Living with their families — and not leaving the family home until they get married — is the social norm for many young women in most geographical regions, especially rural and semi-urbanized communities. The values of family honor and respect create a family expectation of sexual abstinence for single daughters. A daughter's decency and good reputation, and a mother's competency to teach moral values to her daughter, are defined through principles of *moralidad, decencia y buenas costumbres* (morality, decency, and good social mores) — the code of sexual morality established in Mexican society since the early twentieth century (Carrillo 2002). In addition, gender inequality interacts with family politics to control female heterosexuality. Unlike the case of single young men, a single woman may deprive herself of an active sex life before marriage as a way of protecting her family from dishonor and disrespect. As a consequence, the fear of family punishment and coercive marriage due to pregnancy out of wedlock may prevent a single woman from engaging in premarital intercourse. The socially learned fear that her future husband may scorn her for not being a virgin at marriage may also reinforce social control over a woman's sex life.

In most parts of Mexico, it is the practice for a young woman to have a *noviazgo* — a courtship relationship — with her boyfriend. After a period of time, and after becoming engaged, the young man visits her family home in order to propose to her, and then to formally inform his future bride's parents of his intention to marry her. Through this traditional ritual, called *pedir la mano de la novia* (to ask for the girlfriend's hand), the future husband makes their marriage commitment official. In urban and in some semi-industrialized social contexts, an excited future bride may receive (if the future husband's socioeconomic status allows it) an engagement ring from him before the couple's formal commitment to get married.

In most social contexts (urban, semi-industrialized, and pre-industrial rural areas), marriage is the idealized moral rite of passage that a hetero-sexual virgin woman goes through in order to officially become sexually active. Aside from regional and cultural variations (i.e., among indige-nous groups), for a middle-class, virgin, heterosexual woman (or a non-virgin lucky enough not to get pregnant), the traditional social norm for her first marriage includes a series of Westernized socially constructed rituals.

In theory, it is the family that gives a daughter the moral authorization to become sexually active, and that, only after marriage. Only within mar-riage is a woman morally entitled to an active sex life. Through marriage, a woman's sexuality and her identity are transformed from being her fam-ily's property into her husband's possession. The most symbolic indica-tion of this process is a woman's traditional change of her name after mar-riage. Where she once used both her father's and mother's last names, she now changes her name by deleting her mother's and adding her hus-band's after her father's name using *de* — meaning "of" or "from" (which in semantic terms expresses possession or ownership). Someone named Laura Ríos Juárez, a single Mexican woman, for example, would become Laura Ríos de García after she marries a man whose last name is García.

As she becomes aware of the above gender dynamics, a woman may either conform to them or contest them, or search for ways in between to explore, reclaim, and possess her own sexuality. These possibilities take place within specific and social contexts wherein gender inequalities also shape men's lives.

Female Heterosexualities and Popular Culture in Mexico

The most visible social expression of the multiple female heterosexual identities that exist in contemporary Mexican society can be seen in the three expressions of Mexico's popular culture: music, movies, and theater. During the 1980s and 1990s the new wave of *rockeras* singing *rock en español* offered a clear social representation of the *mujer atrevida* (the woman who dares to transgress social and moral regulations controlling female heterosexuality). The most controversial and famous of these singers is Gloria Trevi. An attractive and polemical *rockera* born and raised in Monterrey, Trevi became famous for inviting her male fans to join her in singing her socially provocative songs on stage while she seductively undressed them. She even produced a calendar that showed her in sexu-ally explicit poses. In addition, one of Trevi's musical productions included a CD whose suggestive title caused controversy. *Más turbada que nunca,* which means "more disturbed than ever," was given a semantic twist by most Mexicans, so it came out "mas-turbated than ever."

Controversy enhanced Trevi's popularity among her fans, some of whom include well-known intellectuals living in urban and semi-industrialized contexts, where her musical productions were successfully marketed via television, records, and magazines. But her popularity began to wane after she disappeared during the late 1990s, when she was accused of participating in the sexual abuse of minors who participated in her artistic activities. After she was captured in Brazil, she became the center of a legal scandal and was imprisoned there in January 2000 while she fought extradition to Mexico, a battle she eventually gave up. She was then sent to prison in Chihuahua, Mexico, where she stayed until a verdict freed her on September 21, 2004. While being convicted of the offense, in a symbolic way, she was also paying the price of her immoral insubordination. Gloria Trevi might be the reflection of earlier, equally controversial entertainment personalities, such as Irma Serrano ("La Tigresa") and Isela Vega, who have pushed social norms on television and in the movies since the 1960s.

In some recent films, the moral transgressions of heterosexual women are not only accepted or tolerated but acclaimed by the Mexican masses. Nationally and internationally celebrated movies, like *Como agua para chocolate* (*Like Water for Chocolate,* 1992), depict female characters who are no longer merely the objects of male sexual desire. Instead, the women themselves now have become subjects whose own sexual desires are manifest. In *Como agua para chocolate,* Gertrudis pleasurably identifies and enjoys the intense aphrodisiac effects of her sister Tita's love dish made with rose petals. Gertrudis's intense sexual desire is graphically represented, as she desperately runs away from the dinner table to immerse her naked body in a rudimentary shower built inside a wooden shack. Her burning sexual desire is metaphorically represented by the steam generated as she sensually bathes her voluptuous body. Her sexual urge is symbolically satisfied when she gets out of the shower and, naked, rides away on a horse with an attractive revolutionary who opportunely passes by.

More recently, *De noche vienes Esmeralda* (*Esmeralda Comes by Night,* 1997) portrays the obsession of a sensual and assertive woman who marries one man after another without bothering to get divorced. When Esmeralda is tried for her morally erratic behavior, the prosecutor (like all of her other lovers) falls helplessly in love with her and becomes her next husband. Based on a novel written by the highly respected Mexican novelist and writer Elena Poniatowska, *De noche vienes Esmeralda* might be a social counteroffensive to the commonly accepted phenomenon known as *la casa chica*. This is the socially tolerated practice in which a married man establishes and often supports a separate household (or households) without divorcing. Whether it represented a rebuttal to *la casa chica* or not, *De noche vienes Esmeralda* received excellent reviews and played to great acclaim throughout Mexico.[4]

In addition, the celebrated blockbuster film *Sexo, pudor y lágrimas* (*Sex, Shame, and Tears,* 1999) depicts the many relationship complexities experienced by two yuppie heterosexual couples living in contemporary Mexico City. Loving relationships, marital conflict, the search for love and spirituality, blurred boundaries between friendship and sex, unresolved old flames, and marital infidelity by both sexes connect the lives of the six characters in the film. *Sexo, pudor y lágrimas* was a huge success at the box office all over Mexico in 1999.

More recently, three movies in particular have capitalized on sexualized themes. *Y tu mamá también* (*And Your Mother, Too* 2001), which was well received in the United States, portrays the sexual adventures of a threesome made up of a young adult woman called Luisa and two younger men, who literally take an "erotic journey" as they travel together. Four priests are at the heart of the controversial *El crimen del padre Amaro* (*The Crime of Father Amaro,* 2002), but the movie highlights Amelia and her mother, two devout Catholic women who have romantic and sexual relationships with two of the priests. Finally, the Academy Award winning *Frida* (2002) is a colorful Hollywood biopic of the acclaimed painter Frida Kahlo and her bisexual amorous relationships. Interestingly, in all three movies, the main women characters — who are transgressors in more ways than one — die in the end.

In the theater, female heterosexuality and its expressions of pleasure are enacted by women who become agents openly expressing their sexual desire for men. In a production accurately entitled *Sólo para mujeres* (*For Women Only*), female heterosexual agency is purposely stimulated by a group of attractive male singers and actors who dance seductively and undress sensually in front of an intense female audience that cheers, yells, and screams as the men expose their well-sculptured bodies. *Sólo para mujeres* is a mix of a North American Chippendale strip-show and a Broadway musical that shows a group of men who ostensibly spend hours every day working out to achieve highly desirable muscular bodies. Groups of Mexicanas have attended presentations of the show at locations all over Mexico. *Sólo para mujeres* was recently performed for the enjoyment of Mexicanas and Latinas living in Los Angeles and the San Francisco Bay Area. The show was also released on video in 1999.

Gloria Trevi, the women protagonists in these films, and the many real-life women who have enjoyed the production *Sólo para mujeres* highlight some of the avenues through which popular culture grants social permission to Mexicanas to express their traditionally repressed sexual agency and eroticism. Only recently have the sexual desires of women been portrayed in Mexican popular culture in ways that do not demonize them — for example, a prostitute might be identified as a *fichera* or a *cabaretera,* or as *la amante* (literally, "the lover," but often meaning "the other woman"). In part, this new openness reflects the impact of globalization and neoliberalization on Mexican popular culture. Like entrepreneurs elsewhere, Mexican businessmen and women have learned they can tap into new markets by commodifying male sex objects. These representations are also important because they transform Mexicanas as objects of men's sexual desire into sexual subjects possessing agency. They are women with their own desires — *desiring* women.

To what extent do these emerging social images reflect changes in real Mexicanas' sex lives in recent decades? Do they represent a counterforce in popular culture by challenging the traditional values and ideologies attached to female heterosexuality? How do these representations affect the sex lives of real Mexicanas living in the transition between two centuries? These questions are beyond the scope of this book, but my point of departure is that sexuality is constantly in flux, even in remotely located hinterland areas of rural Mexico. In the following chapters, I explore the nuances and complexities of this process by examining the sex narratives of sixty Mexicans, before and after migrating to and settling in the City of Angels. What do these women think and how do they feel about virginity and premarital sex? How did they experience their first sexual encounter? What do men have to say about what these women reveal? To what extent does that reveal the men's own sexual and family biographies? The next chapter will explore these questions, whose answers become more complicated as danger and eroticism meet in a continuously evolving, fluid, and sophisticated yet patriarchal society.

CHAPTER 2

Beyond the Hymen

Women, Virginity, and Sex

"I will preserve my virginity until I get married," said Eréndira. "Not because of religion, but because of myself. I will preserve it to avoid many problems, like pregnancy, and also to better concentrate on my studies, among other things." An immigrant from Guadalajara, Eréndira has lived in Los Angeles for more than ten years. She has never wed, and at the age of thirty-two, she is adamant about waiting until she marries to have sexual intercourse for the first time.

Lorena, a thirty-four-year-old housewife who has lived in Los Angeles for a decade after migrating from her small town in Jalisco, says: "It is terrible to have sex before marriage. You lose your dignity as a woman. I was a virgin when I got married and now I do not have any problems with my husband. I have a happy life with him, you know. I have my own home and everything. Many women lose their virginity before marriage and then they don't live well. Many women have problems with their husbands for that reason."

These accounts provide evidence that some immigrant women from Mexico deeply value virginity, but they also challenge explanations that attribute that attitude to Catholicism (see, e.g., Paz 1950; Guerrero Pavich 1986; Espín 1986; Amuchástegui 1994, 2001; Zavella 1997; Reid and Bing 2000). The Catholic Church has held powerful control over the sexuality of Mexican women, but the moral standards of Catholicism are only one variable influencing women's ideas about virginity. Gender dynamics also shape women's attitudes toward premarital sexual abstinence.[1] As Eréndira's and Lorena's accounts suggest, virginity has complex social meanings that go beyond those usually considered by academic and popular writings on the subject.

In this chapter, I examine the many ways in which Mexican immigrant women construct the meanings of virginity. Sexual purity is socially assembled as a life-enhancing resource; it becomes what I call *capital femenino*. That is, virginity takes on a social exchange value that Mexican women, a subordinate social group in a patriarchal society, use to improve and maximize their life conditions and opportunities. In addition, pre-marital abstinence is tied to socially articulated family and gender dynamics. It is interwoven with a complex ethic of *respeto a la familia* (respect for the family), which links family honor with a daughter's virginity. The ideal of preserving sexual purity until marriage stems from a woman's knowledge that men prefer to marry virgins. The loss of virginity creates risks, and women's heterosexual experiences exist along a dynamic continuum between danger and pleasure. The overwhelming majority of the women in this study (70 percent) were not virgins when they were married. The women's first sexual experiences reveal the moral and social contradictions that control their sexualities, as well as their capacity to explore sexual autonomy, agency, and pleasure.

In addition, I incorporate men's views. As men articulate perceptions of women's understandings about sexuality, they reveal multiple expressions of masculine identity. These identities question monolithic images of masculinity. Men's reactions to women's fears surrounding first sexual encounters also reveal the complicated relational nature of sex and gender — from women and men's participation in egalitarian relationships to unequal sexual experiences between the genders.

The Cult of Virginity

Writings on the sexuality of Mexican women consistently focus on two strands of religiosity — Spanish and pre-Columbian — that have blended over the course of almost five hundred years (see Lavrin 1989; Rocha 1991; Tostado Gutiérrez 1991; Tuñón 1991; E. Tuñón Pablos 1991; J. Tuñón Pablos 2000; Amuchástegui 1994, 2001; Rubio 1997). This unique mestizo combination of beliefs and practices has molded Mexican morality.[2] The cult of virginity relates to dominant religion in three ways: (1) it is *normative,* to the extent that the Catholic Church insists on virginity for women at marriage; (2) it is *coalitionist,* in terms of the Church's alliance with a patriarchal society that lowers the moral status of women who cannot or will not maintain virginity; and (3) it is *coercive*, one result of the social mechanisms of moral control that have historically defined a sexually inexperienced woman as "sacred and pure" and a sexually active woman as "profane and impure" (Amuchástegui 1998).[3]

The role played by pre-Hispanic religions has not received as much attention. Yet virginity was valued, ritualized, or promoted by the Aztecs, Tzotzils, and Zapotecs (Domecq 1992), and by other Mesoamerican cultures (Amuchástegui 2001).[4] Pre-Hispanic traditions may have reinforced Catholic values.

Finally, the ethic of virginity has been codified into a series of dichotomous categories: passive/active, good/bad, or virgin/whore (see Paz 1950; Almaguer 1993; Alonso and Koreck 1993; Amuchástegui 2001). Women's intact hymens represent sexual purity, honor and decency; those with a ruptured hymen represent dishonor, profanation, and lack of virtue. Octavio Paz's *El laberinto de la soledad* (1950) offers a literary perspective that associates a woman's body and her sexuality with cultural interpretations of femininity and masculinity. Since the Mexican ideal of manhood consists in never having to *rajarse* (to crack, or split, oneself), Paz associates a woman's inferiority with the penetrable nature of her sexualized body. Octavio Paz's provocative literary analysis of *la rajada* (the wound), for example, maintains that virginity is embodied in an intact hymen. From this perspective, bleeding after the rupture of the hymen would be the most reliable way for a man to "have proof" of a woman's virginity. This essentialist view seems to be accepted by many in Mexican society. There is strong evidence of the overwhelming social value that an intact hymen receives as a verification of virginity throughout Mexico. Juanita, one of my a study participants, gave this illustration: "One of my sisters was very concerned because the day she got married she did not bleed, and she says that she feels sad because of that. I asked her, 'Has your husband ever said anything about it?' and she said, 'No, no, he hasn't said anything, but I feel very sad because even though I was a virgin it hurts not to have bled that day.'"

Even more dramatic and explicit are the advertisements circulated by Dr. Guadalupe I. Solís, a physician in Northern Mexico who promises to "repair" a woman's virginity. Dr. Solís has performed *himenoplastía* — plastic surgery to restore a ruptured hymen — on Latina women (90 percent of them rape survivors) since 1968. Her patients have come for hymen reconstruction services from Mexico, South Texas, Spain, and Central and South America (Solís 1998). She guarantees that the women she has "repaired" will bleed when their hymen is re-ruptured.

Beyond the Cult of Virginity

Mexican women are often portrayed as subservient and submissive, but in my study I found that immigrant women actively challenge and rebel against Catholic sexual morality. The overwhelming majority of the women who participated in this study (39 women out of 40) were raised in the Catholic Church but describe it as morally fractured and in need of progressive social change. At the same time, these women did not abandon their faith. With regard to sexuality, they found creative ways to selectively reconcile the contradictions in their faith.[5] Of the non-virgins-at-marriage in this study, 70 percent were critical of Catholic morality.[6] Their non-virgin status, however, was not just an act of rebelliousness against the Catholic sex ethic; other factors were involved.

FAMILY POLITICS AND VIRGINITY

"I think it is because of a family tradition," Macaria said proudly. "My grandmother always said that all of her granddaughters had 'to get married right.' I think that is the reason why I am still a virgin." She used the expression *casarse bien* to mean marrying in accordance with social conventions of decency and morality.[7] Macaria, who migrated from Mexico City, has worked in Los Angeles for nine years. She has never married, and at thirty-seven has never experienced any type of sexual encounter, except for once having been assaulted, with no vaginal penetration, as an adult woman. For women like Macaria, virginity must be preserved as part of family honor, dignity, and tradition, values a woman learns from the authority figures (parents, grandparents, uncles, aunts, older siblings, etc.) within her own family and that cause her lack of sexual autonomy and, thus, sexual agency. Macaria and the other women in this study whom I identify as "virgins-until-marriage" relate that *respeto a la familia* is a major reason for a woman to renounce her sexuality. For them, a woman's virginity, and hence her sexuality, becomes a family possession. When a woman disowns her sexuality and surrenders total control of it to her family, it becomes more than a family value. For women like Macaria, *casarse bien* becomes one way to demonstrate family respect.

To marry well represents purity, virtue, and goodness. In addition, it guarantees economic and social benefits later in marriage: *casarse bien* means *vivir bien* — to live well. Lorena, a thirty-four-year-old from a small town in Jalisco, made this clear. When I asked her whether she would have liked to have had sex before marriage, she exclaimed, "No! Not having sex before marriage is something beautiful; that is something that my parents imposed on me, to be a virgin, and that was right!" She went on to describe how for her and her sisters, keeping their virginity had translated into a stronger socioeconomic status and the promise of marital stability and happiness: "In my family all of the women were virgins when we got married, all of us married right. Now we all are living well with our husbands and we all have our own homes, independent and everything."

Lorena's words may suggest self-sacrifice and sexual renunciation, but they also reflect the social reality of Mexican women as a subordinate group. Although quality of life (i.e., education, employment, health, etc.) for Mexican women has improved in the last decades, studies of their living conditions show that access to marriage is still a woman's most important means of survival. The more marriage is valued by women, the more virginity matters. Constraints on female sexuality are more rigid in rural areas or small towns, where there is a dearth of resources and few opportunities for women. In these social contexts, virginity, as a personal quality, acquires a higher "exchange value" (Szasz and Figueroa 1997, 13).

For women like Lorena and her sisters, preserving one's virginity translates into an increased likelihood of access to a financially stable, conflict-free marriage. Ultimately, it lessens vulnerability and improves the odds of a more secure personal life. Lorena's testimony resonates with the experience of other Mexicanas from rural Mexico. In her research on the sexual initiation of young women and men from Mexico City, Oaxaca, and Guanajuato, Amuchástegui (1994) identified rural women as those who perceived premarital virginity as an asset that could be exchanged for financial support via marriage. Similarly, hymen reconstructive surgery represents an attempt to reverse the depreciated exchange value of a damaged hymen. Dr. Solís began doing hymen reconstructions in the late 1960s after listening to the pleas of desperate mothers concerned about the future for their young daughters who had been raped. Bleeding after the hymen is re-ruptured not only becomes a woman's virginal guarantee, it also makes her sexualized body an instrument for improving her living conditions within the context of inequality between the sexes.

Virginity had a clear exchange value for Lorena and her sisters, for Amuchástegui's rural informants, and for Dr. Solis's patients. Based on these observations, I have proposed the term *capital femenino* to identify virginity as a form of social endowment. In this, I am expanding on other scholars' work on social exchange value of virginity (e.g., Twinam 1989; Tostado Gutiérrez 1991; Amuchástegui 1994, 1998, 2001; Szasz and

Figueroa 1997; Zavella 1997; and, Córdova Plaza 1998).[8] Premarital virginity possesses the following characteristics: (1) it is a form of *social capital* only women possess and use in the marriage market of a patriarchal society; (2) women as well as men actively participate in socially constructing virginity as a life-enhancing resource; (3) these dynamics have their historical roots in Mexican colonial society; and, (4) virginity functions as a transaction commodity. Depending on the social context, it may acquire a higher or lower social value. The stronger the gender inequalities and/or sexual moralities in a given social context (e.g., in small towns and ranches), the higher the value of virginity as *capital femenino*. Mexicanas struggle for survival through marriage, but they are not alone; their experience unites them with women living in similar circumstances in other countries. As Rosemary Hennessy writes: "It is just recently, and only in urban industrialized economies, that for most women there have been any alternatives to marriage as a route to subsistence, since the patriarchal household was the only place where women's economic security was protected, and the social as well as the economic position of a wife was often preferable to that of unmarried sister, daughter, or aunt. Across the globe, the economic security marriage continues to offer women is often an incentive to marry or for staying married" (2000, 64).

VIRGINITY AS COLLECTIVE PERFORMANCE

Given that the marital contract is such an important means of sustenance for women, virginity becomes crystallized as a social construction after a wedding takes place. And as both women and men participate in this social event, their respective families become involved in reproducing the heterosexual interpretation of abstinence and premarital sex. In some cases, a family's celebration of a daughter's marriage "the right way" may be understood by the woman's parents as a gift from their son-in-law. This increases the likelihood of a conflict-free and harmonious relationship within the extended family for both the woman and the man. Fidel, for instance, boasted, *"Yo soy el consentido de mis suegros"* (I'm the favorite son-in-law), as he explained:

> My wife is the only one who got married wearing white in her family. In other words, her sisters also wore white but they were already pregnant. And I took my wife out from her family home wearing white! I asked her parents [for her hand in] marriage in advance. As my wife says, "You paid all the respect due to my parents. You took me out of my family home while respecting every single rule."

In Fidel's case, respect for his in-laws was closely connected to an ethic of reverence for women. Abstaining from physical intimacy with a girl-friend, however, did not preclude adolescents from experiencing sexual initiation with prostitutes, as Fidel and his friends did. Hirsch's inform-ants also associated *respeto* with abstinence during courtship but not to the exclusion of external sexual contacts. As with Fidel and several of my informants, some of Hirsch's informants also described the pride they felt when their brides were able to wear white, a symbol that the marriage was taking place "the right way" and not by eloping (Hirsch 2003, 78).

Fidel described his wife as a happy, full-time homemaker who had ded-icated herself to providing care, attention, and love to him and their three daughters since they had established a modest yet financially stable life in Los Angeles. Then he revealed the secret of their marital bliss: "[Most] married couples have problems because of sexual relations before getting married." Furthermore, Fidel was harshly critical of men (including acquaintances and some of his brothers) who have extramarital affairs. He described the fidelity and satisfying sex life that he and his wife had devel-oped throughout eleven years of marriage. As we wrapped up our con-versation, he recalled joyfully:

> It [having sex with his wife after marriage] was a beautiful experience that I cannot compare with anything. How can I explain it? It's like my wife once told me, "I was saving it [my virginity] for you, in order to give it to you as a gift the day I would marry you, and now it is yours."

Women like Lorena, men like Fidel, and their respective families, par-ticipate in what Bourdieu (2001) identifies as an *economy of symbolic exchanges*. A woman learns to perceive her premarital virginity as a form of social capital that she may use strategically. A woman's decision not to engage in premarital sex also offers symbolic capital to her family. Similarly, a man may perceive virginity as a symbolic value: it guarantees a stable and happy married life. In Fidel's case, virginity represented an inaugural gift to a sexually satisfying and emotionally stable life, which included the extended family. These symbolic exchanges and reciprocity take place in other Latin American countries (Burgos and Díaz Pérez 1986; Paternostro 1998; Boyd-Franklin and García-Preto 1994), and in Mediterranean, Middle Eastern, and North African societies where moral integrity and family honor are frequently associated with a woman's vir-ginal status (Youssef 1973; El Saadawi 1997; Shahidian 1999).[9]

The symbolic value of virginity is also embedded in the metaphorical language some women and men use to define it. Sebastián, for example, used the expression "Take care of your little treasure" to educate his teenage daughter about sex and the negative consequences of early pregnancy. Alfonso's triumphant feelings became evident when he stated, "To be the first man in a woman's life is like winning the Olympics." He alternately referred to virginity as a "gold medal" or a "trophy" while celebrating his wife's virginity at the time of their first sexual encounter.

In addition, sexual purity may be amplified through family coercion. When I asked Azalea about the most important reason for her to follow religious beliefs about sex, she exclaimed, "The fear that [my] parents would do something to [me]!" Unlike most of the women in the study, Azalea held religious values with regard to sexuality, but fear of family punishment was the main reason she preserved her virginity until marriage. Virginity also served as a safeguard against potential risks such as pregnancy and family punishment. When I asked Olga if she had received religious teachings with regard to virginity, she replied:

> Yes, but I did not follow them because of religion, I followed them because of fear . . . of my mother! I was afraid of my family . . . because you have your family inveighing against you if you get pregnant, that is why I was terrified . . . to get pregnant, to not be able to go to school, and to become like those women with many children and all those problems.

Fear of family condemnation surpassed fear of God for many women in this study. Tearfully, Soledad noted, "More than [concern about] committing a sin it was the fear of getting pregnant! And fear of my mother! She was so abusive, just the way she talked, she would be furious while talking to me. She always said, 'No! You will be a virgin until the day you get married! Or else men leave and you are left pregnant with problems!'"

None of the men in this study reported fear of being punished by family for being sexually active before marriage. Nevertheless, family had been an important influence on these men's views of sex and heterosexual relationships from an early age. Coercive marriage, for example, was a common denominator for both genders when premarital sex resulted in pregnancy out of wedlock. A fear of being forced to wed the "wrong woman" was the reason why some men refrained from premarital sex with a *novia,* that is, a steady girlfriend, or even a casual acquaintance. For these men, being a frequent customer of a sex worker represented a morally safer alternative. A second choice for men — especially when they were in adolescence — was to maintain a sexual relationship with an older women (either a friend or acquaintances) who could take charge of contraception and become their sex mentor.

Virginity and Sexism

Finally, virginity was seen as protecting women from external dangers. "A woman is like a piece of bread," said Azalea. "If you have been touched all over, who is going to want you? It's like when you go to buy bread; you take the one that hasn't been touched by anybody! It is the same with men. They are *machistas;* they want a woman that has never been touched by anyone." For women like Azalea, preserving virginity was not just about family politics — it was also a protection from the hazards of gender inequality. That Azalea's fears were justified was confirmed by more than one of the men I interviewed. According to Fermín:

> When they marry, [most men] want to be with a virgin. . . . It's like buying a new car. You tell yourself, "I want to buy a new car, but I want one that nobody has ever touched, one with zero miles." Right? You don't want to have the one that everyone's driven all over. [You say,] "I don't want that kind of thing." And if you buy it like that, you don't feel comfortable with regard to the other persons that used it. Then, you say, "Well, it wasn't new." So, you want to open up the package that nobody has ever touched. I believe that all of us [want that].

Fermín's language becomes gendered as he describes a woman's body. For him, as Peter Murphy observes, "The most powerful cultural metaphor for masculinity is the machine, a cold, disembodied, efficacious piece of equipment" (2001, 17). The narratives of Fermín and Azalea also resonate with Juana A. Alegría's reflections in her book, *Psicología de las mexicanas*: "Men expect women to be virgins because they are upset when women have belonged to other men before them; this excuse implies another concept: belonging" (1974, 147–48). A man expects a woman to be virginal in body and soul because it is a reassurance that she will be his exclusive property. In addition, any type of sexual activity may provide a woman with a frame of reference for comparing a man's sexual performance. Although these beliefs are not universal, half of the virgins-until-marriage in this study remained sexually abstemious to prevent future husbands from throwing their transgressions in their faces. Five of the six women who held strong views on this subject were from small towns in Jalisco. Only one was from Mexico City. The concept of regional patriarchies explains such variations in gender patterns across geographical areas.[10]

Mothers not only embraced rigid sexual beliefs for themselves but, more importantly, for their daughters, hoping that virginity would protect them against the hazards of sexism. Being a virgin at marriage guarantees respect, which in turn, reduces marital conflict. "I have always had a good relationship with my husband," said Lorena. "We never have arguments where he could complain that I was with another man. [By comparison,] I see that many women who get married [but are not virgins] have problems." Fidel expressed a similar opinion. He and Lorena were born and raised in different towns in Jalisco, which suggests that people from rural areas may share a belief in abstinence as a necessary element for marital stability. This prescription is also present in other parts of Mexico, such as rural Guanajuato, where a woman who voluntarily has had sex before marriage may even lie to a potential husband, telling him that she lost her virginity through rape (Amuchástegui 2001, 292). This is to quell feelings of jealousy. Salomé described how a widowed friend is still paying the consequences of her husband's distrust regarding her non-virgin status at marriage. "Men throw it in your face for as long as you live!" she said. "I was thinking about what happened to a friend of mine whose husband is always throwing [premarital sex] in her face. And on top of that he would not let her watch her favorite *telenovela, Te sigo amando* (*I Still Love You*), because he thought it reminded her of her first husband." Three other women offered similar testimonies:

> *Eréndira:* Your mother will tell you that if you [have sex before marriage] you are nothing, a man will not respect you anymore . . . won't look at you the same way . . . Besides, if you get married without being a virgin, the man is going to throw it in your face all your life.
>
> *Romelia:* My mother said, "When a man touches you, you are worthless, you are not a virgin anymore." And ay! Oh my God! I did not let the boys touch me.
>
> *Victoria:* Mother used to say that we should not allow men to touch us; when you get married you have to be a señorita, because if you are not, your husband will not want you.[11]

These narratives reflect the same concerns Amuchástegui observed. Some of the women she interviewed reported that they had not revealed their sexual activity to their husbands for fear of rejection and potential conflict (2001, 291). Also, all the rural men in Amuchástegui's study reported that it was a male privilege to "accept or reject a young woman who is suspected of not being a virgin" (330). Some of the women in that study expressed similar feelings. Finally, some of them described "single young women who are not virgins as women without honor and, therefore, as lacking any social value" (384). The virgins-until-marriage in my study have learned a lesson: virginity is a "guarantee seal" respected by husbands, and it offers women a greater possibility for happiness.

Virginity is not always a safeguard, however. Although Azalea was sexually abstinent until marriage in the hope of gaining her husband's respect, things didn't turn out that way.

> My husband always asked me why I got wet when we were having sex, and we argued a lot because of it. He always told me that a woman should not be that way, that a woman should be dry and clean for her husband. But how dirty could I be if he was the only man? I never thought about being with someone else. And he always asked me if I was a whore. . . . We did not stay married for that long . . . nine years, and then he looked for another woman.

To Azalea's husband, the normal physical reaction of vaginal lubrication during intercourse represented a lack of virtue and goodness. To men like him, a virginal vagina is not only one that has never been penetrated but also one that does not know how to respond to any type of erotic pleasure or physical sensation.[12] Azalea felt sadness and guilt when she discovered her husband's extramarital affair. Her story echoes that of Saúl from rural Guanajuato, one of Amuchástegui's informants who described his paradoxical feelings when he first had sex with his virgin wife: "[He felt] disillusioned during his first sexual relation with his wife, [but also] satisfied in finding her to be an ignorant in terms of sensuality" (307).

The story of intercourse between Azalea and her husband shows that the sexual act does not occur in a social vacuum. Behind the man's jealousy and ignorance about female physiology lies a mechanism of social power and control: the man defines the woman's sexuality, while the woman does not have the right to own her body or to experience sexual or erotic pleasure. Furthermore, the man enjoys an exclusive privilege: through adultery, he can dispose of a woman he considers no longer useful as a sexual object and replace her with another. By having a lover, men like Azalea's husband validate not only an erotic need but also a political one: he can take a mistress when his wife does not meet his expectations of womanhood and sexuality. Other than the testimonies of twelve women who had experienced sexual violence, Azalea's story was the most extreme expression of masculine control and power in this study.

Virginity, Men, and Gender Sensibility

All of the male informants in this study were single when they had intercourse for the first time. Those who experienced sex with their wives before marriage, or who married women who were not virgins, reported that their spouse's premarital sexual experiences were rarely at the center of marital discord. They said that conflict with their partners was rather due to factors such as inadequate communication, economic hardship, children's education, or other sex-related issues, but rarely to their wives non-virginal status at marriage or premarital sex history. Some of the men explained how their own sexual initiation prior to marriage became a rite of passage into manhood. This was not always voluntary or pleasurable. It created stress and anxiety especially when, as young boys, they were coerced by an adult male to have sex for the first time with a sex worker or a considerably older woman. Men consistently reported that male chastity was not a moral expectation. On the contrary, a lack of sexual experience could be the source of stigma.

What did the men in the study think about the women's narratives about virginity? I presented the following statement as part of our interviews: "Some women told me that one of the reasons why they decided to be virgins until they got married was because they were afraid that men would throw sexual involvement in their faces. Have you observed situations like that? What is your personal opinion in that respect?" Most men reported having witnessed or having heard of similar situations. In their responses, some men expressed feelings of empathy, compassion, and understanding toward the women. Their responses were complex and shared some commonalities. Some reported having been exposed to and convinced by gender-sensitive ideas learned from teachers, professors, and mentors in their biology, psychology, or sociology classes in school.

In addition, gender sensitivity was embedded in these men's families. As I listened to them, I felt as if I were talking with the brothers, sons, and cousins of the women I had interviewed earlier. Alejandro, for instance, described arguments between his parents. A cousin had raped his mother when she was a young teenager, and the fact that she wasn't a virgin at marriage became the catalyst of marital conflict. Alejandro recalled, "My father, he was *machista*. [Since childhood] I used to see that problem in men. How is it possible for a man to be so sexist? In Mexico they say that the woman has to be a virgin at marriage, and that the woman has no right to talk, only the man. The woman becomes a second-class citizen."

Mauricio became similarly upset while describing the challenging conversations he used to have with an uncle about the man's suspicion that his wife was not a virgin at marriage: "[Such] men are so close-minded, very *machistas*. One of my uncles says, 'My wife did not bleed.' So just because she does not bleed, she's not a virgin? The men who [care about] those things are wrong. What if someone raped the woman? Now the woman, who was not even responsible, is being condemned!"

Ernesto agreed: "I used to listen to [my sisters] talking about virginity, all the time. [They said,] 'I have to be a virgin at marriage because otherwise I am going to have problems.'" Daniel did not want to characterize his relationship with a young relative with whom he used to talk about sex before migrating. He merely said, "I had someone in my family . . . she trusted me and I trusted her. And she told me that she had problems with her husband because of that, because she was not a virgin [at marriage]. And that created a lot of fear in her."

Family life was the first school of gender consciousness for these four men. Feelings of love and concern for their female relatives prompted both sensitivity toward women and non-hegemonic expressions of masculine identity. Emotions and feelings had shaped both their masculine self-definitions and their views of women and virginity (see Chodorow 1995). Men from Mexico City were particularly severe in condemning those who would judge a woman for not being a virgin at marriage. These men used the term *machismo* in their statements more frequently than their Jalisco counterparts. Alfredo, for instance, explained that female virginity was at the center of the many heated conversations he had had with friends. "The country where we live, where we come from, is *machista*," he stated, after relating the following conversation with one of his friends:

Friend: Hey! You know what? I got married and my wife was not a virgin.

Alfredo: And what about you? Idiot! Were you a virgin when you got married? If you are demanding virginity, you have to be a virgin at marriage as well! I do not [care about] that little membrane they have.

Like Alfredo, many men engaged in thoughtful reflection, either defying or reinforcing their assumptions about the need for women to be virgins at marriage. Diego condemned sexism in Mexico by citing anthropologists who see the origin of virginity at marriage in pre-Hispanic cultures. Fermín, Sebastián, and Marcos highlighted the importance of mutual acceptance between partners, regardless of a woman's previous sexual experiences. They described with sadness the stories of friends or acquaintances who had separated or experienced marital conflict because of allegations that a wife had not been a virgin at marriage. Joaquín and Raúl explained that emotional and sexual bonding before marriage was crucial for a satisfying marital life, more so than a woman's virginity. Raúl noted that some men are still raised to believe in the Mexican expression that makes him chuckle: *"La mujer es nomás para el metate y el petate"* (The woman is only good for the kitchen and the bed). Alfonso said he did not believe in outdated sexual taboos, yet interestingly, he had earlier gloated that taking his wife's virginity made him feel like an Olympic gold medal winner. Recognizing the apparent contradiction, he noted, "We say that we are not sexist, but perhaps there is machismo in all of us." He said that he would not have rejected his wife had she not been a virgin, but the postponement of sex as she played hard to get helped to build up the excitement of their first sexual encounter, which he repeatedly described as pleasant and loving.

Emiliano and Vinicio both said that they did not believe in the dumb things some men are raised to believe. Fidel celebrated his wife's virginity, but as Nicolás did, objected to men's use of a woman's past sex history to stir up marital conflict. He recommended that men should have probing conversations with their girlfriends before marriage to prevent "surprises." Jacobo reported that some men's obsession about virginity originated in their ignorance about what is really important in loving relationships. With a big laugh, he confessed that he enjoyed teasing and creating doubts in his friends who brag about their wives having been virgins at marriage. Eugenio was the only man whose responses did not match those of the rest of my male informants. He was convinced that "a woman who is not virgin at marriage . . . has lived life without moral restraint. She is an irresponsible woman."

These multiple expressions invite us to explore the ambivalent nature of women's and men's heterosexual experiences. While it is essential to examine the sexual histories of women like Azalea (for whom the long-awaited first sexual encounter was the first step in a hazardous journey), the inclusion of men's testimony may do more than just confirm women's experiences of sexual inequality. By articulating a "she said/he said" perspective, we are able to better explore the dialectics of heterosexual love and sex. This perspective is inspired by Jessie Bernard's (1972) notion of two points of view ("her marriage" and "his marriage") as part of the same union. I have benefited from this analytical framework, which has sensitized me to how heterosexual scripts are written through social interactions. An inclusion of family life and relationships between the two genders has the potential of expanding our feminist horizons.

Women and Sexual Initiation: Between Pleasure and Danger

For the women in this study, diverse forms of female sexuality are reconfigured along a bipolar continuum joining pleasure and danger.[13] At one extreme, I examine sexual stories that offer the possibility for Mexican women to reclaim sexual autonomy, agency, and pleasure. At the other end, I identify the moral and social contradictions shaping Mexican women's sexuality. A wide variety of mechanisms of social control linked to a woman's loss of virginity emerge between these two extremes. These tendencies are not equally balanced; the danger end of the continuum is over-represented in my data. The sexual behavior described by my respondents includes the following characteristics along the pleasure–danger spectrum:

1. Pleasure. A woman may question the various dynamics controlling her sexuality and may come to reclaim it so that she can experience it freely. The stories shared by the women who identified with this tendency illustrate the ways that women living in patriarchal societies can enjoy their sexuality. The women's testimony also indicates that women have the capability to experience sexual agency and autonomy, and to enjoy sex and erotic desire as positive feelings and opportunities for exploring emotional intimacy with a partner before marriage.

2. Sexual risks and threats. A woman may take a risk in claiming and experiencing sexuality while encountering dangerous situations and experiencing painful repercussions: (a) the risk of pregnancy and, in a worst-case scenario, coerced marriage; (b) guilt for not complying with an ethic of family respect; and (c) feelings of shame, fear, confusion, frustration, ambivalence, worthlessness, and failure, or *fracaso,* as a result of their earliest sexual encounters.

3. Danger. A woman faces the risk of being sexually coerced or victimized and of involuntarily losing her virginity due to sexual violence (i.e., rape, incest). For one-third of the women who had premarital sex, rape and/or incest were their first sexual experiences. That is, 80 percent of women survivors of sexual violence in the study were virgins when they were raped. Their testimonies reveal mechanisms of sexual control and power hidden behind sexualized gender relations.

Each one of these three female heterosexual experience patterns resounds with feminist theorist Lynne Segal's proposal to acknowledge the existence of multiple female heterosexualities. Segal writes: "Once we look for sexual diversity and fluidity, the fluctuating nature of heterosexual encounters or relation-ships [*sic*] is obvious: some are pleasurable, self-affirming, supportive, reciprocal or empowering; others are compulsive, oppressive, pathological or disabling; most move between the two" (1994, 260).

The sexualities of most of the women that I interviewed do not neces-sarily move symmetrically between the two extremes identified by Segal. Risk and danger surround the heterosexual encounters of many of these women. Many women born and educated in underdeveloped and devel-oping nations still face multiple sources of gender inequality. Never-theless, Segal's framework offers an alternative for exploring both the pos-sibilities for Mexican immigrant women to claim their right to sexual autonomy, pleasure, and agency and to identify the social, cultural, and political forces that oppress women involved in heterosexual relationships.

By adopting this continuum, I do not deny women's simultaneous exposure to both pleasure and danger in sex. I use this model exclusively to represent how they interpret their first sexual encounters. Some of the women I interviewed revealed how in some situations pleasure and dan-ger can occur simultaneously. Danger and pleasure are not mutually exclu-sive and, at times, the former may enhance the latter. For example, some women recalled how as teenagers hiding from or lying to a parent about a boyfriend enhanced their expectation and excitement of an intimate encounter with him. Prohibition enhanced desire; their challenge was to find ways to keep the thrill alive while challenging the proscriptions that kept them from pleasure.

After analyzing the women's sexual narratives, I found Segal's aware-ness of "the fluctuating nature of heterosexual encounters" and what she calls "relation-ships" fascinating. Her notion of female heterosexualities was also an invitation to listen to the men's stories, in a dialogue of sorts between the two genders.

Erotic Love, Emotional Pleasure

Not all of the women in this study who had sex before marriage experi-enced guilt, shame, fear of sexism, or family persecution. A small num-ber, five out of twenty of those who had premarital sex, experienced it in a positive way. They had no regrets. Instead, having sex for the first time had a special meaning: it had been an expression of trust in and deep love for a man:

> *Graciela:* I felt good, not nervous or anything, and I never regretted it. . . . I
> really loved him, I had sex with him because I really loved him.
>
> *Rosalía:* I felt happy because he was my first boyfriend and I did it for the
> first time with him and felt happy. I have never regretted it.

Lolita: Since I trusted him . . . and I loved him . . . I did not feel bad. In other words, I felt good.

Zenaida described her first sexual encounter in a tone of elation: "I felt happy because I adored that man. . . . I never felt nervous because I knew what was happening, and I did not feel afraid either. All I remember is that I felt so happy, and so in love with him . . ." When I asked if she had noticed a change in the relationship after having sex, she replied, "It got better; we got closer to each other. We had a great time." Oralia's sexual experience was like Zenaida's, exciting and pleasurable: "I never felt bad, quite the contrary, I felt . . . as if he was already a part of me. When I looked at him from the distance, I really rejoiced. [The relationship] got better. Yes, it got better."

What is required for a man educated in a patriarchal society to experience sexuality in ways that are similarly positive? In this study, three men had sexual relations for the first time with women with whom they had developed a steady relationship. Raúl had sex for the first time when he was nineteen or twenty, with a beloved girlfriend who was a year or two younger than him. Tenderly, he described the deep emotional relationship he had with her. Emiliano had intercourse for the first time when he was fifteen. With a wistful sigh, he recalled the woman, who was five years older than him, as *el amor de mi vida* (the love of my life). Daniel, the youngest of the men from Jalisco, had sex with a girlfriend about a year younger than him. He also described their relationship as emotionally meaningful.

A commonality in the life of this manly trio was the influence of education on their personal perceptions of sexuality and gender relations. Raúl explained that by the time he had sex for the first time, he had already found answers to many of his questions about reproduction and human sexuality in his psychology classes at the Colegio de Ciencias y Humanidades — the CCH. CCH is the equivalent of a senior high school at the Universidad Nacional Autónoma de México (UNAM) — the largest public university in the nation, located in Mexico City. Coincidentally, Emiliano reported that although he stopped attending school after he had finished *secundaria* (the equivalent of ninth grade), his older cousin had become his mentor with regard to human sexuality during his adolescent years. Emiliano reported that his cousin, like Raúl, was completing his education at the CCH. Daniel reported that a middle-school teacher had a powerful influence on his perceptions of sexuality and gender relations. That teacher eventually became the school principal. He was a respected yet controversial figure in Daniel's small town for openly teaching his students about reproduction, human sexuality, and for promoting equal rights between women and men. During our interview, Daniel realized that his teacher had been a substitute for his absent father, who had died when he was a little boy. Raúl, Emiliano, and Daniel echo the experiences of other young Mexicanos. In a study of more than three hundred young Mexican men, Stern et al. (2003) found that some of their informants approached their male cousins and uncles who were attending *preparatoria* or college in order to ask them questions about sexuality. The men's stories also resonate with Hirsch's findings for women: those who embraced views of sexual intimacy within marriage — as opposed to those who were more "reproductive oriented" — had completed higher levels of formal education and had been exposed to school-based sex education programs (2003, 224).

Besides education, the three men shared similar personal histories, which were also a factor in shaping their expansive sexual views. They described loving relationships with the women with whom they experienced sex for the first time. They used the term *nervioso* to describe feelings of anxiety during their first sexual encounters. In their cases, the first sexual experience had intensified emotional bonding and improved the quality of their relationships:

> *Raúl:* I felt as if she had become part of my life, and I think that I also became part of her life.
>
> *Emiliano:* It [the relationship] improved a lot, and ah . . . we, we understood each other well; I think it was much better that way. . . . Happy. I felt good. It surprised me because [I thought] because she is older, she has more experience, and it was not that way. It was very tender and affectionate.
>
> *Daniel:* It [the relationship] became more open; better, with more tranquility and everything. . . . I developed more love for her.

The three men noted that their respective partners had been virgin women, but that they had felt no moral obligation to marry. They rejected the idea that a man's decision to refrain from sexual relations with a girlfriend was a sign of *respeto a la mujer.* Nevertheless, they were aware that unexpected pregnancy might have led to marriage. They asserted that the decision to preserve virginity until marriage was a woman's personal choice and not a moral obligation. None of these men married the women with whom they explored heterosexual desire for the first time, but they remembered those love experiences with nostalgia. Interestingly, the two men from Mexico City continued to engage in sex as part of later dating experiences, a practice that at some point resulted in unexpected pregnancies and coercive marriages with women they were not sure about.

Daniel is still single and dreaming of a woman with sexual desire and experience with whom he can explore erotic pleasure, commitment, and love.

For both women and men, the decision to have sex before marriage and experience it with pleasure was a consequence of social awareness (via education) and the recognition of an emotional connection between love and sex. For women in particular, questioning Catholic Church teachings on sexuality was a factor. Zenaida, a college-educated woman from Mexico City, spoke passionately when I asked about religion's influence on a woman's sexuality: "Sexuality, for both men and women, is something personal, it's an intimate issue. [No one should] tell you what you can do and what you cannot do, not even the Church!"

Oralia, who had sex before marriage, saw things differently. While talking about her deep Catholic faith, Oralia said that although she did not regret having sex (and her husband had never complained about it) she had experienced feelings of guilt later in life. "I know I offended God in that way as in many other things," she said. "I know it wasn't right, because He didn't want me to do it. I am sorry because I offended God, but I know He already forgave me and He knows I love my husband and that I would not do it with anybody else."

Unlike Oralia, none of the men in the study reported feelings of guilt and remorse related to religion. The testimony of women like Oralia, and that of the other women, discussed earlier, bring us back to the sex experiences of women who dare to explore pleasure and joy before marriage while trying to disentangle themselves from a web of moral condemnation.

How is the first sexual encounter experienced when it happens before marriage and does not lead to pregnancy? A third of the women who had voluntarily had sex before marriage experienced fear, guilt, confusion, disappointment, shame, physical pain, frustration, and a sense of worthlessness and failure, or *fracaso*:

> *Norma:* I felt disappointed because I always thought it was something special, beautiful . . . like everybody had told me.
>
> *Diamantina:* I was scared . . . because I did not know about it, and the next day I was afraid and I could not look him in the face because I was ashamed of myself.
>
> *Deyanira:* I did not like it . . . you know, it hurts and then you bleed and I did not like that at all. . . . He did not do it roughly or anything, but I remember feeling bad.
>
> *Felicia:* I felt very bad and very strange. He did not force me, and I would not know how to explain it to you . . . but I felt strange. I did not know what sex or love was about.

> *Idalia:* When I did it the first time I felt worthless. . . . I thought every-
> thing was gone for me. I felt *fracasada*, I felt like a failure.

Idalia further explained the meaning of *fracaso* to me: "Well, *yo fracasé*, that means that I failed, that I did not get married, following the custom that says that I have to walk down the aisle [as a virgin]." In relation to premarital sex and pregnancy out of wedlock, *fracaso* was also used by some of the men I interviewed.[14]

In short, having sexual relations before marriage was morally confusing for this subgroup of women.[15] For women who voluntarily experience premarital sex, sexual activity flows between two extremes. At its worst, sex results in pregnancy out of wedlock and leads to coerced marriage. At its best, sexual activity does not result in pregnancy but creates feelings of guilt or regret for not having complied with the ethic of family respect. Although none of the men were faced with a girlfriend's pregnancy as a consequence of their first sexual encounters, some were exposed to coercive marriages later in life when they had to deal with a partner's unexpected pregnancy. In addition, some men felt that they were constantly watched by their families. In that respect, the women and men shared similar risks, but the extreme dangers were reserved for women.

Rape of a Virgin

Being educated in a patriarchal society where a devotion to virginity is still pervasive may magnify the trauma of rape in a virgin woman. Eight women in the study (four from Jalisco and four from Mexico City) described the emotional ordeal of rape in detail. They related the horror, agony, confusion, shame, and guilt that were brought about by the rape, and of the damaging impact rape had had on their lives. The following are condensed accounts of their stories.

Nora. A Mexican man she had dated raped her in Los Angeles. Her only daughter was the consequence of this assault. During our interview, she showed anxiety when the topic of virginity came up. Nora had refrained from any sexual activity for twenty-eight years; all her life, she had dreamed of marrying in white. Being raped and becoming pregnant as a result dashed her hopes. At the time of our interview, she was living without benefit of marriage with a Mexican man she described as kind and understanding.

Victoria. She remembered vividly the fear of being killed after a man she did not know kidnapped her and took her to his house, where he raped her, when she was an adolescent. She still swallows tears when she sees that her son, the result of the rape, has the rapist's face and gestures. She is married to a man she describes as handsome and good, but who at times complains because she was not a virgin at marriage. He knows her son but not the whole truth about what happened.

Candelaria. She came to the United States to escape her rapist, a neighbor who had forced her to have intercourse with him many times over the years, beginning when she was very young. Immediately after she was told that she had given birth to a little girl, Candelaria cried and prayed that her only daughter would never have to go through the same kind of experience. She married an immigrant man she met in Los Angeles. Under the influence of alcohol her husband complains that she was not a virgin when they married. He doesn't know about the rape. She also recalled feeling "embarrassed, ashamed, and confused" after her older brother "touched her in inappropriate ways" more than once when she was ten or twelve.

Tomasita. She still cries in silence and confusion, trying to forget the ways in which her uncle sexually abused her when she was five or six years old. She is separated from her last partner and lives with her children.

Belén. Her father forced her to have repeated intercourse with him from the time she was nine years old until adolescence. As with many incest survivors, Belén's sexual ordeal did not stop with her father — two cousins also abused her and, as a young adult, Belén was the victim of date rape. She still recalls fears of being rejected by men as the main reason why she maintained a relationship with the boyfriend who raped her and finally married her. They are still together and they live in Los Angeles.

Irasema. Unlike the vast majority of the study participants, she described herself as a former "Daddy's girl" who owned a garment shop. She was an upper-middle-class young woman in her native Mexico City. When she was nineteen and riding in a car with her boyfriend, he took an unknown detour and drove to a hotel, where he raped her. She is currently in a relationship with an immigrant man that she described as a great lover, gentle and compassionate.

Fernanda. She is extremely protective of the two daughters she is currently raising. She cries and thinks of them as she experiences flashbacks of her uncle molesting her and her younger sister while both were spending Christmas in their relatives' small town. A Latino man who came out of the dark as she walked down the alley leading to the sweatshop where she works in Los Angeles sexually assaulted her. She has had different types of relationships, at times rough and at times marked by love. She is currently unmarried but living with a man.

Diamantina. She identified her father's alcoholism as the main reason why he would wake her up at night, touching her genitalia, when she was eight or ten. Similar incidents happened with one of her brothers. She recalled both experiences as a dream, something impossible to believe. She does not know if she "technically" lost her virginity because of those experiences. (The "technical" aspects of virginity were also a concern for Macaria, who had been sexually assaulted with no penetration. At the end of our interview, she asked whether a gynecologist would be able to tell if she was still a virgin or not.) Diamantina ended her story by describing her current relationship as not the best in terms of sexual satisfaction. Her husband works long hours to be a good provider.

The women had been sexually victimized under varying circumstances, and they differed with respect to the quality of their relationships. Yet they all shared certain commonalities. They all had felt morally devastated, devalued, and ashamed after losing their virginity in a violent and offensive way. For some, losing their virginity as a result of rape meant that they had been robbed of their *capital femenino* and engendered fears of not being able "to marry right." Some women experienced bitter regret about having to forfeit the cherished dream "to marry in white." Being raped also meant experiencing shame. Embarrassment and confusion were reasons why the women had not revealed their experiences to their families. Several were afraid of being blamed for their own victimization. Their ultimate concern was to learn what to do as mothers so as to spare their daughters the same fate. Elsewhere, I have examined these stories in more depth with regard to the negative consequences of rape on the women's emotional lives (see González-López, forthcoming).

Men and Sexual Violence

> *Though an appalling number of men do rape, most men do not.*
> *It is a fact of great importance, both theoretically and practically,*
> *that there are many non-violent men in the world. This too needs*
> *explanation, and must be considered in a strategy for peace.*
> R. W. Connell, *The Men and the Boys*

What do the men in this study think about sexual violence against women? When I asked male informants that question, some replied in one sentence while others gave complex answers. The overwhelming majority made the male figure solely responsible for acts of violence against women, while also naming the psychological factors they believed might explain a rapist's behavior: lack of personal control or self-confidence, selfishness, alcohol and drug use, and so on. Men from Mexico City were more likely to attribute sexual violence to sexism, while men from small towns in Jalisco were more passionate and severe in the judgments, using terms such as "beast," "brutish," "savage," and "animal" to condemn rapists. A similar pattern emerged in the men's opinions about husbands who complained about their wives' earlier sexual involvement and the women's fear of sexism. Men from Mexico City were more likely to blame gender inequality for rape than their rural counterparts. This pattern follows my argument about fluid yet systematic variations in masculinity and patriarchy depending on socioeconomic context. Only a minority of the men alleged that a woman's attire and behavior could be held as a cause of rape.

Unlike the women in my sample, only one man reported his first sexual experience as having been abusive. Although he did not elaborate, Vinicio briefly stated that an adult man in his family had attempted to sexually molest him when he was about five years old. Although the vast majority of men did not report sexual abuse, some had been profoundly affected by violence against women. Like Vinicio, they were moved when that subject came up during the interviews. They exhibited the same emotional responses as the women's concerning recriminations from the women's partners for their not being virgins at marriage. For Alejandro, Ernesto, Diego, and Sebastián, sexual violence against the women they love — including mothers, sisters, wives, and daughters — is part of their personal histories.

Alejandro asked me during our interview whether I could provide a professional referral for his wife. He explained she had been raped in her early twenties, while still living in her native town on Mexico's Pacific Coast. He explained that although sex between them was sometimes pleasant, tensions still emerged in moments of intimacy because of the rape she had experienced. "All I do to help her is give her lots of affection and support," he said. One of the reasons why he had learned to be sensitive and caring toward his wife was the rape experience of another woman he has always loved: his mother.

Ernesto, who is forty-three, had migrated from his native Guadalajara to Los Angeles when he was twenty-three. Not long afterward, he had married a Mexican divorcee who was also an immigrant. Early in the marriage, Ernesto learned about her painful past, which eventually led to conflict between them. Like Alejandro's, Ernesto's sex life was negatively affected by the physical, sexual, and emotional violence his wife had experienced. "I do not sleep with her. For a long time, I have not slept with her, I have my own room," he stated with deep concern.

Like Alejandro, Ernesto has also encouraged his wife to seek professional help but without success. Despite his sexual frustrations, he is proud of his behavior as a married man. "I have always been faithful," he said. "I am not like those people who need to be with one woman and then another one. I firmly believe in being faithful to my wife."

Alejandro's family history helped him to develop compassion toward his wife. In the early stages of our interview, we explored the reasons why he believed that women and men should have equal rights. He explained that, while attending elementary school, he had begun to notice conflict between his parents. Although his father was not physically violent toward his mother, Alejandro witnessed the emotional abuse she endured and that made him especially caring toward her, his sisters, and women in general. For both Alejandro and Ernesto, falling in love with and marrying a rape survivor had led to tolerance, acceptance, and self-sacrifice.

Both men's stories resonate with a pattern I discuss elsewhere: the relational nature of gender and sexuality via motherhood (González-López 2003). The mothers in that study taught their daughters about the value of virginity on the basis of their own sexual histories. Similarly, married men like Ernesto and Alejandro who are involved with rape survivors become sensitive toward their partners when women in their families of origin have had similar experiences. The rape of a sister or a daughter had different — but no less painful — consequences on a man's life. Diego, for example, harshly condemned violence against women as he described his own feelings after learning that his sister had been raped:

> One of my sisters . . . over there in Mexico, someone took advantage of her. When I learned about it, I experienced a stunning feeling of impotence. You feel rage, of course. You feel like going to look for him, giving him a lesson, leaving him half dead. You feel so indignant; she is blood of your blood! Someone, an asshole, a coward gets there and abuses her just because he wanted to and she didn't, so all he had was force, right? It demoralizes me not only about my sister but also about all women.

Diego explained that although his parents had an exemplary marriage, his only two sisters had married abusive husbands from whom they were now legally separated. Diego, one of the most eloquent of my informants, firmly condemned violence against women and children. Sebastián whispered that his daughter had been raped at the age of seven or eight by a family relative while still living in Mexico. Now a teenager, the girl was nearby, listening to our conversation. Discreetly, Sebastián reported that his daughter had never exhibited behaviors or attitudes suggesting that she had been raped. Nevertheless, he was bent on protecting her from further abuse.

In short, women whose first experience of intercourse was rape have undergone moral, spiritual, and psychological devastation. This type of gender violence also affects their sons, husbands, brothers, and fathers. From sexual desire to coercive sex, the continuum captures the paradoxes of patriarchal institutions and ideologies that selectively affect women as well as men.

In this chapter I examined how sexuality is a malleable social process for both genders. A woman's decision to preserve virginity until marriage goes far beyond the values imposed by the Catholic Church. Virginity is socially constructed as a resource that Mexican women can use in their search for marriage opportunities. As *capital femenino,* virginity possesses a social exchange value that women deploy to improve life conditions and expand opportunities. Because marriage is still a means of subsistence and upward social mobility for many Mexican women, virginity increases the likelihood that they will have conflict-free and financially stable marriages. In addition, virginity is a safeguard against risks like pregnancy out of wedlock, family punishment, and sexism. As shown by the testimony in this chapter, women are not alone in their use of sexual purity. Men actively participate in, and some benefit from, the construction of virginity as a social asset.

Women may explore erotic desire, pleasure, and emotional intimacy within loving relationships. Nevertheless, for many in this study, their first sexual contact was tied up with acts of domination. The men's testimony tended to confirm the women's reports of sexual violence, affirming rather than contradicting the feminine voices. The same testimony also revealed that virginity is a social exigency for women, more so than for men. On the other hand, the men's narratives suggest multiple expressions of masculine identity, some of which may promote gender equality. Education and family life in varying socioeconomic contexts (i.e., rural and urban) shape heterosexual masculine identities.

The social processes discussed in this chapter are continuously being reproduced through negotiation, conflict, and accommodation between women and men. The next chapter goes beyond the feminine silhouette to examine men's sexual initiation experiences as essential components in a comprehensive study of Mexican immigrant sexualities.

CHAPTER 3

Pleasurable Dangers, Dangerous Pleasures

Men and Their First Sexual Experience

Masculinities are not homogenous but are likely to be internally divided. Men's lives often embody tensions between contradictory desires or practices.

R. W. Connell, *The Men and the Boys*

"In other words it was not a satisfying experience because eh . . . I remember that I was with her in the sex act . . . and some of the prostitutes do it for money, and for them, the sooner you are done, the better for them." Fidel was explaining about the first time he had had intercourse, at a brothel in his small hometown. "And I remember that I . . . , I was afraid and I could not finish. I could not finish, and she told me '*¡Ándale!*' to hurry me up. 'Come on! They are waiting for me. So-and-So just arrived!' Then, when I did it . . . In other words, I finished by the force but with fear and . . . In other words, it was not an experience, let's say, unforgettable, I would not say. It was an experience that had to happen and it happened."

Fidel exemplifies the vulnerability some men experience during their heterosexual sex initiation in a patriarchal society. As they discussed his story, Fidel and the other men also revealed an unfolding process and my thesis about the men's first sexual experiences: a young man's sexual debut is a rite of passage into manhood often orchestrated by peers and sexual initiation is not just about a young man exploring the erotic with a woman for the first time. A sexualized experience that is shaped by class, this ritualistic process exposes young men to wide variety of emotions, feelings, contexts, and situations, including anticlimactic, unexpected, and dangerous ventures. Sexual initiation may expose men to many risks. As each man follows a personal version of this basic pattern, each embraces his first sexual experience in a unique and subjective way. Multiple and nuanced expressions of masculinity both shape and emerge from first sexual experiences. As part of this sexualized process, a young man may engage in sex as a way to be accepted as a man by his peers. And as illustrated by Fidel, some men may seek pleasure even as they are subjected to difficulties and pain. So, if a woman's first heterosexual sexual experience takes place along the pleasure–danger continuum, what is the equivalent of this continuum for men? How do the men's experiences influence or shape women's sexuality? Why? To what extent? This chapter explores answers to these questions through the examinations of the men's reported first sexual encounters.

Erotic Paradoxes: Men's First Sexual Experiences

Some men (in an equal proportion to women) reported their sexual initiation experiences as pleasurable, intimate, and erotic, while others recalled the pain, anxiety, and confusion of a coercive sexual initiation by adult men. Between both pleasant and painful possibilities, the men's accounts of their first sexual experiences also reflected the multiple ways in which patriarchal societies construct and promote painful expressions of heterosexual masculinities.

The sexual experiences of the men reveal the wide array of social challenges men encounter while dealing with social prescriptions of masculinity that shape men's sexual initiation expectations and actual experiences. As a social group, however, women were still at a disadvantage, as illustrated by the high incidence of rape and incest, coercive marriage due to pregnancy caused by the first sexual experience, and feelings of shame and guilt attached to family respect — circumstances of sexual initiation rarely reported by the men. On the other hand, the men's testimony also highlights social pathways that explain why both men and women contribute to the social construction of sexual expression that disadvantages women but that also creates situations of injustice for men in distinctive ways.

In the following section, I will discuss the sexual initiation of some of the men with sex workers. Their stories expose how a highly anticipated first sexual encounter may be transformed by a series of unexpected uncertainties that may go beyond erotic desire and pleasure.

Sexual Disenchantment: Between Fantasies of Pleasure and Commercial Sex Pressures

> *Like most of my friends, I lost my virginity to a prostitute at the age of thirteen. An older acquaintance was responsible for arranging the "date," when a small group of us would meet an experienced harlot at a whorehouse. It goes without saying that none of the girls in my class were similarly "tutored": They would most likely become women in the arms of someone they loved or thought they loved. But love or even the slightest degree of attraction was not involved in our venture. Losing our virginity was actually a dual mission: to ejaculate inside the hooker and then, more importantly, to tell of the entire adventure afterward.*
>
> Ilán Stavans, *The Latin Phallus*

The sexual honesty of Mexican-born and raised novelist Ilán Stavans offers a reflection of the first sexual experiences reported by many men in this study. Nine out of the twenty men I interviewed had their first sexual experience with a female sex worker. Interestingly, two-thirds of the nine men were from Jalisco. Mainly from small towns, the men collectively expressed an ethic of *respeto a la mujer* as one of the reasons for having engaged in their sexual initiation rite with a sex worker. This rationale was not an exception for the men from Mexico City. However, the men's stories of sexual initiation with sex workers reflect how both women and men construct collective expressions of masculinity and femininity differently, depending on whether they are educated in rural vis-à-vis urban socioeconomic contexts. This dynamic is one among many that define feminine and masculine identities and that mutually interact within the complex relational dynamics taking place between women and men.

For the men, their first thoughts of sexual initiation had begun to unfold as they constructed graphic sexual fantasies through conversations with their respective groups of friends. For most of these men, however, these fantasies had vanished at the very moment when they were supposed to be coming true. Their first sexual encounters were rather surrounded by feelings of numbness, disappointment, indifference, discomfort, fear, guilt, curiosity, stress, and tension due to the pressures generated by the circumstances surrounding commercial sex. When I presented the question, "How did you feel the first time you had sex?" regardless of their places of origin, many of the men recalled less than wonderful experiences:

> *Fermín:* Oh! I felt very bad, very frustrated. In other words, because buying sex for me was not like . . . I thought it was going to be something like . . . I was hoping that, you know, that being with a woman and having sexual relations was going to be something wonderful, right? But no! In other words, when I got there and the woman, the first thing that she tells you is "Hurry up!" or "Don't touch me!" and is very . . . It's like you say, what is this?! Because . . . you know, I had my friends and they used to tell me, "Being with a woman is, you know, you feel like this." In other words, you create your own fantasies and it's not that way.

> *Eugenio:* Well, normal, like nothing. I thought I was going to feel something delicious, something full of flavor, a nice experience but I felt like a robot, as if nothing have happened. Then, eh . . . it seemed like another person was pushing her with some voices because it was a little room. Then, they were pushing her. Then, it was something uncomfortable, and what I wanted was to be done and get out of there, ¿no?

> *Marcos:* It was not really a big deal. In other words, it was not that kind of satisfaction that you think about, no. Why? Because you are one more client. Then, the more customers they have, the more money they make, right? Then, quick! run! And you go and go, and that's it! Let's go! And the next one comes next. Then, it's not, it was not an experience like . . . neither pretty nor ugly. In other words, it was something that happened, as if I was drinking a Coca Cola just any day, either thirsty or not.

These men's narratives also show how the older and more seasoned sex worker is in control of the sexual encounter with a younger male novitiate and even how she deals with the tensions and pressures of her job. Lastly, the men's stories reveal some of the social forces underlying the regional differences and the specific socioeconomic contexts in which sexual initiation is experienced by men. Men from Mexico City included Eugenio, Fermín, and Alfonso. And men from Jalisco included Fidel, Joaquín, Marcos, Felipe, Ernesto, and Gabriel.

Eugenio and Fermín requested the services of a sex worker in order to experience sexual intercourse for the first time because of an important dynamic haunting the sex lives of many of the men from Mexico City in this study: fear of pregnancy out of wedlock and coercive marriage. In this study, all of the men who had experienced various expressions of coercive marriage after their girlfriends became pregnant were from urban areas, mainly Mexico City and Guadalajara. For Eugenio and Fermín, for example, a sex worker offered a safe door leading to sexual intercourse without the potential consequences of an unexpected pregnancy and the subsequent moral responsibilities of an undesired marriage. As Eugenio said:

> You bring with yourself the idea that women can become pregnant and that it is not easy to have sexual relations with a woman. Eh . . . it can happen with a prostitute, or a woman of the streets, but because that is her job. But a woman like . . . Back then, having sexual relations with a young woman, a girlfriend, it meant having a great responsibility. In other words, you had to be willing to get married.

Similarly, Fermín identified commercial sex as a strategic avenue to explore sex for the very first time. "I was always careful so I would not get a woman pregnant. No! That was the trap!" "A trap?" I questioned. He then offered,

> Yes, because over there they forced you to get married, right? Therefore, if at times you wanted to do it, you know, if we did something, we had to do it carefully, or not at all. In short, we had to respect women, right? Never getting a woman pregnant because you knew that if the girl became pregnant, then you had to get married.

Besides respect for the woman, pregnancy out of wedlock, and the possibility of coercive marriage, Fermín had also been affected by seeing the marital experiences of about half of his male friends who gotten their girlfriends pregnant. During the interview, he explained that he had followed very closely, as a critical observer, the quality of his friends' marriages. What he learned had made him even more careful to refrain from premarital sex. When I asked, "What was the destiny of your friends who were forced to get married?" he said:

> They gave a bad life to their wives, they did not love them. In other words, there was not a good relationship. They maltreated them, and then they got drunk, they did not want to go home. It was that way.

Fermín's descriptions of his friends' marital problems seemed to be stereotypical, but he explained that the unhappiness his friends revealed to him in their conversations had had a profound influence on the way he explored sexuality with the many women he dated. Although he

enjoyed all aspects of sexual exploration with his dates, he also strategically avoided intercourse at all cost, even with protection. The stories of
his friends' forced marriages were always in his mind.[1]

In addition to respect for the woman, fear of pregnancy, and coercive
marriage, what additional circumstances surrounded the first sexual experiences of these men from Mexico City?

First, as Eugenio explained to me, his first experience of intercourse,
at the age of twenty-seven, was a result of intense peer pressure. A forty-
three-year-old, never-married man who identified himself as both an
alcoholic in recovery and as being shy with women, Eugenio explained:
"I was ashamed that my friends and my brothers would know that I had
never had sexual relations before ¿no? Then, I did not want to be
ridiculed by them, and my friends. So I had to get drunk and then went
out and hired her." Like Eugenio, other Mexican men have similarly
identified peer pressure and group acceptance as the reasons they had
accepted sexual initiation with a sex worker as a way to prove their manhood to a group of male friends (see Amuchástegui 2001, 273).

And second, the social and economic contexts surrounding the sex
lives of little boys and young men living in a large metropolis may
expose them to precocious sexual initiation, especially when intransigent
poverty is part of their daily lives. Alfonso, thirty-three, was born and
raised in a family that had survived on the collective income from each
and every one of the family members, including all minors. With a
chuckle, Alfonso used the term *mil usos* to characterize himself (a *mil usos*
is a person who survives by means of numerous informal, part-time jobs).
Alfonso had started working when he was still in elementary school, sell-
ing Jell-O and chewing gum, and cleaning car windshields on the busy
streets of Mexico City: "Precocity has no age, and I, unfortunately, was
taught to work since I was little. I did not have an adequate childhood."
Alfonso went on to explain that while he was contributing to the survival
of his family he had developed friendships with the female and male prostitutes with whom he shared an urban workspace. As he struggled to contribute to the economy of his family in the mid 1970s, Alfonso's sexual initiation had occurred with one of these friends in the mid-1970s, during
his elementary school years.

> My father used to work at the Hospital General de México, in the downtown
> area of the city. Eh . . . and what you find nearby is lots of prostitutes. I always
> went out because I used to work at night. Then, I used to hang out outside
> and went and talked. . . . The girl I met was a young girl, if I recall well
> enough, she was fourteen or thirteen. I did not know that she was a prosti-

tute girl because I was a little boy, a lot younger than she was. We were friends, and my father had given me my allowance. I had money. She said, "O.K. there is no problem." They used to have some rooms. We went up, and we had a short conversation, eh . . . I did not have that sexual desire because I was still a little boy. Then, the girl was playing with me until I had my erection. Then, she practically . . . she did her job and that was it. But it was nothing that I would . . . simply, I felt fear.

Alfonso is representative of the phenomenon Latin American social scientists call *los niños de la calle* — the children of the streets. As of 2003, at least 1,799,000 children live in Guadalajara, Mexico City, and Monterrey in circumstances similar to those described by Alfonso (CIMAC 2003).[2] Alfonso's story reveals the possible implications on the sexual initiation and sex lives to youth being raised in an increasingly urban Mexico.

Thus, for men living in urban areas, the reasons for experiencing sex with a prostitute were neither uniform nor monolithic nor static. While there are common patterns, these are always fluid and deeply connected to the social complexities that surrounded the men's lives. The heterosexual initiation experiences via paid sex for some of men from Mexico City reveal their fears of impregnating their girlfriends and being forced into coercive marriage, as well as the force of peer pressure and the complex ramifications of urban poverty. The personal experiences of the men from rural Jalisco offer an additional dynamic.

Sexo en El Pueblo

> We agreed to go, we were young boys, and we went over there. And yes, yes, yes, you get there [the brothel] . . . but it happened among friends, I was part of a bunch of young men. "Ándale, let's go over there!" And it happened.
>
> Felipe, interviewee

The men from Mexico City reported their sexual initiations as personal experiences, something I interpret to be an expression of individuality and a modern lifestyle within a larger urban context. The men from Jalisco, in contrast, more frequently narrated collective experiences of sexual initiation. These would typically take place while they were visiting a well-known cantina where sex workers might offer their services. For the men from Jalisco, their sexual initiations took place when they were between the ages of fourteen and seventeen and they were usually arranged with excitement and great expectation by a group of friends. Like Felipe, Marcos rejoiced in recalling those memories of sexual initiation:

> One makes plans to go. Let's go! Come on! And I don't know how many things you talk about. Then you say, "We'll go on such and such day." Because now you have to save money in order to be able to pay. Then, some of them get paid for it. "No problem! I pay for it! Let's go!" And then you go. But well, really, at that age, in other words, the most you can drink, you cannot stand more than four tequilas, right? Then, you have to drink one or two tequilas, and now, what else do we do? Right? Let's go, let's go! Why? Because in my personal circumstances I was not in a position to spend money.

Most of the Jalisco men recalled that they were either attending *secundaria* or were in a trade school in their small towns when their sexual initiation took place; some others were attending *preparatoria* (high school) not far from their places of origin. Regardless, the absence of an income in the lives of young men like Marcos required a well-thought-out plan. However, if sexual initiation was prompted by the enthusiasm spontaneously generated while conversing about sex among a group of friends, making loans and at times financial sponsorship of the sexual initiation might become part of the ritual of collective sexual initiation among friends. Felipe laughingly recalled how one or another of his friends would brag about having been his financial sponsor: "I made him a man!" The men would boast about facilitating the sexual initiation of some of their friends at a brothel. Felipe also explained that in some of the small towns nearby where he grew up, some cantinas would hire sex workers who specialized in the sexual initiation of young men. Felipe explained that older men, including fathers, friends, or other male relatives, would use the expression "I am going to take you to have your first communion" to indicate that they thought it was the right time for them to be sexually initiated by a sex worker. This use of religious ritual terminology as metaphorical language for sexual initiation with sex workers was also identified by Héctor Carrillo in his research with homosexual men in Guadalajara. Carrillo (1999, 232) described how one of his gay informants reported being "baptized" when his brothers took him, at the age of sixteen, to experience sexual initiation with a female sex worker, as a strategy "to fix" his homosexual identity and to initiate him into heterosexuality. In other sexualized contexts, "being baptized" may have other connotations. Flaca, a homosexual informant of Annick Prieur, used the question "You know about the baptizing?" as he began his recollection of being gang-raped by almost thirty men while in prison (Prieur 1998, 215). As illustrated, for these male informants, sexual initiation was linked to specific social processes. First, the social anticipation of a first sexual encounter was surrounded by friendly camaraderie among men. And for many, this experience of sexual anticipation was more exciting than their highly anticipated and fantasized first sex act per se. As reported by the men, their sexual fascinations and fantasies before initiation often exceeded the actual experience. Second, peer pressure and group expectations played an important role in the sex lives of these men. Sexual initiation was not an individual decision but the result of this collective construction of eroticism. Ross and Rapp have shown that young men participate in the organization of sexual values and practices in many cultures, so that "peer regulation of sex and marriage is crucial to the politics and economics of both family and community life" (1997, 157). Third, for these men, sex is not exclusively about the erotic per se but is also about gender, in this case, masculine identities. These men's narratives suggest that masculinity may find its life through erotic/sexual expressions; the men use sexual initiation as a social vehicle to construct important aspects of their masculine identities (see Stern et al., 2003). In this way, "for young Mexican men, sex is not always an expression of eroticism but one of the main forms to represent and affirm their masculinity before other men" (Amuchástegui 2001, 375). And finally, the emotional and subjective dimensions of a young man's first sexual experience are manifest in the voices of these same men, now adults, who candidly revealed their sighs of emotion and nostalgia as they recalled and reconstructed the fear, concern, enthusiasm, excitement, anxiety, bliss, and frustration, among others emotions, which surrounded their actual sexual initiation experiences.

Rural men experienced sex for the first time in an anticlimactic atmosphere, a commonality they shared with their urban counterparts. Similar to men from Mexico City, men from Jalisco expressed the same discomfort emerging from the pressure surrounding the working conditions of sex workers. This experience was particularly difficult for the men who learned about the marketing of commercial sex for the first time. Observing that men had to wait in line to receive the sexual service provoked feelings of disenchantment of the first sexual experience. In addition, for some of these rural men, fears of moral prosecution and potential family punishment accompanied them on their first visit to the brothel. Felipe expressed these fears — "If they see that I am here, what's going to happen? — as he recalled the first time he went with his friends to a bordello. He explained that some of his friends had been beaten when their fathers found out that their sons had visited a brothel. Felipe was no exception, and he was afraid of potential corporal punishment by his father.

A sexual paradox in the lives of men like Felipe, the practice of heterosexual initiation with a sex worker is expected from young men like him, even though such behavior may also be punished if it is done voluntarily or without the consent of a family authority figure. Many of the male informants from small towns reported that a majority of their friends had been sexually initiated by sex workers, but that these events had taken place against their will and on the initiative of an older brother or the father. This was not an experience that was exclusive to rural areas; some men raised in urban areas also reported that they had also been forced by older brothers and friends to have sexual initiation with a sex worker.

Finally, besides fear of family punishment, some rural men also reported a concern about being attacked by the husbands, boyfriends, or lovers of the sex workers.

Joaquín was not from rural Jalisco but from Guadalajara. However, he was one of the men who experienced confusion and fear during his coerced sexual initiation. He went into a lot of detail concerning how his older brother had taken him to a brothel to be sexually initiated when he was fourteen or fifteen years old. The experience took him by surprise. His older brother and three of his friends had driven him to a neighborhood far from his house. They entered a building he had never seen before, and his anxiety increased as he observed many rooms all in a row with a woman standing next to each one of them. Then his brother pointed to the woman with whom Joaquín was going to have sex for the first time, against his will, intoned with his deep voice: "Over there you have the woman who is going to make you a man!" As Joaquín continued to describe his experience, I asked him, "How did you feel while all this happened?" He said:

> I don't know [giggles]. I wanted to run away, to get out of there! It was the whole thing because, I don't know, to be left alone with the lady, no way, even the way of looking at her and getting undressed, right? I . . . well, I have never been through an experience of that magnitude, let's say it that way. I did not know what to do, run away! And when I wanted to get out of there, my brother was right there ¿no? And the other guys as well.

Joaquín went on to explain that after feeling anxious, agitated, and after shaking for a while, he felt more relaxed and willing to follow the sex worker's instructions. He described her as a caring and sensitive woman who made him feel more relaxed by telling him that she had professional experience in the sexual initiation of young men like him.

Joaquín's story and his emotional reaction to being initiated into sex against his will is not an isolated case. Marcos, for instance, explained that all of his friends had been sexually initiated in the same way:

> I have a friend from high school who, when he was in middle school, they had to . . . [giggles] they had to run after him in order to get him back again into the room! Because he went out running, right? While pulling up his pants.

Besides Joaquín, other men in this study had intercourse per the decision made by an older adult friend or relative. Their stories of forced sex with a sex worker are not isolated cases. For other Latin American men, the coercive sexual initiation of young boys with female sex workers has been a rite of passage into manhood (Díaz 1998; Pérez and Pinzón 1997). And some men have indicated the experience allowed them "to be accepted as members of the group of men and experience a profound transformation in their gender identity" (Amuchástegui 2001, 370). Coercive initiation with sex workers may also have been used by some parents and older adult brothers as a preventive or corrective measure against homosexuality in young men (Carrillo 1999; Castro-Vázquez 2000). Being forced as young men to comply with the expectations of the hegemonic culture concerning expressions of masculinity — that is, being male, heterosexual, and sexually knowledgeable — provoked tension and discomfort in the men I interviewed, and they paid a high emotional price. These young men's experiences resound with those of the football players Messner (1992) interviewed, who endured intense training, sore muscles, and even broken bones in order to live up to hegemonic expressions of sport masculinities.

The sexual initiation stories of my male sample are striking when compared to those of Gutmann's working-class informants, among whom only one man ever visited a sex worker, or to his finding that none of his informants had been coerced into sexual initiation by adult men who sought out sex workers as partners for them (1996, 132–33). In addition, the testimony of rural men with regard to the sexualized group rituals they engaged in to collect and save money for a young man's sexual initiation at a brothel reveals the nuances surrounding the sex lives of some men educated in some modest rural backgrounds. Their testimony also invites us to reexamine Gutmann's assumption that "going to prostitutes may be more of a tradition among young men from the middle and upper classes" (133).

Sex with a sex worker may not necessarily require a monetary transaction nor involve feelings of distress, anxiety, or disappointment in a sexual novitiate. For instance, Ernesto reported a pleasant sexual initiation with a sex worker, although he was the only one to do so. He did not have to pay for the service, however, and his experience grew out of an amicable relationship with her. While visiting a brothel with a group of friends at the age of sixteen, he had sex for the first time with a twenty-six-year-old sex worker he met there through one of his friends. After dancing and engaging in a pleasant conversation with her, she invited him to come to her house, where they had sex. When I asked Ernesto, "How did you feel when you had this experience? Some men have told me that at times they were afraid," he replied in a high-pitched voice:

¡Uy! Very happy! I did not get scared, no. I did feel . . . I opened up my mind completely. In other words, I felt very relaxed, feeling . . . In fact, the next day I talked to my friends about the way it had happened, everything. Yes, I had a great time; there was no trauma, nothing.

Erotic pleasure does not end when the sex act is consummated. For Ernesto, sexual desire continued to be stimulated and constructed as he shared his first-time experience with his group of friends. After a reportedly pleasant first time, Ernesto developed a steady relationship with the young woman. But the relationship turned out to be conflictual and barely lasted a year.

In general, the men from Jalisco were more likely to have experienced sexual initiation with sex workers than their Mexico City counterparts. The reasons for this difference had to do with socioeconomics, which also affected rural versus urban women.

Socioeconomics and Women's Sex Lives

Men from small towns were more likely to have intercourse with a sex worker for the first time in part because of the surrounding socioeconomic context in which rural women live. The fact that women born and raised in rural areas are less exposed to employment and education opportunities makes marriage an essential vehicle for their socioeconomic survival. Thus, virginity develops a higher value as a form of capital. Under these circumstances, a woman's need to avoid premarital sex becomes fundamental. This proscription is also shaped by the limited variety of sexual discourses, which indicate that her reputation is continually at stake and that there is a greater pressure to conform. This process is articulated within the dynamics identified by both women and men, such as a man's need to refrain from sexual activity with a girlfriend as an expression of *respeto a la mujer.* Accordingly, a rural woman learns sexual attitudes and behaviors that are aimed at preserving her premarital virginity, and a rural man who experiences intercourse for the first time with a sex worker and not a girlfriend has specific reasons for doing so. Fidel explained the reasons why he, as well as many of his friends from his small town, did not have sex for the first time with their girlfriends:

> I think that . . . we expressed a lot of respect toward women because they did not even give you the chance to do anything. In other words, they would reject our sexual advances because they had that belief that the woman had to be a virgin at marriage. Besides that, women would demand our respect, perhaps because they were afraid of their parents.

Felipe made clear how the relationship between women and men, as well as the family as an institution, was instrumental in constructing a gender identity within the context of inequality. This dynamic is neither linear nor one-dimensional but complex.

Socioeconomics and Rural Femininities and Masculinities

For rural women and men, limited socioeconomic opportunities are associated with hypermoral gendered prescriptions regulating both women's and men's heterosexual experiences. The fact that women from small towns were more likely than urban women to report both fear of sexism and actual recriminations from their husbands for not being virgins at marriage illustrates how relational patterns of both femininity and masculinity exist in mutual interaction in a specific socioeconomic context. Women's fear of sexism and actual exposure to gender inequalities may create sexual distance and caution between a rural heterosexual couple as part of their courtship experiences. The restricted socioeconomic possibilities responsible for a limited repertoire of sexual discourses seem to further enhance this dynamic.

As discussed in chapter 2, Fidel rejoiced in the virginal purity of his wife when they became married, a fact he also associated with becoming the favorite son-in-law within his extended family. However, as a young adolescent, he had experienced mixed emotions as he felt erotic pleasure and desire for the woman who would later become his wife. At times, he had tried to persuade her to have sex with him. However, he reported that he was glad that she had not accepted his invitations. As he explained, "Sometimes, when you have sex with your girlfriend, you lose interest in the woman. What comes to your mind is '¡Pinche vieja fácil!' [Damn easy woman!] You tell yourself, 'If she had sex with me that easily, she could have sex with someone else.'"

Fidel's words confirm the justification articulated by the women in this study who refrained from premarital sex as a way to protect themselves from being stigmatized and recriminated against (see also Hirsch 2003, 105). Idalia, also born and raised in a small town, explained the behavior of men like Fidel in this way:

> In small towns, it is very different . . . sex for men is different than for women. Because, over there, men can go out with all the women they want and not get married. They go out with prostitutes and go to bars and all that, and nothing is going to happen to them. In other words, he is not devalued, but the one who is devalued is the woman.

Thus, virginity becomes a multilayered protection mechanism for a woman. And a sex worker becomes a viable option for a young rural man's sexual initiation in the midst of a sexualized, gendered puzzle. That is, feelings of desire for a girlfriend are surrounded by rigid prescriptions of both femininity and masculinity. This confusion is resolved to some extent as men are exposed to the social construction of erotic desire taking place among groups of friends, which further promotes the hyper-sexualization of sex workers. The corresponding influence of discourses of modernity on sexuality (as promoted by media and schools in urban areas) has been identified by Amuchástegui, whose study similarly found that rural men over twenty years old hired the services of a sexual worker, whereas younger men from urban areas expressed their desire to have sex with a girlfriend (2001, 376). This process seems to invigorate the hyper-sexualization of sex workers as marginal and morally devalued but nevertheless central and socially acceptable in the sexual initiation of young men.

For the rural men in this study, the sex workers were sexual objects, while "the official" girlfriends both deciphered and participated in the creation of rural expressions of femininity and masculinity. However, rural prescriptions of masculinity do not only affect rural sex workers and the young women who refrain from premarital sex. As discussed, men whose first experience of intercourse is through coercive or voluntary sexual initiation as young boys at a brothel also experience painful uncertainties and dilemmas concerning masculinity. For instance, Marcos reflected on his and his friends' sexual initiation experiences. All of them had sex as young adolescents with sex workers in his small town. He explained that the common ritual of sexual initiation included an older brother (sent by the father) or the father himself requesting the sexual initiation of boys with sex workers, a widely accepted and enforced social practice in his town. However, Marcos objected to the practice of sexual initiation and expressed his hopes for a change for a new generation of men:

> I think it is a bad practice. I think they should leave the young boy to make a decision on how he wants to have sex for the first time and with whom. A man should even have the option to be a virgin at marriage so he can discover the new experience with the woman with whom he will spend the rest of his life.

Marcos's words indicate that even though some gender patterns are present in the lives of men raised in rural contexts, gender relations and masculine identities are not static but fluid. A man's gender consciousness and contestation of masculine identities that are selectively oppressive to both women and men indicates that masculine identities in rural contexts may become multiple and fluid.

Ni Vírgenes, Ni Putas: Sexuality and Gender as Relational

> *The Virgin Mary and Miss Colombia cannot continue being our role models. We need to introduce an alternative to the dichotomy between a "good woman" and* una mala mujer; *there is something between mother and whore. The definition of "good" need not entail being virginal and submissive. To be self-assured and independent does not mean we are whores.*
>
> Silvana Paternostro, *In the Land of God and Man: Confronting Our Sexual Culture*

So far, I have explained some of the reasons why rural men experienced sex for the first time with a sex worker in their pueblos. As a group, however, almost half of the male sample experienced sex for the first time with a sex worker. Why? The overused and traditionally accepted "good/bad," or "madonna/whore," paradigm comes in handy to explain this pattern. In this regard, Ana Amuchástegui argues: "The Guadalupe–La Malinche duality constitutes the two faces of female sexuality, which have remained as emblematic of Mexican culture since then [the conquest]: the mother, pure and virgin, and the whore, voluptuous and a traitor. The images related with this duality have been used as a local translation of the traditional Catholic division of female sexuality between Eve and Mary. These two types of women represent opposite images of distinct moral value, and they have been used as norms for the construction of gender" (2001, 76).

Octavio Paz's (1950) views of traditional sex roles in Mexican society may explain the popular social categorization of *mujeres buenas* and *mujeres malas* (good women and bad women), as identified by Ilán Stavans in his literary writings on Mexican culture (1996, 150), and that Héctor Carrillo similarly incorporates into his discussion of gender roles and the "gender-based categorization" of sexual identities in Mexican society (2002, 37–59). Using the good woman/bad woman paradigm as a point of departure, one might argue that Mexican women who are taught to be "good" learn the lesson that they must be "decent and virgin" at marriage. And women with the opposite fate, such as sex workers, learn to be "bad and loose," as their social destiny will be to satisfy a man's premarital sexual needs and provide him with the sexual experience for marriage (as well as satisfying the unsatisfied sexual needs of married men). This dynamic would seem to argue that traditional "roles" should be even more emphasized in rural areas, where a lack of modernity might serve to emphasize the good woman/bad woman dichotomy. Though appealing and partly convincing, this perspective explains only a small portion of the picture, from a literary and archetypal perspective but not a sociological one. The model is too difficult to sustain if one wants to explore the complexities of gender relations at a deeper level. Gender theorists have relentlessly challenged notions of gender that are based on fixed categories and identities, while highlighting the relational, contextual, and situational nature of gender (see, e.g., Connell 1987, 2002; West and Zimmerman 1987; Butler 1990; Kimmel 2000).[3] Moreover, Juárez and Kerl have challenged the static dichotomy of the traditional versus the liberated with respect to Latinas by identifying the many social, cultural, and historical complexities shaping their sex lives. They show that "Latinas may have unique ways of expressing sexualities, but are neither as repressed nor as oppressed as both popular culture and scholars would have us believe" (2003, 7).

Neither virgins nor whores. Sexuality is fluid and complex and quite far away from fixed, culturally determined, monolithic gender identities or typologies. The madonna/whore paradigm blurs the relational nature of gender and its nuances and complexities in everyday life. It not only promotes cultural stereotypes while neglecting the dialectical sophistication of gender, it also obscures the possibility of social and political change. Everyday life, love, and sex relationships are more complicated than the opposing dualities that the cultural images and icons of the Virgin of Guadalupe and La Malinche would seem to suggest. For instance, in the more than 180 hours of in-depth interviews that I collected, nobody mentioned, suggested, or associated either of these two cultural symbols to suggest that their decisions about whether to have sex or not with a girlfriend or a sex worker (in the case of men) or a boyfriend (in the case of women) were influenced by them. As I illustrate in this book, gender relations and their nuanced complexities within the context of power relationships between women and men and family life take place within specific socioeconomic contexts. And these are the processes ultimately responsible for women's and men's decisions with regard to the meanings attached to virginity and premarital sex.

The good woman/bad woman framework is problematic and simplistic. The sexual paradoxes and contradictions experienced by my male informants in their sexual initiation experiences with sex workers, as well as their own sexual desire for and prohibition from the women they loved, reflect a multidimensional spectrum of possibilities with regard to female identities and experiences of heterosexuality. As indicated in the previous chapter, the men who experienced sex for the first time with a girlfriend described the enhanced emotional intimacy and the feelings of profound love and respect they felt for their girlfriends after sharing the cherished moments of sexual and erotic pleasure. Those men did not stigmatize their girlfriends.

In addition, even though sexual initiation with a sex worker was not always a pleasant or satisfying experience, some of the men who experienced sex for the first time in this manner did not necessarily demonize those women. In fact, some of them humanized the sex workers. Joaquín, for example, explained that, after he had become a regular customer at more than one brothel in Guadalajara, he developed very close relationships with *las trabajadoras de noche,* or the night workers — a term he considered less offensive than *prostitutas*. He explained what he thought many men who visit bordellos ignore about the personal lives of the women who sell sexual pleasure to them at night:

> Almost all of them, and I tell you based on my experience, all of them have one child, at least. But you know what? I talked seriously with them many times, with these women, and all of them came to the conclusion that because of their parents at home, because of problems, because of pressures, because of all that, they have decided to leave their family homes, to run away with the boyfriend, or with the first boyfriend they had, to have a child, without being married.

So, what happened after that? They started to have problems with their husbands, and the man was not an expert either. I talked a lot with many women
that way. And . . . so what was left as a choice? Some of them had no education, not even the basic education, let's say elementary school, not even
trained to be able to work at a factory, they were fearful. Therefore, what was
left for them to do?[4]

Similarly, Ernesto developed a personal and sexual relationship that
lasted about a year with the twenty-six-year-old sex worker with whom he
had sex for the first time as a teenager. As he talked about his first sexual
experience with her, he expressed: "I say that what I like the most about
her is that she smelled very good, she was very pretty, and I saw a lot of
cleanliness in her body."

If the good/bad dichotomy is not the answer, why are these men, as a
group, more likely to have sex for the first time with a sex worker? Besides
the previously discussed socioeconomic context in rural areas, which constructs various expressions of masculinity and femininity, there are additional dialectical relationships between women and men. These processes
generate multiple yet parallel femininities and masculinities, and their
respective sexual expressions with regard to heterosexual relationships.

First, as shown, some of the men whose sexual initiation was with a
sex worker worried about pregnancy out of wedlock and the subsequent
coercive marriage if they were to have sex with a casual girlfriend. This
rationale was more frequently cited by men from Mexico City. And
most men who had been coerced to marry their girlfriends when they
became pregnant out of wedlock were from Mexico City or Guadalajara.
Thus, for urban men, premarital sex with a sex worker was a viable option
that protected them from this threat.

Second, an ethic of *respeto a la mujer* was created and reproduced by
both women and men. This ethic takes on different emphases and specific
characteristics depending on socioeconomic context, but in general it
indicates that a man who invites a woman to engage in sexual activity is
being disrespectful. One can identify the effects of this ethic in the narratives of those urban women who felt uncomfortable after having sex.
Amuchástegui interviewed women from Mexico City who similarly felt
their future had been placed at risk because of their premarital sexual experiences (2001, 341). Besides the lack of education and paid employment
opportunities for women, the limited access to sexual discourses that is
prevalent in rural areas may accentuate these dynamics (Amuchástegui
and Rivas 1997).

And third, regardless of their places of origin, both urban and rural

men refrained from engaging in premarital sexual relations with their girlfriends (and thus looked for a sex worker) based on a socially learned fear.
Men are taught to believe that making sexual advances or expressing their
sexual desire might be perceived as offensive by the woman they love.
Thus, a negative reaction from a girlfriend (e.g., anger) to such a sug-
gestion risks an undesired rupture and perhaps the painful loss of a loving relationship. The women Hirsch interviewed confirmed this: sexual
advances in a courtship relationship may be perceived by a woman as disrespectful and as a good reason to terminate a relationship (2003, 107).

This dynamic, however, was further shaped by specific regional
differences. For example, when I asked Marcos if he thought that one of
the reasons why men experienced sexual initiation with sex workers was
because of the risk of pregnancy out of wedlock and potential coercive
marriage, he said:

> I believe that more than, I think that more than pregnancy, it's the fact that you
> are truly in love with that person and you are afraid of losing her. Then, if I
> ask her to go to bed with me, and she has solid moral foundations that we are
> going to go to the hotel only for the honeymoon, and if I tell her to do it, with
> whom am I comparing her?! Or with what object am I comparing her?! Then,
> I could lose her. Then, since I do not want to lose her, I better control myself,
> right? I do not believe that oneself thinks about the pregnancy in that moment
> that you are all excited, right? You think more than anything about the other
> thing, about losing her. And if I do not want to lose her, I better think about
> it and right at that moment.

For some men educated in small towns, the fear of losing a girlfriend
after asking her to have sex is further emphasized by the idea that the
woman is being compared with an identity of femininity that is marginalized and devalued (i.e., the sex worker), and she is thus not being
respected as a woman. As part of the gender prescriptions to which
women and men are exposed in this rural context, such an invitation may
become a moral offense for a woman who has learned to be reserved and
cautious with regard to sexuality and as she tries to remain a virgin until
marriage, not only as a way to assure survival and a stable marital relationship but as a sign of respect for her family.

Men from urban centers, Mexico City in particular, also reflected on
the fear of being rejected and thus losing a relationship with a girlfriend.
Some of these men refrained from sex with a girlfriend for the same reason men like Marcos from a small town did. However, the urban men did
engage in premarital sex with other women and not necessarily sex work-

ers. Men from Mexico City, when compared to rural men, were more likely to have a wider exposure to a variety of heterosexual opportunities, a more diversified and extended social and geographical space, and a wider variety of expressions of femininities, which offered them a wide array of premarital sex avenues. Next, I will discuss the social dynamics of first sexual experiences with *amigas y conocidas* — friends and acquaintances.

Friendly Pleasures: From Erotic Exploration to Sexual Mentorship

Most of the men who experienced sex with acquaintances and friends were from Mexico City. For the eight men in this category, the moral prescriptions against sex appeared to be less forbidding in an urban context, and it is also the case that urban women have greater possibilities of employment and education, which in turn makes for more egalitarian relationships between men and women. For both sexes, urban areas offer more discourses on sex, including socially progressive ideologies. As was the case for their rural counterparts, however, there was an ethic of respect for *la novia,* which in the case of urban men motivated them to explore sexual alternatives beyond the common scenario of commercial sex.

This arrangement of the prospect of sexual initiation in a non-commercial context presented the men with both positive and negative consequences, as well as paradoxes and contradictions. Their stories offer a rich variety of sexual exploration opportunities, even including the sexual mentorship that a considerably older female friend or acquaintance may offer.

Alfredo, a thirty-six-year-old from Mexico City, recalled vividly the series of personal experiences that prompted his sexual initiation when he was about twelve years old. Back then, he had informally met and developed a friendship relationship with an adult single man in his mid-twenties. Their relationship evolved as Alfredo's adult friend told him the colorful details of his sexual adventures. Alfredo called the man a *mujeriego,* or womanizer, and explained that his friend also introduced him to alcohol as he related the stories of his many simultaneous affairs and sexual relationships with both single and married women. As the relationship between the two men deepened, Alfredo explained, he would lie and cover up for his friend when many of his friend's sexual partners tried to interrogate and confront Alfredo in order to know if his friend was seeing and having sex with other women. Alfredo noted that he had become the mediator who facilitated his friend's polygamous sexual relationships. Alfredo said that he felt safe in the friendship until one day his friend posed a question for him: "Hey! Have you ever been with a woman?" Alfredo responded to him candidly. And one day, while accompanying his friend to see one of his sexual partners at a hotel, Alfredo learned about the surprise his friend had planned for him.

> Then, he took this woman to a hotel and he comes down and tells me "Come on up." But she did not know anything about it, and I think he told her "I will be right back or, stay there, I will be right back." Then, he came out and I got inside. And then, when I get inside and I see this woman right there, she was naked. In other words, it happened with this woman. And she said, "What are you doing here?" I replied, "I do not know, why don't you ask him?" Then he said, "You know what? He has never been with a woman and I want you to teach him about it." "You are an asshole! You treat me like a whore!" Then he said, "Well, if you were not, you would be with your husband, not with me. But I don't care; I want you to teach him. If you don't, go back and we break up right here, I do not want you to look for me ever again." In other words, he manipulated her, and she was a married woman.

Left alone with his friend's lover, an attractive woman in her early to mid-twenties, Alfredo had intercourse for the first time. He recalled:

> Well, first you feel confused, because you say, what am I going to do? In fact, I was so nervous about being with her and about touching her because she would hold my hands and would put them on her legs, and on her breasts. "Don't be afraid!" "No, I am not." But I was feeling nervous. "Do not be afraid!" "I am fine, don't worry." Everything was fine, but I was the one who was not reacting well.

Alfredo said he felt more relaxed and comfortable as his anxiety diminished and he gradually explored his first heterosexual encounter. When I asked him about how he felt after his experience, he replied: "Well, I felt like a real man, I felt good." Then Alfredo described the excitement he experienced when he shared the details of his new experience of sexual discovery with his classmates. With a spark in his eyes, he had boasted to his friends: "You know what? I already had sex with a woman, and she is older than me, she is very pretty and has a great body!" Alfredo said he became the envy of his friends. For Alfredo and other men, a pleasurable first sexual experience did not end after the actual sex act took place. The sharing of the first sexual experiences with their friends promoted further sexual desire through group conversations. Thus, sexual desire is not only constructed a priori as men create fantasies and romantic visions of what the first time might be like. A posteriori, it continues reproducing and influencing the sex lives of the protagonist and other men. The excitement is lived over and over again as the man relates the sexual adventure to other men. In addition, when men share their sex stories in all-male company, they may facilitate the reaffirmation of their masculinity (Szasz 1998; Stern et al. 2003).

Alfredo talked about the subsequent sexual encounters he had with the older woman. At some point, their encounters became a routine that lasted for about two years. The woman became Alfredo's sexual mentor, even as he simultaneously established an official dating relationship with *la novia de la escuela,* or a school date, who was about eleven or twelve years old. When I asked Alfredo if he ever thought about having sex with his school date, he replied, "No, I respected her." Interestingly, at some point, Alfredo did have sex with an informal or casual girlfriend, who eventually became pregnant and with whom he decided to cohabit due to the birth of their first child.

Alfredo's interview was one of the longest and most informative and colorful interviews. His sexual initiation story is also the one that showed the widest range of age difference between partners. His first sexual experiences led Alfredo into future relationships with other older women who, at some point, also became his sex mentors, including a woman who was attending college while Alfredo was still in middle school. Some of these relationships were conflictual and difficult.

Like Alfredo, other men experienced sex for the first time with friends or acquaintances who were older and who had accumulated previous sexual experience. For some of these men, also raised in urban areas (Mexico City and Guadalajara), an initial experience of heterosexual sex with an older woman set the stage for subsequent encounters of various levels of sexual mentorship and erotic exploration and learning. Three of the men who fit this category were Diego and Sebastián from Mexico City, and Jacobo from Guadalajara.

Diego had intercourse for the first time, at the age of nineteen, with his best friend's sister during a trip to his friend's town. A single mother raising her child from a previous relationship, she had more than one sexual encounter with Diego. Interestingly, he said that he had consciously refrained from any sexual activity in his early adolescent years because of fear of getting the girl pregnant and being forced to get married to someone he did not love. But Diego very soon forgot about those old fears during a vacation trip to Michoacán. He immersed himself in the romantic scenario that began when he and his best friend's sister gently seduced each other while sitting next to one another in the back seat of his friend's car. Diego and his good friend had arranged a dating group, which brought about the romantic and bohemian tale he now enjoys sharing. Eventually, Diego and his first sexual partner ended up in the bedroom.

> I think it was after I had finished singing and we still had the flavor and the memory of what had happened in the car, and as soon as my friend turned around and left, I put the guitar on the side and we were like two magnets, we hooked, we got together. I was very awkward, for the moment, and that was the first experience, very quickly, right? Very quickly. Ah . . . it was . . . I felt bad, I felt bad because of all the things that I have heard. I thought about my friend Rosaura, I remembered many things, and said damn it! No! Why is it that it did not last longer? Right? But it was intense, very intense.

Diego reported feeling concerned and anxious about his sexual performance and his inability to be a good lover the first time he had sex. At some point, he said, he apologized to her in case their sexual encounter had not been satisfactory for her. Why did Diego feel that way? Prior to his first sexual encounter and while still living in Mexico City, Diego had enthusiastically participated in long group conversations with Rosaura, a friend in her thirties who would give Diego and one of his friends informal lectures, recommendations, and tips on human sexuality, sexual intimacy, and lovemaking. Diego explained that besides the many conversations he had with male peers and friends about the highly discussed "first time," he had learned his most important lessons about sex from Rosaura. She was a friend and a coworker who made powerful statements that came to his mind the very first time he had intercourse. Diego recited one of the most compelling lessons he learned from Rosaura, when he was still a young adolescent: "There are many men who masturbate in a vagina, they do not care about feelings, they do not care, the woman has a different timing, distinct."

For men like Diego, pre-established ideas about masculinity, manhood, and heterosexuality came from both peer conversations as well as from the sexual mentorship he received from an older woman who might be perceived as an authority figure. Other than their endless discussions about human sexuality, Diego never had an actual sexual experience with Rosaura. He deeply respected her, characterizing her as a *revolucionaria* who possessed wisdom, maturity, and progressive and enlightening ideas about sexuality and loving relations between women and men.

Diego and Alfredo had some things in common. Both would refrain from having sexual relations with a woman with whom they would become emotionally involved later in their lives. And both would either marry or cohabit with a woman as a consequence of premarital sexual activity. However, unlike Alfredo, Diego did not cite an ethic of respect for women as the rationale for his not having premarital sex.

Sebastián is the third man from Mexico City who had sex for the first time with a woman older than he. After developing a casual friendship with a married woman about five years older, Sebastián had intercourse with her for the first time when he was about nineteen or twenty years old. Both had lived in the same neighborhood and had known each other for about six years by the time they engaged into sexual activity. Sebastián described his experience as a positive encounter that gradually evolved. When I asked him if their sexual encounter was a consequence of a common agreement between both, he replied:

> Yes, well . . . no, I was not expecting it. I was not the aggressive one, but I was surprised at that moment when things started to happen. When I . . . , by the time I realized, she told me, "Do this." And I did not know how to do it. In other words, but we were, both of us were almost embracing each other, we were embracing each other. Then, I was not, I was not able to say "No." Besides that, I had the desire to do it.

Sebastián talked about the anxiety and vulnerability he experienced while getting naked for the first time in order to have sex:

> [I felt] very nervous because . . . well, it's a thing that . . . Well, you know what will happen. You know what you have to do or how you have to do it. But at the moment in which you feel naked, at the moment when you take out your intimate parts, and say "Oh! A thing that you have never done in front of anybody else . . . !" You do not know what to do, you do not know how that works.

As he talked about his emotional experience, I asked him if he had felt that he had been forced to have sex. He confirmed for me his own firm desire to do it, as well as the many sexual encounters that had followed his first time with her. He explained that after their initial encounter, they had experienced regular sexual activity twice a week. The pattern became a routine that lasted more than a year, without the apparent knowledge of his partner's husband. He explained that he stopped their periodic encounters after he met and established a steady relationship with his first formal girlfriend — his wife at the present time. Like Alfredo and Diego, Sebastián also married his girlfriend as a consequence of apparently unprotected sex that resulted in her unexpected pregnancy.

The last man who experienced sex with an acquaintance older than he was Jacobo. A native of Guadalajara, Jacobo had a series of spontaneous encounters and conversations with a neighbor that eventually translated into his first sexual experience. "Oh! finally something good happened to me!" he exclaimed with a big laugh while explaining that even though he did not initiate their first sexual encounter, he had been longing for it with special curiosity. When I asked him about the type of relationship that existed between the two of them, he replied:

> Well, the truth is that she was not my girlfriend; she was a girl a lot older than me. And I think that it could be considered that . . . yes, she seduced me, by the fact of being older than me and with more experience. It could be said that she seduced me and for a period of time, we continued having sexual relations. I was . . . I was not even sixteen, and she must have been like eighteen, nineteen, I believe.

Jacobo explained that the first sexual experience offered him a feeling of satisfaction and no negative consequences or "trauma." And like Alfredo, Diego, and Sebastián, Jacobo later developed emotional relationships with different women. Like the other men, he also engaged in regular sexual activity with a girlfriend he dated and eventually was forced to marry her due to pregnancy out of wedlock. The dynamics connecting the lives of men who experienced sexual initiation with older women and who at some point coincidentally had sex with a girlfriend (an experience followed by unexpected pregnancy and coercive marriage) are discussed in the next chapter.

As I listened to and then transcribed these men's experiences with older women, the sexual assertiveness of their female partners made me think of such movie characters as Mrs. Robinson in *The Graduate* (1967) or Dorothy in *Summer of '42* (1971). The existence of similarly empowered sex mentors within Mexican popular culture three decades later may suggest the slowness of Mexican society to accept the sexual initiation and mentoring of young men by older and more experienced women who are not socially devalued or marginalized, as are prostitutes or *cabareteras*. Characters equivalent to Mrs. Robinson and Dorothy have surfaced in two recent Mexican movies: *Y tu mamá también* (2001) and *Un embrujo* (*Under a Spell,* 1998). The latter tells the story of a schoolteacher who gets sexually involved with her adolescent student.

Among my respondents, there was a second group of three men who had sexual relations for the first time with women about their age. In these cases, the men — Alejandro, Nicolás, and Vinicio — had established a casual or informal dating relationship with the women but never thought about marrying them.

Nicolás and Vinicio were from small towns in Jalisco and had experienced sex with women with whom they had casual relationships. Nicolás related that his first sexual experience had happened when he was about twenty-two or twenty-three years old, and it had been the consequence of a temporary relationship. Reserved and curt in his answers when the topic of sexual initiation came up, Nicolás explained that his first sexual relationship had been "simply something new, a new discovery" with a woman, as he clarified, who was not exactly his girlfriend. When I asked Nicolás if he had had sexual contact with any of the women he had been in love with as a younger man, he explained, like many of the men, that he had refrained from having sex with them as a sign of respect.

Vinicio, also from a small town, had sex for the first time when he was between sixteen and seventeen years old with a woman who was about two years younger than he. Vinicio responses to my questions about his first sexual experience were brief but not as reserved as Nicolás's. Interestingly, he said he did not remember the very first time he had had sex with the young woman from his town he identified as a "'novia,' entre comillas" — a 'girlfriend,' quote unquote.

Finally, sexual initiation by a female relative was not frequent but it is worth mentioning because of the social significance of gender relations within families. Mauricio, a native of Mexico City, experienced intercourse for the first time when he was twelve years old. With a giggle and an expression of nervousness, Mauricio explained that while visiting his "distant relatives" in the country, he had explored sex with an older distant cousin, or *prima lejana,* who gradually had seduced him.

> Well, in one occasion that my parents and I went to visit with her. In other words, we went to see the family and we went to swim to the river, right? And she started to kiss me and hug me, and then, it happened right there.

Even though sexual initiation with female relatives was not frequently reported by the men in this study, sexual exploration with older female relatives was disclosed at least twice. For instance, Sebastián explained how circumstances had exposed him to his early erotic feelings with a female cousin back when he attended elementary school.

> My father had a niece and . . . I was about ten, she was fifteen. And she was already changing; she had her breasts and everything. And eh . . . in one occasion, well, I believe that my father did not expect me to start being awake to

sexuality because he would tell us, "You go to sleep right there." Or he would tell her, "You know what? Go and sleep with the boys." But . . . in other words, they look at us as young children. And the experience that I had, I started to touch her, there was no penetration, there was nothing. But, come on, I was already beginning to awake to sexuality.

The stories of Mauricio and Sebastián are revealing. First, in both stories it is interesting to observe how young boys might be perceived as desexualized individuals by their parents, a perception that may facilitate sexual exploration or initiation with older female relatives under circumstances that appear to be relatively safe. Second, a young boy might be perceived by his blood-related, older adolescent *prima* as providing a harmless opportunity to explore her more developed and assertive sexuality. This possibility offers an interesting contrast to the testimony of my female informants who had experienced emotional pain after they were coerced into sex with their older male relatives, including brothers, cousins, uncles, and fathers.

Thus, while taking into account a sensitive awareness of mental health professions' definition of incest, heterosexual exploration between relatives flows along the danger–pleasure continuum, depending on the participants' ages and power differentials, as well as an individual's sense of personal agency. The Mexican expression *"A la prima se le arrima,"* meaning "You can get physically/sexually close to your female cousin," comes to mind to suggest the social acceptance of such arrangements. This expression indicates the woman's potential sexual danger within family relations, including her sexual objectification within the family context. For example, the meanings of such popular expressions as they relate to women may be altered as a result of the gendered censorship of human relations. During a visit to Mexico, a friend of mine clarified this for me by explaining that "A la prima se le arrima" as an expression was incomplete. She expanded the expression with a perfect rhyme in Spanish, exclaiming: *"A la prima se le arrima/¡Y si se ataruga, se le enciman!"* meaning "You can get physically/sexually close to your female cousin/And if she is not alert, you might get on top of her!"

Another expression, *"Entre primos y primores nacen los amores"* (Between cousins and beauty, love is born), similarly justifies romantic love within extended families. Even though it was not the case for any of the informants in this study, it is worth mentioning that issues of class may shape this kind of social practice. In some rural areas, marital relationships between relatives are used by some families to maintain and reproduce capital investment, real estate, and family inheritance within the same blood lines (Chávez Torres 1998, 153).[5]

Generational differences and the nature of the sexual encounters make a significant difference in how such encounters are perceived. In the case of my female informants, their sexual experiences with male relatives were not disclosed in the same context as the experiences of my male informants. Female informants who had sex for the first time with male relatives experienced it under violent circumstances and with men who were considerably older than they. The points of view of the women in the stories related by Mauricio and Sebastián would be interesting to analyze. Unfortunately, testimony that could speak to these types of sexual experiences was not disclosed by any of the women in this study.

The final case presented here is that of Alejandro, a man from Mexico City who had his first sexual experience at the age of twenty. He recalled his many dating experiences with special gusto. Alejandro related that, as a teenager and young adult, he had experienced deep excitement by being a *noviero*. *Noviero* is a concept that derives from the terms *novia* and *novio* (literally, "girlfriend" and "boyfriend"); it is used in Mexican society to identify a single man who has a long history of dating many women, without necessarily falling in love or having sex with any of them. A *noviero* may follow this pattern in either a monogamous or a polygamous fashion. The latter was the case with Alejandro. He explained that even though it was costly, in terms of time and money, he had dated and had had physical relationships with about five women at one time. As we talked about the emotions involved in the relationships he had with each one of the women, he said more about the nature of his sexual experiences with the women. One of them, for example, would eventually become his first sexual partner, a woman he identified as *mi amante* — my lover. Then, he exclaimed, "There was one, *la elegida*! [the chosen one]," to explain that only one of the women had been *la novia,* or the object of his true love and respect.

> Well, *la novia,* in other words, my girlfriend, the one I was in love with, eh . . . I always respected her. What I would do, just the way people used to say: *"de manita sudada"* [holding and sweating hands]. I would hold her with a lot of tenderness. Eh . . . I would kiss her that way, kind of very tender, that way, something very beautiful.

As we continued, I asked him, "So with four of them you would have sex, but not with her?" He replied: "Maybe, maybe not. But, no, no, no. In other words, the one for whom I felt a great sense of appreciation, affection or love, she . . . I always respected her. In other words, taking into account that she might become my future wife, right?" Alejandro said that perhaps he was a hypocrite for having put into practice his keen awareness of the distinction between a woman who could be a potential wife and the woman with whom he could have sex. In this clear split of female gender identities, the former is identified with the expression consistently used by some men in this study, *respeto a la mujer.* At the center of this ethic of respect for women, a potential wife is desexualized by some men and thus forbidden as a source of sexual pleasure before marriage. Thus, the latter woman — *la amante* — becomes a suitable sexual possibility before marriage and is hypersexualized.

The code of values with regard to female identity and heterosexuality was a credo Alejandro had learned. He said he was proud to have learned it from his parents at an early age and that he has maintained this belief uncontested to this day. As he talked about his many relationships that at some point became potential opportunities for marriage, he used the term *noviazgo limpio* to emphasize the "clean" and morally acceptable nature of his formal courtship relationships. Then, he explained: *"Mis novias . . . ,* I respected them a lot, a lot. Only, if I was able to see that, or when I had the opportunity to have sexual relations with another person, then I would do it."

Even though Alejandro's experiences suggest the existence of a madonna/whore dichotomy, the sex lives of men like him are more sophisticated than this bipolar paradigm would suggest. The ethic of respect for women that apparently is responding to the good woman/bad woman prescription is the result of a deeper, more complex dynamic that intertwines with a man's decision to avoid having sex for the first time with his love object. As Alejandro talked about his struggle to control himself sexually with the women who were suitable for a potential marriage, he explained that an intense fear of *fracaso* frequently invaded him. I posed this question for Alejandro: "Why do you have to control yourself sexually if you are so in love with her? He struggled to reply:

> Well, I . . . in other words, I controlled myself a lot because, let's say . . . ah . . . in other words, respect. And I said, well, no . . . in other words. In other words, it used to come to my mind to tell her, "You know what? I would love to have sexual relations with you, but . . ." In other words, I had a fear of, in other words, fear that for saying that it would become a fracaso.

I probed, "What did you think would happen?" He continued, in a high tone of voice, "Yes, in other words, [she would say] 'Stop right there! And we break up right here, and this is the end of it!'"

When it comes to sexual initiation, men like Alejandro use the same expression as women to describe their greatest fear: *fracaso,* or failure. In the case of men, the term is used for failing to comply with a code that would translate into the potential rejection and loss of a beloved woman who could become a wife. As we continued our discussion, Alejandro explained that proposing sex to a potential wife might represent an offensive comment for her, which might become a reason for conflict within the relationship and an inevitable breakup. Alejandro's decision to explore sex with a constellation of other women, anyone but *la elegida,* might have been based on the same dynamics utilized by rural men like Marcos — the belief that sexual initiation with a sex worker was the safest avenue to avoid such a regrettable loss.

In sum, when it comes to love, sex, and heterosexual relationships, both rural and urban men share a commonality: fear of losing a beloved woman. However, their social contexts define the variety of scenarios and dynamics through which rural and urban men enact these sexual possibilities. An urban man may have a wider variety of heterosexual alternatives, whereas a rural man may have fewer opportunities in his smaller and more morally restricted social circumstances. Urban women versus rural women are similarly exposed to these geographic subcultures of sexuality. Thus, the stories of sexual initiation of both women and men suggest the existence of multiple femininities and masculinities and their corresponding types of patriarchy.[6]

The testimony of my respondents leads me to conclude first, that heterosexuality — through at times coercive sexual initiation rituals — is central in the construction of masculine identities. The men's narratives confirm Connell's conclusions (1995, 104) about men being exposed to compulsory heterosexuality. Men are also vulnerable to social pressures to become "sexually available" to women (and their peers); it is not only women who are susceptible to similar dynamics with regard to men (see Rich 1980). Second, the Mexican women and men in this study were exposed to various types of socially constructed patriarchies. Regional patriarchies are those that are constructed in the diverse geographical regions of Mexican society and include the following characteristics:

1. They are fluid and contestable, depending on the socioeconomic and political contexts in which women and men live. The fewer opportunities women and men have to obtain equal education and paid employment, the greater the gender inequalities (Amuchástegui 2001) and the more emphasized the regional patriarchies.

2. Not just men, but also women, actively participate in the social reproduction of different expressions of gender inequality, femininities, and
   multiple masculinities in contemporary urban and pre-industrialized
   colonial societies.[7]

3. These dynamics have their historical roots, in part, in the formation
   of the Mexican state, which has been constructed through and within
   local hegemonies that have promoted and reproduced regionally
   specific constructions of social and political power and control since
   the early 1930s (Rubin 1996), and through regional expressions of
   bourgeoisie and proletariat shaped by international capital and free-
   market economies in contemporary society (Besserer 1999).

Based on these narratives, I also identify two modalities, which I call
rural patriarchies and *urban patriarchies*. The former term identifies the
hard-core and more intense expressions of patriarchy and gender inequalities that appear in small provincial locations, or *pueblos*. And the latter
identifies the disguised or de-emphasized gender inequalities more commonly seen in the larger urban metropolises, such as Mexico City. In
urban social contexts multiple possibilities for education, paid work, well-
informed sex education and training, and organized women's organizations may expose women to social circumstances that enable them to
challenge gender inequalities (Figueroa Perea 1997). Similarly, young
heterosexual men from Mexico City are more likely than rural men to perceive their female counterparts as being more equal in their sexual encounters and heterosexual experiences than are rural men (Amuchástegui
1994).

My conceptualization of urban-versus-rural expressions of patriarchy
neither essentializes nor polarizes the ways in which gender inequalities
are reproduced; my concept deals exclusively with the extreme yet fluid
expressions of patriarchy within Mexican society. One could argue that in
highly urbanized contexts, such as in the cities of Monterrey or
Guadalajara, the expression of urban patriarchy still exists to some degree,
but these cities are still far less open, volatile, complex, and sophisticated
than is cosmopolitan Mexico City. Comparative sex research in these three
urban locations has shown, for instance, that women and men living in
the Monterrey and Guadalajara are more likely to value female premarital virginity than those in Mexico City (De la Peña and Toledo 1996). At
the same time, rural patriarchies are different: in some Zapotec Oaxaca
locations, for example, the social sexualization of women and men may

expose both of them to a wider diversity of sexual and gender expressions (see Stephen 2002) than in areas that embrace the hard-core *charro* cultures of Jalisco. Thus, in terms of sexual morality, the term *urban patriarchies* does not necessarily mean liberal and progressive, and rural does not necessarily imply rigorous and restrictive.

Both types of patriarchies are fluid and may be emphasized, weakened, or strengthened depending on socioeconomic and political contexts. For example, the expression Fidel used, "Pinche vieja fácil," to stigmatize a rural woman who has premarital sex is an expression of rural hegemony. However, the same expression is also used in larger urban contexts, such as in Monterrey, where I heard men using it, to convey the same meaning. In contrast, rural and urban men also embrace multiple expressions of masculinity that are not hegemonic and that at times may cause them pain. Regardless of the geographical region, the social reproduction of gender inequality is closely associated with *la doble moral*, or the double standard, of morality (Szasz 1998).

In sum, the sexual initiation experiences of the women and men who participated in this study indicate many contrasting differences between genders and across specific social and economic contexts. In addition, all of my respondents coincide at the very core of their relationships; all of them have special reasons to be apprehensive and worried with regard to a first sexual encounter. Looking beyond cultural and social prescriptions of gender identities, sexualities, and patriarchies, we are left with an additional component flowing through the sexual histories of these women and men, that is, the emotions and feelings that encompassed their first sexual encounters, as well as the meanings and interpretations they attach to sexuality in general.

Women and Men in a Culture of Sexual Fear

At their core, sexuality and gender are interconnected processes, and for all of my interviewees they engendered a personal yet collective emotion that was reported during my individual interviews: fear. Fear was the dominant emotion involved in the social construction of their sexual experiences. For both women and men, fear had a wide array of intensity levels and was expressed in the myriad reasons given by both men and women for not wanting to have premarital sex with the partners they loved. For the women, these reasons included fear of pregnancy out of wedlock and its potential negative consequences (e.g., not completing an education, becoming a single mother, or being coerced by the family to marry); fear of family punishment via the maternal figure; fear of experiencing negative feelings; and fear of sexism and recriminations from a future husband, resulting in marital conflict and potential abandonment. For the men, these included fear of a girlfriend's pregnancy and undesired marriage; fear of inappropriate sexual performance; fear of peer pressure and rejection; fear of corporal punishment by the paternal figure; fear of moral prosecution; fear of offending and being rejected by a girlfriend; fear that if a girlfriend is not a virgin then she must be a "morally loose" woman; fear of *fracaso* or of being a moral failure; and fear of the loss of a loving relationship.

The diversity of fears reported by my female and male informants reminds us of the individual and subjective component of sexuality. At the same time, the collectively shared parallels and similarities highlight the social and cultural elements of the sexual. These two dynamics confirm the pioneering sociological insights of Gagnon and Simon, who describe sexuality as being both internal, or intrapsychic, and external, or interpersonal (1973, 20). The interaction between both of these elements is also found in Chodorow's (1995) reflections on the construction of gender as personal and cultural. As she states: "I suggest, that is, that gender cannot be seen as entirely culturally, linguistically, or politically constructed. Rather, there are individual psychological processes in addition to, and in a different register from culture, language and power relations that construct gender for the individual" (517). Thus, sexuality and gender not only share both subjective and social dimensions, but these dimensions interconnect and mutually shape one another.

The emotional reaction of fear — reported individually and shared collectively — suggests the existence of a socially constructed and individually experienced culture of sexual fear in Mexican society. Neither static nor monolithic, this culture of sexual fear is shaped by the specific rural and urban ideologies, socioeconomics, and regional patriarchal processes that alternately create more restrictive or more permissive sexual discourses, and more intense or less intense sexual fears that accompany them. For example, in the sexual advice column of a Mexican magazine called *Desnudarse* (*Getting Naked*), topics and concerns related to sexuality are often discussed. The column offers many examples of the same fears and concerns that were reported by the women and men in this study. Two examples are reproduced below. "Amelia" and "Matías" each ask the advice of the celebrated yet controversial sexologist, Doctor Anabel Ochoa:

Doctora,

I am not a virgin anymore and that worries me. I have heard that virginity can be reconstructed. Is it true that there is some kind of surgery to accomplish it? I am interested because I broke up with my boyfriend (the one who inaugurated me), and I don't want the man I marry to reproach me about it some day. I would love to be the way I used to. Please, give me some guidance.

Amelia, 18 years old, Morelia, Michoacán

Doctora,

I want you to clarify something for me. My girlfriend swore to me that she was a virgin, that I was the first one, and I believed her. That was the very same reason why I respected her for a while. But now that we finally had sexual relations, she did not bleed and I feel as if I have been fooled. My friends tell me that she fooled me, that for sure she had been inaugurated already, but at the end nature makes sure to uncover liars. I hate her, Doctora. Besides, she continues lying. She does not even accept it. She cries and cries and spends the time crying and swearing to me that it is not true, that she cannot even explain herself why she did not bleed, but that she is a virgin. Do you believe her, Doctora? At times, the dignity of men is respected very little, and I tell you this because you have the habit of defending women. Well, I want you to know that I feel betrayed and I deserve some type of compensation.

Matías, 19 years old, Saltillo, Coahuila[8]

My conceptualization of a culture of sexual fear is inspired by Barry Glassner's book *The Culture of Fear: Why Americans Are Afraid of the Wrong Things* (1999). Glassner examines the hidden dynamics responsible for the social fears permeating the daily lives of North American mainstream society (i.e., fear of crime, drugs, and diseases, among other dangers). He reveals how these fears are used, manipulated, and reproduced by the political establishment and other social institutions, generating high expenditures of money, energy, and time on the part of a frightened white middle class that is being deceived. In a similar way, the first heterosexual experiences of the Mexican women and men in my study were shaped by a sexual panic that emerges from the patriarchal mores, gender inequalities, and social prescriptions of femininity and masculinity that determine Mexican women's and men's heterosexual relations. This culture of fear is embedded in Mexican institutions and in the larger ideologies of the nation. While North Americans pay a high price for their socially inflicted and politically sustained fears, Mexican women and men pay a sexual cost. Sexual threats and dangers deny them the right to a meaningful first experience of erotic pleasure and intimacy within the context of a loving relationship. In general, exploring sexual pleasure may become an emotionally exhausting journey within the context of heterosexual relationships. Deciphering sexual desire within a culture of sexual fear takes time, energy, and emotional work. There is a social puzzle that needs to be decoded by any woman or a man who attempts to embrace sexuality and experience eroticism. This gender maze disadvantages women as a social group, but it also shapes the sex lives of men in intricate and enduring ways.

The narratives of male sexual initiation presented here reveal the many complex ways in which patriarchal ideologies speak through the heterosexual initiation experiences of men. As I have shown, gendered beliefs and practices not only control and shape women's sexualities, identities, and heterosexual relationships, but men's as well. The sexual initiation experiences of men are embedded in paradoxes and contradictions that take place along a pleasure–danger continuum. At its best, a man's first sexual initiation was an opportunity for emotional bonding in loving relationships, but the event became a nostalgic memory that did not translate into a long-term relationship. This gradually became more dangerous for some men when sexual initiation became the first stage of an exciting process of sexual learning within non-committed premarital relationships, including sexual mentorship by older women, but this sexualized process became a psychological ordeal within high-conflict or emotionally detached relationships or with non-available partners. As danger increased for others, sex became a highly expected and voluntarily planned event of exciting masculine initiation and a ritual of coming of age as a man, but this passage became a painful experience of sexual disenchantment characterized by feelings of stress, anxiety, fear, and frustration, especially when sexual experience took place with a sex worker. And, finally, at is worst, a young adolescent man's idealized sex fantasy of his "first time" became materialized, but it was the traumatic, unexpected, and involuntary experience of sexual coercion by an older adult or through unexpected casual sex that shattered his sex fantasies. The bittersweet nature of the men's heterosexual relationships is highlighted by their recollections of the unanticipated pressures on the sex workers they seek out, the anguish of coercive sexual initiation, and the effervescent emotions that may be prompted by the sexual mentorship of a considerably older sexual partner. Beyond the sadness of sexual disenchantment and the joy of erotic discovery, the men's stories also reveal the social mechanisms and circumstances through which women may be in charge of the negotiation and control of the sexual scenario. Such controlling women include sex workers who skillfully exercise power in their sexual negotiations and encounters, married women who develop and sustain extramarital affairs with younger or single men, well-seasoned and mature single women who explore pleasure within casual relationships with sexually novice younger men, and older *primas* who may feel safe enough to explore erotic desire with a younger *primo*. Differences with regard to age, marital status, and sexual capital (i.e., accumulated sexual knowledge and skills) appear to be the salient factors facilitating these experiences of sexual exploration and power for these women, whose relationships with the men would be only temporary. An inexperienced but aroused young man may profit from these sexualized opportunities as he becomes the main protagonist of these encounters. How would these Mexican women describe their experiences of sex and the erotic? The sociology of gender and sexuality behind the sexual stories of Mexicanas who embrace a sexually empowered female image has yet to be heard.

Besides their pleasurable dangers and their strenuous adventures, the women and men participating in this study share many of the commonalities that take place within a culture of sexual fear. Sexual knowledge, beliefs, values, anxieties, desires, taboos, pressures, ideals, feelings, emotions, ideas about deviance, and a longing for intimate and meaningful sexual relationships flow through their heterosexual experiences. For both the women and men, all of these dynamics are embedded in an important social institution, *la familia*. In the following chapter, I will discuss how the various dimensions of sexual interaction are interconnected at the very core of this important institution.

CHAPTER 4

Sex Is a Family Affair

Nurturing and Regulating Sexuality

"They forced me to get married," Irasema said. "My father said, 'We're not going to leave it like this!' And he grabbed me and let's go! Boom! He took me to the house of my husband and I do not know how many things they said . . . that he had to repair the damage." With tears in her eyes, Irasema explained that her first sexual encounter had resulted in an unexpected pregnancy, which led to a coercive marriage with someone she would not have chosen as a husband. For Irasema and other women in this study, premarital sex and its consequences were not only a private and intimate experience; they became a public and a family affair.

Diego described how he also wound up in an unexpected marriage at the age of twenty-three: "I married her because of honor. I had to come out and face the bull, to protect her image and her name." Like Irasema, Diego's having sex with his girlfriend became a family affair, leading to an intense conflict for the young woman. When her father learned the two of them were having sex, he became physically and emotionally abusive to her — and Diego felt the need to protect her. Values that he had learned about masculine responsibility and premarital sex validated his desire to shelter her, and he convinced her to elope with him.

Irasema and Diego's stories show how society and its families selectively defined, shaped, and controlled the sex lives and relationships of the study participants. Their parents rarely taught them about reproductive health or biology. Many of the women received only basic menstrual hygiene information, usually from their mothers, older sisters, and aunts.[1] However, as illustrated by Irasema and Diego's cases, parents shaped the ways in which my informants perceived and lived their experiences of sexuality, including virginity, premarital sex, dating, courtship, marriage, and the ideal of heterosexual love. Their erotic desires and drives were neither an individual nor an intimate experience. Their sex lives were collective, public concerns that took place within the confines of family regulations, expectations, and norms.

Family Politics and Coercive Marriage: Pregnancy Out of Wedlock

> *A woman who has been seduced or raped, far from finding protection*
> *and understanding from her family or society, finds in them her*
> *most blind, brutal, and compassionless executioners.*
>
> Dr. Miguel Padilla Pimentel,
> *La Moral Sexual en México*

"Pregnancy makes sex visible; it converts private behavior into public behavior," writes Constance Nathanson in her book on adolescent women's sexual behavior, *Dangerous Passage* (1991). For the women in this study whose sexual activities became visible through pregnancy out of wedlock, the loss of their virginity was transformed from an intimate experience into a public one that ultimately became a family affair. A daughter's premarital sexual activity fractured family honor and caused shame, and the moral damage done to the family had to be repaired by coercive marriage. In Mexico, some families attempt to repair that damage by forcing their daughters to marry, even when pregnancy is the result of rape. In such extreme cases, the daughters are actually forced to marry their rapists.

Mexican colonial society linked female sexuality with a woman's moral virtue (i.e., her virginity), socioeconomic status, and family honor (Espín 1986; Twinam 1989; Tostado Gutiérrez 1991; Ramos Lira, Koss, and Russo 1999). This principle is well understood also by the women from Degollado (Jalisco) and El Fuerte (Michoacán) who shared with Hirsch their recollections of being kidnapped and raped by men, "so that she would be forced to marry to save family's honor" (2003, 87). Mummert similarly observed that in, a village in Michoacán, courting was under strict parental surveillance until the 1960s because "violent abductions and forced unions with virtual strangers were not uncommon" (1994, 194).

Families may pressure a man to marry when a young woman gets pregnant in many other Latin American (Youssef 1973, 340) and Middle

Eastern countries, such as Turkey (Cindoglu 1997), where forced marriage may be decided based upon a virginity examination (Frank et al. 1999). However, evidence of sexual activity in a young woman may become a reason for marriage even when there is no pregnancy or when sex was by force. This practice has been carried to the extreme in Turkey (Frank et al. 1999) and in at least a dozen Latin American nations, where a rapist may be exonerated if he promises to marry his victim (Paternostro 1998, 31).[2] In the early twentieth century, white families in the U.S. South forced marriage as a consequence of out-of-wedlock pregnancy more often than African American ones. Whites were more likely to use threats, resulting in "shotgun weddings" that would coerce the young man involved to marry a pregnant adolescent because of social stigma and shame (Pagnini and Morgan 1996).[3]

Coercive marriage came into play in the lives of three of the women in this study. Two of them, Irasema and Trinidad, were from upper-middle-class families, born and raised in Mexico City. As previously described, Irasema had been raped by her boyfriend and was then forced by her father to get married. Our interview was the first time she had ever talked about her rape and pregnancy. Trinidad had become pregnant during a casual relationship with a boyfriend she had never considered marrying. Like Irasema, she experienced intense feelings as she recalled the day she was forced to marry:

> My mother was kind of strict, and she wanted me to be a virgin until I got married. But since she realized that *"me comí el pastel antes del recreo"* [I ate the cake before recess] she sent me to get married. I pleaded with her. I cried, I begged. I did not want her to force me to get married. She said, "No, no, she has to get married. After she gets married, she can get divorced if she wants to."

Out-of-wedlock pregnancy suggests that the family has failed to provide good moral guidance and a "pro-decency" sex education to a daughter.[4] Coercive marriage then becomes a solution to save the social image of the family, or *las apariencias* (appearances), a concept Irasema used as she explained why she had a religious wedding ceremony: "You wear white in front of society, in order for you to be okay with them. But then after a few months you give birth to your baby. The week after I got married I was already wearing dresses for pregnant women because I already was five months pregnant."

Both women experienced a psychological ordeal after their first sexual experience, long before they knew about their pregnancies. Being raped was Irasema's first sexual encounter. She cried when she described her emotional collapse:

> Oh my God! I felt so dirty; I did not even want to see my parents. I felt as if they were going to point the finger at me, like they were going to guess what had happened to me. But you know, I got home all relaxed with all my makeup on, pretending nothing had happened to me. I felt so dirty and guilty. I used to share my bedroom with one of my sisters and I did not even want her to touch me or get close to me. And I cried and cried because I asked myself why?

Trinidad also struggled with the issue of having had sex with someone she did not love and then having to face the various forces that combine to expropriate a woman's sexuality: a mother's controlling and threatening teachings about morality and virginity, fear of pregnancy, and Catholic guilt:

> I do not love him, I hate him! So why do I let him touch my body? I did not know what was happening, but I knew it was not right. My mother's warnings to avoid sex, about my future, and morality as well . . . that I risked getting pregnant. And she said, "Who knows what you are doing? You do not want to tell me. But whatever you do, if you overstimulate yourself sexually without having intercourse, that will create sexual deformations." All that made me so afraid, and then you know, Catholicism, that I was not supposed to do it before marriage. That created a lot of guilt in me.

Both women tried to abort but failed. Irasema gave birth to a daughter who is now attending college in Los Angeles. Trinidad had a son whose mental retardation might have been caused by her two unsuccessful attempts at abortion. Since abortion is not legal in Mexico, Trinidad tried to induce abortion — without telling her mother — by taking an herbal formula she had purchased from a *hierbera* at the market.[5] A medical doctor was also unsuccessful in inducing an abortion.

Both women were also suicidal. Irasema tried to kill herself when she learned about her second pregnancy, by a man she did not choose to marry. And Trinidad, after giving birth to her son, was depressed to the point of being suicidal for years. She is grateful to a support group in Los Angeles for helping her through this painful experience.

Trinidad told me how she had learned about human reproduction when she was seven or eight years old. Her mother, a gynecologist by profession, gave her a tour of a museum exhibit in Mexico City which showed the chronological evolution of human embryos and fetuses preserved in formaldehyde. Women like Trinidad may develop some knowledge of reproduction, especially if they are educated in urban areas, where this type of information is more likely to be available. However, family ethics may still covertly define the ways in which women are supposed to interpret the knowledge they receive. The message is: "This is the information you need to know about sex so you do not get pregnant before you get married and shame our family."

Fernanda, born and raised in Mexico City, is the third woman in the study who was forced to get married after her family found out she was pregnant.

> I wanted to die. I was eighteen, and I was studying to become an art educa-tion instructor. Then everything collapsed for me because of an unwanted pregnancy. Like my mother says, "Nobody made you to do it," and nobody had made me do it. I was forced to get married, and I did.

Fernanda was sexually assaulted by her uncle and three adult men when she was thirteen. Later, as an older adolescent, she agreed to voluntary sex for the first time, but only because she was under the influence of alcohol:

> I did not do it consciously. I did it after a party. I was kind of drunk and I was not completely aware. I think I drank alcohol to feel more encouraged, less like a coward. But after I woke up and I looked at myself, I started to cry and felt so ashamed of myself. And I felt also ashamed because *había defraudado a mi mamá* [I had defrauded my mother]. My father, fortunately, had died three years ear-lier . . . because if he had been alive I do not think I would have done it.

Defraudar in Spanish has the same meaning it has in English: to defraud, which means "to deprive of a right or property by fraud; cheat." In just that way, Fernanda learned that *defraudar* meant being a transgressor by cheating, disappointing, or disillusioning her mother. This is a common experience for many women, as I discuss in the next section.[6] Paternal property rights with regard to sexuality are also clear in Fernanda's story: the death of Fernanda's father had made it possible for her to possess her own sexuality.

Fernanda also looked to abortion as a way to terminate her pregnancy, but a physician at a clinic talked her out of it. Other women in the study experienced similar pressures to marry. Tomasita, for example, explained that she finally married a man with whom she cohabited and had children "because of family pressure." She recalled that she had been embarrassed to see her children throwing rose petals in the aisles of the church on her wedding day. Margarita did not tell her family about her pregnancy. Instead, she immediately asked her boyfriend — a college student — to marry her as a preventive measure. The man, who is now her husband, still cites their hastily arranged marriage as the main reason he was not able to finish college.

The men's stories of coercive marriage offer parallel yet contrasting gender dynamics. Five out of the twenty men in this study were forced to get married after the women they were dating became pregnant. Diego is a thirty-six-year-old immigrant from Mexico City, who came to Los Angeles at the age of twenty-one; he has supported himself through a series of part-time jobs since arriving in the United States. An articulate and eloquent man raised in a middle-class Protestant family, he married for the first time at the age of twenty-three after having had sex with a member of his church, the daughter of a Mexican immigrant pastor. The couple did not marry because of pregnancy, however. If they had never had sex, Diego said, he would not have decided to marry her, but he had felt pressured to do so after they had sex, for several reasons. When the girl's father learned about their sexual activity, he had abused her physically and sent her to a boarding school. Diego felt humiliated and enraged and compelled to protect her from the abuse. He also felt a moral obligation to marry as a way to repair what he called a *falta social* — a social offense. He related the story of how they came to decide to marry without her father's consent:

> She did not ask me to marry her; I was the one who told her. "Do you want to marry me?" "How?" "We get away right at this moment!" It was about eleven [o'clock] in Riverside, and that night I took her to Las Vegas. I drove all night long. I believe I had $100 or $120, I don't remember. We arrived to Las Vegas when it was dawn, we rented a motel, we looked for a chapel, and with $30 in hand that you needed to pay the service. But with the money left, I took her to a mall and bought her a long white dress with little black spots, a pair of pantyhose and shoes, and some makeup because her mouth was still bruised after her father had slapped her on the face. I got married wearing my tennis shoes, blue jeans, and a leather jacket. A strange guy led the marriage ceremony, you know, a Las Vegas type of man. And you know what? Right after we leave the chapel, we go to the motel and that is when she gets pregnant! [Laughs]

I asked Diego, "Where did you learn that you had to get married, and about your responsibility? Where did you learn all this?" He replied, "At home, listening to things. That I had to be a man, that I had to be responsible for my actions."

Through the institution of the family, society creates and reproduces principles of masculinity that teach young men like Diego that a lack of personal responsibility for premarital sexual activity may compromise manliness. In order "to be a man" — and thus to show responsibility for the consequences that might follow premarital sexual activity — Diego felt he had no choice but to get married. For Mexican men like Diego, being *un hombre de verdad* — a real man — meant to be *responsable y cumplidor* — a man who lives up to his commitments — central attributes of masculine identity (Cazés 1993; Stern et al. 2003). Protecting a girlfriend who has run away to flee abuse is also connected to this principle. Such a sense of honor and feelings of guilt have been observed in other Mexican men in similar circumstances. For instance, Amuchástegui found that some of her informants also felt a sense of obligation and decided to marry the young girls whose honor they had compromised by having had sex with them (2001, 386). "The sexual activity of the men seems to be regulated through a sense of honor and guilt clearly connected with masculinity, in the sense that they feel the obligation to marry the woman from whom they stole virginity. By not doing it, they would be considered cowardly and irresponsible with regard to the word of honor they have invested" (417–18).

Diego said he had done his best to be a good provider for his wife and the two children born of the marriage. However, an extramarital affair resulted in a painful separation and divorce from the woman he had once loved so deeply and their two children, who he spends time with on a periodic basis.

Raúl, a thirty-four-year-old technician who migrated from Mexico City to Los Angeles in 1988, also married after he learned that the Mexican immigrant woman he had been dating was pregnant. They had broken up and lost communication, but she reestablished contact with him a couple of months later to notify him about her pregnancy. "I felt pushed by her," he said. "I felt emotionally pressured." His decision to marry her was preceded by DNA tests, mixed emotions, confusion, shock, discomfort, and pain. She had been dating other men and he had not been sure if the baby was his.

I prompted Raúl with the incomplete sentence, "If she had not become pregnant . . ." and he said, "I would not have married her. I did it because of that, and that was the reason. Then, we got married and had our daughter." Later on, he added, "And yes, I married without loving her. I am going to be honest with you, but . . . [I married] with the purpose of making sure that my daughter would be raised in a family environment."

As with Diego, the dilemma of an unexpected pregnancy and the decision to marry revealed values of respect for the family of origin. But unlike Diego, Raúl did not associate his decision to marry because of her pregnancy with a sense of manly responsibility. Rather, he felt strongly that a nuclear family would be the way to assure his child's psychological well-being, even at the expense of the quality of his own marital life. His values supported a single woman who became pregnant while having multiple partners but who also wanted a stable family life. Established in the midst of emotional turmoil, the marriage soon fell apart, and after a few failed attempts to save it, ended in divorce. Raúl is currently raising his daughter with the support of his parents and the rest of his family.

The third man who married after he learned that his girlfriend had become pregnant was Sebastián. Like Diego and Raúl, he was born and raised in Mexico City. Sebastián was forty at the time of our interview, and he had been working as a technician since arriving in Los Angeles in 1995. He had attended college in Mexico City but did not complete his third year due to an accident. Back then, a steady relationship with the young girl he was dating had resulted in an unexpected pregnancy. He had planned to marry her, but only after finishing college. Sebastián explained how his decision to marry sooner came about as a result of undergoing both his family's and his girlfriend's scrutiny. A son who "gets a girlfriend pregnant" was not a new experience to Sebastián's parents; his two oldest brothers had also married after their respective girlfriends became pregnant. Sebastián paraphrased his father's reaction when he told him about his girlfriend's pregnancy: "*¡Róbatela! ¡No te cases, róbatela y sigue estudiando!*" (Steal her! [meaning, Kidnap her! or Run away with her!] Don't get married; continue studying!). His girlfriend's father, on the other hand, had no information about her pregnancy. Sebastián understood the rationale behind his own father's proposal, since by eloping they would still be legally married, but without the expense of an official religious ceremony and a wedding reception.[7]

The concept of *el robo de la novia* (the theft of the girlfriend) has many linguistic and social interpretations.[8] With some exceptions, couples who agree to run away eventually do legally marry. Running away with a girlfriend is one way to get around family disapproval. For example, Fermín, from Mexico City, explained that some of his friends had run away with their girlfriends because it was the only way they could marry them. "Parents deny permission to their daughters to go out with their boyfriends," Fermín said. "So if a young man and his girlfriend ran away, her parents would have no choice but to accept the marriage." Some of Hirsch's informants had, in fact, established conjugal relationships in this fashion (2003, 86).

As in the case of Sebastián's father, many Mexican fathers educating their sons in urban Mexico are seriously concerned with developing the human and cultural capital of a young son who has to be well prepared to survive in an increasingly competitive and complex society. Some urban fathers may therefore reject the "respect for the family" ethic and its corollary, an immediate and traditional coercive marriage. Instead, they may be more concerned about their son's education and economic future. In addition, Sebastián was one of five sons, in a family with no daughters.

If his father had had to face a daughter's out-of-wedlock pregnancy, he might not have suggested running away as a way to deal with it.

Sebastián's mother was practically invisible in the decision-making process with regard to his marriage, but she had a strong reaction to his girlfriend's pregnancy: she became ill. His father seemed to be completely in charge. The reverse was true in his girlfriend's family, where the mother actively pushed for the marriage. According to Sebastián, his future mother-in-law told him, "But you are going to marry her, asshole, aren't you?" She also kept the pregnancy a secret and never informed her husband about it. Here, she was playing the mediator role, protecting her pregnant daughter both from a potentially angry father and from the stigma of single motherhood.

Sebastián did marry his girlfriend, but he never had the opportunity to complete his college degree. Of all the women and men who married because of pregnancy out of wedlock in this study, he is the only one whose marriage has not ended in divorce.

The fourth man who was forced to marry a pregnant girlfriend was Emiliano, a forty-three-year-old native of Mexico City. Like Diego and Sebastián, Emiliano had to rush into a marriage with a steady girlfriend he might have married some day in the future. He had a good job (he traveled across Mexico to perform special assignments as a technician working for a construction company), but like Sebastián, regular sex and an unexpected pregnancy changed his life and career plans. Emiliano described how the pregnancy happened:

> We had sexual relations for about a year after we met, and from that moment she was really fast. Suddenly, she said, "I am pregnant." And I said to myself, "What happened? What did not work?" And what did not work is that we were not using anything, we did not use any protection!

He went on to explain that between the ages of seventeen and eighteen, he had encountered obstacles and had been stigmatized when he had tried to explore alternative ways to experience safe sex. He had had problems while trying to get condoms from doctors, and again when he had tried to buy them. "Incredible! I remember that one time I went to a pharmacy. I told the pharmacist, '¡Hola! Recommend something to me [to have safe sex].' And he said, 'Get out of here, young boy!'" Thus, in spite of the government's active promotion of the use of contraceptives since the 1970s (especially for married, urban women), young men like Emiliano have also experienced the government's and society's rejection and denial of the sexual activity that takes place among youth and single people (see Amuchástegui 2001). Despite these obstacles, Emiliano did not refrain from engaging in regular sexual activity. And like Sebastián, he immediately talked with his father after learning about his girlfriend's pregnancy. But Emiliano was cautious. He did not tell his father about the actual pregnancy. Instead, he wanted to see his father's reaction if he only said that they were having sex.

> [He said] that I had already had sexual relations with her and that it was my obligation to be responsible as a man. I do not know, if whether it was a falta or an offense, but I had to be responsible as a man.

Like Diego, Emiliano's father embraced the male ethic that promotes a man's responsibility for a potential or real pregnancy. He was also aware of his son's stable employment and secure economic situation. Unlike Sebastián's father, he did not suggest other alternatives, like eloping. Emiliano was not a college student; he had a decent job. As far as the father was concerned, an unexpected marriage would not affect his son's future financial stability. Instead, he offered support to his son with regard to the formalities preceding a marriage, including asking for the young woman's hand.

Emiliano got married, had three children, and enjoyed a relatively stable marital life. However, his career opportunities in Mexico gradually dried up. The former construction technician became a bus driver and developed a drinking problem. Like Diego, Emiliano had an extramarital affair that hurt his marriage and led to a temporary and difficult separation—his main reason for migrating to the United States. Unlike Diego, Emiliano and his wife are now in Los Angeles, living together again while struggling to heal past wounds.

Jacobo, a thirty-five-year-old man from Guadalajara, is the fifth and final male informant in this study who married because of his girlfriend's pregnancy. An articulate and eloquent man who used a lot of humor during our interview, Jacobo has a financially stable life, having worked for the same company ever since he arrived in Los Angeles fifteen years ago. He started having regular sex with a Mexican immigrant woman soon after he arrived in the United States. After six months of courtship, she unexpectedly became pregnant and he felt forced to marry her.

> *Author:* Did she tell you that you had to get married because she was pregnant? Or was it your initiative?
>
> *Jocobo:* It was the two, the two of us.
>
> *Author:* Were you pressured by either of their families?

> *Jacobo:* Neither one forced me, in so many words, but they did it with their attitudes. [My parents'] attitudes were, *"Deben casarse, tienen que cumplir!"* [You both should get married, you both have to be responsible!] They never said it verbally, but their attitudes did it. My mother said, *"¡Uy!* I cannot even have my confession; I cannot even go to mass!" "But mother! Whatever I do does not have to affect you." "No? Yes! Before the eyes of God yes, I am responsible!" That kind of attitude.
>
> *Author:* That was your mother's reaction. With regard to your father, did he say anything about it?
>
> *Jacobo:* My father was neutral. He only recommended that I think about it very well. "Think about it and think about it, and you will decide what to do." "Perfect!"

In the end, Jacobo and his girlfriend decided to get married, but their decision was very evidently influenced by his parents. He said he did not tell his future in-laws back in Mexico about the pregnancy, and they were not involved in the decision about getting married.

Even though the marriage was relatively stable for the first few years, Jacobo initiated divorce proceedings after he and his wife attended a marriage retreat organized by their Catholic church congregation. The workshops helped him make a decision to get a divorce, he said: "The problem in my marriage is that I got married almost without being really in love with her. I felt forced to get married because of the whole thing with her pregnancy."

Shortly before our interview, Jacobo had remarried. Like Diego, he said he has done his best to provide for the two children from his first marriage, by paying child support and spending time with them on a periodic basis.

These stories illustrate that being exposed to coercive marriage because of pregnancy out of wedlock is difficult for everyone, regardless of gender. However, gendered patterns make the experience different for women vis-à-vis men. These patterns are different, depending on both the gender of the child and the gender of the parent; they are also influenced by the individual sexual histories of the unmarried woman and the unmarried man.

The involvement and reactions of fathers to sons who get a girlfriend pregnant out of wedlock are malleable and multifaceted. At times, these dynamics embrace a male ethic of responsibility for a woman's pregnancy (Emiliano's father), at times they offer some space for negotiation based on what a father considers the best interests of his son (Sebastián's father), and at times they leave the decision to marry completely up to a son (Jacobo's father). In contrast, the reaction of a son's mother can be an acute illness (Sebastián's mother) or religious guilt and manipulation (Jacobo's mother). Similarly, a mother whose daughter gets pregnant out of wedlock may exercise pressure on a potential son-in-law in order to guarantee a marriage (in Sebastián's case). As previously discussed, the maternal figure becomes a mediator of the affair involving the young couple. A mother's parenting skills are compromised if she is the one responsible for the sexual morality of her child and her son or daughter does not follow her teachings. Thus, learning about a child's pregnancy out of wedlock may have a more intense emotional effect on a mother than on a father.

These dynamics were different for the three female informants who experienced coercive marriage due to pregnancy. They reported being denied any type of personal agency with regard to the decision to get married. In the case of Irasema, her father did not allow her to explore any alternatives; he automatically forced her to marry. Trinidad and Fernanda were forced by their respective mothers to marry immediately once they learned about their daughter's pregnancy. In these two cases, the marriages took place before the participants had migrated to the United States; the geographical closeness between parents and a pregnant daughter might have accentuated the need to enforce marriage. Jacobo's girlfriend experienced less family pressure by virtue of the physical distance between her and her parents in Mexico, who were not even informed of her pregnancy.

As we have seen, how people react to an out-of-wedlock pregnancy depends on the gender of the parent and that of the child. In this study, men were not always forced to get married, while women always were. This finding confirms Prieur's conclusions about how and why morality is more ambiguous for men than for women (1998, 196). For sons, a father's reaction is fluid and flexible, whereas a mother is more emotional in her reactions. For daughters, the parent's reaction is stricter regardless of the parent's gender. At times, this dynamic might be mediated by geographical distance, especially when the pregnant child lives on the other side of the border from the parents.

The five men in my study had more than one thing in common. By the time all of them were married, due to the girlfriends' pregnancy out of wedlock, they all had some accumulated sexual experience from previous loving relationships. With the exception of Raúl, all had experienced sex for the first time with women who were on average five years older than they. As previously discussed, sexual mentorship by older women was a special characteristic in the sexual histories of some of the men in this study. For those men, their first sexual experiences were positive and pleasant, and did not result in unexpected pregnancies. In addition, all had been born and raised in urban areas, such as Mexico City and Guadalajara.

In contrast, the female informants who experienced coercive marriage were sometimes forced to marry the men with whom they experienced sex for the first time. An interesting pattern of biological odds and probabilities may expose a young woman to getting pregnant if she has sex before marriage. Her risk of getting pregnant is especially high if sex education and family planning resources have been lacking or limited, and if the responsibility for birth control rests solely on a sexually inexperienced woman. In contrast, a young man of the same age may have been exposed to safer sexual experiences, especially if his initial sexual partner was considerably older. A more sexually seasoned or experienced female partner may come to her sexual encounters with previously learned skills to negotiate or demand protected sex (e.g., condom use). If she is more knowledgeable than her younger male partner with regard to sexual health, she is also more likely to take full responsibility for birth control. Thus, older women may not only offer sexual mentorship but may take care of young men in their sexual encounters. However, this may also have some cost for men. Numerous sexual encounters and a lack of appropriate sex education increased the risk for a man (and his sex partners, including sex workers) of being infected with sexually transmitted diseases (STDs), including HIV/AIDS. In this study, the incidence of STDs was more prevalent and more frequently reported by men than by women.[9]

The men's testimony also show how male sexualities, practices, and expressions are gendered. In Latino cultures, "the definition of homosexuality as a gender problem rather than a difference in sexual orientation fuels and exacerbates homophobia" (Díaz 1998, 64). In the same way, heterosexual practices that result in pregnancy out of wedlock for a single heterosexual man are resolved according to gender: a man has to be responsible for his actions, so getting married becomes an expression of masculinity and manhood.

Beyond gender differences, what are the commonalities among female and male informants who experienced coercive marriage due to pregnancy out of wedlock? Of the sixty study participants, those who experienced coercive marriage — or felt the need to marry due to premarital sex or pregnancy out of wedlock — were all raised in urban contexts, mainly Mexico City, with one participant being from Guadalajara. What is responsible for this pattern? Mexican women and men who come of age in urban contexts experience social and economic conditions that provide them with less rigid gender prescriptions and a wider variety of sexual discourses for defining both female and male heterosexual practices, including socially progressive religious groups within the Church, such as pro-choice Catholic groups. In addition, a sense of personal anonymity and a more developed, modernized notion of individuality and autonomy combine to promote a sense of freer sexuality in both urban women and men (see Carrillo 2002). Finally, urban women's greater exposure to education and employment opportunities may help them to construct expressions of femininity that are less restrictive in their heterosexual relationships. This may help urban women to engage in sexual relations before marriage, and urban men to perceive their female partners as *sujetos de deseo,* subjects of desire (Amuchástegui 2001, 274, 291). However, the same gender patterns that may help urban youth explore premarital sex can combine with social factors to put them at risk of pregnancy and coercive marriage. A recent survey conducted in Mexico City, for example, revealed that only 48 percent of adolescent couples who are sexually active use some kind of contraception, and of them, 20 percent self-prescribe.[10] These youth face the same obstacles Emiliano faced more than twenty years ago. They remain vulnerable if there is no equally shared responsibility or concern for reproductive health and no knowledge or individual responsibility on either side.

Paradoxically, in rural areas, a more rigid pattern with regard to gender identities and a more controlling or restrictive sexual discourse may protect rural youth from engaging in premarital sex and thus risking pregnancy and coercive marriage. The contrast between the urban and rural context is illustrated by the circular migration experienced by Fermín. He was born in Mexico City, but when he was six his parents divorced and he was sent to live with his paternal grandmother in a town in the state of Mexico, the area surrounding Mexico City that is made up of urban, semi-industrial, and rural spaces. "I am from both places, I got the culture from both places," Fermín explained. He had grown up going back and forth, spending weekdays with his grandmother in a small town and weekends with his father in Mexico City. Fermín followed this routine for twelve years until he was eighteen, when his grandmother passed away and he moved permanently to Mexico City.

Fermín was one of the three Mexico City study participants whose sexual initiation had taken place with a sex worker, out of fear of a girlfriend's pregnancy and potential coercive marriage. That had happened to many of his male friends, and he was terrified of following in their footsteps with an unhappy marriage. Fermín was not only aware of the danger, but his movement between the big city and the small town offered him the unique experience of repositioning himself with regard to local sexual practices. He said:

> When the woman became pregnant, she had to get married because that was a responsibility and they had to do it. I saw it a lot then and you had no choice. It used to be more puritanical. In my grandmother's town, that is where I saw

it. But in Mexico City, [sexual activity] was even more, men were careless about it [sex]. But, almost always, they became responsible for their actions anyway.

Being responsible for the consequences of unprotected sex represented a moral responsibility, for many of Fermín's friends and for about 25 percent of my male informants. Some of these men said this sense of responsibility was profoundly linked to their masculine identity and manhood. For many of them, being morally responsible for a pregnancy meant being "a man," while evading responsibility compromised their manhood.

Though a young man may associate a sense of manly responsibility with a girlfriend's pregnancy, coercive marriage because of pregnancy or premarital sexual activity is not a fixed cultural norm. It is a flexible and nuanced social practice shaped by many complexities. For example, Alfredo, from Mexico City, said that when he learned about his girlfriend's pregnancy, he had felt his "responsibility as a man," and accordingly, he had felt there was no doubt that he immediately had to talk with the girl's parents about their need to get married. However, Alfredo said, he could have never imagined the reaction of his girlfriend's parents when he told them he wanted to marry their daughter.

> Her parents became furious when we talked to them about it. [They said,] "That man is not good for you, leave him! We are going to support you and your child!" And you know what? That is very confusing. When you assume your responsibility as a man, they close the doors to you. And I threw it in my in-laws' face. [I said,] "You know what? Haven't you seen other people, other families, who argue and fight because they want their pregnant daughter to get married? And now that I am assuming my responsibility, you say that I am not a good catch for your daughter?"

After that conversation, which took place in the late 1980s, Alfredo and his girlfriend decided to live together. He said he is not surprised by the tension and conflict that has characterized his communication with his in-laws since then. In spite of it, Alfredo and his live-in partner of more than ten years produced two children and established a relatively stable relationship. They live in Los Angeles, but they have recently experienced emotional stress and escalating marital discord, and Alfredo expects them to separate soon.

Alfredo's story is both similar to and different from Joaquín's, after the latter traveled from his native Guadalajara to a small town in Nayarit (a state just west of Jalisco) in order to meet his girlfriend's parents. Unlike

Alfredo, Joaquín did not know if his girlfriend was pregnant, and therefore, he did not raise that issue when he told the parents he wanted to marry their daughter. He also did not tell them about his sense of obligation to marry the girl with whom he had been sexually active. As with Alfredo, Joaquín's in-laws disapproved of the relationship. Joaquín then offered that he knew of one strategy to use to see if he could get his girlfriend's parents to accept their decision to marry. "I told them that 'we had to' get married," Joaquín said with a big laugh, explaining that he was able to successfully play some "morality tricks" in order to make his future in-laws accept the couple's decision. Joaquín married the young woman within a relatively short period of time. He later left her behind, with three children, after he migrated to Los Angeles in 1994.

Alfredo and Joaquín respectively complied with, or strategically manipulated, their well-learned cultural expertise with regard to premarital sexual activity. Their stories also suggest that rural parents may follow a more rigid sexual morality with regard to coercive marriage when compared to urban parents, who under similar circumstances, may not always agree to deal with a daughter's (real or potential) pregnancy by imposing or accepting marriage. Joaquín's in-laws were from a small town characterized by stricter moral regulations, and they had to protect the moral reputation of a daughter who might be pregnant. They had no option but to give her in matrimony to a man they barely knew. By contrast, the urban socioeconomic circumstances of Alfredo's in-laws ultimately shaped their views of sexual morality and offered additional options to a pregnant young woman.

"Le Fallé a Mi Mamá": I Let My Mother Down

In patriarchal countries like Mexico, the education of children is a mother's responsibility; mothering is considered the ideal vehicle for transmitting patriarchal mores. Gutmann (1996) has noted that in Santo Domingo — the urban, working-class *colonia* in Mexico City he studied — fathers are highly involved in child-rearing responsibilities, more so than men from more privileged socioeconomic contexts. This happens because men from upper socioeconomic strata are more likely to have the means to hire a maid or a nanny. However, Gutmann has noted, "mothers enforce the rules far more than fathers, even when it comes to beatings. Men in Santo Domingo talk of beating their children, just as they were slapped, spanked, and whipped with belts as youngsters. But the most violent punishments inflicted on children today are often at the hands of mothers, a situation many also take as 'normal'" (77).

Gutmann also observed that mothers were the main parental figures "involved in gathering the children to attend church and religious celebrations and, when they were young, to pray" (77). Prieur (1998) cites Melhuus's (1992) anthropological research in Mexican villages, where the mother is blamed for the misbehavior of her children. And Hurtado (2003) says that, among the U.S. college-educated young women of Mexican origin she studied, mothers might speak directly to their children (daughters, in particular) about sexuality and then report back to the father figure (53), but that although daughters would tell their mothers if they had become sexually active, they would discuss the subject far less often with their fathers (57). Thus, we might speculate that this cultural dynamic accounts for the origin of the offensive expression *que poca madre* — literally, "so little mother, meaning so badly brought up" (see Prieur 1998, 56, 217).

For the women in this study, not complying with educational standards and moral expectations means disobeying the mother figure. Yet fathers, more than mothers, own their daughters' sexuality. As the moral guardians of a daughter's sexuality, the mother works for the father, who is the ultimate proprietor. Thus, any failure by a daughter to comply with her mother's teachings indicates the mother's failure to successfully educate her about sexual morality.

Romelia and Xóchitl, both from Jalisco, explained their feelings after having had premarital sex for the first time:

> *Romelia:* I felt very bad because I said "*¡Ya le fallé a mi mamá!*" (I already let my mother down!) In other words, I felt bad, bad . . . I felt . . . and also because of religion and I said "*¡Dios mío!* You were taking care of me, why did this happen to me?" It made me feel so ashamed, so ashamed of myself, and for my mother, because everybody was going to know that I . . . , I felt as if the world already knew about it and I felt so bad.

> *Xóchitl:* *Le fallé a ella* [I let her down], and I felt bad because my mother had offered all her *confianza* [trust] and she used to tell me and my sisters, "If you think about it, there is no need for me to tell you anything about it, you know very well what is right and what is wrong, and I give you the freedom to go out." So, guilt, anxiety, feeling dirty and all that I felt; it's like you have it inside of you. I felt all this inside because I did it without being married.

Romelia and Xóchitl's mothers expected them to follow a code of sexual ethics, and they knew that their fathers would hold their mothers responsible for their sexual behavior. Not being able to comply with one of these principles represented "letting your mother down," or at its worst, not being able to live up the trust she had shown in you.[11] The young women's despair and guilt were aggravated by their awareness of religious rules about female sexual behavior. Romelia knew that she would be punished and shamed by her family, her religion, and society-at-large.

A mother is responsible for her daughter's marital success and sexual adequacy, and the emotions associated with this process may endure beyond generational differences and migration experiences. Romelia's and Xóchitl's testimony is echoed in Hirsch's reflections on mothers' pain when a daughter ends up in a failed marriage (2003, 117), and in Hurtado's, whose informants' mothers expressed "sadness and loss when their daughters did not follow what they considered the proper way to conduct themselves sexually" (2003, 57).[12]

As part of their deep concern about their parents' reaction toward premarital sex, feelings of ambivalence — pleasure and guilt, happiness and shame, joy and sadness — were not unusual for some of the women. Yadira related her feelings about her first sexual experience:

> My experience was nice but at the same time it was sad, because I asked myself "*¿Me voy a casar bien?* [Am I going to get married the right way?] What is my mother going to say about it? What is my father going to say?" I was afraid my parents would know about it. "Yes," I said to myself, "they are going to kick me out of my house!"

Unlike Romelia, Yadira was not concerned about what other people would say about her not being a virgin anymore. However, she was seriously concerned about both of her parents' reactions. During our interview, she recalled how, when she was twenty years old, her father had twice slapped her in the face after serious arguments. Offended by her father's physical and emotional abuse, Yadira decided to leave the family home and move in with her boyfriend — the man with whom she had her first sexual relations and who is now her husband. Cohabiting with her boyfriend transformed Yadira into a major moral transgressor: she was living with and having sex with a man without being married. Accordingly, she was punished by her family (her father, in particular).

> My father said, "You are dead to me, I do not want to know anything about you. All this man wants is to play with you." He stopped talking to me for at least three years or more. Then, after he started to talk with me, I got pregnant. And he stopped talking to me again. But then, one day, *su otra señora* [my father's second wife] held my child in her arms and talked to him about it, and then he did not reject me anymore. He accepted my child and me.

Like those women who were forced to get married because of pregnancy out of wedlock, Yadira's decision to cohabit with her boyfriend became a family affair that was punished by her father's rejection, indifference, and anger, even though, unlike those women, she had not been forced to marry. Yadira had also anticipated her lack of sexual ownership after having sex and had foreseen the potential negative consequences of premarital sex. Her ambivalence (feeling good but fearing her parents would learn about it) clearly revealed this dynamic. And the proof that Yadira was sexually active (her pregnancy) was punished again by her father's indifference and rejection. In Yadira's case, it was her stepmother who functioned as the maternal figure who intervenes as the mediator (Ypeij 1998) by challenging the father's long-term rejection and punishment of Yadira and facilitating their reconciliation.

Yadira's case is of special importance, given its many implications with regard to the father–daughter and mother–daughter relationship, gender relations, and power dynamics within the family in a patriarchal society. "Letting your mother down" is different from "letting your father down." The former implies the unequal relationship between two women due to generational differences: a young woman is morally controlled by the family ethic embedded in the relationship between herself and an older woman who is socially responsible for her sex education. In addition, the mother — or any maternal figure — may become a mediator between daughter and father. In contrast, "letting your father down" emphasizes the evident unequal power relationship between a woman and a man due to patriarchy. This power differential exacerbates generational differences between father and daughter and the family ethic that expropriates a daughter from her own sexuality. A young woman is exposed to the moral control of the maternal figure — who at times may become a protector — as the one who is responsible for her education. But when it comes to the father, a young woman is exposed to the greater risk of harsh punishment due to his power, control, rights, and privileges as the head of the family.[13]

Other stories follow a pattern similar to Yadira's, but with different consequences. Two women, Cecilia and Emilia, recalled feeling ambivalent after their first sexual experiences: they both felt that they had let their mothers down, but they also experienced pleasure while having sex. It was dangerous to talk to their mothers about sex, so they kept it a secret. Cecilia clearly recalled her ambivalent feelings as she described her first sexual experience:

> I felt bad and good: good because I loved him and I felt happy. I felt content because I had had sex with the person that I loved. But I felt bad

because I would not have liked my mother to know about it, so I just kept it to myself.

Emilia was clearly aware of the negative consequences that would result if her mother had known about her having premarital sex. She described the way she felt the first time she had intercourse:

> I felt nervous. I felt bad because of my mother's ideas. I felt bad for her, and I knew I would never tell her about it, and to this day I have never told her.

I asked Emilia what would have happened if she had told her mother about it.

> I think she would have reacted in a very aggressive way. She is like those people who believe that you have to be a virgin until you get married, you know, in order to wear *el vestido blanco* [the white dress].

The emotions the women in my study exhibited were similar to those of other Mexicanas who had experienced premarital sexual activity. Amuchástegui found that for a group of women living in other regions of Mexico, premarital sexual activity "unfolded fears, feelings of guilt and a sensation of betrayal of their families" (2001, 291).

Men and Their Mothers: Mothering Masculinities

> *Hijo de mi hija,*
> *mi nieto.*
> *Hijo de mi hijo,*
> *sólo Dios.*

> Son of my daughter,
> my grandson.
> Son of my son,
> only God knows.
>> A popular expression I heard
>> while growing up in Mexico

"La mamá es la machista más grande que tenemos en la familia" — the mother is the most sexist member of the family — said Marcos sarcastically with a loud laugh. Of his family life while growing up in a small town, he said:

> Yes, and then they make us, men, responsible for it! And the truth is that the mother is the one who has told you what to do! Why? Because if you are dat-

ing a girl whom people accuse of not having a good reputation, the mother tells us, "No, no, no, my son, do not date that girl. She already dated so and so, and people say that she was messing around with him in the *huisache* trees." Right? But she says, "They say." She has not even witnessed it herself. "It is better for you. Look, date so-and-so. She is such a good girl. She even wears a *rebozo* [a shawl], and the other one already took it off."[14]

Marcos was not the only man who received lessons on women and sexual behavior from his mother. Sebastián recalled the family ordeal that followed his girlfriend's unexpected pregnancy and the decision the two of them made to rush into marriage. When Sebastián's mother learned that her son was going to marry a woman with whom he had been sexually active, she asked him: "Well, was she even a virgin?" When he said no, she was furious. He then recalled what happened on his wedding day: "My mother told her niece that my wife was not a virgin, and then my cousin told her children. And on our wedding day, my cousin's children were asking me, 'Is it true that she was not a virgin?' I replied, 'No! And so what!'"

A mother is in charge of providing a good education to her sons as well as her daughters, and most hope their sons will find *una mujer decente* — a decent and faithful wife — who will provide a good example of morality and decency to their future grandchildren. In that process, however, mothers may engage in a kind of gender-profiling exercise designed to predict the desirability of a potential daughter-in-law. They will stigmatize women who do not comply with their specific expectations of morality, and thus they continue to promote gender inequality via motherhood. This dynamic is neither unidirectional nor static. Men like Marcos become aware of how social stigma and sexism is created and promoted, and men like Sebastián participate in family conflict as they challenge the maternal expressions of gender inequality. As they contest and become aware of gender inequality, they embrace their masculine identities. A paradox at its core, the gendered lesson that men receive on heterosexual relationships reflects the mother's well-intentioned efforts to improve her son's chances for a stable and happy marital relationship. However, attempts to be a good mother end up promoting gender inequality through the mother's efforts to control their sons' relationships.

I asked Marcos about the role his father had played in his coming of age. He replied:

> The role the father plays is for the son to have women. The father does not care about the virginity of the woman. He is interested in the son having women. The mother is the one who places more emphasis on the son having to be with

a virgin woman. I am not saying that the father does not place any emphasis on virginity. I am saying that the mother is the one who emphasizes it more.

Thus, while fathers may also wish for a good marriage for their sons, the father's primary obligation is to help his son develop a sexualized masculine identity. Some fathers may do this by stimulating a son's sexual exposure to many women. It is the young man's job to decipher the gendered, and at times polarized, meanings of motherhood and fatherhood as he explores love and sexuality. In addition, women and men are positioned within a contrasting sexual hierarchy: while a woman is more likely to be expected to refrain from premarital sexual activity, a man is expected to accumulate sexual knowledge before marriage. Their parents may selectively enforce this pattern. LeVine (1993) identified the same dynamic in the lives of the women she studied in Morelos. And Amuchástegui similarly found this gender asymmetry in the heterosexual interactions of both women and men: "While it is expected from the man to have some type of sexual experience before marriage and, therefore, to know how to move and what to do with his partner, a woman should not actively participate in her search for erotic pleasure since that would mean a risk for her probabilities of getting married. That same lack of knowledge with regard to sexual practices is in itself an indicator of her virginity, which in discursive terms, is a condition for the woman to find a husband and to have a family" (2001, 307).

In chapter 2, in the attitude of Azalea's husband, we saw an extreme case of the above paradigm. He complained about Azalea's physical response to their initial sexual relations. To him, vaginal lubrication was a sign of sexual knowledge, and thus proof that Azalea had not been a virgin before marriage.

This pattern is also reflected in my own mother's response, years ago, when I told her that I was going to work on a dissertation about Mexican women and sex: *"El hombre espera ser el primero en la vida de una mujer, y la mujer espera ser la última en la vida de él"* (The man hopes to be the first one in a woman's life, and the woman hopes to be the last one in his).

Like Marcos and Sebastián, other men described how mothering could become a vehicle of social stigmatization of women who do not comply with normative ideals of morality. For example, when I asked Raúl, from Mexico City, if he had ever had sex with a sex worker, he replied:

No, I was afraid of them, and it was not because of the sex act but because of my parents. And then we go back again to the moral aspect. They used to tell me that these women were rotten. "They are very pretty on the outside, but they are rotten on the inside," my mother used to tell me. And that, I had it inside of me, right? So, for that reason, I never did it.

Mothers also vigilantly watch for their sons' actual sexual behaviors from an early age. Emiliano recalled that his mother had punished him when he was a little boy after she learned that he had been playing doctor with his neighbors. She had also played the role of mediator, Emiliano recalled. "She was the one who always made sure that my father would not become aware of many things. She was the one who intervened." In a pattern that had been established gradually, as he got older and became a young adult Emiliano's mother continued to watch out for her son's safety: "She always worried because I would get home late."

With regard to specific sexual behaviors, my other male informants from Mexico City reported on the various maternal messages they had received. Alejandro, for example, recalled the intense fear he had experienced the first time he had sexual relations with a girl he was dating. When I asked why, he said: "Because of the influence that my mother gave me, mainly that I should be careful with women, because they could get me infected or something, and I did not use any protection."[15]

Interestingly, when men from rural areas talked about mothers and sex education, they referred to the mothers of their girlfriends. Some men from small towns recalled the behavior of their in-laws in safeguarding their daughters' moral integrity. For example, when Felipe got married, he learned immediately about his wife's family's rules with regard to marriage. He recalled:

> We were accustomed to practicing respect. For example, we were in fact already married by el civil, which is the legal marriage, and her mother would come with us wherever we had to go. Her mother would come with us if we had to take a wedding invitation somewhere, or to work on the wedding preparations, or to go to the church to the premarital classes, or you name it. She would gently push us forward and she would walk behind us. In other words, it was very strict.

Felipe's mother-in-law's role as a chaperone is examined by historian Vicki L. Ruiz (1992) through the life histories of a group of adult Mexican American women living in the 1940s. These practices are not a thing of the past, however. They are still prevalent in U.S. communities of Mexican origin, as Aída Hurtado (2003) illustrates in her research with young, college-educated Chicanas.[16] Ruiz and Hurtado explain how women — more than men — are subjected to specific morality standards.

Interestingly, none of the women I interviewed reported being chaperoned during courtship and dating. They may have taken it so much for granted as not to be worth mentioning, or it may have created only slight discomfort or tension for them. For men like Felipe, in contrast, this practice may be more easily identified because men may have enjoyed more freedom than their sisters. Their freedom is conditional, however. When a young man starts to date, his sexual behavior begins to be regulated beyond his family context: his girlfriend's family sets the rules for dating and other sexual behaviors, not only for their young daughter but also for her boyfriend.

This expression of an ethic of respect for women, exemplified by Felipe's mother-in-law — that a young woman should not have sex until both legal and religious ceremonies are performed — was not exclusive to rural areas, where a good reputation is vital. In urban areas, it was promoted and enforced in a different way. Alfredo recalled the clear messages he received from his mother, a widow who had not remarried and who had raised her son by herself. His decision to avoid sexual contact with his girlfriends reflected the ethic of *respeto a la mujer* she had promoted since he was a young boy. Of his sexual behavior with a steady girlfriend he loved deeply, he said:

> I did not have sexual relations with her either, because of the same reason. My mother used to tell me, "The day you get married, you have to take her out of her house wearing white, you have to walk down the aisle, you have to be respectful." That stays with you. The woman you love, if you are dating her, you have to respect her, and I would respect that rule.

The message Alfredo, Marcos, and Sebastián received from their mothers was the same: sexual permissiveness may be allowed with some type of women, but respect is always reserved for the one who may become your wife.

The experiences of the men in my study confirm Gutmann's (1996) observations of some mothers' active participation in the reproduction of masculinities that promote gender inequality in contemporary Mexico.[17] They also reflect the history of the interaction between state-formation and gender relations I discuss in chapter 1. For example, a mothers' regulation of attitudes toward a son's sexual conduct may have some of its roots in such legislation as La Real Pragmática de Matrimonios, established in 1776, which legally punished couples who married without parental consent (Tostado Gutiérrez 1991, 119).[18] More recently, young newlyweds who do not have the financial means to establish a separate household have no option but to live with the man's parents. This decision often means that a young wife will be under her husband's parents' moral surveillance, usually his mother's (Varley 2000). Writes Ann Varley: "Ironically, it is women who, as mothers-in-law, have taken on themselves the task of maintaining control over their sons' wives and, in doing so, of reinforcing patriarchy" (2000, 247).[19] And Mummert examines how, until the 1960s, parental control over a heterosexual couple was evident in some rural areas, an arrangement in which the newly married woman "served, literally" her husband's mother until the couple became independent (1994, 195). Thus, the relationship between a young wife and her mother-in-law may be perceived by the former as intrusive and controlling (LeVine 1993, 83). It is important to mention, however, that for other women this relationship may become supportive and understanding — even more so than the relationship they have with their own mothers (LeVine 1993, 101).

Though it was not reported by my informants, upper-middle-class and wealthy families in Mexico may become highly involved in their sons' dating choices. As an adolescent and young adult, I witnessed cases of young women from working- and middle-class backgrounds who were firmly rejected by their wealthy boyfriends' parents for one specific reason: they did not belong to *una buena familia* and that meant they were not eligible to become a wealthy son's wife. The future of the family name is carefully safeguarded, as the parents of a young man train him to become more selective — and to stay within his own socioeconomic group — in his romantic decisions. This pattern is often depicted in Mexican *telenovelas* (soap operas) that are aired in Mexico, other Latin American countries, and on Spanish-language networks in the United States.

Mothering a young man's sexuality in strict ways is often seen as well intentioned, even by the boys. Some of the men I interviewed described their mothers as being genuinely concerned about their precocious sexual behavior in childhood, as well as the risks they might encounter as they became older, such as sexually transmitted diseases and commercial sex. But in trying to enhance her son's possibilities for a satisfying marital relationship, a mother promotes the social stigmatization of other women, who may be perceived as morally incompetent. In many cases, the main predictor of marital stability and happiness revolves around a central concept: the bride's virginity.

Vestida de Blanco: Virginity and Its Social Symbolism

> *Yo voy a casarme*
> *vestida de blanco*
> *va a dolerte tanto*
> *te arrepentirás*
>
> I will get married
> wearing white
> it will hurt you so much
> you will regret it
>
> "Vestida de blanco,"
> a popular Spanish song

Cecilia explained why she did not "deserve" to wear a white dress on her wedding day and why she felt she ultimately was not entitled to have a religious ceremony: "I felt like I was fooling myself because for me, to walk down the aisle wearing el vestido blanco, the woman should be a virgin, clean, pure, white, just like it is represented by the dress. But since I was not, I decided that I should not do it. That is the reason why I did not even get married by the Church."

Mexican social prescriptions impose marriage as the moral and official passport society uses to endorse women's sexual activity. *El vestido blanco* is the seal stamped on that passport. It is the most important symbol representing what a patriarchal society can bestow on a woman on her wedding day. *El vestido blanco* (a highly valued garment usually worn by a woman only once) carries in itself a social burden and a moral responsibility. Wearing the white dress was unthinkable for Cecilia and the other women who associated premarital sexual relations with fear of parents and family disloyalty; their awareness of the morally charged social expectation made it impossible.

After several conversations with a priest, Yadira allowed herself to marry in the Church after having cohabited with her husband for more than fourteen years. She explained her reasons for wearing a beige dress instead of a white one:

> When you shine wearing a white dress, *los azahares* [orange blossoms] represent the purity of the bride, but when there is no virginity you cannot get married wearing white. I decided to have *los azahares*, but I decided to wear a beige dress because I already had my children and everything.

Yadira made some personal accommodations (she chose to carry an orange-blossom bouquet), but wearing a white dress was clearly impossible for her. She felt she had already transgressed its meaning by conceiving children. She did not possess the virginal purity that entitled her to wear white. In whose eyes? Felicia offered an answer: "[Virginity] is something traditional, and more in Mexico, because it is very important for her husband when a woman walks down the aisle being a virgin and wearing white." Felicia's words echoed the feeling of pride that men like Fidel and Alfonso reported when they talked about having been "the first" in the lives of their respective wives.

For other women, family politics became part of the decision to have a religious ceremony and to wear a white dress. Emilia decided to wear a white dress to satisfy her mother's need to follow a social tradition: when a daughter gets married — and therefore walks out of the family home — she must be wearing *el vestido blanco*. Emilia recounted her conversation with her mother:

> I told my mother that we were planning on getting married but that I was going to get married only by el civil [civil marriage], but you know . . . for the very same reason that she has those ideas of her religion, you know, that you have to walk out your home wearing white and all that. She was the only reason why I married in the Church, just to satisfy her need.

Emilia was not a virgin at marriage — something she has kept from her mother to this day in order to avoid her mother's resentment. She decided to wear a white dress to honor her mother socially and morally while protecting herself from the potential negative consequences of her honesty. She was keenly aware of the symbolism of the white dress she would wear: *el vestido blanco* symbolized her mother's ability to appear as a morally and socially competent mother who had been successful at overseeing and securing her daughter's appropriate moral behavior.

Being dressed in white goes far beyond honoring virginity at the time of marriage; virginity is also honored and worshiped when an adult virgin woman dies. Tomasita, a woman from a small town in Jalisco, described how two of her adult relatives (a cousin and an aunt) were each buried in an *ataúd blanco* (white coffin) when they died. Paloma, Tomasita's cousin, had died from a serious hemorrhage subsequent to being raped by a neighbor who broke into her house late one night. Her family was informed by the physician who conducted the autopsy that Paloma had been raped. Tomasita recalled:

> They put her inside an *ataúd blanco* because she was not responsible for [the rape]. When they did all the investigations and the doctor looked at her, they found out that she had been raped. I looked at her in one of those pictures, because in those pueblos they take pictures of the dead, and I remember she had a lot of flowers around her head.

Paloma's story is revealing. She had not voluntarily agreed to have sex, so morally speaking she was still a virgin for her family when she died. As a virgin woman who had been forced to have sex, Paloma may not have had the tangible or physical evidence to prove her virginity (especially if she has been vaginally penetrated) but, she had retained it spiritually and morally, which was more important. In her case, her family recognized and celebrated her chastity even beyond death. The preservation of virginity was praised and became a family affair.

Tomasita's aunt Carolina had a similar experience. When Carolina died, she was fifty years old, but her honeymoon tragedy was well known — she had not been able to bring herself to have sex with her husband on their wedding night. An extremely religious young woman, Carolina had received no sexual education and had no idea what she was expected to do on her wedding night. Tomasita explained:

> She was from Guadalajara and she was a señorita when she got married. The next day, after her wedding, the husband woke up in one home and she woke up in a different one! When we talked with her, she said that she had been afraid of *el instrumento del esposo* (the husband's instrument). When she looked at it, she got scared and ran away. He must have thought she was crazy.

Carolina went back to live with her family and spent the rest of her life committed to religious activities. On her deathbed, Carolina called her husband to ask for his forgiveness, but he refused. Carolina's family knew her life story and, when she died, they honored her virginity by burying her in an *ataúd blanco,* like Paloma.

Like the women, the men had also been exposed to the symbolic meaning of virginity as part of family life. Alfonso, a thirty-three-year-old who was born and raised in Mexico City, recalled his extended family's rituals around virginity. He described how his maternal grandmother and aunts designed, sewed, and embroidered *la mantilla blanca,* a white bedsheet with a hole close to the center that is embroidered with the names of the bride and groom, as well as the date and place of their wedding ceremony. Alfonso still remembered the bedsheets that his aunts received from his grandmother on the occasion of their respective wedding ceremonies. Alfonso explained how, when he was a child, he had listened silently during a family gathering in which his grandmother and his aunts discussed the ritual of making the bedsheet and talked about the wedding night that was to follow:

> I must have been eight or nine years old when they started to talk about it. My aunts were so excited because all of them started to ask about the person who

was going to work on the design, and the one who was going to do the em-
broidery, and the one who was going to choose this and that, especially if they
were going to write something. And also about the nervousness that the bride
felt, and my grandmother was indicating if it was going to be painful or not.

Alfonso recalled that he listened quietly to these conversations but did
not really understand his aunts' and grandmother's excitement or what
they were talking about. When he grew older, the women's conversations
began to make sense. "Before he died, and two years after my aunt got
married, my grandfather told me about it and about the way the man uses
the bedsheet on the night of the sexual relationship. He told me then that,
if she was not a virgin, he had the right to kick her out of his house."
Alfonso also learned the mechanics behind this family tradition, "They
covered the woman completely with the bedsheet and then he got
there and they had their sexual relationship. It [the hole] was for the
penetration."

> It was a white cloth, a bedsheet, and they would put a perforation in the mid-
> dle so the woman would put her part right there. If the woman leaves a blood
> spot on the bedsheet, she was a virgin. Then she had the right to be part of the
> man's family; otherwise, she would not. Then, in my grandmother's family,
> they talked a lot about it and said that it was good, that it was best for the
> woman to be a virgin, because she was pure and chaste, and that was because
> she had not had sex with any man. In other words, it was her treasure.

In a family that for generations had regarded virginity as precious,
there was an equally symbolic place where the bedsheet would be de-
posited. When I asked Alfonso if he knew what they did with the bedsheet after the wedding night, he said:

> They would put it inside a coffer. It would come with things that they had
> since they were little, such as a piece of hair, a tooth, the confirmation crucifix,
> or the baptism crucifix, or whatever they had accumulated, little things, and
> then the last one: you have the bedsheet. Then, after that, the grandmother
> may keep it most of the time, or the person in the family to whom all that
> belongs.

Alfonso did not know if the evidence of their virginity remained on the
embroidered bedsheets of each of his twelve aunts. He explained, however, that even though his mother had been a virgin at marriage and had
followed this ritual, she had been trapped in a destructive marital relationship that led her, Alfonso, and his siblings to a life of poverty. Some
of his mother's younger sisters had continued with the tradition, but his

mother did not promote the ritual with her own daughters; modernity had further disrupted this family tradition. Neither Alfonso nor his sisters adopted the family custom. Yet, such a powerful tradition left a social imprint on Alfonso's perception of virginity. As indicated in chapter 2, he called virginity a "gold medal" and a "trophy" in explaining his feelings of pride when he became aware of his wife's sexual innocence.

Like Alfonso's mother, aunts, and grandmother, other women may undergo similar, if more modest practices to show proof of virginity and thereby protect themselves from a husband's potential rejection. Joaquín recalled his surprise when he opened the mysterious little bag he found inside one of his wife's dresser drawers:

> It was a piece of a towel, a rag, I don't know, something like that. She cleaned herself, and I did not even see her when she did it. Can you imagine? That was in case I wanted to ask her: "Are you a virgin?" I think that was a proof of it, it comes from old-fashioned mothers [who say] "Keep a proof of it, save it." It's like me; that is what I am doing with the letters, I am saving copies of the letters and checks I send [to Mexico], I have a copy, I get copies. I think that is what she told her: "When you go to your wedding night, save the evidence." [Just in case] "What? Am I not a virgin? Of course I am! Here is the evidence!"

Joaquín realized his wife was embarrassed to be talking about the piece of cloth with soiled bloodspots that she had saved since they had sex the first time three years before. He told her: "I love you anyway. But I am glad you saved it as a sign that I am your first man."

The rituals Alfonso and Joaquín shared with me may justify, in part, the requests made by those Mexicanas who have visited Dr. Guadalupe I. Solís in northeastern Mexico since the late 1960s in order to have their hymens reconstructed. The testimony of my two male informants also indicates the similarity of such rituals and practices, and the cultural meanings they contain, for women and men living in different regions of the world.

Public symbols of loss of virginity are constructed in other cultures, including but not limited to Middle Eastern societies, for the same purposes they serve in Mexico. Until ten or fifteen years ago, Moroccans would display the evidence of a woman's virginity by parading a blood-stained bridal sheet through the streets (Buitelaar 2002, 485–86). In some areas, after the wedding night, "it is said to be fashionable not only to display on a platter the underpants stained with blood, but also to adorn them with a certificate of virginity duly obtained from a doctor and attached to the garment with a safety pin to prevent it from slipping" (Mernissi 1982, 187). In Turkey, the in-laws of a woman very frequently wait for "the 'blooded sheet' as proof of both the bride's virginity and the groom's virility," and if bleeding does not occur, it may become the main reason for virginity tests after marriage (Cindoglu 1997, 253, 258). As is the case in Mexico for the women Dr. Solís has "repaired," women in modern Turkey have also had their hymens reconstructed to cover up premarital sexual activity. But unlike in Mexico, "the physician's reputation as well as his or her medical license may be in jeopardy if a groom takes him/her to the court on the basis of helping the woman to deceive him over her virginity" (Cindoglu 1997, 258). In China, stories are told about rural men rushing out of the marital bedroom during their wedding nights when they have discovered that their bride has not bled (Zhou 1989, 280).[20] In Sri Lanka, the honeymoon night may become a bridal nightmare for the newlywed woman: during a ceremony called *poruwa,* the couple receives a piece of white cloth, which is placed on the marital bed on their first night they spent together in order to test her chastity (Basnayake 1990). Some families follow up the ritual by officially inspecting the piece of cloth a day after the ceremony, while others may wait to conduct their inspection until after the couple returns from their honeymoon. More rituals unfold depending upon whether the woman passes or fails the test. If she passes, she may wear red and be greeted with red flowers for the homecoming. If she fails, she is often humiliated in public for her lack of purity at marriage. And finally, there is this description. Hammed Shahidian explains the ritual utilized by a group of Iranian immigrants living in Canada: "I have observed a few cases when the bride's family insisted upon presenting the 'proof of virginity' — the blood-stained kerchief or a physician's written testimony — as an unquestionable proof that they have raised an honorable daughter. I have also heard rumors of several cases of reconstructive surgery to 'sew back' the hymen" (1999, 207).

Virginity is not created in a social vacuum nor is it divorced from society. In Mexico, losing or preserving virginity goes beyond the bedroom and transcends stained or unstained bedsheets. Virginity is inherently public. Pregnancy out of wedlock, having children, wearing a white dress or carrying orange blossoms on the wedding day, leaving a blood-spot on an embroidered bedsheet or a modest rag, and being buried in a white coffin are important indicators of the social nature and meaning of virginity throughout a woman's life course. Each of the symbols used in these rituals positions a woman's sexuality within the public domain of family and society. Each symbol makes visible what is personal and intimate; each makes public what is private. A woman's loss of virginity does not become a family affair if she does not get pregnant — the issue may remain intimate and silent. In contrast, pregnancy makes sexual activity evident and then a woman is often coerced into marriage by her family. A woman who does not wear white may jeopardize her moral integrity and decency; a woman who does wear white honors herself and her family. Wearing white when it is widely known that one is not a virgin may prompt whispered rumors and social censorship. All these visible symbols make public what is private and reveal to society what a woman has lived in her intimate moments. They link a woman's virginity, as part of her sexuality, to important processes of social significance and control.

The stories of my female and male informants about premarital sex, dating, courtship, pregnancy out of wedlock, coercive marriage, and the symbolism of virginity confirm the centrality of family life in the social construction and regulation of sexuality and heterosexual relationships. These stories of sexual activity and pregnancy out of wedlock begin to map the exquisitely gendered paths women and men must tread with intense emotions, anxieties, moral turbulence, family tension, and conflict. Within the patriarchal family system, prescriptions of both female and male identity are nurtured by the maternal figure, the ultimate mediator in charge of sex education and morality. The maternal figure reproduces the various expressions of female and male identity. The woman may be stigmatized as a bad mother if she does not comply with the moral establishment that regulates sexuality. This is not the case for the man. The father may be a central authoritarian figure, but he may also be flexible and he is a marginal figure with respect to the sexual education he provides to his children. The white dress, the ribbons and lace, and the white bedsheets all speak of the social meaning of virginity. In a society where virginity is still venerated and embodied by religious, moral, and creative social and symbolic expressions, young women and men must find a way to reconcile both tradition and the challenges of modernity and a more urban and globalized society.

The social processes exposed in my interviews with my Mexican women and men informants are fluid and continuously reproduced throughout their lifespans. Each one of them has actively transformed and reproduced these dynamics as they faced new challenges in their adult lives. As they migrated to the United States, sexuality and heterosexual relations were transformed through myriad social and economic circumstances that unleashed an endless array of sexual expressions. The following chapters will examine the multiple reinventions of their sexuality the women and men created as part of the migration experience which brought them across the Mexican border to the United States. The social processes they encountered, including new socioeconomic opportunities, the dangers and risks of the hosting society, new employment, social networking and community life, Spanish-language media, and parenting a new generation of women and men in the new land, among others, offered new scenarios and circumstances that reshaped their sexualities and their heterosexual lives. In the following chapter I explore my informants' immigration journeys by examining the sexual transfigurations they created as they dealt with immediate sexual challenges, that is, the social paradoxes and contradictions influencing their sexuality as they established a permanent life and become part of U.S. society.

CHAPTER 5

Sex and the Immigrant Communities

Risky Opportunities, Opportune Risks

"This whole thing about *el país de las oportunidades* [the land of opportunities] . . . I will change the name, I will change the version. I will call it *el país de las enfermedades* [the land of diseases] because you get sick for any reason at all." Eugenio, a forty-three-year-old from Mexico City, spoke in a melodic Spanish rhythm as he described the various health problems he has suffered in the United States, including relapse and recovery from alcoholism and a pattern of addiction that sometimes made him behave in sexually risky ways.

Diamantina, a thirty-one-year-old, also from Mexico City, complained: "I already told my husband that if he continues working here [in the United States], I better go back to Mexico, because I am just like a piece of furniture here." Diamantina explained that her husband's strenuous schedule made her feel emotionally devalued, and that the emotional and sexual intimacy of their marriage had deteriorated. Returning to Mexico would be one way to deal with her personal circumstances, but the fear of economic hardship if she went back made her tolerate her current dissatisfaction.

For Eugenio and Diamantina, their incorporation into the labor force of an advanced industrialized economy has provided them with the opportunity to survive and improve their financial situation. However, for them and for many of the study's informants, becoming part of a highly urbanized capitalist society had also presented them with contradictions and challenges to their everyday survival, and these situations ultimately affected their sex lives. This chapter examines how after migrating and establishing a permanent life in Los Angeles, poverty, segregation, and incorporation into the labor market, among other forces, exposed these immigrants to hazards that would reshape their sex lives. These risks, along with the capitalist society and the fast-paced life found in the United States, would exacerbate an already existing culture of sexual fear, which would take new forms in Los Angeles.

American Dreams, Mexican Realities

Olga, a thirty-two-year-old woman from Mexico City, explained: "I do not know about Mexico, but here, life is screwed up. That is the truth, and more with children, the whole thing about rape of girls, and that kind of thing. And AIDS, as well. And also the whole thing about boys who hang out in gangs." Olga's words reflect the disenchantment and vulnerability that surrounds the migration experience of the overwhelming majority of the informants in this study. They also echo immigration studies that have described the inadequate health care Latino immigrants receive in the United States (Brown and Yu 2002; Freire 2002; Hayes-Bautista 2002; E. Díaz et al. 2001) and the deterioration in mental and physical health they experience as they are assimilated into North American society (Portes and Rumbaut 1996; Scribner 1996; Rumbaut 1997).[1] For the immigrants in this study, becoming part of American society did not necessarily improve their health and general lifestyle, and certainly not their sex lives.

Most informants reported that living in the United States was more dangerous than living in Mexico. Some have witnessed shootings in their neighborhoods or felt threatened by gang activity, fights, police arrests of neighbors involved in drug trafficking, INS apprehensions, and drug dealing on the streets. They have witnessed or personally experimented with drugs and have faced language difficulties, xenophobic laws and racism, emotional isolation and loneliness, a lack of paid employment, crowded housing, homelessness, and prostitution.[2] All of these conditions make them vulnerable, but informants also identified some as specifically influencing their sex lives. These included the additional risks associated with sexual violence against young girls, alcohol and drug use, gang activity, and sexually transmitted diseases (AIDS in particular). And these risks are not experienced in a social vacuum. Gender issues and the socioeconomics of their communities, both in Mexico and the United States, also shape the ways in which immigrants interpret, negotiate, and cope with their new lives.

Sexual Abuse of Children

The sexual abuse of children was of special concern for all of the women in this study. Regardless of their place of origin, women were more likely than men to be concerned that their children were more vulnerable to sexual abuse in the United States compared to Mexico. This is not to say that fathers did not express their love and concern for their children's welfare; many of them openly did. However, a mother's direct responsibility for her children's education seemed to be the reason why the women worried about their children being raised in the United States.

The women's perceptions of the sexual abuse of children shape their views of sexuality. How? Mainly through the sex education they gave to their children, especially daughters. Some of the women worried about how permissive they should be with their adolescent daughters. They also were concerned about the "when" and "how" of talking to their children about sex and coercive sex, as well as the need to be protective and vigilant regarding their children's sexual behavior. These mothers were keenly aware of sexual violence. Said Norma:

> I would have liked to stay in my country precisely because many things happen at a very early age over here, and in Mexico it is not that way. That is the concern I am experiencing here, and I know that my daughters are taking a higher risk over here than if I went back to live in Mexico. That is the only reason why I would like to go back to Mexico, so they have more safety because of the malice that we have over here. Had I stayed in Mexico, sex education [for my daughters] would not have been the same because I learned many things over here, and I learned about the malevolence that exists in the U.S., which I didn't know about.

Women like Norma do not deny that sexual abuse also happens in Mexico (some of them reported incidents of abuse in their own childhood or adolescence). However, discussions about the kidnapping of children on television talk shows and in the print media, plus the women's own isolation, poverty, marginality, and language barriers all contributed to making the women feel that they and their children were more susceptible, vulnerable, and at greater risk in the United States.[3]

Jimena stated her concern for her adolescent daughter this way: "Sometimes they [potential rapists] give young women something in their drinks so they fall asleep and then two or three men abuse them. That is what I tell my daughter 'See?' Because we don't give our daughter permission to go anywhere." Based on the stories she had heard since migrating, Felicia said: "I have changed because of the violence we have these days. You find all these maniac characters who rape children and girls. So I tell them to be very careful. I tell them what they may find out in the streets. Because these days there is a lot of drugs, lots of gang violence, and sex. 'A drug addict can rape you, even kill you and leave you half dead in the middle of the street.'"

Such fears and anxieties about the potential for sexual violence were emphasized more by mothers who had a personal and family history of sexual molestation. In my essay "De madres a hijas" (2003) I explain how an immigrant mother's personal history of sexual violence shapes her views on women and sexuality, sexism, and the sex education she wants to give to a daughter with regard to virginity. For example, Candelaria, who tearfully spoke about her fears that her daughter would be a victim of sexual violence, cited the statistics on sexual violence in the United States to justify her overprotective attitude. And Deyanira also expressed fears for her youngest daughter, based on event that had happened within her family. "I feel like I changed here. My sister had a daughter and she was raped. She was about five; it happened here."

Mothers said that they used their best parenting skills to cope with these threats, and they also turned to networking with other Latina/o immigrants, workshops on sexuality at community-based agencies, and the Spanish-language media. For example, Romelia explained how she uses talk shows to teach her children about these dangers. She relayed the message she gave her two adolescent daughters as all of them watched a talk show in Spanish: "Look, you see all these young girls who are talking about the same thing you are talking about? 'I know how to take care of myself, I know how to do this and how to do that. And look at what is happening!' I tell them so they can take care of themselves out in the streets."

The mothers' keen awareness of the greater dangers their daughters may face in the United States compared to Mexico seems to be accurate. Even though sexual and domestic violence is a harsh reality for women living in Mexico, a study showed that "U.S.-born Mexicans were three times more likely than Mexico-born Mexicans to have been sexually assaulted."[4]

Alcohol, Drugs, Gangs, and Sex

The men in this study primarily reflected on their vulnerability to drug and alcohol use after migration; none of the women reported this pattern.[5] As mainly working-class immigrants, the men's socioeconomic marginalities and migration- and settlement-related psychological stressors make them susceptible to alcohol use (Portes and Rumbaut 1996). They match other Mexicanos (Brandes 2002) and men from developed nations in their vulnerabilities to alcohol when compared with women (Connell 2000, 180). These risks did not happen in isolation. Men with a previous history of substance abuse became more vulnerable after immigration, due to such contributing factors as emotional distress, geographic dislocation, economic hardship, racism, uncertain legal status, language limitations, isolation, peer pressure, and crowded housing. But immigrant men are also exposed to social and economic forces that may offer potential coping mechanisms.

The parallel lives of Eugenio and Fermín exemplify the experiences of some immigrant men. Both began to use alcohol and drugs while they lived in Mexico City. In the United States, a sense of anomie and peer pressure made it hard for both men to stay sober. When I asked Fermín if he knew why he started to use alcohol, marijuana, and cocaine in Los Angeles, he replied, "Well, I think it's because when you come over here, you don't end up living with a family. In my case, I came by myself, and wherever I ended up living, I had to take it." Fermín had struggled to cope with peer pressure where drug use was part of everyday life, as he tried to fit into a new environment.

Poverty and a lack of medical insurance or access to professionals who might help them overcome their addictions coincided in the lives of both men. However, they both found a way to cope with their addictions in the United States through the Catholic faith they had previously practiced before migrating. Both men said they found that swearing a *juramento* — an oath made to God or the Virgin of Guadalupe — had been the best way to remain sober. The *juramento* as a strategy to cope with addictions is a common practice among many Mexicans raised in the Catholic faith (Brandes 2002).[6] Said Eugenio: "From July 1993 to this day, I have not drunk any alcohol. In other words, I have tried to keep my *juramento* that I made to the Virgin of Guadalupe, and I already have seven years without drinking." Said Fermín: "Religion is the best thing that ever happened to me." He used, and periodically renews, his oath to God as a way to stop drinking and using drugs in Los Angeles.

For both men, practicing their faith did more than reshape their addictive behaviors. Sobriety made them aware of the sexual dangers existing within their communities (i.e., HIV/AIDS) and led to changes in their sexual behavior. Eugenio described his sex lifestyle after becoming sober:

I have not had sex for five years. Then, when I go out to the streets, I do not have the desire to have sexual relations. I go out to the street and if I see a woman, and she smiles with me, I look at her appearance, and I ask her questions, and I see what she does for a living. If I see that she is a prostitute or she uses drugs, I do not get involved with her.

For a married man like Fermín, becoming sober through his *juramento* not only meant developing a keen awareness of potential dangers but also revisiting some values with regard to marital life and sexual behavior.

These days to have sex with another woman would be very, very, very difficult for me. To betray my wife would be . . . ah . . . first, I would not do it because . . . first, there's AIDS, right? So, having sex with a woman these days is like flipping a coin and telling yourself, "She has AIDS or she does not have AIDS," right? You don't know anymore who is infected at this moment. Many women are having sex with many men, and men are having sex with so many women that who knows with whom they are getting involved. So that is what worries me. And religion is the other thing that does not allow me to do it; it's adultery.

Eugenio and Fermín's stories illustrate how men coping with addiction may make use of cultural expressions of religiosity within the immigrant community to achieve not only sobriety but to develop a safer sex lifestyle. The other end of the spectrum is represented by the risky sexual behaviors that emerge out of the combined effects of drug and alcohol use, gang activity, and the social lifestyles of some groups of immigrant men.

A twenty-six-year-old man from Mexico City, Mauricio talked about his many experiences as a gang member before and after migrating. When I asked him if some of my questions had been controversial or difficult for him, a stimulating dialogue on the intersection between gang activity, sex, and drug abuse ensued. He began by recalling his early experiences with drug use as one part of his gang activities. "When I had just arrived in this country, my friends were more liberal, my friends were more crazy [laughs]. Because if a woman wants to belong to a gang, the woman has to have sex with all the men." He had participated in gang-related activities in Mexico, but he had not witnessed coercive sex as an initiation ritual for *las pandilleras,* his female gang counterparts. Since migrating, he explained, he had participated in these collective sexual rituals on at least three occasions. He recalled being part of groups of ten or twelve men who would take turns having intercourse with a girl whom the women members of the gang had previously beaten up. I attempted to get a clear picture of the initiation ritual, which many times involved drug use.

Author: When you talk about the girls and their gangs, and the fact that the woman has to have sex with all the men, are the other men looking while she is having sex with one of the guys?

Mauricio: Yes, yes, in fact, you are touching her. One is on top, and the other guys are there, kissing her, touching her.

Author: How does she react when all this is happening?

Mauricio: Sometimes they enjoy it, sometimes they cry. For example, the first guy did it already, and then the woman does not want to do it anymore, she may leave but the same women tell her, "Do not be stupid, if you put up with one, put up with the rest." But at times, they cry and leave.

Author: And what do the men do if she cries?

Mauricio: They swear, they curse, they call her names, they force her. At times, they tell her that if she tells the police, her family is going to pay the price. They threaten her.

Mauricio seemed remorseful and reserved as he remembered these events. I asked him what other issues he found hard to discuss during the interview. "The one on sex with men," he said. As I probed, he explained the surprise he felt after learning that some attractive women he had met at bars in Los Angeles were actually "homosexuals dressed up like women": "By the time you realize, you already kissed them and did everything." Of his sexual involvement with other immigrant men, he said:

> My friends had homosexual friends, but they had them only so they could give them oral sex, not to have sexual relations. I have had oral sex with homosexuals, when I had just arrived to this country. But not relationships in which they penetrate.

Mauricio's ideas about sexual relations stemmed from pre-migration social and cultural constructions of masculine identities and sexuality. In Mexican society, self-identified heterosexual men who have sex with men (MSM) do not identify themselves as homosexual when they play the active role during anal penetration (Carrier 1976, 1977, 1985; Almaguer 1993; Alonso and Koreck 1993; Flaskerud et al. 1996; Díaz 1998; Szasz 1998), or when they receive oral sex (Bronfman and López Moreno 1996). In addition, for self-identified heterosexual MSM who play the insertive role, penetration may become an expression of honor, power, and masculinity (Alonso and Koreck 1993; Bronfman and López Moreno 1996, 59; Prieur 1998). This "split" between the sexual and the emotional

(Rubin 1983, 113) may facilitate the men's sexual involvement with other men. Even though penetrating another man does not compromise a man's sense of masculinity, being penetrated by the other man may. This pattern became evident when Mauricio insisted that he had not been penetrated by homosexual men in the United States. Prieur's (1998) ethnographic work on Mexican homosexual identities illustrates how men like Mauricio and his self-identified heterosexual friends actively participate in the gay subculture in a Mexico City working-class suburb. Prieur's informants might call Mauricio and his immigrant friends *mayates,* meaning "men who have sex with other men without being feminine and without seeing themselves as homosexual" (179).[7]

Eugenio, Fermín, and Mauricio's narratives confirm that gender and sexual identity are socially and culturally constructed. The social aspect of sexuality is also reproduced in reciprocal interactions between an individual's emotions and their subjective interpretations and meanings (Chodorow 1995). Gender and sexuality are social but also personal and emotional. I asked Mauricio, "As a man, how do you feel after having sex with a person of your same sex?" He replied, "I feel bad. If I am with my buddies, I am talking with my friends, I will never tell them *'Me eché a un maricón'* [I screwed a queer] because they would tease me. They would give me a hard time." Besides fear of peer pressure, social stigma, ridicule, and homophobia, other emotions shaped Mauricio's subjective experience of masculinity and sexuality. Though male bisexual practices are frequent in Mexican society (Liguori 1995), bisexuality is not necessarily accepted (Prieur 1998).[8] I also asked Mauricio if he liked men or if he felt sexually attracted to them. He reacted emphatically, "No, no! And that is what I think about. And I ask myself, Why? In other words, when I am drunk, I do it. But then, after I do it, I do not like myself. But then I say, what if later on I begin to feel attracted to men?"

Mauricio has kept his sexual practices from his circle of close friends, but he is open about them with casual acquaintances and roommates. His voluntary and involuntary sexual contact with other immigrant men when he felt peer pressure or was under the influence of alcohol and drugs had provoked a roller-coaster ride of mixed feelings in him. When I asked him if he remembered on how many occasions he had received oral sex from other men in Los Angeles, he said,

> About twenty times or more. Yes, and with different men because they would arrive at our apartment and when you get drunk or drugged, and I did not know, by the time they told me, they had already got me undressed, but I was not aware of it when they did it. I did not like it.

Mauricio was not alone in his sexual experimentation with other men. He reported that some of his self-identified heterosexual migrant friends had had similar experiences. In Mauricio's case, he had begun experiencing same-sex activities as a young adolescent in Mexico City, when he was seduced by a friend he identified as homosexual. He explained that he had felt obliged to have sex with his friend on three or four occasions: the man had helped Mauricio get a job and had offered him a room to live when he was younger. However, there was one common denominator in all of Mauricio's sexual experiences, both pre- and post-migration. For Mauricio, being under the influence of drugs or alcohol always accompanied and facilitated his sexual activity with other men.

Mauricio has struggled to stay sober. Fear of being arrested by the police, as well as concerns about the safety of his two daughters and maintaining a relatively stable relationship with his wife were some of the reasons he gave for having withdrawn from both his gang activities and from sexual activity with other men. In addition, he described his growing awareness of sexually transmitted diseases (i.e., AIDS). Indeed, alcoholism and drug use are the primary risk factors that propel Latino men like Mauricio into unprotected sex with its accompanying high risk of becoming infected with HIV/AIDS (Marín, Gómez, and Hearst 1993; Hines and Caetano 1998; Marín et al. 1998).[9]

Other informants also mentioned the combined effects of drug and alcohol use, peer pressure, and isolation on their sexual behavior and on the behavior of male friends. Alfredo and Alejandro, who are from Mexico City and who both said they are now sober, talked about what they had observed among their immigrant friends. Sounding defensive, Alfredo described an incident at a bar:

> When they drink, it's like homosexuality takes over, because they say, "I like you, I love you," that kind of words. It's okay for them to say to a person, "I am fond of you, I love you, I like you as a friend," within what's normal. But when they get drunk, they get closer and they want to hold you and that makes you think . . . [They have told me,] "I even feel like giving you a kiss." [And I say,] "Hey! Get away from here!"

With a similarly guarded attitude, Alejandro made sure I understood he did not hang out with immigrants who had homosexual desires, although he knew some:

> Men do it out of loneliness. A friend of mine, well, he is not my friend like that, right? He told me that he used drugs and also alcohol and then he started to have an inclination toward men. So it was loneliness. He found out

that he was alone and perhaps his friends pushed him to do other kinds of sex acts.

Researchers have noted the link between alcohol use and eroticism between men. De la Vega (1990) examined how some self-identified heterosexual Latino men who live in the United States engage in sex acts with other men when they are under the influence of alcohol and other substances. Bronfman and López Moreno (1996) studied a group of rural immigrant men living in Watsonville, California. The authors note that the men explained that sex that took place "under the influence of alcohol did not count. . . . Alcohol consumption constituted another effective mechanism to protect masculinity and reinforced the separation of roles" (59). In his research with Mexican men, Gutmann identifies alcohol as a trigger for homosexual desire in "even the most macho" (1996, 126). Carrillo has argued that *hombres normales* (normal men) who have sex with both women and men may engage in sex with the latter if they are exposed to the "right kind of encouragement, sometimes through alcohol consumption" (2002, 90). And Brandes has shown how, for a group of working-class men in Alcoholics Anonymous in Mexico who are now in primary loving relationships with women, "homosexual wishes and encounters are part of their dark alcoholic past" (2002, 127). Interestingly, this pattern seems to indicate that "becoming straight" is part of an alcoholic man's recovery, as heterosexuality becomes the ideal of sobriety.

In addition to the influence of alcohol and drug use, similar behaviors emerge from emotional isolation, socioeconomic segregation, and overcrowded housing conditions. Of his difficult years after arriving in the United States, Raúl said:

> I lived with these buddies, and they were about fifteen men living in one apartment. They lived like sardines inside the apartment. Suddenly, *el albur* [sexual wordplay] made them start touching each other on their buttocks because they did not have anyone to socialize or even go out with.

El albur refers to the very popular, nuanced games that use words with sexual connotations and double meanings. Such games are widely played by Mexicans in a variety of social contexts and circumstances. They may even predate the late colonial period (Stern 1995).[10]

Raúl's story confirms research in Mexico that describes the variety of sexual exchanges — including collective sex, body-touching, and joking and bragging about sex — that take place among working-class men in such all-male settings as neighborhood streets and soccer fields (Szasz 1998). In a similar vein, Alfredo reported: "I lived with these five men in an apartment, who were also immigrants, and every week they rented pornographic movies. And I did not like to join them, because you see that movie with a group, and then what? In fifteen minutes your sexuality changes, you end up doing things you shouldn't. That is when some men reveal their homosexuality."

Alfonso went on: "I have seen men who have sex with men because they cannot find women, because if you want to have a woman over here, you need to have money." Though that had not been his experience, he had been deceived while dancing at a bar with "a pretty transvestite." Other informants talked about same-sex eroticism before and after migrating. Sebastián described the avowals of romantic love he had received from a male friend. Diego recalled the sexual advances of a man he had met at work in Los Angeles. Fermín explained that as a naive adolescent he had accepted an invitation from an older man to have coffee with him. He had allowed the man to touch him, but when he started to perform oral sex on him, Fermín had thrown up and run away. Emiliano had had a similar experience when he was fourteen when a man in his early fifties had seduced him. Like Fermín, he resisted and ran away. Fidel recalled a story about "the mayates from Guadalajara" that he had met as an adolescent. Joaquín explained that since "homosexuals prefer ugly, strong men," he was not surprised to have received so many proposals from *"maricones."* Marcos recalled incidents of men flirting with him when he had used public transportation in Los Angeles. Felipe talked about *"los homosexuales del pueblo"* and of how he had successfully avoided their advances. Even though he had "just observed," Ernesto graphically described the group sex among men that he had witnessed on at least one occasion. And Nicolás said he had frequently been chased by homosexuals but always rejected them with respect and honesty. Other men recalled being similarly chased, seduced, or harassed by transvestites; or of being either attracted to them "by mistake," or of sexually teasing them, either in their adolescent years or, at times, after migrating.

The men's reports of their own and others' same-sex desires, erotic innuendo, and actual sexual practices among immigrants who self-identify as heterosexuals differs remarkably from Gutmann's (1996) findings for a Mexico City neighborhood. Like Prieur (1998, 190), I am also struck by the fact that only one of Gutmann's informants revealed having experienced sex with other men (1966, 125). However, knowing that I am a psychotherapist might have made it easier for my informants to disclose these experiences. Unlike the men in my study, the women rarely reported same-sex experiences.[11]

Besides reflecting on the influence of drugs and alcohol on the sexual

behavior they observed among groups of men, some of my male informants discussed the impact of their drug and alcohol use on their sexuality
and on the quality of their heterosexual relationships. Alejandro, who was
proud of his current sobriety, revealed that he had experimented with
marijuana, LSD, peyote, mushrooms, inhalants, and other substances
while still living in Mexico. In college, Alejandro had become a passionate reader of sociology and psychology texts, which, he claimed, had
helped him decide to stop "these habits," a decision he was proud of. He
was critical of some of the couples he had met in Los Angeles who were
involved with drugs and alcohol, and particularly concerned about the
effects of their use on women. "Risks are more for women. The woman
is affected a lot, because let's say the man, when he arrives in this country, becomes an alcoholic or a drug addict, right? If they are in a relationship, many problems arise, such as economic, sexual, and at times,
domestic violence."

Joaquín, a forty-four-year-old from Guadalajara, reflected on his sobriety while expressing concern about the drinking habits of his roommates,
who had lived in Los Angeles for five years. "Many come with the desire
to work, and I have met many people who send money to their wives. But
then, many of them, 60 or 40 percent of them start using drugs, wine. I
have lived with people who are that way." He associated his friends' alcohol and drug use with the deterioration he had noticed in the quality of
the men's long-distance marital relationships. He noted that many men
were involved in non-monogamous relationships on both sides of the
border. I asked, "How often have you seen men who are involved with
other women in the United States while still having their wives over
there?" He replied:

> Out of twenty friends, ten have done it. It's like now, I live with two friends,
> and one of them drinks beer every day and the other one uses drugs. Both are
> married. I am not a saint, but I stopped doing all that. I have told them:
> "Many men use drugs within their groups of friends, they are drinking, but
> then your sex appetite goes down, you are killing yourself that way, you are
> locking yourself up inside a circle and you are not going to get out of it."

In one of my longest interviews, Joaquín talked about the many individual and group conversations he had had with his friends about sexuality and of how he has shared with them his own journey of psychological evolution after migrating. As I will discuss in the next chapter, for
Joaquín, and for many women and men in this study, networking became
a way to discuss and examine their concerns about sexuality.

The variety of backgrounds and immigrant experiences of the men is also reflected in the complex similarities and differences among them. Like Alejandro and Joaquín, Emiliano, Fidel, Jacobo, and Daniel also talked about drug or alcohol experimentation that they had overcome before migrating. Others, like Vinicio, said they had been pleased to discover and attend Alcoholics Anonymous meetings shortly after migrating. But regardless of their personal coping mechanisms or their past histories, most men associated substance abuse in the United States with their immigration and settlement experiences. Even though not all rural men had difficulties in adjusting to urban Los Angeles, men who had migrated from urban areas in Mexico were more likely to report that they had already been exposed to similar risks in the home country. For example, Jacobo explained:

> I am from a barrio in Guadalajara where we had all sorts of stuff. We had drugs of all calibers, alcohol, prostitution, everything. Right there in the barrio, there was a part of the neighborhood where many prostitutes lived. They worked in San Juan de Dios. So, I was exposed to all that, and had invitations to do everything. I just did not want to take it.

Eugenio, who clings to his *juramento* to help him cope with alcoholism in Los Angeles, explained how he confronted his friends: "Look, you know what? I come from Mexico City, I come from a very poor barrio, I know all this stuff from A through Z, I can even give you a lecture on it."

Some men used their previous experience of growing up in an urban center in Mexico as a coping strategy to avoid the use of alcohol. But others used liquor as a strategy for solving the problems of legal uncertainty, emotional isolation, and sexual urges. Sebastián told of a popular bar where his immigrant friends would go to drink and dance at night. "Out of curiosity, I went once to know what the hell was going on at that place. I said to myself, this can't be real!" He described what he observed:

> A lot of old women go there, or fat women, the kind of women who would not be able to get a man in a different way. And young men go over there to get their papers, their legal documents, or they go to get a woman so she can buy a car for them. I know someone who caught this woman at this place, I think she has houses in Tijuana. Anyway, he has a truck, and he does not work, and he has money and everything.[12]

The use of alcohol and drugs are post-migration risks that can affect men's sex lives and their heterosexual relationships. Men are vulnerable because of the social, economic, legal, and emotional stresses they face as part of the immigrant experience although a man's vulnerability is mediated by the quality and the intensity of his immigration experience, as well as by his personal history. Emotional isolation, peer pressure, and gang activity may evoke experiences of a painful past and enhance danger. But desperately looking for an alternative or renewed faith within the community may offer a chance to some.

El SIDA

Gender selectively shapes the risks faced by women and men, but both women and men identified a ghost that haunts their lives after migration and settlement: el SIDA — AIDS.

Both women and men reported being fearful and concerned about their own health and the health of their children when the topic of AIDS was discussed. This was especially true for those who knew or were related to AIDS victims, or whose partners had or were having extramarital relationships. A few, mainly those from rural towns, reported not having any information about the disease. Those who were more informed said that their main source of information was the Spanish-language media — radio, magazines, brochures — and workshops, or *pláticas,* they attended at clinics and schools, as well as other community-sponsored programs.

As I analyzed my data, I found that gender strongly shaped women's and men's reactions to the risk of HIV/AIDS. And often, gender was shaped by socioeconomic background.

As a group, women expressed feelings of concern about the potential negative consequences of infection on their marital relationships and the possible consequences for their children (i.e., the death of one or both parents). Regardless of their place of origin, about half of the informants reported that the AIDS epidemic had helped them to open up conversations with their partners about sexuality-related issues. However, when I asked them if the AIDS epidemic had affected their sex lives, women from rural Jalisco were more likely than urban women to report that they had not experienced changes in their actual sexual behavior. Rural women less frequently reported fear of AIDS when compared to either their urban counterparts or to men from all locations. Rural women were also more likely to use the phrase *"Le tengo confianza a mi esposo"* (I trust my husband) to explain why they did not worry about AIDS/HIV infection.

Women from Mexico City were more likely to report the use of condoms as a protection against AIDS. This was especially the case for women whose husbands had had extramarital affairs, or who knew people infected with the virus. Women who had engaged in their own past extramarital affairs or temptations were more likely to be from urban areas, and were also more likely to express feelings of apprehension and regret regarding the epidemic.

The socioeconomic contexts in which the women were educated often shaped their views and behavior with regard to AIDS. In particular, the social prescriptions they learned for gender relations defined these women's ways of caring for their own bodies and health. The social acceptance by rural women of a husband's extramarital affairs offers an example. Beatriz, who is from a small town, reported what she recommended to her husband:

> I am careful, and he is the same way. We have to take care of each other because you never know what may happen, at least with men. I tell him, "If you are going to go out with another woman, you have to be careful." So, in that way, we take care of each other. That has helped me a lot.

Gabriela, a woman who is aware of gender inequality, articulated her rationale differently. "Many men are macho, I know, and they do not protect themselves," she said. "Therefore, I talk with my husband a lot and I tell him to take care of himself."

Thus, as long as it is perceived to be safe, an extramarital affair and sex with a secondary partner may not lead to a change in the quality of a marital relationship. However, for some women, a husband's potential extramarital adventure not only represents a health risk. A woman may also use an affair as a strategy in preventing both the risk of infection and a deterioration in the relationship. Deyanira explained how this might be the case for some rural women:

> I would not like my husband to cheat on me, but I tell him, "The day you want to have sex with another woman, you better wear *el gorrito* [the "little hat"]. If you are going to have sexual relations with someone else, I do not want to have sex with you. It would be better if we treat each other like siblings."

Compared to the women, the men's answers offered some consistent patterns and also some differences. The overwhelming majority of the men said that AIDS had shaped their opinions about sexuality. Their views of sex were infused by feelings of fear, terror, concern, risk, and curiosity about learning more about protection.[13] Fear of infection as a result of casual, extramarital, or commercial sex lay at the core of the vast majority of the men's testimony. However, as they discussed changes in their actual sexual behavior, some patterns emerged. Like the women, the men from Jalisco reported more changes in their opinions about sex due to AIDS, but not in their sexual behavior. Men from Mexico City were more likely to report changes in both attitudes and sex behavior. A broader exposure to a variety of sexual discourses, earlier and easier access to health-related information, and education and employment opportunities may have helped women and men educated in urban areas to develop a greater concern about their bodies and their sexual health.

Regardless of their places of origin, many of the men identified different strategies to protect themselves from infection, including a decrease in the frequency of casual or commercial sex and in extramarital relationships. But only a minority reported they had become monogamous or totally abstinent because of the AIDS epidemic. Even though embracing these strategies was a challenge for many, knowing someone who was living with the HIV virus made it easier. As illustrated in the next chapter, some immigrants experienced changes in their view of sexuality after they had interacted socially with other individuals living in their immigrant communities. Emiliano, who was fearful of HIV infection and identified himself as completely monogamous at the time of our interview, told about four friends he had met at various stages in his migration who had died of AIDS. Similarly, Marcos described the ways in which he had learned to discipline his body out of fear of infection while recalling the experience of one his friends. His friend had told him, *"¡Híjole mano!* [Gee whiz, man!]. Now to know who the hell was the one who infected me! I have taken many women to bed and which one is the one who infected me?"* Marcos, who did not report any alcohol or drug use problems, explained that he had developed *"la disciplina del cuerpo"* (discipline of the body), a value emphasized by his Catholic faith and which he used to practice abstinence and to protect himself from sexually transmitted diseases.

Even though a link between religion and the lack of risky sexual behavior was present in the lives of only a few men, their cases are relevant because they show the contrasting ways in which some immigrant men cope with the risk of infection. For Eugenio and Fermín, who are single and married, respectively, a religious oath offered a way to remain sober and also led to a concern for their sexual health. Eugenio reported that he had been sexually abstinent during the previous five years. Fermín said he had never experienced casual sex while single, nor had he had an extramarital relationship. In contrast, some men took risks even though they knew they might become infected. However, these men may protect themselves by assessing their risk of infection in distinctive ways. Alejandro used the term *"mujer limpia"* (clean woman) to explain that he had learned to protect himself from infection by exploring the personal history of a potential partner through in-depth conversations. Likewise, Raúl said he had always known that his ex-wife was a *"mujer limpia"* and so he had not worn a condom when they engaged in premarital sex.[14]

About half of the men from both rural and urban areas said they did not use condoms due to physical discomfort and the anticlimactic effect on the sexual experience. Regardless of their places of origin, the remainder said they were amenable to wearing a condom if their wife or a sexual partner demanded it. In this group were some of the urban men, including Mauricio, Diego, and Emiliano, who had reported extramarital affairs or secondary partners. But some of the men who reported discomfort with wearing a condom had an additional reason to avoid using one: the possibility that its use would provoke conflict in the relationship. I asked Joaquín what he would do if he went back to visit his wife in Mexico and she asked him to use a condom. He imagined the dialogue that might take place between them:

> I think that she would make me think, "Why do you want me to wear a condom?" That is what I would say, kind of defensively. "Why do you want me to put it on?" "Because I don't know in what condition you come from." "Ay! You don't trust me!" And then we would go: "Yes." "No." "Yes." "No." So, I would not put it on.

A second man, Alfonso, gave a similar answer.

> Well, I would feel lack of trust toward her. Why, after all these years, is she asking me to do this? If I ever had to wear a condom, it would be because she is sick or I am sick, and that's it.

During our interviews, Joaquín and Alfonso talked about the unprotected sexual contact they had at times engaged in within extramarital relationships. Avoiding the kinds of struggles over trust and power they described in their interviews might be one of the reasons why, upon returning to Mexico, such men, who may not know they are HIV-positive, are very likely to engage in unprotected sex with a compliant primary partner (i.e., wife) who perceives sex as a marital obligation (Salgado de Snyder et al., 2000).[15] Even though Joaquín and Alfonso are from Guadalajara and Mexico City, respectively, their behavior might be associated with the following migration-related patterns related to HIV/AIDS in Mexico:

1. Migrants who have lived in the United States represent twenty-five percent of rural Mexican men infected with HIV (Magis-Rodríguez et al. 1995).

2. Heterosexual transmission is the primary cause of HIV infection in rural Mexican communities that send farm workers to the United States (Del Río Zolezzi et al. 1995).

3. Mexicans make between 800,000 and 1,000,000 round-trips between Mexico and the United States every year; most of these travelers are young men between twelve and thirty-four years old (U.S.–Mexico Migration Panel 2001).

4. In general, heterosexual sex is the leading cause of women contracting HIV in Mexico (Chávez 1999). (The attitudes and behaviors reported by both rural women and men in this study — for example, that rural women do not change their sexual behavior even after being educated about the risks of AIDS, that they are less in control of their sexualized bodies, and that they are influenced by more rigid moralities — may exacerbate this problem.)

The men and women in this study who reported having a satisfying marital relationship identified monogamy and lack of condom use as an expression of mutual love, respect, trust, and intimacy. This finding echoes that of another study whose respondents associated "unprotected sex as the most intimate kind of sex" (Hirsch et al. 2002, 1230). Two of my male respondents, Sebastián and Fidel, boasted about being faithful to their wives and felt that this behavior was reciprocated. They used the expression "I trust my wife," as they expressed their preference for unprotected sex. Fear of infection, however, was at the core of these decisions.

> *Sebastián:* Because of the diseases you find here, because of the promiscuity that you find over here, that is the only reason, that is the reason why I have refrained from having another relationship. I do not understand how people can take those risks. But it happens and we are seeing it.

> *Fidel:* I am afraid because of all the diseases, these days. I have been married for twelve years, and I have a very stable family life. I could blow it or make a mistake, right? But I have tried to avoid it. I am afraid of having extramarital relationships, especially because of AIDS.

Some of the women and men reported that migration had made them more concerned about the cruel reality of AIDS. Others characterized the disease as an international problem, one they had also witnessed in their places of origin. For instance, Cecilia said that her cousin, who was living with AIDS in Mexico, had asked her to buy a special treatment for him that was not available in Mexico City. Similarly, Idalia talked about an AIDS case that had become controversial in her small town.

In sum, my informants' perceptions and interpretations of the dangers of sexual violation of children, alcohol and drug use, gang activity, same-sex eroticism, and the AIDS epidemic arose as part of their settlement and immigration experiences. These fears influenced in many ways their sexual health, as well as the quality of their sex lives and their heterosexual relationships in the United States. For some of them, the use of alcohol and drugs, and participation in gang activity, had brought erotic pleasure and emotional comfort, but always in the shadow of serious threats and potential harm.

But why are immigrants exposed to these dangerous situations that selectively shape their sex lives? They are responding to a "political economy of risk," a concept introduced by Rayna Rapp (1999) in her investigation of women of diverse racial or ethnic, class, religious, and national backgrounds and their decisions about using or refusing new reproductive technology. Inspired by Rapp's work, Castañeda and Zavella (2003) have utilized this paradigm to study immigrant Mexicana farm workers in north-central California. The farm workers face dangers to their sex lives within the context of economic, political, and social forces. Similar forces also threaten the sex lives of Mexicans migrating to and settling in Los Angeles, but they are played out in distinctive ways.

Los Angeles has become the main destination of undocumented immigrants coming to the United States (Valenzuela 2002).[16] Mexicans represent over 95 percent of those who have been apprehended during the last two decades (Portes and Rumbaut 1996, 10). Many immigrants arrive in L.A. financially needy, legally vulnerable, and looking for work. They first settle in segregated yet resourceful communities that provide them with kin, a familiar language, and a familiar culture (Valenzuela and Gonzalez 2000), along with places to exchange goods and services (Sassen-Koob 1984). These vibrant communities witnessed an increase of more than 300 percent in the Latino workforce from 1970 to 1990 (Grant 2000). However, in 1990, two-thirds of the foreign-born, lacking a high school diploma, were hired for jobs at the bottom of the occupational hierarchy, and they had the highest poverty rate. Immigrants concentrate in specific occupations in part because those who are already established help the recently arrived to get jobs. "By 1990, 72 percent of Mexican immigrants worked in occupations that could be classified as Mexican immigrant niches" (Ortiz 1996, 257). Businesses that depend on economic migrants use these social networks to fill vacancies that are low-paying and frequently boring, dirty, hazardous, and without prospects for advancement (Cornelius 1998; Waldinger and Lichter 2003). This low-wage labor force is described by employers as reliable and diligent and willing to work hard and for less pay (Portes and Rumbaut 1996; Waldinger and Lichter 2003).

As a "global city" (Sassen-Koob 1984), Los Angeles depends on immigrant labor, which has become part of an international division of labor indispensable in the United States, a country with a widely uneven distribution of wealth and a widening gap between rich and poor (Valle and Torres 2000).[17] These forces include the process of *segmented assimilation* (Portes 1995; Portes and Rumbaut 1996, 255–56), which drove many of the immigrants I interviewed into the inner city and other neglected areas of Los Angeles. There, insecurity, segregation, and poor-quality housing exist hand-in-hand with devalued real estate and low rents (Vigil 2002). Some Mexican immigrants jokingly refer to these urban settlements as "Hell A" and "Lost Angeles."

The culture of sexual fear that shaped the lives of the women and men I interviewed as they grew up in Mexico takes different forms in the United States. Old fears around sexual matters are transformed in a different society as people get older and become parents. The social forces that affect their fears and their coping mechanisms include some paradoxes: socioeconomic segregation versus job opportunities, xenophobia versus avenues for social change, new social connections versus anonymity and isolation, and the Spanish-language media and immigrant communities versus language barriers. Some informants, for instance, said that fears of sexual danger are in part promoted by Spanish-language talk shows, where deviance is paraded and terrible stories are discussed by panelists.

In Mexico, fears often revolved around premarital sex. In the United States, parents share those fears, but they are also fearful of sexual abuse and rape, gang violence, drug use, and AIDS. During periods of social and political turbulence, sexual fears can merge into a more general culture of fear. Cyclical waves of xenophobia, illustrated by the anti-immigrant Proposition 187 in California, and, more recently, by racial profiling at airports after the September 11 terrorist attacks, affect the hierarchy of immigrants' concerns. Such fears never completely paralyze these women and men, however. As I show in next chapter, my respondents cope with their fears (and with a wide variety of sex-related concerns) through the social networks they construct within their communities. In addition, everyday survival in a large metropolis can create distinct interpretations of what they perceive as dangerous.

The words "risk" and "danger" might be synonymous; both possess a similar linguistic meaning. Socially speaking, however, class, ethnicity, gender, and legal status may give an additional semantic twist to these words. As immigrants, these women and men identified additional paradoxes surrounding their personal lives. When I told Alfredo that some of the women that I had previously interviewed had stated that HIV/AIDS, alcohol and drug abuse, violence, and crime were risks many immigrants faced, he exclaimed, "What risks? Not having a job, that's what I call a risk! The rest of the stuff isn't a risk. My risk, for me, my preoccupation is not to have a job." Similarly, but paradoxically, when I presented Felipe with the same statement, he replied, "Well, a risk? What I call a risk is that practically all you do in this country is to work."

Even though men like Alfredo and Felipe may give contrasting interpretations to their employment experiences, attaining a paid job in a capitalistic society may be linked to an immigrant's sex life in a particular way: sex is vulnerable to the pressures of time. At times, sex improves, at times, it degenerates. It all depends on how sex is organized by the demands of busy schedules and efforts to survive in a contemporary society that craves more and more time.

With the Clock by the Bed: The Taylorization of Sex

> "My beau and I travel a lot for work and have a zillion social
> and professional commitments," says Fergusson, a self-employed
> marketing consultant and triathlete whose name has been changed
> for this article. "I am totally organized and anal retentive. My life
> is planned in 15-minute increments. So we schedule time for sex.
> Quite frankly, I would be surprised if most people don't."
> "Making Time for Sex Makes a Difference,"
> San Francisco Chronicle, 2001

Work, time, and sex were intimately connected in the lives of the immigrants in this study. Diamantina is a married, full-time housewife who lives with her husband and their two daughters. She said her husband's busy schedule has hurt the quality of her sex life. "I think my sexuality is fading in this country," she said intensely, "because *en este país puro trabajo, puro trabajo!*" [in this country, it's just work, work, work!]. The deteriorating nature of Diamantina's intimate life is part of her immigration experience, but it has parallels in the personal lives of the white, middle-class people Arlie Hochschild discusses in her book *The Time Bind: When Work Becomes Home and Home Becomes Work* (1997).

Hochschild examined how the personal and family lives of working women and men were damaged by busy routines, the demands of work, financial needs, fears of losing one's jobs, and a sophisticated culture of the workplace that exists at every level in the workplace, even among companies that claim to promote "family-friendly" policies. Interestingly, Hochschild did not look at her subjects' sex lives.

Diamantina started to notice a deterioration in her sex life with her husband after migrating to the United States:

> *¡Puro trabajo! ¡puro trabajo!* The man works day and night, so his sexuality fades away. When he comes home, he is so tired he just goes to sleep and that's it! He doesn't even pay attention to the girls, or to me, either.

Unable to earn enough in his former day job, Diamantina's husband now works around the clock for the transportation company that hired him as a trailer driver some time ago. His busy schedule has created an emotional and sexual distance and tension between them, and Diamantina worries about the future:

> I feel bad because then you get older and then you cannot do anything, and then I believe the menopause will come. And then, what if I do not want to do it and then he wants to? What is going to happen? He is going to look for someone else. But I am a woman, so I would not dare to do something like that.

From a feminist perspective, Diamantina's fears have important implications. They reflect a central mechanism of sexual power: a woman's sexual potency deteriorates with age and therefore she becomes devalued. A woman is more likely than a man to be abandoned if she does not satisfy her partner's sexual needs; and, unlike a sexually dissatisfied married man, a sexually dissatisfied married woman is inherently constrained from looking for another sexual partner. At one point, Diamantina blushed and admitted that her frustration had led her to think about having a lover.

What would happen if a woman like Diamantina pursued her sexual fantasies of looking for a lover? How would that be interpreted by an immigrant man? When I interviewed Emiliano, he said he had been lucky enough not to be personally affected in his sexual life by the pressures of survival in the United States. However, he asserted that Mexican women change sexually when they come to the United States. "They become more liberal," he said, "because the man does not dedicate enough time to them." Emiliano had reached that conclusion because of the story an immigrant friend, who worked a strenuous schedule in order to support his family, had confided to him.

> A friend of mine works a lot. He is a baker, so he has to start working, I don't know, about 3 or 4 A.M., and he gets off from work around noon or 1 P.M. And then, he still goes somewhere else to bake more cakes, and to work at I don't know how many places. And I saw it, when his wife was cheating on him, and then he realized that she was being unfaithful to him.

For men like Emiliano, a busy routine of survival in Los Angeles may trigger the fear that a man will be abandoned and betrayed if he does not find enough time to satisfy his wife's sexual needs. In light of the view of masculine identity as being that of the breadwinner and also maintaining the quality of the marriage, how did the men in this study sexually react to the demands of their busy schedules? What do men like Diamantina's husband have to say about the effects of the fast pace of a highly industrialized capitalist society on their sex lives?

When I interviewed the men, I asked them if the fast pace of their daily routine in the United States had influenced their sex lives. Most nodded, while noting that they didn't have much choice: hard work was their only legal avenue for survival in Los Angeles. A few explained in detail how their daily survival routines had reshaped their sex lives. Diego observed, angrily:

> Los Angeles, California, is an urban plantation. It is a large factory. Here, you work in the morning, you work in the afternoon, and you work at night . . . and in your spare time, you also work! It absorbs your life, the pace of work in this city is overwhelming, it does not allow you to do anything. The city has one thousand hours to work in it, and one thousand distractions to spend your earnings. You are tied to the city, you live in a chain, there is no social life in the city, there is no social bonding.

Diego used the expression *"Mi tiempo es sagrado"* (My time is sacred) to explain why he had deliberately chosen to survive on a series of part-time jobs in order to have a modest but enjoyable routine. He proudly explained how his flexible schedule allowed him to have a close relationship with his children, whom he periodically visits; a romantic partner with whom he claims a satisfying intimate and emotional life; and an active social life with his friends.

Though Diego says he is careful not to allow his schedule to invade the privacy of his bedroom, he is aware of the negative consequences of a busy life on the sex lives of immigrants he has known in Los Angeles.

> The woman gets off from work and the man gets off from work, they invested eight hours at their work places, and two hours of overtime, and after that . . . do you think she is going to be willing to flirt with or to be teased by her husband? Or to wear intimate and beautiful underwear? Or to allow her man to be romantic with her? Or to have a glass of wine before going to bed? By 8 or 9 P.M., they are fried. All they want to do is to lie down and go to sleep. The little time left after a meal is dedicated to the children, or to watch the news at Channel 34, 52, or 22, which are always fighting against each other to show you who killed more people in the city. And then, they go to sleep. The man falls down on the bed, just like the woman does, anesthetized. And then, sexual relations? Well, I have become aware — which is not my case — that they are not that frequent, once a week, or once a month, as something extraordinary, something I am against. . . . So there is more mental and physical exhaustion in this city. In Mexico, there is more chance to relax.

Diego's criticisms of how daily survival routines structure the family and marital lives of many immigrants were echoed by other men, especially those from small towns. Said Vinicio, who is from rural Jalisco: "That is the punishment you have to pay at times. People tell you this is the land of opportunities, the country where you can get everything, but you have to pay a price." He added, "Do you want to live earning the greenback? Well, you have to deprive yourself of many things." Vinicio then outlined how his post-migration routine had shaped both the quality of his family life and his marital relationship with his wife, who works full time as a clerk:

> In my ranch, we used to have breakfast at 8, lunch at 2, and supper at 8. That way, you have the opportunity to be with your family. But not here. Here, you start working at 6 A.M. because you have to work for the rich, right? Then, you miss breakfast with your family. Then, you also miss lunch, because you don't get off from work until 3 P.M., or not until dinner.

Vinicio also said that his work schedule cut into the intimate times he had to be with his partner:

> It happens to me because my wife many times has to start working at 5. Then, she wants to go to sleep at 8 so she can get up at 4 to get dressed and ready for work, and I want to be more relaxed watching TV up until 11 at night, and I cannot wake her up, I have to respect her sleep. Even when she is off, the days when she does not work, I have to work. So, it affects me as well.

Fidel, also from a small town, explained the strategies he and his wife (a full-time housewife) follow, as he works forty hours a week, plus five or six hours of weekly overtime periodically. I asked him if his work schedule had influenced his intimate life with his wife. Sensitively, he said:

> I think it does, but you have to overcome that in order to have a sex life with your partner. At times, my wife gives me the chance to sleep, but then about midnight I wake up to have sexual relations with her. Or at times she sleeps and I go and wake her up. The fact that she is at home all day is not a honeymoon for her because I know it is really difficult to put up with the kids. They can be terrible!

Even men whose sex lives were not hurt by their work worried about that happening in the future. Jacobo, from Guadalajara, talked about the radical decisions he might face:

> Well, that is not my case at this moment, but I would consider it as very important because when I remarried, I remarry with the idea of having a very good relationship, one we could share, and I do not see how we could share a relationship if we have different schedules. So, if I am going to start working at 8 A.M. and she starts working also at 8 A.M., but if she starts working at 6 P.M., definitely, we are not going to have time to share. So, I think, that would affect me. I would not like to be in that kind of situation. But if I had to live that way, and that is what I say, I better get a divorce and look for another woman with whom I can really share a relationship.

Fermín had similar concerns. He was recovering from an accident that had placed him on disability for nearly a year, and had been taking care of his daughters while his wife worked full-time. As the day for him to resume working got closer, he began to think about the potential changes in the quality of his marital relationship. He used the word *"distancia-miento"* to explain that he was afraid of emotional distancing in their marital relationship:

> I would not like it, but what else can I do? She will have to work in the morning and in the afternoon. Then, we are not going to see each other that much because of the girls. I have to take them to school in the morning, and she has to take her classes in the afternoon. We cannot stop working until the girls grow up. So, I see it coming. When I get back to work, it may create some problems for us.

For women like Diamantina, their sexuality and sex lives were defined by their husbands' busy schedules, which seemed out of anyone's control due to the limitations and realities of their lives as immigrants. In addi-

tion, Diamantina explained the reasons for her overwhelming routine —
all a part of her immigration experience: her full-time obligations as a
housewife; the many doctor's visits she made on foot to various free clinics in order to take care of the health of her two daughters; her commitments at her Protestant church; and her daily struggle to find a paid job.
As we have seen, Diamantina is not alone in her capitalist predicament.

Unlike the white, middle-class employees and professionals Hochschild interviewed, these women needed to survive in a new country. But
both groups shared the experience of having their intimate lives redefined
by the world of work in a highly industrialized capitalistic society.

Diamantina's expression, *"En este país puro trabajo, puro trabajo!"* and
Diego's complaint, "Here, you work in the morning, you work in the
afternoon, and you work at night . . . and in your spare time, you also
work!" may have the same linguistic equivalent in English. However, in
sociological language, they may have more than one meaning. "Time,
work-discipline, and industrial capitalism" is also an accurate translation
of these statements. The line is the title of a chapter in E. P. Thompson's
book *Customs in Common* (1991), in which he analyzes time management
as a crucial transitional component between pre-industrial and industrial
societies. Thompson examines how industrial societies implemented
time regulation and measurement as the ideal way to control and manage
labor and work. He explains how the task-oriented system utilized in pre-
industrial societies (i.e., the family economy of a small farmer in the nineteenth century) as a way to manage and control labor was replaced by a
system of time measurement resulting from the multiple mechanisms that
emerged in industrial societies, such as employment of labor, division of
labor, discipline between employer and employee, production needs, and
so on. The concept of time — its efficient management and its place in the
history of capitalism and industrial development — is also central in
Hochschild's book *The Time Bind* (1997). She cites Frederick Taylor (the
engineering genius who studied and established the principles of time
management and efficiency in factories almost one hundred years ago) to
argue that "family life gets Taylorized" as work invades family life. That
is, family life comes to be designed and lived based on principles of time
efficiency learned at the workplace. The cult of time management and
efficiency that her informants worship at work is carried home.
Hochschild describes how some of these dedicated employees learn to
cover all their family needs on time and in a very efficient manner. This
experience is not an easy process and requires a great deal of investment
of emotional energy (and needless to say, it also requires more "time").

In my study, Diamantina, Diego's and Emiliano's friends, Vinicio, and Fidel were already paying a "sexual cost," and Jacobo and Fermín were keenly aware of the possible high price to their sex lives. Their sex lives were clearly deteriorating as a result of the demands of survival and the pressures of time and work in an industrial society. A few of my informants, in contrast, had experienced "Taylorization" of their sex lives, which, interestingly enough, had had a positive effect.

"Yes, it is nicer! It is terrific to do it once a week or once every other week!" exclaimed Rosalía. She added, "It is nicer than having sex every day because everyday sex gets kind of boring." Being responsible for six children and working full time had made Rosalía redefine her sex life in a "timely efficient manner" by establishing a sexual agreement with her husband of less than a year. With great excitement, she talked about how working full time had created the need for them to establish a schedule for their sexual encounters. Interestingly, waiting for the appropriate day to have sex had created an atmosphere of sexual excitement in her marital life and a "sexual gain" as part of her life in the United States. Coordinating work within a busy schedule has turned out to be an aphrodisiac, she said.

> Sometimes when I do it once every eight days, or once every fifteen days, we are happy because it is like doing it everyday. Because when we make it once a week or once every two weeks, I give myself more. It's like . . . you do not give yourself the same way when you do it every day.

Rosalía reminded me of the highly attuned ways in which other informants — beyond the context of work and time — had perceived different expressions of prohibition as sexually exciting. For them, forbiddance had increased sexual yearning and passion. Felipe, for example, told me he still remembers the rainy season in his small town with special pleasure. Back then, a rainy day was a golden opportunity for him and his friends. "When it rained, we would watch carefully to see when women would raise their long skirts," he said with a giggle. "Now, with miniskirts, well, it's not the same."

Immigrant women like Diamantina and Rosalía may not be aware of the changing rhythms in the history of industrialization and capitalism. However, the important transitions in their sex lives do allow them to measure the contrasts of time management and economy between a developing nation, like Mexico, and the United States — the mecca of capitalism, modernity, and industrialization, and the place where they have to survive as immigrants.

As part of my own personal experience in the United States, I have observed that North Americans use the expression "Thank you for your time" to express their gratitude after someone has spent "time" helping them with a particular issue. In my years living in Mexico, I never heard anyone use its equivalent in Spanish, *"Gracias por su tiempo."* In general, in Mexico, people would use the expression *"Gracias por ayudarme"* (Thank you for helping me). Socially speaking, in capitalistic societies "time" seems to have a higher value than "help." Time means capital, time means money.

Diamantina and Rosalía's stories bear on the discussion of employment, personal empowerment, and sex that I present in chapter 7. An immigrant woman may develop a sense of sexual autonomy as a consequence of obtaining paid full-time employment outside the home, earning a salary, and becoming financially independent. As a full-time housewife who is financially dependent on her husband's income, a woman like Diamantina may not have much power in negotiations with him. In fact, she may be in a devalued and disempowered position and therefore lack control over negotiations involving her sex life. Therefore, she is more likely to experience negative changes in sexuality. By contrast, Rosalía — a full-time employee in a paid position outside her home who shares household expenses equally with her husband — may have the opportunity to experience a positive transition in her sex life.

Unlike women, men reported more elaborate and sophisticated responses with regard to the negative influence of a busy and fast-paced routine, on their sex lives as well as on their marriages and their families. This pattern is important given the sample size, forty female versus twenty male informants. Some explanations may include the following:

All the men had full-time paid employment, whereas 60 percent of the women had part-time or full-time paid employment. Men's sex lives seem to be more directly negatively affected by survival when they are the breadwinners in an economy of time. In addition, men more frequently complained about the intrusion of work and schedule on their family lives. Whereas a full-time housewife with no paid employment may develop a closer bond with her children and home, the demands of economic survival may increase a man's feelings of isolation and disconnection from his family and marital life.

As a group, women appeared to be socially trained to be more tolerant of sexual frustration and more reserved with regard to their sexual needs and desires when compared to men. It is significant that the only two women who clearly noted "sexual costs" (Diamantina) or "sexual gains" (Rosalía) as a consequence of their busy schedules in the United States were from Mexico City. As a consequence of more education and employment opportunities in urban centers, women living in industrialized areas may feel they have more social and cultural permission to identify and express their sexual needs, desires, and frustrations when compared to their rural counterparts. Amuchástegui observed in her sex research in Mexico: "There seems to be a greater awareness and acceptance of sexual desire among women participants who have had more contact with urban culture and formal education" (2001, 291). This is consistent with research that concludes that urban women are less disadvantaged with regard to negotiating preventive sexual practices when compared to their rural counterparts (Del Río Zolezzi et al. 1995). Diamantina's and Rosalía's testimony, as well as the testimony of Amuchástegui and Del Río Zolezzi's informants, seem to have a connection with recent reports by the Instituto Mexicano de Sexología which indicate that women from urban Mexico are twice as likely as rural women to report that they have experienced an orgasm (Gómez Mena 2001). This finding also coincides with research on rural women from Michoacán who complained of lacking sexual desire because they were sexually dissatisfied or had never experienced an orgasm in their heterosexual encounters (Bronfman and López Moreno 1996, 64); and on rural women from Jalisco who reported a lack of negotiating power in their heterosexual encounters and perceived intercourse not as a voluntary act but as an apparent marital obligation (Salgado de Snyder et al. 2000).

Women who have learned to perceive sexual intercourse as a marital obligation may experience a sense of relief from not having to be sexually available to an absent or physically exhausted husband who is too busy working. Thus, within a traditional family arrangement, a busy economy may hurt an immigrant man's sex life, but it may give a break to a woman who doesn't enjoy sex. In chapter 7, I examine this notion of sex as a marital obligation within the nuanced, everyday life contexts of Mexican women migrants.

The women and men in this study revealed the sexual vulnerabilities and paradoxes for immigrants settling in the ultra-industrialized city mecca of the capitalist system that is Los Angeles. As shown, these challenges unfold through specific social mechanisms. Even though many of the immigrants shared their awareness of their susceptibility to crime, violence, and drugs, among other things, they identified only some of them as having prompted changes in their views of sexuality or their actual sexual behaviors and attitudes. The discourses and realities of child sexual

CHAPTER 6

Sexual Discourses and Cultures in the Barrio

Networking

"Turn on the TV! Turn on the TV so you can see!" Victoria's neighbor was shouting. The woman was urging her to tune in to a Spanish-language channel where a video on sexuality was being advertised for sale. After watching the endless sexual promises of the seductive propaganda, Victoria ordered the cassette. It turned out to be an important event. In many ways, her ideas about women's sexuality were transformed after watching the video and discussing the new information about sex with her neighbor. Victoria also became the confidante of her neighbor by listening as the woman attempted to find ways to satisfy her husband's sexual urges so he would never be unfaithful to her.

Similarly, Alejandro described the many private conversations he has had with many immigrant *amigas*. "They are open. In other words, they tell me, 'Look, this is what I did with my husband last night. And he came once or twice, but I did not come, not even once, and I was unsatisfied.'" Alejandro would react by telling his friends: "Talk to him, write a little letter to him and tell him, 'Look, you know what? Look, I do not like this about you. Let's say you made a mistake or I am not happy about it. We can change in some way, or in some aspect of the relationship so I can feel good about it.'" Alejandro said he had learned a great deal about marital relationships, intimacy, and sexual practices by listening and giving advice to his immigrant friends from various Mexican regions and Latin American countries.

Like many of the participants, Victoria and Alejandro are actively transforming their sexuality through the process of immigration and settlement.

Their stories about sex-related conversations with Mexican and other immigrant neighbors, friends, and relatives expand on the arguments presented in the previous chapter on danger and survival, socioeconomic segregation, and work within the fast-paced environment of the United States. Becoming part of the labor force in U.S. society may expose Mexican immigrant women to vulnerabilities and challenges in their sex lives. However, they are not passive social actors. Beyond the social hazards and socioeconomic contexts, women and men forge relationships with their Mexican and Latina/o immigrant relatives, neighbors, and friends to create multiple immigrant communities and cultures. These bonds include conversations about sex. In this chapter, I examine the dynamic reconstruction of Mexicans' sexuality within their immigrant communities. The sex lives of the informants in this study were transformed through networking. Though this phenomenon was more frequently reported by women than by men, both sexes reported that their conversations with fellow immigrants had helped them to actively construct new prescriptions and standards for socially acceptable sexual beliefs and practices, ideals of femininity and masculinity, gender relations, and new social norms to promote or challenge inequality between women and men.[1]

Sociological studies of Mexicans that examine their experiences of immigration to the United States address the importance of networking as an essential, dynamic, and complex part of life in their new land (see Rosenthal-Urey 1984; Portes and Bach 1985; Massey 1987; Massey et al. 1987; Chávez 1992; Hondagneu-Sotelo 1994; Woo 1995, 1997; Cornelius 1998; Waldinger and Lichter 2003). The sociology of sex research indicates that networking becomes one of the most important social vehicles in reshaping individuals' sexuality in a particular context. Laumann and Gagnon (1995) write:

> The social networks in which individuals participate, despite the invisibility of actual sexual performances, have a number of important effects on patterns of sexual conduct. Networks offer both opportunities for and limitations on the formation of ties in which sexual activity can go forward, and they provide audiences for the public behavior of individuals as they form and maintain ties that have a sexual component. While such third parties to the sexual interaction are only sometimes privy to the actual sexual performances of other persons, such network relations are deeply influential in terms of legitimating many of the specific sexual practices of persons in sexual relationships. (198)

For the women in this study, social networks represented an important avenue to revisit and reinvent their sex lives. Talking about sex with other immigrant women gave them the means to exchange advice, personal support, and information about sex while coping with their sexual difficulties. In some instances, these personal interactions had a profound and impressive impact on their sex lives. At times, these exchanges involved U.S.-born and -raised women and multicultural friends whose social life was centered in predominantly Latino neighborhoods. They took place in many social settings, including schools, clinics, workplaces, churches, or in the privacy of the discussants' homes. These groups and gatherings were informally constituted.[2]

Emancipatory Networking

Having groups of friends and actively exchanging information with them worked to reshape the sex lives of some of the women in this study; the transformations that occurred were liberating and awakening. The story told by Romelia, a woman from Jalisco, illustrates the networking dynamic. For Romelia, learning that it was morally acceptable to discuss sexuality openly was only the beginning in a series of changes she would undergo. Romelia became part of a multicultural friendship group that formed in Los Angeles, a result of her having become a community activist and organizer for immigrant rights. The ambience of these informal talks among friends helped her to overcome some taboos with regard to sexuality, to feel more comfortable with her own sexuality, and to explore new information about sex. She described how the group helped her to change the way she thought, felt, and talked about sex as part of this process:

> Well, the trust they give you to talk. Nobody is going to criticize you because you talk about sex. And nobody would tell you that you are of the worst kind for talking about it. There is more freedom to talk here.

I asked Romelia where she thought that freedom came from. She said:

> It is the atmosphere in which we live here in this barrio. All of our friends are very open and we have them from everywhere, North American, Argentineans, Guatemalans — it is a multicultural group!

Romelia described her multicultural friends as respectful and open while talking about sexuality-related issues. She was proud that some of them were well educated and informed about matters of sexuality. Their conversations about sex were unplanned and occurred during informal encounters, such as at parties, on trips to the beach, and when the women went together to their favorite cafes. Romelia described how their conversations about sex emerged as part of a common effort to help, support, or offer orientation to some of the group members who were experiencing concerns about their sex lives. When I asked her who in particular she talked to about sex, she said:

> With all of them. At times, all of us get together, and at times two or three of the couples come and talk. Or my neighbor comes and says, "Well, I have this problem, what do I do?" Don't worry, come over! And we go and see that person and we see what we can do about it, or we go and see someone else. But we always get together as a group.

Romelia was excited and enthusiastic about the changes that had taken place in her sex life since exchanging information about sexuality with her friends. She described how her marital life, and her sex life in particular, has been favorably influenced by these talks.

> Before, making love was something that I had to do, and now it's like something that can be enjoyed. I look at it now as more pleasant. Now, if there's the need, both of us have to agree. Now I see it more as a right than an obligation.

I asked Romelia how this change had taken place.

> Everything has happened because of my friends. We have talked a lot in a way that opened my mind up. It's like in the last four years we have enjoyed our sexual relations more.

As illustrated by Romelia's story, such informal groups offer a safe social space for women to discuss personal concerns about sexuality and to collectively transform ideas about and experiences of sexuality. Romelia said she had never been stigmatized or judged harshly by anyone in the group. In addition, Romelia was then able to facilitate potential sexuality transitions in the lives of other immigrant women by organizing a sexuality workshop for a group of immigrant women in her neighborhood, including friends, neighbors, and acquaintances.

Emilia and Norma described how talking about their sexual concerns became part of the conversations they had with their Central American and Mexican friends. Norma talked about exchanging information on sexuality in her *"reuniones de parejas"* (couples' groups), which were predominantly heterosexual. "I have learned that they have a lot of mental freedom to think about sex as something pleasant or as something important." When I asked her if she had experienced changes in her sexual behavior as a consequence of these conversations, she replied:

> Yes, in a positive way. I did not know that sex was such an important part of being married, and I do not know why they coincided. In less than two weeks, two or three people told me about the same thing. That was a positive change because I am more concerned about my partner when we have sex. Well, and I think this has been positive for me, too.

Talking about sex within this group context gave Romelia, Emilia, and Norma the chance to explore their sexual concerns in the presence of their husbands and facilitate change. Romelia and Emilia's stories exemplify how Latina networking may promote the transition to emancipatory sexuality for heterosexual Mexicanas. Both women transcended their perceptions of heterosexual love within the context of marriage; they redefined their understanding of sex, from a marital duty into a right in which they, too, should experience sexual pleasure. These changes may further shape their views of sexuality as they educate their daughters in the United States.[3] And Romelia and Emilia also confronted the inequality embedded in their apparently dissatisfying sexual experiences.

For other women — especially those not involved in a relationship — networking played an important role in exploring sexuality. For Azucena, for instance, who periodically met with Latina friends at their homes, networking provided a social space in which they could talk about their sex lives as single women. Azucena described her circle of friends as being composed mainly of separated and divorced women and single mothers ("mature women"). Though all were sexually experienced, they learned a great deal about sexuality and aspects of their own sex lives from these conversations with one another. Their informal meetings were the ideal forum to exchange ideas, feelings, and opinions, Azucena said, as she described how she and her contemporaries were rethinking the meaning of sexuality in their personal lives and in their future relationships with men:

> As mature women we look at things in a very different way. In other words, it [sex] is necessary, why? Because your body is asking for it, it is normal, you are a woman, you are functioning! But it is not a thing, a goal that we have to have a man just to have him to go and sleep with him. So then, all of us start looking at this and we talk to see if it is necessary to have a partner for other kinds of things.

The self-confidence and ease with which Azucena described these conversations reminded me of the women in Lillian Rubin's book *Women of a Certain Age,* where she writes: "Sexuality breaks the bonds of early repressions and gathers force and power as they [women] move into midlife" (1979, 101). Thus, it was immigration and settlement that had brought about the formation of Azucena's and other groups, but it was becoming midlife adults in Los Angeles that had facilitated the dialogue.

Romelia, Norma, and Azucena's stories illustrate how meaningful changes in Mexican immigrant women's views of sexuality take place as they participate in social networks. Their stories also reveal the participation of immigrant (i.e., Latino) and non-immigrant (i.e., North American) men in the process of sexual transformation.

The male informants in this study reported various forms of networking about sexuality, but they mentioned participating in couples' reunions and informal groups of couples less often. Gabriel, who comes from a small town, reported that he and his wife had been consulted by their married friends on a variety of marital topics. "Some of them [talk to us] because of the problems they have with their partners, or about sex as well. Some of them complain about the partner not wanting [to have sex] or not taking enough time to have sex, and that kind of thing." These were relaxed, informal conversations about sex, "informal chatting, or mockery and jokes."

Besides the casual arrangements previously described in the context of social groups, other women came to reexamine issues of sexuality through one-on-one conversations with neighbors, friends, acquaintances, and sisters. For example, Irasema felt confused about her husband's desire to have anal sex. What happened illustrates how networks of women can sometimes confirm a woman's fears and attitudes. Deciding she needed to learn more about anal sex, Irasema approached two neighbors and asked them if it was a common practice.

> I had to ask for . . . not help, but I had to talk about it with another woman, my neighbor, who lives right here and the other neighbor who lives a little bit ahead to tell me about it because it was horrible for me! It was like . . . I did not let him touch me. He was going to touch me and I pushed him away. It was kind of ugly. It was one of the most horrible things that ever happened to me.

Irasema was reassured to learn that her two neighbors had had similar difficulties with both anal and oral sexual practices. She felt understood and validated in her personal struggle after talking with the first neighbor, a woman in her forties who had migrated many years before from El Salvador.

She told me that she had been through something similar. The same thing I was sharing with her. I was telling her something that she had experienced with her husband, both doing it orally and anally. "The same, the same, the same! Imagine!" she said. "I am reliving it!"

Irasema described her conversation with the second neighbor, a Mexican immigrant woman in her fifties, who again disclosed her own struggle about allowing anal sex. This neighbor gave Irasema specific information on how to cope with her physical discomfort while experimenting with anal sex:

> After talking with her I felt relaxed because I had felt like I was not the only one in this world who was going through this. And after we talked, she told me that, yes, that it would hurt a lot but that I needed to do it carefully and that I needed to be patient and that I should not tighten myself so it would not hurt that much, and also to do my best while doing it with him. But for me, it was horrible!

After she talked with her neighbors, Irasema felt more comfortable with her new knowledge. Anal sex never became a pleasurable sexual practice for her, but she learned specific strategies, such as using a lubricant, to avoid physical discomfort.

Victoria, Eréndira, Amparo, and Graciela, as well as Alejandro and Diego, also described changes in their knowledge and views of sexuality that came from personal conversations about sex with their neighbors, friends, and relatives. As already mentioned, Victoria attributed her change in attitude to her neighbor's advice to buy and watch a video on human sexuality. After Eréndira converted to Protestantism in Los Angeles, she began to talk about sexuality with her friend, an immigrant man from Mexico City whom she had met at their Adventist church. Later, they had regular telephone conversations about sex. Eréndira explained how they teased each other on the telephone while sharing their personal sexual experiences. She recalled that the most important advice she received from him was: "Do not be foolish. Sex is not dirty, it's healthy. But just take care of yourself!"

When I asked her if the conversations she had with him about sex had influenced her, she replied:

> Yes, because the image of sexual relations that I used to have was like sex was a sin. Even thinking about it, having any sexual temptation in my mind was sinful. So, after talking with him, I do not feel guilty if I think or talk about it. If I have sexual fantasies, I do not feel guilty. I think it is healthy.

Other men in the study also reported having conversations about sex with friends and acquaintances of the opposite sex. Alejandro often had such conversations with his Latina immigrant friends: "I talk a lot with my [women] friends about sex. I try to help them or to manipulate them because they are women and they have the same rights as men."

Alejandro had been born and raised and attended college in Mexico City. He had studied sociology and psychology in a large urban center, which might have helped him (as well as men like Eréndira's friend, who was also born and raised in Mexico City) to comfortably talk about sex-related issues with their female friends and to promote views of sexuality that were designed to help women take more control of their sexual lives. Interestingly, Alejandro and Eréndira's friend, and their respective female friends, created a hierarchy in their conversations. The men played the role of sex mentors in the women's lives. Paradoxically, Alejandro noted that he "manipulated" his female friends, with the intention of helping them improve their status as women.

In the opposite direction, some men from Mexico City said that it was *their* views of female sexuality that had changed as a result of their conversations with women. Diego, for example, said he had never believed in women practicing sexual abstinence before marriage and that his conversations with women had reinforced that point of view.

> Because for the woman it is a very difficult experience, it is a very tough experience. I have heard from many women for whom the first sexual experience was horrible, a torture, very difficult . . . traumatic, many times, and that, in fact, it has left a deep imprint in their lives! She should know what she is supposed to do when she gets married, so she needs to accumulate some experience. That would be the ideal, but I respect people. If some women want to be virgins at marriage, go ahead.

Diego's redefined views of female sexuality have not only shaped his views of women and their first sexual experiences, but the sex education he wants to give his daughter.[4]

Amparo, a woman who had lived in Los Angeles for twenty-five years, said that informal conversations about sex with one of her sisters had helped her to see women's sexuality differently. She had talked with her sister about how to better educate their daughters with regard to sexuality. While still struggling with some of her own traditional views, the exchange of ideas helped her to become more open-minded with regard to the way she is educating her adolescent daughter. With sadness and resignation, she said of her sister:

She has three adolescent daughters and they are completely free. The three of them have sexual relations, and I think all this is helping me to accept that the same will happen with my family some day.

Finally, Graciela described the nature of her conversations with a Guatemalan friend: "We talk a lot about sex, what we should do and what we shouldn't, or about things we hear here and there about sex, or if we had sex with our partners. You know, we talk about how good it felt."

So far, I have described how some of the women in the study have reshaped their sex lives through the social interactions they maintained within groups and through individual networking. In addition, other stories depict how the women in the study played the role of networking facilitator as they influenced the sex lives of their friends, neighbors, and relatives. The stories told by Juanita, Candelaria, Xóchitl, Jimena, and Azalea demonstrate how immigrant women play an active role as confidantes to other Latinas (immigrant and non-immigrant), who, in turn, provide them with sexual advice.

For Juanita, who is from Jalisco, providing support and understanding for some of her friends who were coping with sexual difficulties was part of her routine as a full-time housewife. Before we started our interview, Juanita asked me if I was a counselor who might offer my clinical services to some of her friends who were survivors of domestic violence or sexual abuse. Juanita described the trust her friends have placed in her by sharing intimate issues about their sex lives and in looking for emotional support:

Some people tell me such stories, incredible but it's the truth! Some people look for me and tell me, "I can't believe how after I speak with you I feel so relaxed!" There are some people who call me to talk about it [sex]. I have some friends who call me and say, "Oh! I feel so comfortable when I speak with you about my problems!"

Candelaria and Xóchitl, who are both from Jalisco, talked about the specific messages they would offer to their relatives and friends who were experiencing sexual difficulties in their marital relationships. Candelaria, for example, gave this *"consejo"* (advice) to her aunt:

Well, my aunt sometimes used to tell me that she did not have sexual relations with her husband and I gave her *consejos*: "Motivate him! If he does not want to have sex, well, you can start by teasing him!" Because she wanted him to be the one to initiate it, and I advised her that the initiation was mutual, from both of them.

Candelaria later described the advice she gave to a friend who complained that she could not experience orgasms. She had first recommended that her friend read some literature on women's sexuality. When
she realized that her friend was illiterate, Candelaria gave her specific
things to say to her husband during sex:

> I told her, "Tell you husband that you do not feel anything, so he can explore
> the way to make you feel something because that is necessary for your body
> to feel relaxed and also to feel good."

Following a parallel pattern, Xóchitl described some of the conversations she had had with many of her friends who suffered from sexual
difficulties in their relationships. She offered as an example the case of a
Latina immigrant friend who shared a small home with an extended family, and whose sexual and marital life had been affected by a lack of privacy. She told her:

> "Look, Eugenia, if you did not live with them, I think you would have a nicer
> relationship; otherwise, you cannot do it [sex]. I think that by living with other
> people, you lose your privacy."

Xóchitl talked enthusiastically about the sexual stories she had heard
in conversations with her married friends. She explained, for example, to
one of her U.S. born and raised Mexican American friends that wearing
seductive lingerie was an important part of successful foreplay with her
husband:

> I told her, "It's different when they [men] see you carelessly dressed wearing
> an old robe. What kind of emotions can be provoked that way? However, if
> you take a shower, change clothes, get dressed, when the man looks at you,
> what's going to happen next will be different!" And she said, "I think you are
> right, I will buy that type of clothes."

At first glance, it might seem that Xóchitl's advice makes the woman
responsible for creating an appropriate sexual atmosphere. However, her
recommendation has the potential to offer her friend a clear avenue for
exploring sexual pleasure and excitement. At some point during the
interview, Xóchitl told of the excitement and enjoyment she had experienced going through this same preparation ritual for a sexual encounter
with her husband. In addition, while discussing the extent to which she
believed her recommendations to her Chicana friend were part of a
woman's responsibility for sexual satisfaction in marital life, she com-

mented: "I do it to please him and also to please myself. I do it for both of us."

Jimena and Azalea, who are both from Mexico City, mentor their younger and less experienced female friends. Playing the role of older sister, they give them advice on how to take care of their bodies, how to prevent pregnancy, on contraceptive pills, condoms, and abortion, and on how to have a healthy reproductive life. Jimena talked about the ways she has tried to teach her younger friend about reproductive health:

> What happened to her is that this young boy got her pregnant and then abandoned her. She had many problems with her family. I have known her for years. I told her, "There are so many ways to prevent a pregnancy. What are you going to do if you get pregnant again?"

In a similar manner, Azalea described how she wanted to teach her young friend to be a responsible parent while learning to develop an appropriate family-planning method. When I asked Azalea what she and her friend talked about, she replied:

> I have asked her, "Why don't you use condoms? There are clinics out there where they can give you contraceptive pills or something else." I have told her many times, "If you already have three girls, why don't you have surgery so you don't get pregnant again?" She told me the other day that she had had sex not only with her husband but with someone else, and now she does not even know who the father of the child is!

In general, networking has three important functions in the sex lives of these immigrant women:

1. Networking represents a source of social and personal support. Mexican women use this social process in two ways: to cope with sexual difficulties they have in their relationships and to maintain their psychological equilibrium with regard to their sexual health.

2. Networking provides alternative sexual ideologies that challenge and modify previously established value systems and actual sexual behaviors.

3. Networking gives immigrant women a chance to educate each other about sexuality.

Historically, networking has been used in many times and places to exchange knowledge and experiences on sex- and reproductive-health-related issues. Stern examined how women in late colonial Mexico used networking to create local reputations or rumors while promoting mutual solidarity, support, and mediation "in a given village, barrio, hacienda, or cluster of ranchos" (1995, 103). Hirsch has shown how, in one of the transnational contemporary communities she studied, conversations about oral sex would occur as women gathered to knit and chat (2003, 215). Bronfman and López Moreno examined how women from a small rural community whose men had gone to Watsonville, California, used all-female networking as a way to vent their sexual frustrations and explore ways to enhance their marital relationships (1996, 64). And Ross and Rapp (1997) showed how networking among rural and urban women in pre-modern Europe functioned as a way for women to share information about reproduction. "Urban females' networks also were sources of information, and pre-World War I British evidence suggests that abortion was more common in urban areas at least in part because such information networks could operate there" (159).

The sexual transformations I have discussed seem to promote a socially progressive sexual morality, which may have led some of the women in this study to a wider repertoire of sexual beliefs and practices. Immigrant women, in addition, may help each other improve the quality of their personal lives and of their loving relationships, as they teach one another about U.S. laws that protect women from domestic violence — a development that many of the men I interviewed view with discomfort and resentment.

Some of the men I interviewed became part of women's sexual networking experiences through their participation in these conversations with groups of friends, at couples' reunions, and in one-on-one conversations with the opposite sex. The men were less likely to report one-on-one conversations with other immigrant men as a way of exploring intimate sexuality-related issues. Interestingly, the minority of men who reported that they *did* have a confidant with whom they could share sexuality-related issues were the younger men in the study, like Mauricio, Daniel, and Alfonso. These men belong to a younger generation that seems to be experiencing the influence of modernity on views on sexuality and other sex-related topics, a change that allows them to openly talk about these issues with their peers and friends. Yet some of the older men reported that they have a relationship with a best friend or a male relative whom they may seek out as a sounding board to solve conflicts in their marital and family relationships. About half of the men reported being confidants for some of their immigrant friends with regard to these same issues.

Thus, gender seems to shape sexual networking for women. The emotional bonding among mothers and daughters that emerges from the mothering arrangements in the traditional patriarchal nuclear family (Chodorow 1978) is further enhanced in some Mexican families, as a constellation of women who belong to the extended family (i.e., aunts, grandmothers, cousins, and godmothers) may get involved in the education of children (Segura and Pierce 1993). In addition, women's assigned responsibility as the brokers of love and emotionality in heterosexual relationships may mobilize them to seek help to solve their sexuality concerns as part of their marital and partner obligations. It is no surprise that in Mexican immigrant communities mothers, more frequently than fathers, seek professional help as a way to solve their families' emotional distress (Falicov 1982).

The above gender patterns are not rigid, however. They are fluid processes in constant negotiation and redefinition as women and men are exposed to new migration-related social contexts and situations, including the world of employment and work in the United States.

Discussing Sexuality at Work

As discussed in the previous chapter, the issue of employment and survival within a fast-paced capitalist society has invaded some immigrants' bedrooms and shaped their sex lives. In the opposite direction, sex may similarly invade the workplace, when time allows or when the need to make a routine more pleasant invites it. As Emilia noted, "When we do not have that much work, we talk about [sex]." For Emilia and other women in the study, the world of work has exposed them to the sex lives of other Mexican and Latina immigrant women. Listening to and joining informal conversations about sex at their workplaces was a frequent experience for some of the women. Most importantly, being part of such conversations about sexuality allowed the women to revisit and redefine their own sex lives. For a woman like Emilia, being exposed to the ideologies of young women at the office where she works represented both a change and a challenge in the way she perceived her own sexuality and sexual behavior. Emilia reported that her friends, who are mainly from Central America, were *"amigas liberadas"* who had exposed her to a more liberal ideology with regard to women's sexuality.

> I have had conversations with my friends about sex, you know, young women, who tell me, "I do this and that, and if he wants it fine, and if he doesn't, it's fine, too." And then when I think about it, I tell myself, "They are right. If men do this, why shouldn't I? If we are all the same, why am I going to stay behind? I have the same needs!"

Her attitude toward sex had changed, she said.

> Now, I tell my husband, "You know what? I want to do this," or "I do not feel
> comfortable when I do this." I am not saying we have a great communication,
> but now, sometimes, I reject him if I don't want to have sex. In other words,
> now I think more about myself.

Emilia feels that living in the United States makes it easier for a
woman to express and to own her sexuality. In addition to networking at
her workplace, Emilia also has received new information on sexuality and
women's rights through the Spanish-language media, talk shows in particular. Interestingly, within the context of work, Emilia was able to both
challenge and change some of her friends' sexual practices — casual sex, in
particular — while reflecting on the sexual morality she had learned from
her family.

> Sometimes we talk and they are very explicit, they are very open. What I do
> not like about them, for example, I do not like about a woman — perhaps
> because I have my mother's values — is that you should not "offer" sexually to
> one person or to another, even if they are your friends or coworkers. Or if you
> want sexual pleasure, go and have sex with someone just like that, or go and
> have a cup of coffee and then go to bed.

Like Emilia, Fernanda was exposed to information that led to some
changes in her sex life. She described the curiosity she felt after having
heard about the many sexual practices, such as oral sex, that were openly
and graphically discussed by her friends at the garment shop where they
work.

> I have not changed the way I think about it [sex], because my way of think-
> ing is different than theirs. But sometimes their comments made me have ideas
> and I feel like asking questions. I feel curiosity because of what they do sexu-
> ally! The change I am experiencing is that now I have many doubts about what
> really happens in a sexual relation.

Emilia showed some resistance to accepting her friends' practice of
casual sex, based on values mainly learned from her mother. Fernanda, on
the other hand, was held back by fear and embarrassment. She did tell her
sexual partner, a Mexican immigrant man, about her friends' conversations, but she felt embarrassed and afraid that he would judge her, which
kept her from exploring such practices as oral sex with him. When I asked
her if she had changed her sexual behavior with her partner after listening to these conversations about sex, she replied:

No. Like I said, I feel embarrassed. I can't get to that point with him and doing all that kind of things because then what is he going to think about me? [Laughs] "Where did you learn to do that?"

In their interactions at work, Emilia and Fernanda exhibit the influence of two mechanisms that have shaped women's experiences of sexuality: family control, via the maternal figure in Emilia's case, and a fear of sexism in Fernanda's. However, these women's experiences of sexuality are not static processes. Women may use networking to revisit and reconsider new possibilities to express and experience desire.

Some men reported having similar yet contrasting conversations about sex at the workplace, with the difference being that sex was always the central theme of jokes and mockery. In rationalizing why such joking took place, some of the men offered concrete examples of the content of their playful sexual conversations. Being playful about sex protected their sense of masculinity, and joking about it was safe and uncompromising. Even though none of my informants offered examples of how men sexually objectify women, like the men studied by Manuel Peña (1991), some used networking to reinforce their sense of manhood and expressions of hegemonic masculinity.

For example, Jacobo used the word *apantallar* (to show off, or to impress others) to explain why some of his coworkers talked about their sexual experiences, including describing new positions they had learned for the sex act or telling stories about their many sexual adventures. At times, however, Jacobo explained that some of his friends at work approached him to ask for serious advice on educational material about sex, such as magazines or videos. Similarly, Daniel explained that his coworkers used sexuality-related conversations as a way of engaging and teasing each other while trying to liven up their monotonous routine at work. Daniel said that making jokes about sex would eventually lead to recommendations with regard to their actual sexual behavior, such as condom use or avoiding casual sex, as in, "Look, watch out, take care of yourself. Do this or that so you don't regret what you're doing."

For some immigrant men, the concept of work goes beyond the walls of a factory or job site. While looking for work, immigrant day laborers who meet at employment centers often talk about sex. During one of my longest and most informative interviews, Joaquín offered a colorful example of this dynamic. He began by explaining how small groups of men might gather while waiting to be called and assigned to a potential employer at the center. They had met at the center and had gradually become friends. As they developed a closeness and trust, they began to share their personal lives. Sooner or later, they would be confiding their sexual experiences to one another. Joaquín explained how he initially gotten the men talking:

> I start by telling them "How do you do it [sex]?" "Well, why do I need to wear a condom? I know I have to wear it, but why?" "You can transmit that [AIDS] and that is the reason why you cannot have sex without a condom. So tell your son, your brother, and your cousin about it."

"That is the way I start having these conversations about it [sex], and I end up with a group of people around me," Joaquín said. He gradually became a *consejero*, giving advice about such sex-related topics as condom use, sexually transmitted diseases, homosexuality, loving relationships between women and men, premature and delayed ejaculation, impotence, drugs and sex, and aphrodisiacs. Joaquín and the men would also share their collective yearnings and nostalgia for the partners they had left behind in Mexico, especially during winter. Many of them missed having a sex partner in bed.

One of the reasons why Joaquín enjoyed talking about sex with the day laborers who became his acquaintances and friends was that the conversations helped him pass on the knowledge he had learned from other immigrants, who had taught Joaquín about sexual performance, intimacy, and heterosexual relationships. Joaquín went on to briefly describe his conversations with the group about *el retardador chino,* a Chinese spray one of his friends had bought and successfully used to lengthen his erection and delay ejaculation. His friend had claimed that he had felt like "a champion" and had learned that the quality of sex with a woman can be enhanced when the man refrains from ejaculating while making an erection last longer. The spray did not give Joaquín the same result when he tried it, but he said he did not hesitate to recommend it to his friends, for one reason: "Frankly, I don't know if the man feels something powerful, but you are doing it mainly so the woman can feel happy to be alive."

As one of the most fervent advocates of women's rights in this study, Joaquín felt it was important for men to know about the importance of women's need to be sexually satisfied during sex. Discussing female anatomy with his friends was the best way for him to convey these ideas. Joaquín related a typical conversation:

> "Do you know what the G-spot is all about?"
> "Yes, I have heard about it."

"Have you ever done it? [pointing at other men] What about you, have you done it? And what about you?"

"No, nobody has done it."

"Well, based on my personal experience, I have done it. And here in the United States, I did it with one of the ladies I dated."

Joaquín used his own sexual experiences in an attempt to help his friends and their partners improve their sexual health and their intimate lives. He did not want to brag to his friends about his knowledge of female sexuality but rather to share what he had learned through life experience. These conversations influenced his own sexual behavior, he said. "I have learned to speak more seriously about these things, about sexually transmitted diseases, gonorrhea, syphilis, and all that."

Lastly, Joaquín said that in his conversations with men he also used some of the information he learned from the Spanish-language media. Vinicio also reported this type of experience. He and his coworkers would use a controversial topic that had been presented on the popular TV talk show *Cristina* to start off a group conversation about sex during their lunch break. Vinicio said the topics might include "homosexuality, double marriages, extramarital relationships, people who live together in love triangles, and other topics considered as taboo, topics that are criticized by people, some I thought were disgusting." Vinicio said that his views of sexuality had not been changed by watching such shows and engaging in such group conversations, but others' had.[5]

Thus, for the women and men who engaged in sex-related conversations on the job, the exchange of information led to changes in their experience of sex at two levels. It changed their social perception of sex as they considered others' views and experiences of sexuality. And, simultaneously, it selectively incorporated these sexual redefinitions into their own lives. Women like Emilia and Fernanda, for example, based on their conversations with coworkers and friends, redefined and created new expressions of femininity that enhanced their sexual autonomy and curiosity as women. Jacobo's coworkers teased one another and laughed at the workplace in efforts to enhance their hypersexual expressions of masculine identity. And immigrant men like Joaquín actively promote alternative, non-hegemonic expressions of masculinity, as they try to convince other men about the importance of women's sexual satisfaction, the connection between emotional intimacy and sex, and men's self-care and sexual health.

These are not isolated cases. Hirsch found immigrant women in Atlanta who had sexualized conversations at work similar to the ones presented here (2003, 228). But dialogues about sex happen beyond the confines of the workplace. And dialogue between women does not always promote progressive or emancipatory ideologies. Moreover, like Joaquín, there are other men who advocate among their friends for egalitarian relationships between women and men.

Gender Crossroads: Sexist Women, Feminist Men

"Look, women are guilty of their problems with men!" exclaimed Soledad. She was condemning her friends who consistently sought her out for advice and orientation as they looked for solutions to their marital difficulties. Soledad talked about the many stories she has heard from women who complained about their husbands' infidelities.

I discovered that Soledad and some other women had internalized the sexism that promotes beliefs and certain behaviors that accentuate women's social inequality. I use the term *internalized sexism* to identify a dynamic wherein women participate in the social reproduction of sexism while simultaneously stigmatizing themselves.[6] At the core of this combined psychological and social process, women create new tools by which they can effectively control and negatively label other women. In some contexts, networking may help Mexican women share information and learn sexually liberating methods and insights. In others, these connections may aggravate their sexual inequality.

The following stories show how internalized sexism can be spread via networking. The stories told by Irasema, Irene, Oralia, and Macaria illustrate how these immigrant women were exposed to the internalized sexism of their confidantes. The experiences described by Yadira and Soledad reflect how some women in the study may promote gender inequality while offering sexual advice to their sisters, sisters-in-law, and friends.

Even though the sexual experiences shared by Irasema, Irene, and Oralia happened under different social circumstances, their stories share a common denominator: a confidante who reinforced an ideology that promoted the belief that married women are responsible for their husbands' sexual satisfaction, and that failing to comply with this principle is an excuse for a man to look for a lover. Irasema, who learned from her two neighbors that anal sex is a frequently practiced sexual behavior, described the specific recommendations of one of her neighbors who emphasized the importance of satisfying her husband's request for anal sex. Irasema explained that her friend cautioned about what would happen if she did not comply with her husband's request.

> I see that other couples do it and now I see it as something normal, and I feel more relaxed. And then she told me, "Be patient, talk to him and everything, relax and try to do it. Look, like this, this way or this other way. Because if you do not do it, he will look for it somewhere else."

To comply with her husband's sexual needs, and out of fear of being betrayed and later abandoned, Irasema had forced herself to endure the pain of anal sex. She repeatedly said, "Yes, and I said: no, no, no, I have to be able to, I have to be able to, but for me it's horrible!" I asked her, "After you go through all this, what motivated you to finally have anal sex with him?" She replied: "So he would not go out to the streets to look for it. It's like, if they have what they want at home, they don't look for it elsewhere."

After Irene learned of her husband's extramarital affair, she had a conversation with a close friend, who made her think that it was her inability to satisfy her husband's sexual needs that had provoked him to find a lover. "She told me that, with regard to sex, perhaps it was my responsibility for the change in my husband's sexuality. Perhaps I was guilty because I did not give him what he was asking for."

Later in the interview, we explored the negative effects of her friend's comment on her sex life. Irene struggled to defend herself from her friend's pronouncement on her inability to sexually satisfy her husband. I asked, "Did her making these comments affect you sexually?" With tears in her eyes, she answered:

> Yes. I say sometimes to myself that I am guilty and I have that inside my head, that I am guilty. But, on the other hand, I say that it is not possible, I have not failed! But I do not know how to have a different kind of sexual relationship other than what I know!

In the same vein, Oralia's story also expresses a woman's concern over keeping her husband sexually satisfied to protect herself from being betrayed or abandoned. Oralia talked about some of her conversations with other married women, about the importance of wearing lingerie and taking care of one's personal appearance to make sure a husband is sexually satisfied and to guarantee a happy marital relationship.

> For example, the other day, una señora came and told me that her husband had told her, "I would never leave you for another woman," and I said, "That's

great!" I asked her about what she did and she said that she always wears makeup even at home and that she is always all dressed up and that when her husband gets home, she always has a good attitude and a smile for him. So, then that's what I try to be, okay with him, and to look good.

Earlier, Oralia had told me that her husband had had an extramarital affair while they were still living in their small town in Jalisco. She believed that if she followed her friend's advice, she could keep that from happening again in the United States. Interestingly, one of Oralia's reasons for coming to Los Angeles was to put some geographical distance between her husband and his lover.

The last story in this section illustrates a woman's need for the moral support and advice of a friend after being sexually victimized. Macaria talked about the confusion and pain she experienced after her boyfriend sexually assaulted her in a violent way. She talked with one of her friends to find support for her decision to terminate the relationship. But afterward, she said, she still felt anxious and confused.

> I have a friend who tells me not to make a decision that quickly. She has had this type of experience but it does not compare to what I went through. She has told me, "Look, do not take it impulsively, do not make a decision like that. Time will take care of it."

Some of the women in the study promoted gender inequality when they offered advice or support to their sisters or sisters-in-law. Yadira's female relatives regularly sought her out to talk about their marital difficulties. She described the advice she gave her sister-in-law when the woman revealed that she and her husband had not had sex in three months:

> I think that by her avoiding contact with him, he will go somewhere else. Even worse, if she does not do it with him for two or three months, it's natural that [men] would look for it somewhere else! I think that you as a woman have to do a lot to make sure the man is relaxed at home so he does not go out to look for another woman, because it is the woman who sends her man into another woman's arms.

Yadira espoused the same principle as the one presented in Irasema, Irene, and Oralia's stories: the woman must satisfy her husband's sexual urges, and if she does not, she is responsible for his reaction. Soledad's conversations with her friends who were looking for her advice concerning sexual matters in their relationships echoes a similar pattern. By saying that the women were responsible for their problems with their men, Soledad was arguably also making the women responsible for their husbands' extramarital affairs.

Some of the men's stories, in which they challenge the sexism of other immigrant men, represent the other side of the coin.

"Why the fuck do you get married if you want to have the lifestyle of a single man?" Sebastián would ask his married friends who invited him to go out at night to drink and dance. Some of these men told Sebastián that their wives complained about their going out to dance at night by themselves, and he responded by talking to them about marital relationships, betrayal, and monogamy. He was proud that since migrating by himself in 1995, he had refrained from getting involved sexually or emotionally with another woman. Of the lifestyle he followed after his wife had finally arrived in the United States, he said:

> If I am going to go somewhere, I always take my wife with me. Why do I look for something else if I already have something that is mine? Besides that, what I described for you is not one case, there is more. I have met people who at times I feel like beating up. The truth is that men can be assholes. Women are right when they defend themselves. So . . . why do these men want a wife? To keep her locked up inside the house? Later on, she will be locked up inside the house, but with another man!

Some of Sebastián's friends resisted his arguments and explanations — and they in turn tried to convince him — but he said that his conversations with them neither affected him nor changed his views of sexuality or marital relationships. "I feel my moral principles are firm," he said, while expressing his concern about the communication problems and the emotional distancing in his friends' marital lives. Hirsch (2000) also identified contrasting expressions of masculine identities (men who seek extramarital affairs versus men who engage in monogamous and emotionally intimate relationships) in her research with immigrants living in Atlanta.

In a similar vein, Raúl analyzed the views and behaviors of the men he lived with after coming to Los Angeles, all of whom had migrated from extremely poor rural areas. "I had them under my microscope," he said. Even though Raúl was not as confrontational as Sebastián, he was similarly critical of the men's perceptions and practices of heterosexual relationships and sexuality. When I asked Raúl if he had had conversations with them about sexuality-related issues, he replied,

> Yes, sexual, about sexuality, quote unquote, because they had no education. They were people who were completely poor. I respected them because in

order for them to leave their country with that type of education and that type of ideology, that is something that requires a lot of courage. But they used to talk about beating up women, "Do not be an idiot, beat her up, get the fucking hell out of here so she can educate herself and so she does not do it again." That is typical, that is very typical.

Diego, a third man, from Mexico City, said that at work he had quietly listened as the men talked about their extramarital relationships.

I am telling you, there are people who talk 90 percent sex. Fantasy or reality? I do not know. But they talk about it, sex, and graphic matters about sex. And they do not talk much about their wives, but about their potential lovers, or imaginary lovers, or people they met at work. It is kind of embarrassing, but that is the way it is. But, for example, they say, "This woman takes this position that makes me crazy, this one kisses me in this way, this one does this, this one does that."

Where Sebastián was direct and highly involved with his friends, Raúl and Diego appeared to be more cautious and reserved. However, their critical attitude toward the other men's views and practices of sexuality and heterosexual relationships seem related to their middle-class, Mexico City background — and, in the cases of Sebastián and Raúl, their college education. This process may go hand in hand with other forms of social awareness. Hondagneu-Sotelo's urban and middle-class informants reported their keen awareness of the discrimination and racism immigrants are exposed to in the United States (1994, 182–83). Sebastián, Raúl, and Diego (more frequently than their rural counterparts) were also alert of these social inequalities. And as for those immigrants Hondagneu-Sotelo interviewed, class differences within these three men's immigrant communities also prevailed. In the case of Raúl and Diego, their stories suggest the emotional and social discomfort arising between men of different socioeconomic backgrounds who embrace contrasting masculine identities and sexual ideologies. These factors increased the distancing between them and some of their immigrant friends who had been raised in more disadvantaged locations. Like Hondagneu-Sotelo's better-educated informants (1994, 182), Raúl was critical of the poor pronunciation of the Spanish language that he heard from the illiterate and rural immigrant men he had met at work.[7]

Joaquín, a fourth man, from another urban area (Guadalajara), not only promoted gender-sensitive sex education at the center for day laborers, he, like Sebastián, actively tried to get his friends to reflect about the quality of their loving relationships. In one case, Joaquín attempted to offer support to his roommate, who had struggled with a drinking problem and violent behavior in his relationships with women. As he did with his day-laborer friends, Joaquín did his best to help his friend understand the importance of egalitarian relationships between women and men, and he followed different routes to accomplish this goal. As discussed in chapter 2, some men in this study described the difficult experiences of the women in their families in an effort to show their sensitivity with regard to the issue of virginity before marriage. Following the same principle, Joaquín attempted to manipulate his friend's feelings of love for his female relatives in order to develop his gender sensitivity. He told his friend, "Remember that our mothers are women as well." Gender sensitivity seems to be emotionally experienced (Chodorow 1995), and Joaquín tried to promote equality by stirring up his friend's gendered emotions and feelings.

Even though these men tried to promote equality, some of their own experiences revealed the complexities of gender relations and sexuality. Joaquín's life, for example, was a paradox. In spite of his efforts to promote gender equality with his friends, Joaquín said he would not use a condom if he ever went back to Mexico and his wife asked him to wear one for protection. He also said he had had many extramarital experiences before and after migrating. Other men revealed similar gendered traps in their networking narratives.

Fidel, who comes from a small town, talked about becoming the confidant of a long-time friend who felt anxious after finding out that his wife was not a virgin on the day they were married:

> I have a friend here in California, and when he got married, he tells me, "I want to talk with you, buddy." And he told me, as if he was a little boy, "She was not a virgin, she was not a virgin!" I believed him because she dated other men and she had physical contact with them. So, *otro tuvo que haber estrenado a la muchacha* [another man might have inaugurated this young woman]. He said, "Well, yes." And I told him, "Look, sexuality at times, in other words, women who are no longer [virgins], at times they are not because they do not bleed and that is because they fell off their bikes or they fell down, or something happened, do you understand me? Or they got hit and lost their virginity." Then I tell him, "So what happened?" And he says, "I had sex with her and it went well." "Forget about the rest of the stuff, asshole! *Pos ya te casaste, ya te chingaste* [You got married, you are fucked up], forget about everything, life begins right at this moment." And then he said, "You know what? You are right."

As we saw in chapter 2, Fidel was proud that his wife was a virgin when they married, and he gave that as the secret of their marital success. Even though marrying a virgin was not possible for all men, he attempted to ease his friend's disillusion and protect him from a potentially bitter marriage or from blaming and abusing his wife. At the same time, his language revealed some forms of gender inequality. First, the verb *estrenar* literally means "to wear for the first time" or "to inaugurate." So, *"Otro tuvo que haber estrenado a la muchacha"* suggests an objectified view of the sexualized body of his friend's wife. And second, *"Pos ya te casaste, ya te chingaste"* suggests the possibility of a man's learning too late that he had not married a virginal woman; marriage is indissoluble and irreversible and he has to resign himself to accept her "as is." Fidel seemed happy that his friend was able to overcome his disappointment and develop a permanent and satisfying marital relationship.

As illustrated by the majority of the women in this study, networking provided Mexican immigrant women with the resources to alternatively contest or reproduce their own gender inequality. On the one hand, networking provided them with an arena where they could discuss their sexual difficulties, marital problems, and reproductive health issues. In general, it served to expand their knowledge of women's sexuality. On the other hand, these interactions also might expose them further to sexist ideologies perpetuated by other Mexican or Latina women.

In the case of men, they talked about their conversations about sex within the context of groups of friends, couples' reunions, and one-on-one talks between a woman and a man. Because of the social prescriptions of masculinity, they seemed less likely to engage in one-on-one conversations about their private sex lives with other men. However, this was not the case for the few who developed close friendship or confidant relationships. Similarly, the men less frequently reported the ways in which they might have personally promoted gender inequality via networking with women or other men. Quite the contrary, some of them may have promoted gender equity, as they exposed the reportedly sexist attitudes of their immigrant friends. Regardless, networking recreates the social circumstances that Mexican women and men use in order to create various kinds of sexual discourse that may either challenge or promote gender inequality within their immigrant communities. Through these sexual discourses, they expose their own sex lives and heterosexual relationships to other women and men by, first, selectively transforming various aspects of their sex beliefs, behaviors, and relational practices, and second, by creating and reproducing new expressions of femininity and masculinity.

The experiences of sexuality and heterosexual relationships dynamically created by these women and men selectively embrace continuity and change between their country of origin and their new immigrant communities. Social networks served the following functions:

1. They were a meaningful source of information that had the potential to provide sexually liberating ideas to many of the women, and in the case of men, they provided a way to explore and develop non-hegemonic expressions of masculinity with regard to sexuality and heterosexual relationships.

2. They offered a source of information so that both women and men could become more "sexually literate" as a result of the continuous exchange of information about adult sex education.[8]

3. They may have influenced the actual sexual behavior of both the women and men, although it should be emphasized that my respondents were not passive but active social agents who scrutinized the information they received before either accepting or rejecting it.

Beyond the confines of mainstream society, the Mexicans in this study actively established many immigrant communities and cultures where talk about sex became part of their everyday life experiences. These narratives show the nuances and complexities of the lives of these women and men, and they challenge monolithic and stereotypical views of Latinos' and Latinas' sex lives. Their stories call for a revision of the increasingly popular concept of "sexual silence" promoted in Latino/a sexuality literature across disciplines, which argues that Latinos and Latinas experience difficulties in talking openly about sex-related issues (see, e.g., Díaz 1998; Marín and Gómez 1997; Carrillo 2002).

Gender shaped how the women and men participated in the creation of sexual networks and how they perceived the sexualized, Spanish-language media to which they were exposed. The women seemed to participate more actively in the process of assimilating and conversing about the contents of the Spanish-language television shows they watched. But the men also participated to some extent. Women and men both used social vehicles to look for solutions to their sexual difficulties and concerns as they educated each other with regard to sex. In the process, they alternatively enforced or challenged the gender inequalities linked to their sexual ideologies and actual behaviors, and they constructed social mechanisms and discourses that prompted new expressions of female and male sexual identities in their immigrant communities. These social mechanisms may either improve the quality of their own sex lives and those of future generations, or they may further reinforce the sexist ideologies and practices that were socially learned in Mexico. However, these processes are not always smooth and unidirectional, and they are shaped by additional social forces.

The next chapter looks at how the women sexually reinvent themselves as they experience erotic desire within additional social and economic contexts, including exposure to paid employment outside the home, as well as financial independence, urban anonymity, and laws protecting women. The men's perceptions of these redefined female sexual identities reveal the tensions and contradictions that range from a woman's potential sexual empowerment to a man's fear of losing his patriarchal entitlement. Looking at the wide array of gender subtleties that emerge between both extremes of female and male identities both confirms and complicates our view of Mexican sexualities.

CHAPTER 7

Sexual Bargains

Work, Money, and Power

"When I arrived here, I was working. I was completely in charge of the household expenses, rent, everything, and I supported my mother. So I think I had the right to enjoy some type of freedom, more sexual freedom, too. I no longer had to ask my mother for permission to go out with a man," said Eréndira, a thirty-two-year-old single woman who has lived in Los Angeles since she immigrated from her native Guadalajara eleven years ago.

Azalea is a forty-three-year-old woman who immigrated from Mexico City twelve years ago and is an apartment manager in a predominantly Latino immigrant neighborhood. Is she under her husband's thumb? "That ended a long time ago! I do not have to cry if he doesn't give me money, or if he doesn't give me enough to buy groceries. I don't even have to have sex with him. I do not depend on him. It [sex] is not an obligation anymore."

A third informant, Eugenio, a forty-three-year-old never-married man, described his experiences as a day laborer: "Some employers have offered money to have sexual relations with me. It is very difficult to get a job here, so some men do it, out of need or lack of education. They exchange sex for money."

For Eréndira and Azalea, working full-time outside the home, earning a salary, and attaining financial autonomy or responsibility became part of their sexual emancipation in the United States. In contrast, poor, working-class men like Eugenio and his fellow day laborers may be forced to engage in commercial sex out of necessity.

This chapter examines the impact of immigration and life in the United States on the sex lives of study participants while exploring how their heterosexual relationships are shaped by socioeconomic forces that promote or challenge an individual's sexual agency. I also build on the women's experiences by incorporating men's narratives about Mexicanas and sexuality, as a way to examine the nuances, contradictions, and tensions surrounding female sexuality and heterosexual relationships within migration and gender relations. Finally, this chapter includes men's sexual experiences within the context of migration.

Employment and Sex Life in the United States

"You came over here and you changed," Azalea's husband told her, claiming that her behavior in the bedroom had changed since they left Mexico City and she became an L.A. apartment manager. "He can be kind of machista, but I don't put up with it any more," said Azalea. "I can support myself, I can live without a man. So now I have sex only if I want to, not just because he wants to." The changes Azalea and her husband experienced are similar to those studied by Rae Lesser Blumberg (1991). After conducting research with women in many Third World countries, Blumberg developed a theory of gender stratification, whereby "the greater women's relative economic power, the greater their control over their own lives" (1991, 100). She goes on to say that:

a. The greater a woman's relative economic power, the greater the likelihood that her fertility pattern will reflect her own perceived utilities and preferences (rather than those of her mate, family, state and so forth).

b. The greater her relative economic power, the greater her control over a variety of other "life options," including marriage, divorce, sexuality, overall household authority, and various types of household decisions. (100–101)

Blumberg shows that many of the changes in a woman's life unfold as economic power redefines gender relations between men and women at the individual level or in marital relationships. She cites the work of Martha Roldán (1982, 1988) with a group of women from Mexico City to explain that as Mexican women contribute more to the household income, they get more control over decisions involving fertility. And that as Mexican women earn an income, they develop a sense of control over their own lives, which, in turn, enhances their self-esteem. Blumberg's theory also explains changes in the gender roles of women from rural

Mexico who are exposed to industrialization and paid employment opportunities. As a consequence of their salaried labor at a strawberry processing plant in Quiringüícharo, Michoacán, women took a more active part in decision making at home, including, but not limited to, deciding whether and when to marry and whether and when to have children (Mummert 1994, 207).

These changes among Mexican women, with regard to their decisions about sex and reproduction are one result of historical changes within Mexican society. As discussed in chapter 1, industrialization, urbanization, the employment of women, the growth of contraceptive use, and the AIDS epidemic, among others, have acted to reshape social norms on women's sexuality. Migration, settlement, and the powerful presence of Mexican communities in the United States are also part of this process of social and historical change. As Mexican women migrate to the United States and experience socioeconomic transformations, their sex lives are also transformed.

The analytical frameworks cited above provide us with important theoretical tools with which to examine the sexuality transformations of the Mexican immigrant women in this study. These women developed a sense of personal control and self-sufficiency as they improved their socioeconomic status, primarily due to the financial independence attained by working and earning money in the United States. Important changes in their sex lives and in their perceptions of sexuality unfolded as part of a process of power rebalancing in their relationships.

Unfortunately, these theoretical frameworks also have some limitations. While helpful in analyzing the redefinition of power in couple relationships, they need to be expanded to incorporate many important social factors that influence Mexican women's sexuality beyond the marital scenario. For immigrant women, employment, earning and controlling an income, and the redefinition of power within their relationships are linked to the social construction of female sexuality. Moreover, there are two additional social processes outside the marital context that control Mexican women's sexuality and are linked to these redefined power dynamics:

1. The ethic of "family respect" that controls a daughter's sex life may be challenged by a single immigrant woman with no partner as she develops financial independence and responsibilities within the family economy as part of her immigrant experience in the United States.

2. Earning an income and being exposed to the world of work may empower an immigrant mother by transforming her perception of

sexuality and, accordingly, helping her redefine the kind of sex education she wants to provide for her children in the United States.

In this section, I will analyze the stories of three women to illustrate how working full time outside the home becomes an instrumental component within a dynamic process of sexual emancipation in the United States. I also include men's respective views of female heterosexuality as these changes take place.

Women in Loving Relationships

Azalea was divorced at the age of twenty-five, after nine years of a high-conflict relationship with her husband. After her divorce, and while still living in Mexico City, she established a permanent cohabitation relationship with another man she calls "mi esposo" (my husband). Since the beginning of their relationship, he has been the family provider for both her and their son. Eventually, in 1985, they all migrated to the United States. During our interview, Azalea recalled with great pride and enthusiasm some of the positive transformations in the quality of her sexual encounters with him, as well as the changes she has experienced in her own sexuality since becoming financially autonomous in Los Angeles. "When I had just arrived to this country, he forced me to have sexual relations with him, but not any more!" I asked her what she would tell him if he tried to pressure her to have sex. She said:

> I tell him "No" because I support myself. If he supported me and he gave me all the things that I need, then perhaps one might have to do what they [men] tell you. But since here, all we women work, we support ourselves and we help our parents.

A woman's financial independence clearly alters the power dynamic in which her sexual encounters take place. A woman who is financially self-sufficient may feel less of an obligation to have sex with a partner as a way to reciprocate for his being the family provider. In Azalea's case, her collective gender consciousness ("all we women work") is a consequence of her attending sex-education presentations at a community-based agency.

Azalea's story meshes with the experiences of other Mexican immigrants who associate women's access to economic resources and financial independence with feelings of power within their heterosexual relationships (Harvey et al. 2002; Harvey, Beckman, and Bird 2003). It also echoes the lives of the *American Couples* that Blumstein and Schwartz (1983) analyzed, with regard to the equalizing effects of money, power, and work on the power balance of marital relationships.[1] During our interview, Azalea talked about the sense of self-worth and self-confidence she gets from her work as an apartment manager. She has become an authority figure who makes important decisions for the welfare of her community, and her partner sees the respect and acceptance she inspires — all of which may affect their sexual relationship.

The men in this study reacted in various ways to what women like Azalea have experienced in the United States. Some celebrated the fact that full-time paid employment and financial independence had improved the women's personal and family lives. Others expressed their resentment at losing their authority within the family. Eugenio, who felt the patriarchal status quo of immigrant families was threatened, explained why he thinks Mexican women change after migrating:

> Because of the economic situation over here, there are more possibilities for a person to grow. So what happens to a marriage that does not have a good foundation? It falls apart. It falls apart because there is supposed to be a guide in the family, and that is the husband, the father. When the woman realizes that she has possibilities to excel, she forgets that the family has a head and starts to rebel against her husband.

Daniel, whose teacher had exposed him to ideas about women's rights at an early age, had the opposite view. "While they are living in Mexico, women's worst fear is a husband leaving, and that is because they are financially dependent on him. They depend completely on their husbands, who say 'You don't work, I am the one who gives the orders.' So financial dependence makes them stay with their husbands. But over here the woman has more financial independence, and she has more freedom to abandon a husband." He added laughing: "And that is good! Because that forces us men to behave well. Otherwise, she may send you to hell!"

Like Eugenio and Daniel, other immigrant Mexicanos realized that paid employment offers immigrant women the possibility of becoming empowered in their relationships with men (Hirsch 1999; Harvey et al. 2002; Harvey, Beckman, and Bird 2003). With regard to sex, however, the men I interviewed did not make the link between women's employment and their sexual assertiveness. Neither did they see sexual activity as a woman's obligation within the marital relationship. Intercourse, some said, was *"un acto de amor"* (an act of love) on the woman's part, not a way of reciprocating for a husband's financial support. When I asked men if they thought that married women had an obligation to have sexual relations with their husbands, some men from urban areas firmly rejected the idea, sometimes passionately. "I have never, never, never thought that," said Emiliano. "In fact, I have always told my wife, 'The day that you don't want to, we won't.' What for a forced situation? I think that is even worse than buying sex with a prostitute." In highlighting the equal rights between women and men, Joaquín said, "It's not a woman's obligation, because a woman is neither a machine nor a sex object. She is a wife, she is a man's partner, and you don't do it unless both agree." Sebastián was critical when he said, "I remember reading in 'La Epístola,' which said that the woman had the obligation as a wife to please her husband. No, no! It is not only from wife to husband, but from husband to wife as well." Sebastián was referring to "La Epístola de Melchor Ocampo," a Mexican government document that spelled out the civil code of marital ethics and that judges used to read to couples during their marriage ceremony. "La Epístola" went into effect in 1859; the reading of the original text during civil marriage ceremonies is no longer practiced (see Tuñón Pablos 2000, 52).

Other men's views of sex as a marital obligation illustrate how socioeconomic factors shape social prescriptions of femininity and masculinity with regard to sex within marriage. Fidel, who celebrated his wife's virginity at marriage, explained why he believed that women who were married had the obligation to have sex with their husbands:

> If you are a married woman, and you don't want him to cheat on you, you have to satisfy your marriage. If not, you run the risk of losing it, or you run the risk of your husband abandoning you for another woman. The woman also has to use her head a little bit. "If I want to have my husband at home comfortable and happy, well, I also have to do something on my part."

Rural men interviewed in other studies have expressed similar views. Some of them describe marital sexual relations as a man's need and a wife's "undesired obligation" (Szasz 1998). Hirsch similarly observed that a woman may perceive vaginal sex (but not oral sex) as an *"obligación"* within marriage, which nevertheless has the purpose of satisfying a man's sexual needs and preventing him from engaging in extramarital affairs (2003, 216, 223).

In my study, Fidel, from a rural background, had learned a more rigid prescription that emphasized the woman's responsibility for the couple's appropriate sexual functioning and the husband's sexual behavior, but these gender arrangements were more flexible for other men. Mauricio, who came from Mexico City, offered a contrasting opinion:

I think that supporting women is an obligation. That's what I call an obligation. Having sexual relations is not an obligation. If she wants to, that is okay.
Before they live together, they are supposed to have a good relationship and
a good communication, so later on they do not feel like those women who feel
that sex is an obligation.

Between discourse and practice, subtle complexities may arise both for
rural men like Fidel and urban men like Mauricio. Fidel, for example,
recalled several episodes of sexual tension between him and his wife but
then praised their current sex life. He proudly explained that, unlike some
of his brothers and other men he had known, he has always been faithful
to his wife, a kind woman he loves and respects deeply. As for Mauricio,
though he is a financially responsible family man, he has had lovers outside his primary relationship; his rationale for doing this was his periodic
sexual dissatisfaction with a woman he was not sure he loved. Thus, men
may be exposed to more or less rigid social prescriptions of sexuality and
heterosexual relationships, depending upon their socioeconomic context
of origin. However, the feelings and emotional meanings of their actual
relationships with wives and girlfriends further shapes these gender-
related attitudes.

The very few men whose wives worked full time in the United States
did not report any changes in their wives' sexual behavior. However, some
men in this study expressed mixed feelings when their partners used intercourse as a vehicle to resolve conflicts or to obtain material goods within
their relationships.[2]

The Mother-Daughter Relationship

The mother-daughter relationship is the second dimension in which
employment and financial autonomy have led to the sexual emancipation
of Mexican women. When an unmarried woman earns an income and
takes charge of household expenses in the United States, she acquires
more financial and personal autonomy. If she lives with her mother in the
new country, she may question the ethic of family loyalty and respect regulating her right to make decisions about her body and her sexuality.

"It was fair for me to set myself free!" exclaimed Eréndira, thirty-two.
With tears in her eyes, she described some of the problems she had experienced with her mother, who disapproved of her dating. Eréndira was
twenty-one when she and her mother migrated together from Guadala-

jara. Earning an income and assuming total financial responsibility for their apartment expenses had transformed her. She had never had a boyfriend before, she said, and being in Los Angeles made her free to want one. As mentioned at the start of this chapter, becoming a legal adult had helped Eréndira claim the freedom to have her first date without her mother's permission. She said, "I asked for her permission to have a boyfriend here in Los Angeles, but she did not want me to. So I said, 'Well, now I am informing you that I will be dating this young man.'" Eréndira could have never imagined the resulting consequences, however:

> She wanted both of us to go back to Mexico. She took all of my belongings and moved out of the house. At some point, she asked me to go and live with my cousin. When we got to his house she hit me, but that was the last time she hit me. I defended myself, I did not let her hit me anymore. Then she got some of my paychecks that I had been saving and said that we would go back to Mexico. She called me a bad word. She said I was a . . . [weeping].

Eréndira did not agree to go back to Mexico, and when I asked her about the current status of her relationship with her mother and if they were still living together, she changed the subject. Later, Eréndira said that even though she has never had intercourse, she has gradually learned to give herself permission to reclaim her sexuality. For instance, she said that she had learned to enjoy what she called *"libertades sexuales"* (sexual freedoms) and *"caricias atrevidas"* (risky caresses) with the few men she has dated in the last ten years. Looking back at her personal ordeal, she said that she wished she had done so earlier in her life.

Eréndira's story is a sociological portrait of a power revolt across generations and beyond borders. The chaotic but equalizing power balance that emerged between mother and daughter is more than evident: Eréndira's personal control resulted from her improved economic status and the financial responsibilities she assumed, and these, in turn, set up a challenge to her mother's control over Eréndira's personal life. Her mother was aware of Eréndira's empowerment and resented its repercussion on family politics.

Similar stories have been presented in other research conducted in the United States and in Mexico. Vicki Ruiz (1993) studied second-generation Mexican American women who developed a feeling of independence and a desire to leave the family home after getting jobs and earning a salary. Similarly, Annelou Ypeij (1998) found that as young adult women in Zamora, Michoacán, started earning money at the local refrigeration companies, they were better able to negotiate with their parents. These young women developed a sense of personal freedom and self-confidence that altered their relationships with their mothers. For example, they started making decisions about fashion and wearing makeup without their parents' consent.

How do men perceive the changes experienced by single women like Eréndira? None of the men in the study felt that attaining full-time employment and earning a salary per se should influence the sex lives of single immigrant women. (As I will discuss later, they attributed these changes to additional factors.) A few men said that having money might help women to buy makeup and more fashionable clothing and look more sexually attractive in the United States. That made me think about women less fortunate than Eréndira, such as the poor, single women I had met in Houston in the late 1980s when I taught ESL classes as part of an amnesty program. Many of them were too busy looking for work or putting in long hours of underpaid employment while trying to learn English to even think about love or sex. For these immigrant women, survivors of extreme poverty in Mexico, sex was a luxurious pleasure to be postponed and redefined. A long struggle to meet the basic needs of food and shelter may supersede sexual needs for poor women. When I interviewed Gabriel, I thought about the similarities of the women he had met in Los Angeles to my students in Houston. Gabriel related: "I have met women who barely had the means to buy meat in Mexico. When they get here, they eat and eat until they get sick. I have also seen women finally dye their hair, who over there didn't have the money to do it." I also thought about the unknown love lives of domestic workers who live in personal isolation. As live-in maids, they lack regular social interaction with family and friends, and work an average of sixty-four hours per week (Hondagneu-Sotelo 2001, 2002). Their sexual stories are yet to be heard.

Women, Their Children, and Sex Education

The next story illustrates the third dimension in changes in sexual beliefs and practices as immigrant mothers' perceptions of sexuality are transformed and they gain a feeling of empowerment to talk with their children about sex. In telling her story, Rosalía exclaimed, "Here, you become *despierta* [alert, with your eyes wide open]. *¡Se siente más valor!* [You feel more courage!]" Embracing financial responsibility by working full time to support her six children had helped Rosalía become emotionally stronger and more alert in her perception of sexuality. Becoming *"despierta"* had also translated into feeling less intimidated, shy, or weak when talking to her children about sex. Describing what would have happened if she had had to educate her children in Mexico, she said:

> I would have felt more intimidated; I would have not felt the courage to talk with them about it. Here, you feel más valor [more courage], but you do not know if it is because of the change of country or because you have to protect yourself from everything. Over there, I felt shyer, weaker, like I was not going to be able to talk with them about sex. But here, it was very different.

When I asked where that courageous feeling of "más valor" came from, she said, "From me striving to make it every day, to make sure I can support them and help them get ahead."

Some of the women in the study explained that as mothers they sometimes felt devalued in terms of their authority within the family and that they lacked the power to provide sex education to their own children, particularly their sons. This was especially true of the women who had lived in small towns, where gender inequality and particular forms of patriarchy are emphasized. Romelia is from Jalisco, and when I asked her if she would give the same information to her son as she gave her two daughters, she replied:

> Well, it is the same education but only one thing. The way I see it, it is important for the father to be in charge of the boy because he is masculine. He is a man, right? I think he [the son] would take more seriously what the father has to say because he is the father.

Unlike Romelia, Rosalía was born and raised in Mexico City, where some forms of regional patriarchy are not as strong. Her words reflected her redefinition of the power relations in her family, one result of her earning a salary, working in a full-time job, and being completely financially responsible for her children. By taking advantage of the malleability of the Spanish language, I will use Rosalía's words to argue that women like her may acquire "más valor" in two ways: "more courage" and "more value." They may experience "more courage" at the personal level, including being able to talk with their children about sex, one result of their gainful employment, financial autonomy, and complete responsibility for their children and their household. And they may experience "more value" at the micro-social level, that is, by acquiring a higher value as an authority figure within the family context. They are competent to support their children and are automatically more respected as authority figures when talking to their children about sex, even in the case of a mother talking to a son.

What did the men have to say about women like Rosalía? About half of the men in the study argued that mothers change their attitudes and behaviors with regard to the sex education they want to offer to their children after migrating as they become more comfortable with sexual topics. Some men described these changes as desirable or acceptable, and some did not, but none attributed the changes to the women's exposure to paid employment outside the home. For example, they argued that the mothers' enhanced comfort in talking about sexuality was the result of their exposure to instructional material and information within community institutions such as schools and nonprofit or community-based agencies. As discussed earlier, networking and the Spanish-language media also provided some mothers with alternative views and strategies to teach their children with regard to sexuality. In their observations of the mothers they had met, some men identified feelings that paralleled those of Rosalía:

> *Diego:* Now they take more risks, now they are more objective. "Do not get that girl pregnant. Do not be a fool, complete college, concentrate on your studies." So now they talk more frankly. "I don't like that girl you are dating. She looks like this, she looks like that." And I am not saying that over there they are not that way, it's the same. But here I have seen them more determined to hold the power with regard to their children. [And I think] it is very good. There is no mystery, there is no excuse, like "Nobody told me about it, nobody advised me, I did not have anybody." The mother is being straightforward with her son.

> *Ernesto:* Women have changed a lot. Before, the woman was not that free to talk about it [sex]. Now that I attend those meetings and I have been involved with the community, I have seen it. We graduated from a political organizing and community affairs course and that's the place where I have seen women talk about sex with more freedom.

Urban men like Diego and Ernesto celebrated women's potential to develop more progressive sexual values and behaviors in the United States. Other urban men reported that modernity in Mexico had prompted similar changes in mothers' views of sex education, regardless of whether or not they migrated to the United States. And one group of rural men thought that return migration has gradually created less restrictive views of sex in their communities of origin. In contrast, Fidel said, "With people from small towns you don't see those changes; there's still some taboo where we come from." He compared his small town to some of the families of Mexican origin living in his neighborhood in Los Angeles:

> For people who have two or more generations over here, sex is more liberal. They do not get surprised if they marry and she is not a virgin. Why? Because

sexuality over here is more open. Over here there is not that much of a taboo as in Mexico.

Men like Mauricio and Sebastián were critical of child abuse prevention laws in the United States because, they said, they make immigrant parents afraid to discipline their children. And lastly, some men argued that many Mexican mothers in general are not well prepared to offer sex education to their children, either in Mexico or in the United States. Said Marcos: "When they talk about it, they screw it all up. A vast majority are people who haven't even opened a book, or who have never attended a sexuality workshop."

In sum, employment, income, control over income, and financial responsibility had a clear impact on the sex lives and/or perceptions of sexuality for immigrant women like Azalea, Eréndira, and Rosalía. From their shared standpoint as women, employment interacted with the politics of power and sex in many areas within the family and domestic sphere. But there is also the sexual reality for those women who do not earn any income in the United States.

The Commodification of the Sex Act

> *Fingiendo*
> *y mirando al techo*
> *sin decir nada y sin ganas*
> *y por obligación.*

> Pretending
> and looking at the ceiling
> without saying anything and without desire
> and as an obligation.
>
> Irasema's description of her sexual encounters
> with the man she was forced to marry

"I swear to God that I have never been able to have an orgasm. Never, never, neither with him or with anybody else, never!" said Victoria, thirty-four, who was tearfully describing her sex life with her husband. "*¡Lo hago por compromiso, sólo por compromiso!* [I do it because it's an obligation, only because it's an obligation!]" For women like Victoria, the sex act is part of a *compromiso moral*. It possesses an exchange value, as it is part of the erotic negotiation that takes place within marriage. Victoria echoes Fidel's statements, presented earlier, and those of some of the men and women studied by Szasz (1997) and Hirsch (2003).

As discussed in chapter 2, virginity is viewed in some contexts as a form of *capital femenino,* a commodity possessing social exchange value. And a woman who preserves her virginity as part of her feminine capital does not necessarily perceive it as a burden to do so. But virginity is not the only aspect of a Mexican woman's sexuality that has an exchange value. Within the context of marriage and family life, sexual intercourse may be subjected to a process of commodification. Beyond premarital virginity, there are other forms of sexual commodification that exist in the lives of some of the women in the study. The stories told by Victoria and Candelaria exemplify this dynamic.

Victoria, who comes from a small town in Jalisco, was kidnapped and violently raped at age sixteen. This excruciating episode had many painful consequences for her later married life, including not being orgasmic and experiencing a lack of sexual desire. This was exacerbated by the fact that Victoria never received professional help to overcome the rape experience. She felt ashamed and guilty and unable to talk with her husband about the experience or about her feelings during their sexual encounters. The combined effect of all these difficult circumstances, along with Victoria's sense of obligation to have sex with her husband as a way of reciprocating for his being the family provider, made their sexual encounters stressful. Describing her feelings during sex, Victoria said:

> To tell you the truth, it is very rare that I feel like being with him, even though he is a very attractive man. He is very good looking, but I tell my sister, "If you knew the agony I go through!" At times I feel so enraged that I even cry when I am with him.

Victoria's story illustrates the dangerous domino effect on a woman when gender inequality comes from more than one direction. In the eighteen years since the rape, Victoria's sex life has been more like warfare, due to the psychologically damaging consequences of her having been sexually objectified and abused. This has produced agony, rage, and feelings of helplessness with respect to the sexual encounters in her marriage. Moreover, Victoria is a full-time housewife and is therefore not financially independent. The lack of sexual self-ownership and a well-learned sense of her moral obligation, or *compromiso moral,* toward her financially responsible husband have made Victoria's sexualized body the only negotiable asset available to her in her marital relationship. She described having sex with her husband this way:

> It is like a compromiso because he wants to be all over me. He treats me very well, but when he is happy, right? Then, sometimes, he teases me at night and

I ask myself, "If he gives me everything, how come I do not give him any-thing?" And that is when I do [sexual] things with him.

Like many women who live in patriarchal societies, in Mexico, in par-ticular, Victoria has learned a definition of marriage as a moral contract: whether she enjoys sex or not, she has the *compromiso* to satisfy her part-ner's sexual needs, to procreate future generations, and to be a good housekeeper. Her husband, in turn, has the *compromiso* to be a good provider for his wife and their children. Victoria was born and raised in a small town, but her experience matches that of many women born and raised in Mexico City, where more permissive sexual codes may exist in some social spaces but where gender inequalities make change difficult.[3]

Victoria's testimony may be examined within a variety of different the-oretical frameworks. Radical feminist theorists who expose the objecti-fying nature of such marital arrangements argue that these patriarchal pre-scriptions make the woman as a *sex object,* subjugated by the sexual needs of men, while he is a *sex subject* (De Beauvoir 1949; Dworkin 1987). Mexi-can academics have long observed these dynamics. Raúl Béjar Navarro, for example, refers to María Elvira Bermúdez's analyses, conducted in 1955: "The Mexican woman from rural areas, when she gets married, is bought by the man, who then will 'make use' of her, trying as much as possible to take advantage of her" (Béjar Navarro 1986, 69). Padilla Pimentel (1972) has also identified this sexualized gender pattern by stating that for Mexican women, marriage legalizes a form of "domestic prostitution."

A second theoretical possibility is offered by the British scholars Jean Duncombe and Dennis Marsden (1996), who examine "heterosex" to confirm how intercourse may lack "authenticity" for women who ex-perience sex within a social context of emphatic gender inequality. Duncombe and Marsden might agree with Hochschild's notion of "emo-tion work" to explain that women like Victoria do "sex work" as they resignedly submit to intercourse in order to satisfy their basic financial and survival needs.

Beyond the North American and European paradigms of female sex-uality, women's learned labor of sex and love is also built on what Mexican women have inherited throughout centuries of institutionalized sexual obligation. Mexican women have been exposed to religious man-dates that state that *"negar el débito al marido"* (to deny one's obligation to one's husband) and *"despreciar al marido"* (to reject one's husband) are moral prohibitions. These religious mandates were reproduced in many of the confession guides used by Catholic priests in colonial Mexican society (Lavrin 1989; C. Castañeda 1989). During the same historical period, rapists were able to pay *la dote* (financial compensation to their victims) as a form of punishment for raping a woman (Tostado Gutiérrez 1991; C. Castañeda 1989).

These paradigms and the historical evidence serve to explain the sexual experiences women like Victoria live inside their bedrooms. Interestingly enough, some women, like Victoria, may have more sophisticated marriages. Victoria revealed, for example, the contrasting aspects of her relationship with her husband. She explained that at times (beyond the context of her bedroom) she had embraced a rebellious attitude in her everyday life disagreements with her husband. She said she would express herself to him in this manner: "Aha! I am going to take advantage that I am over here [in the United States]," and then she and her husband would joke about how women were treated in both countries. Victoria explained: "Men are more machistas over there."

> People give women a lot of rights over here. The government gives you a lot; you have more rights over here. Now, we have the same rights in both places, but over there [in Mexico] people are more shy, and your life is more constrained. Well, I think we have the same rights everywhere. Now, whether they give them to you or not, that's a different matter!

Victoria's story reflects two important processes. First, gender relations are situational and contextual as they create fluid and multiple feminine and masculine identities, even for the same individual. These identities may emerge as a consequence of the multidimensional nature of some women's marital relationships. For women like Victoria, life in the United States has allowed her to selectively challenge the gender politics that affect some aspects of her family life, if not the ones in her bedroom. Within sexual contexts and situations, however, she says she is highly vulnerable. She feels completely disempowered in the bedroom, and thus a radical feminist perspective or an alternative view of intercourse as "emotion work" is an appropriate theoretical choice. However, she seems to feel relatively empowered in non-erotic circumstances, as is the case for the legal protections she finds in the United States. Thus, a perspective of gender as situational and relational may offer a more complete view for those looking at the possibilities for change (Connell 1995; Kimmel 2000). The puzzle is to be able to continue exploring the social factors that may prompt full-time immigrant housewives like Victoria to transfer their agency from the kitchen, living room, or patio into the bedroom.

After our interview, I asked Victoria if she had thought about engaging in such an exercise. She said she would not know how to do it. As was the case for Azalea, if Victoria were to attain paid employment and some control over her income, that might offer a potential avenue for her personal empowerment. At some point, I learned that her lack of citizenship status, the language barrier, and her limited education and occupational skills had delayed this possibility for Victoria.

Victoria's story coincides with the images men have of women after migration, such as the fact that women feel more legally protected in the United States compared to their communities of origin. This process also reflects the multidimensional and contextualized nature of masculine identities. Some men, for instance, reported that they were critical of sexist beliefs and practices, but these attitudes varied with the context. For example, Alfredo accused his friends of being machistas for expecting their girlfriends to be virgins, but he confessed that he had physically abused his wife more than once. Fidel, who accepted the idea that intercourse and sexual availability were a woman's marital duty, reported that he had never had an extramarital affair, in spite of the sexual tensions between him and his wife. In contrast, Mauricio was critical of the view of intercourse as a marital obligation, but he had had extramarital affairs, rationalizing them because of his wife's occasional inability to sexually please him.

Similar masculinity complexities have been observed by Hirsch (1999), one of whose informants reported that intercourse should always be mutual and consensual, but said he might slap his wife as a way to deal with marital conflict. Hurtado similarly noted that men present in the lives of women of Mexican origin living in the United States may promote egalitarian relationships yet engage in sexist behavior (2003, 214). These contrasting patterns illustrate, to some extent, Gutmann's concept of "contradictory male identities" (1996, 120), as well as his reflections on Gramsci's concept of *contradictory consciousness* in Mexican society: "Working-class men and women share both a consciousness inherited from the past — and from the experts — that is largely and uncritically accepted, and another, implicit consciousness that unites individuals with others in the practical transformation of the world" (15).

Victoria and the men in my study illustrate some of the complexities that emerge as women and men try to negotiate the commodified path of sex within marital relationships. For some women, however, engaging in the sex act or being sexually available acquires an exchange value beyond the context of marriage. Candelaria, a thirty-six-year-old housewife from Jalisco, endured years of sexual coercion and abuse because of her family's economic circumstances. She was first raped, as a teenager, by a fifty-year-old neighbor while living in Mexico, and then continuously harassed by him. He raped her on multiple occasions and eventually got her pregnant. Paradoxically, Candelaria identified the man as "a family friend," because he had often helped her father with money and loans. Because of this financial help, Candelaria had let him touch her body or had sex with him because of her sense of responsibility for her family's well-being. After he got her pregnant, Candelaria had an abortion and left for the United States as a way of escaping the many years of abuse. To this day, she has never told her father, mother, any of her family members, or her husband — a Mexican immigrant she met in Los Angeles — about the abuse. Like Victoria, she has not received any professional help.

Candelaria's story reveals the complex dynamics involving gender, sexuality, and class within economically underprivileged contexts. At the same time, the women's stories also invite us to explore some avenues for change. Incidences of the kidnapping and rape of women have been also identified by Mummert (1994) and Hirsch (2003) for the geographical regions where women like Victoria and Candelaria were educated. In some areas this pattern started to decrease in the 1960s, and such incidents were less frequent by 1970. Fiona Wilson (1990) writes that education and employment opportunities for women, as well as the gender consciousness developed by the mothers of these victims, were crucial factors responsible for the socially progressive changes in these regions.[4]

Finally, these stories illustrate the women's sex lives and their personal lives within the context of their immigration experiences. Victoria, for instance, said her family had been understanding and supportive when they learned she had been raped. They filed a police report, and the offender (a married man) was sent to prison for eight years. After he was released, however, Victoria left for Los Angeles to live with her relatives out of fear of retaliation. She had become pregnant as a consequence of the rape; her child stayed in Mexico and has been raised by her parents.

Consistent with Argüelles and Rivero's (1993) findings, for women like Victoria and Candelaria, immigration to the United States represent a strategy for coping with or escaping the combined effects of gender, class, and sexual abuse. The two women's stories echo the many untold sexual stories of immigrant women whose sex lives are closely associated with their disadvantaged economic status, including but not limited to those Mexican immigrant women who have been forced into sexual slavery to pay off smuggling fees to their *coyotes* (border smugglers) (Skerry and

Rockwell 1998) and women exposed to sexual trafficking involving *coyotes* and cantina owners in the United States (Ayala, Carrier, and Magaña 1996).[5]

How did the men in this study perceive these gender prescriptions imposed upon and internalized by women like Victoria? As indicated earlier, most of them perceived intercourse as an act of love, and they objected to the view that it is a woman's marital obligation. Besides this generalized view of women's sexuality, the men revealed their own experiences of sex after migrating. Their narratives expand and complicate our understanding of men's sexuality within the context of migration and socioeconomic marginality.

What Else Was He Supposed to Do?

> *When two people are in bed, there is always something economic that complements or impels sex.*
>
> G. Derrick Hodge,
> *Colonization of the Cuban Body* (2001)

As men became part of the world of day labor in Los Angeles, their sex lives took unexpected turns, some of which involved gay men. Eugenio, a forty-three-year-old construction worker and painter, explained, "Some of my employers called me many times to offer me a job late at night." Uncomfortably, he elaborated: "They tell me it's easy, that I am going to enjoy it, and that they are going to pay me a lot for not doing much. They are offering me money to have sexual relations. And they are young, older, of all ages. Seventy percent are white men."

Though the offers were financially attractive, Eugenio said he never accepted them. When other prospective employers made similar offers to him on the streets, he reported feeling offended and losing his enthusiasm for the potential job. He said he was not like the immigrant men he saw who accepted money in exchange for sex with men in parks and public restrooms. He would rather be homeless than be a sex worker, he said proudly, though he had faced financial hardship after migrating and had even slept on the streets of Los Angeles at various times. But Eugenio said he would rather be hungry than exchange sex with a man for money, housing, or a meal—practices he said he observed among some of the immigrant men he met while living in extreme poverty.

Alfredo, also a day laborer, reported receiving similar proposals while trying to survive during a short stay in Northern California. He described looking for work at a place in San Francisco's Outer Mission District known as El Cachadero (from "to catch," meaning to get a job), which was often visited by affluent gay men. He recalled what happened after he was hired by a neatly dressed man who drove a sparkling Corvette.

> We arrived at his home and he asked me to mow the lawn. So, I asked, "What else do you want me to do?" "Clean the windows." I agreed. So everything was fine. But when I was cleaning the windows, he was inside his house already wearing this bikini. So, I said to myself, if this guy is gay, he is giving me that kind of a signal. . . . This guy wants something else. Later on, he told me that he wanted me to fix something in the bathroom . . . I tell him, "I have to fix this and that," and the guy is right there, standing in front of me wearing this bikini. "Isn't it hot? Why don't you make yourself more comfortable?" he said. And I replied, "You know what? I am going to feel more comfortable if you pay me and I am going to leave right away because this place requires a lot of work, and I don't even know if you are going to pay me to begin with." He said, "How much do you charge?" "$350," I replied. Then, he said, "Yes, I pay you. Do you want to drink a soda?" Then I told him, "I know what you want from me." "No," he says, "but look, you need to understand" [he pleaded]. So I said, "No, not with me."

Like Eugenio, Alfredo claimed he had never accepted these attractive offers, even in times of scarcity. "This issue is not only about white gay men," he said animatedly. "Did you know that some women hire immigrant men, take them home to work, and then when you get there, they tell you that they want to have sex with you?" Had that also been his experience, I asked. He said:

> No, but I have met some wealthy white women who pick up young men. You realize it because the men do not have anything, nothing from nothing. Then the man's attire changes a lot. A man changes right away when he gets money. At first you wonder where he is getting the money from. You think he might be selling drugs. Later on, the young man tells you about his relationship with the woman.

Marcos, Nicolás, and Ernesto also told stories involving work, money, sex, and white employers. They had heard of or witnessed immigrant men practicing commercial sex out of a financial need. "That is very common," said Ernesto. "That is why I did not like to look for work by standing at the corner, never. I was not going to stand there. Someone could kidnap me and nobody would ever hear from me again. I know you find a lot of racist people over here who may hurt you."

Ernesto once shared an apartment with ten immigrant men from

Mexico, Guatemala, and El Salvador, and they talked about their job-hunting experiences. "One of my roommates was picked up by this homosexual man," he said. "He told me that when he arrived at the house and started to clean, the other man put this pornographic movie in the VCR and started to touch him. And he used to tell me that this man paid him very well." I asked Ernesto if he knew if his friend engaged in that type of activity with his employer voluntarily. "He accepted out of need, he was financially needy," he said. "He had to send a check to Guatemala, so what else was he supposed to do?"

In sum, for women like Azalea, Eréndira, and Rosalía working outside the home, earning a salary, and enjoying control over their income provided them with many sources of personal power. Personal empowerment might also transform their sex lives and the perceptions of their own sexuality within their marital and family relationships, including their interactions with their mothers. For some of the men, paid employment did not have the same impact. Thus, the sexual experiences of women like Victoria or Candelaria were commodified, either with her own husband (in the case of Victoria) or with a neighbor (in Candelaria's case), for some poor, immigrant men the sexual experience was also commodified, but within a larger socioeconomic context. The lives of the *jornaleros* who survive on day-to-day jobs have been depicted in David Riker's moving film *La Ciudad* (1998). As illustrated by Eugenio, Alfredo, and Ernesto, some endure not only sexual harassment and coercion but they may also be tempted into sexualized encounters for money. Other immigrants, not necessarily *jornaleros,* also may engage in commercial sex when they are unemployed or financially needy, as was illustrated by Bronfman and López Moreno in their research with immigrants living in Northern California (1996, 60).

Class, ethnicity, language barriers, socioeconomic segregation, citizenship status, occupational incorporation (as discussed in chapter 5), and the objectification of Latino men within white, gay communities as "exotic, dark, and passionate" (Díaz 1998, 125) combine to make day laborers vulnerable to being sexually exploited. Eugenio and Alfredo had enough basic English skills to understand and reject such propositions, but that is not the case for other men in similar situations. This is of special concern when one considers that between 20,000 and 22,000 laborers are looking for work in Los Angeles County every day (Valenzuela 2002).[6] In addition, while white, gay men may represent the expression of a subordinated masculinity vis-à-vis white, middle-class, heterosexual men (Connell 1995), the presence of disadvantaged immigrant men complicates this picture. As they interacted with the poor Mexicanos in this study, the gay men who hired them became the protagonists of a hegemonic masculinity because of their different class, ethnicity/race, citizenship, and language. Within this dynamic of power and control, the working-class men in these stories are at the bottom of the social structure, yet they feel a certain pressure to fulfill social prescriptions of masculinity: they are expected to be good providers for their families back in Mexico, who depend on their remittances, and this is especially the case for those who have left wives and children behind (LeVine 1993, 83).

The testimony of these men offers evidence in support of Rosemary Hennessy's study of the political economy of sexuality in late capitalism in *Profit and Pleasure* (2000). The white, middle-class, gay men who make sexual objects of the immigrant men get cheap labor while also satisfying their erotic needs, curiosities, or desires within a context of perverse racial and class inequality. Within this structure of exploitation, capitalism gives birth to new expressions of both sexuality and commodification, as a gay employer and a day laborer have their erotic and survival needs respectively satisfied. In that sense, such interactions resemble the negotiations of white men from developed nations who visit Cuba for sexual tourism. Some Cuban *pingueros* (young male sex workers) who engage in commercial sex with foreign men do so only to earn the U.S. dollars indispensable for personal and family survival (Hodge 2001). Thus, the poor men of color who interact with white, middle-class, gay men, either in Havana or in Los Angeles, are vulnerable to new capitalist market relations that globalize and commodify their bodies. But such race and class relations go beyond the seeking out of sex by "white gay men": poor, dark men migrating to Mexico City from rural areas of Mexico are exposed to a very similar dynamic. Gutmann looked at Patricio Villalva's research on the experience of hundreds of *prostitutos* — adolescent, indigenous men who do not identify themselves as homosexual or bisexual, and who are sometimes married and have children — who are hired by often lighter-skinned men from Mexico City who take advantage of these poor men's vulnerability when they arrive in the big city (Gutmann 1996, 127–28).

Interestingly, some of my informants were aware of some of the privileges enjoyed by white gay men. As I explored his experiences in San Francisco, I asked Alfredo, who said he visited gay bars out of curiosity, if he had ever felt sexually attracted to men, or if gay men made him "nervous."

No, no. Although then I saw these tall "buddies" in San Francisco, you know, men with blue eyes, very good-looking, holding hands with another man and I go, "Let me borrow your body! Let me borrow your face! So you can see

what I can do with them!" [Laughs] These men are big and strong, very handsome. What a waste, man!

White skin, a tall, well-built body, and blue eyes are traits of male
beauty for many living in the United States and Latin America, and
Alfredo is no exception. He said he did not consider himself very good-
looking — he was short and dark — and thus he would benefit from having a more desirable body and face, as he talked about the many women
who then would be interested in him. This Western ideal of beauty
becomes a form of capital within heterosexual relationships, but within
same-sex relationships it leads to abuse and loss.

In making fun of gay men, Alfredo used expressions like *"¡Ay papacito!"*
and effeminate mannerisms. Even though Alfredo had assertively resisted
being seduced into commercial sex with a gay employer, in our discussions, that did not seem to convey enough of his disdain for them. His
homophobic remarks could have been an additional way for him to deal
with what he had experienced; homosexuality is what made his employer
vulnerable, after all. Alfredo's envy of a Western ideal of male beauty
might have reinforced his indirect form of resistance. This way of confronting oppression resonates with Messner's synthesis of research by
Peña (1991), Collinson (1988), and Majors (1995) on "how subordinated
and marginalized groups of men tend to embody and publicly display
styles of masculinity that at least symbolically resist the various forms of
oppression that they face within hierarchies of intermale dominance"
(Messner 2000, 77).

Gender, class, race/ethnicity, and sexuality get more complicated as
they intersect. For instance, the stories of poor immigrant men who
become sexually involved with white or other middle-class women via
paid employment also reveal situations that go beyond risk and exploitation. The wealthy white women that Alfredo's friends were involved with
may provide them with more than a one-time or even periodic income.
They may help them attain permanent residence in the United States. This
is similar to the case of the men Sebastián had met in a bar in Los Angeles
(chapter 5), and to the testimony that Hondagneu-Sotelo elicited, about
immigrant men who "abandoned" their wives and children in Mexico and
married U.S. citizens in order to legalize their migratory status (1994,
109), as well as the stories told to Durand by undocumented immigrants
from Ameca, Jalisco, who similarly married U.S. citizens in order to
receive legal documents (Durand 1998).

In sum, the power of money and the objectification of sexual intercourse is part of the sex lives of some immigrant women within the context of both marital and family life. Women's experiences of sexual objectification within a socioeconomic context reveal social mechanisms of gender inequality as well as some avenues for change. As we zoom the lens out to capture a larger picture of society, we discover that the experiences of economically disadvantaged men make this image more complex. Many of the day laborers who migrated for economic reasons could not have realized that they would become sexual objects for some sex consumers in the United States. For them, the labor relationship would become a sexual transaction under conditions of inequality. As they come to understand this, some men may exercise sexual agency by rejecting such offers of sex for work and by protecting themselves from harassment and coercive sex work (i.e., rape). Others may feel they have no choice but to comply, as they continue negotiating the world of paid under-employment. The latter may also feel that they have no alternative but to engage in commercial sex (voluntary or by force), as both a survival mechanism and as a way to send monthly remittances to their families in Mexico or Central America.

In short, under extreme conditions of inequality, both immigrant women and men face painful alternatives. They play out their few choices via their sexualized bodies. Beyond these scant possibilities, in what other ways did migrating to the United States make a difference in the sex lives of the men in this study?

Las Fronteras del Amor

"I had a girlfriend over here after I came," said Alejandro, "and she wanted to marry me, but I did not want to because of the relationship I had with my wife, who was living in Mexico City back then." Shortly after he migrated, Alejandro would flirt and have phone sex with a South American woman. Their conversations soon led to an extramarital relationship, which they maintained for a period of two years in Los Angeles. He revealed the story to his wife after she had joined him in the United States. "Uy! She got really angry!" he said. Since then, he said, "I have been faithful to her. My eyes are for her only." Alejandro said his current marital life is sexually satisfying. I asked him if his sex life changed after migrating, and he replied, "Here in the United States or in Mexico City, it's the same." Men from small towns were more likely to be influenced in their sexual behavior after they migrated, he said, but Mexico City and

Los Angeles are both cosmopolitan and volatile places. Other than an affair that had offered him a new sexual experience, he explained, the immigration experience had not affected his sex life.

Joaquín, Mauricio, Alfonso, and Alfredo also established sexual and romantic relationships in Los Angeles after leaving cohabitation or marital relationships involving children and relative family stability in Mexico. "What hurts the most about coming to the United States is the fact that I left my wife back there," said Joaquín nostalgically. He explained that his satisfying marital and sexual life had deteriorated since he left Guadalajara. He does not know if he is still legally married to his wife, and he has had sporadic sexual and romantic relationships with single and married women from Mexico and Central America since migrating. His lack of engagement in commercial sex is the most dramatic change Joaquín has experienced in the United States. He said he used to have sex with commercial workers in Mexico as a married man, but not here. He explained why: "I barely go out, and I don't have much money." However, his casual romantic relationships had helped him improve his sexual repertoire and they provided him with stories to share in his conversations about sex within his group of *jornalero* friends. In spite of all the things he had learned about women and sex, Joaquín explained, however, casual sex lacks the affectionate closeness he used to experience with his wife.

Mauricio also regretted having to leave a cohabitation relationship and a daughter back in Mexico City. Unlike Joaquín, his sex life with his partner had been stressful because of differences in their sexual temperaments — his was more intense that hers. However, they had enjoyed a relatively harmonious relationship. Mauricio is the man who, although he did not identify himself as homosexual, had reported engaging in oral sex with more than twenty men after migrating. Like Joaquín, he reported sexual and romantic involvements with different women he had met in casual encounters. Mauricio said he had embraced a more free and stimulating sex life since migrating, and he described a number of the new sexual experiences he had explored in Los Angeles, including "un trio sexual" with two sisters from Mexico City. At some point, Mauricio had established a cohabitation relationship with one of his female sexual partners. They currently live together and have a daughter. Since then, he said, he has had casual sex with other women only when marital conflict or sexual frustration with his live-in partner arises.

"I love her very much, I respect her a lot, but the fact that I respect her does not mean that I am not going to have amigas, right?" This was Alfonso, recalling his sexual experiences in Los Angeles during the seven or eight months that his wife was still in Mexico making plans to join him in the United States. Alfonso had a clear count of the casual sex partners he had had in the meantime: two Latinas, two Americanas, and a Russian woman. Even though he had engaged in sex with casual friends and sex workers in Mexico, in the United States he had experimented and learned new sexual practices with non-Latina women, whom he described as "less scrupulous." After his wife joined him in Los Angeles, they experienced conflict and she eventually went back to Mexico. Alfonso had married a North American woman in order to legalize his status, but he later divorced her. After being separated for a year, his wife came back from Mexico and they reunited again. They have been together since. He still has extramarital sex with his "amigas" every two or three months. He feels guilty about those experiences, which his wife does not know about. He says he does it out of curiosity, or, like Mauricio, when he is faced with marital conflicts. He described his marital relationship as "very stable," and one that he would never want to lose.

Alfredo left a cohabitation relationship of more than ten years, involving two children, behind in Mexico. He said he missed his "wife" sexually but not emotionally since migrating. While living alone in Los Angeles, he has hired sex workers on three occasions. He also established an initially platonic relationship with a married Mexican woman. When he experienced economic hardship, the woman and her husband offered to let him stay with them. Alfredo's long-distance relationship with his partner in Mexico deteriorated at the same time that his friend was experiencing marital problems with her husband. From uncomfortably sleeping on the couch, Alfredo ended up having more and more frequent sex with her in the marital bed during her husband's absences. This relationship lasted for a year without her husband's knowledge. However, it ended after Alfredo unexpectedly received a call from a *coyote* who asked him to pay $1,400 so he could pick up his wife. Alfredo's wife had come to Los Angeles illegally without telling him and was waiting for him at a secret place. Alfredo, his wife, and two children established a separate household in Los Angeles. After their reunion, he has become sexually and romantically involved with other women while living in a hurtful relationship with his partner. "I have never cheated on my wife!" he said. "Cheating is when you hide the truth, that is betrayal. I have never lied to her; she knows about my sexual relationships with other women."

Alejandro, Joaquín, Mauricio, Alfonso, and Alfredo all reported that they had enhanced their repertoire of sexual behaviors after being involved in relationships outside their cohabitation or marital arrangements. They are not alone in these sexual adventures. The overwhelming majority of the men I interviewed shared stories of relatives, friends, and acquaintances who had left a wife or formal relationship behind and had established either a temporary romance or a permanent household with another woman in the United States. Felipe best articulated what many of these men said:

> I am going to talk with you, for example, about the men who come while being married. So when they come, they change, they change sexually. Now, you find the person, for example, who is not looking for sex, you know, those who come to work and save, and well, they are waiting to have sex but after they go back. But others, and I know many who live here in Los Angeles, most of them come, they are married. They have a job over here, but they tell their wives that they don't make much, that they are paying rent and send them very little, in some cases. But in other cases, they send them nothing, they forget about their wives over there. And some of them abandon them, and they find another woman over here and they forget about the woman over there. And I am telling you because that has been happening with men in my family, my cousins.

The differences among immigrants that Felipe noted illustrates the pattern Hondagneu-Sotelo identified with regard to immigrant husbands' "ability to withhold from their wives information on the exact amount on their earnings" (1992, 402). Felipe criticized his cousins for being unfaithful to their wives back home, a situation that was painfully familiar to some of the men. For instance, Vinicio severely condemned migrant men who engage in these kinds of relationships. He recalled his own father's journey to the United States decades ago. "I am the son of a man who did it," he said resentfully, "and believe me, it's very difficult to be part of a family that goes through that." While not trying to excuse himself, Joaquín said that about half of his married immigrant friends had experimented with romance and sex with another women since migrating.

Most of the women I interviewed shared similar anecdotes about the paramours of married Mexicanos in the United States. Some were indignant about the men's involvement with "la otra" (the other one), which was how some of them characterized the other woman. Some recognized, however, that some of the women involved in extramarital affairs with Mexican men were Latina immigrants themselves. In that regard, research has shown that, compared to other Latinas (documented and U.S. citizens) or white women living in California, "undocumented Latinas were more likely to be 'living together' rather than formally married" to their male partners (L. R. Chávez et al. 1997, 101–2). Why is that?

First, undocumented women are more legally vulnerable when compared to the other groups Chávez et al. studied, and they may establish cohabitation relationships out of financial need. The story of Jimena exemplifies this dynamic. Jimena explained that while living in Mexico she would have never imagined that some day she would live with a man without being married. "I was here by myself and had no place to go," she said, as she described a series of arguments with her Latina roommate in Los Angeles. Like some of the immigrant women in Hondagneu-Sotelo's study, Jimena's networking experiences with her Latina friend were initially positive but later became negative (see Hondagneu-Sotelo 1994, 138). Jimena felt she had had no choice but to move in with the man she had been dating, the father of her six-year-old son and with whom, at the time of her interview, she was living in a cohabitation relationship. Fermín's recollections of the stories of immigrant women he knew were similar to Jimena's story:

> You find a lot of women who are looking for men, but they are looking for someone to help them, right? Therefore, it's easier for men to find a woman over here, because you find many who are needy. They are not looking for a man necessarily because of love but for someone who can help them. But then, they get involved with them. So what I think is that all those men who come over here will always find someone, even if they are married, because it's very difficult for women.

Second, parental control over a woman's personal life diminishes after migration. The woman's parents are far away, and moral monitoring of their daughter's sexual behavior is less frequently enforced. For example, even though Idalia felt "fracasada" after losing her virginity in Los Angeles, she explained why she had taken the risk of having premarital sex after migrating:

> In Mexico, I did not do it because of respect for my parents. I said, if I do it, they are going to do something to me, they are going to beat me up or something else would happen. And since over here I found myself being alone, that is why I accepted to do it with him. Now that I think about it, I did it because I was alone, without my father or my mother.

Idalia also said that the lack of parental control had helped her decide later on to cohabit with a man in Los Angeles. Her words confirm the reflections of Chávez et al. on Hagan's (1994) research, which found that distance from parents and older family members — usually living in Mexico — may weaken social control over young couples (Chávez et al.

1997, 102). In addition, Mexicana farm workers living in north-central California's agricultural regions similarly experienced more freedom of movement in the United States, which challenged the constraints that tended to control their sex lives in Mexico (Castañeda and Zavella 2003, 137).

Third, many study participants indicated that while some single immigrant men struggle to support themselves in the United States and send remittances home to their families, others have access to more money than before they migrated. This gives some of them the means to go out, dance, drink, and establish casual relationships with other Latina women. For some, a casual encounter may become a permanent relationship. As Gabriel explained:

> Single men? Well, the economic aspect influences. Because, let's say, for example, a single man who lives in Mexico with the lifestyle we have there, if you work you don't even have money to go and visit prostitutes or a place where he can go and meet someone and have sex. However, over here, if he comes and he has a job, even if he does not make much, at least once a week he can visit those places. So, it's the economic system, yes.

Fourth, immigrants' heterosexual romantic and sexual experiences would be impossible without the increased migration of women to the United States (Marcelli and Cornelius 2001) and the emergence of immigrant communities during recent decades (Hondagneu-Sotelo 1992). In these locations, a lively immigrant nightlife has emerged in nightclubs like the ones visited by Sebastián, Mauricio, Alfredo, Alfonso, Joaquín, and Daniel. Castañeda and Zavella (2003) have also documented this phenomenon in their research on Mexican farm worker communities in California.

Some of the women I interviewed talked about their past or current cohabitation relationships with Mexican or Latin American men they had met in Los Angeles. Interestingly, they did not reveal or seem to know if the men had left a wife or a partner back home. Salomé left Jalisco for California in her attempt to look for the husband who had left her behind with children three years earlier and was shocked to learn about his involvement with another woman. Salomé was the woman who expressed discomfort when the topic of masturbation came up as a potential avenue to experience fantasies with Jorge Rivero; she reported she had been faithful to her husband in his absence. However, that is not the case for other women. Even though little is known about the sex lives of the women who "stay behind," some may develop sexual relationships with other men in their husband's absence. Such was the case of La Tasqueña, the woman from Colonia Santo Domingo who had men living with her (one at a time) while her husband was in Detroit (Gutmann 1996, 132).

A contrasting image was articulated by those men who reported a dramatic change in their sex life after migrating to the United States: they said they had become more reserved and disciplined in their sexual attitudes and behaviors. Sebastián, who was critical of his married friends who went out to dance and have sex with women, explained that he and his wife were not naive before he migrated: "We knew that we were taking a chance. If she needed someone, she was going to look for him, and if I needed someone, I might have done the same as well." He said that, unlike many of the immigrant men, he truly loved his wife and did not take any chances, and that he had never become involved with anyone, sexually or romantically. Then he exclaimed, "I was looking for a relationship with a North American person, not to have sex but to learn *inglés!*" He said that a hectic schedule involving a full-time job and attending night school left him exhausted and deprived him of a social life. He had been reunited with his wife and children about five years later, not long before I interviewed him. He described both his pre- and post-migration marital and sexual life as satisfying and peaceful.

Marcos, Eugenio, and Fermín, who would redefine their attitudes about sex from within their respective Catholic congregations in Los Angeles, had developed more moderate sex lives as a consequence of migrating as single men. HIV/AIDS and the possibility of becoming infected with sexually transmitted diseases mediated any possible sexual interactions for all of them, as well as alcohol and drug use, in the case of Eugenio and Fermín.

Diego explained that, "out of nostalgia," he developed an increased interest in his Protestant church during the two or three years right after he had migrated as a single man. In the beginning, he was very cautious sexually. Diego is the man who married a young woman in Las Vegas and whose marital relationship ended in a divorce after he had an extramarital affair he deeply regrets. He now lives in a cohabitation relationship with a woman.

Vinicio became more disciplined in his sexual behavior after joining Alcoholics Anonymous in Los Angeles. He had engaged in casual sex with women after migrating as a single man. At some point, however, he went back to his small town and married a woman with whom he later established a permanent life in the United States. He reported a sexually and emotionally satisfying life with her. From another small town, Daniel explained why he missed dating in Los Angeles: "My love life has changed because I have become more fearful over here. I don't take the risk of going out with just anyone." He explained that people usually know one another in smaller places, something that is foreign for those living in Los Angeles. He has never married, and like Sebastián and Joaquín, he said he works a lot, goes out only occasionally, and calls his personal life "boring." Raúl noted that while his sex life had not changed, like many Latino men he had "hit a huge ice cube" when he migrated. He said he misses the social warmth, emotional connection, and more expressive social life he used to enjoy in Mexico City. A light-skinned, college-educated, middle-class man, Raúl said he did not fit in with the Mexicans he had met in the United States, or with the North Americans. "I did not fit in as a *chilango* — a man from Mexico City," he said. Interestingly, his intended migration was a catalyst for his first sexual encounter, with a girlfriend he loved deeply: "I told her that I wanted to have sex with her, that I was going to feel very sad leaving Mexico without being with her. It was like blackmail, so I told her that I wanted to have sex with her before leaving for the United States. I told her, I may not see you again." He has rarely been involved in casual sexual relationships in the United States. Raúl is the man who married his girlfriend in Los Angeles after she became pregnant.

The men did not describe their sex lives as necessarily having deteriorated after migrating, even those men who had been exposed to harsher personal experiences in Los Angeles. For instance, Eugenio, who has been homeless and sexually harassed by employers, said that those experiences had taught him to become sexually more cautious and alert, but that they had not affected sexual life in any respect, and particularly not in his beliefs and practices.

Those men who reported that their sex lives had improved after migrating said it had nothing to do with migration per se. Fidel attributed the improvement in his marital relationship to the closeness and sexual exploration that had helped him and his wife develop a trusting relationship. Fidel and his wife were newlyweds when they migrated. The same was true of Gabriel, who migrated right after getting married. He described his life after migrating as sexually very active. Fidel and Gabriel had been born and raised in small towns, and neither had experienced premarital sex, out of "respeto a la mujer." They were thinking about establishing a permanent relationship with their respective girlfriends, and both said they had always been faithful to their wives.

Emiliano was a unique case. When his friends and neighbors advised him to migrate to the United States, when he was very young, he said: "What the hell am I going to do on the other side? No, I'm not interested." He didn't realize then that at some point an extramarital affair would force him to head north. Though he had intended to migrate to Canada, he had stopped to visit his two brothers in California and wound up staying. Tearfully, he explained that he had migrated as a way to cope with an extramarital affair that had destroyed his marriage in Mexico City. He had decided to put some distance between himself and his wife, who had asked for a divorce after she learned about the affair. His sex life changed dramatically after coming to the United States. Emiliano, who was deeply affected by the experiences of his immigrant friends who were infected or died of AIDS, was further influenced by the painful consequences of his extramarital relationship. "Now I take care of myself, I am completely monogamous," he said. At some point, he had reconciled with his wife and they were reunited in Los Angeles. He said his marital life isn't perfect, but he has not been involved in casual sex since he migrated.

Lastly, Felipe, Ernesto, Nicolás, and Jacobo said their respective sex lives had not changed significantly since migrating to and living in Los Angeles.

Regardless of the wide variety of their sexual fates after migrating, the vast majority of these men described North American society as a place dominated by "el libertinaje" — a lack of moral restraint. Like other immigrants, many celebrated the economic opportunities the United States has to offer, but they perceived the morality of U.S. mainstream society as fragile and at times inferior when compared to Mexico (see Espiritu 2001). They argued that a more relaxed sexual morality was prompted by a number of different factors, including (1) multicultural diversity, (2) both a mother and a father having paid employment outside their home and thus children not being educated properly, (3) the excess of legal rights given to children, adolescents, and gays and lesbians, (4) high divorce rates, (5) the commercialization of sex, including pornography, and (6) the information bombardment of the media and modern technology, including the Internet. As they reflected on this topic, many men reported that "el libertinaje" could affect both women's and men's sex lives, but the men claimed that women's sex lives changed more dramatically after migrating compared to men's.

Patriarchies at Stake: Men's Views of Mexicanas and Sexuality in the United States

"Through the process of settlement, relatively speaking, women gain and men lose in family politics" (Hondagneu-Sotelo 1994, 147). For immigrants, patriarchy is transformed as part of the immigration and settlement process, becoming less rigid but not disappearing. As a group, the participants in this study said their sex lives had followed a similar pattern. The women, more frequently than the men, reported sexual gains as part of their migration and settlement journeys. Patriarchy was challenged in the process, but it did not necessarily vanish. Some of these gains included the following:

1. Paid employment and control over income helped women to redefine their power relationships with marital partners and/or paternal figures who controlled their sexual autonomy, as illustrated in the first section of this chapter.

2. Women were more likely to report positive outcomes in their sex lives as a consequence of woman-to-woman networking.

3. None of the women in this study reported engagement in commercial sex.[7]

4. None of the women in this study (unlike the men) reported engaging in high-risk sexual activities involving drugs, alcohol, or gang activity and none of them experienced homelessness.

5. Weakened family control, one result of geographical distance, allowed some of the women in this study to explore their sex lives with an enhanced sense of freedom — even though migration did not necessarily challenge the moral double standards.[8]

As these and other changes took place, men became more than keen observers of the sex lives of the women living in their immigrant communities.

"*Aquí la mujer es más aventada* (Here, the woman takes more risks)," said Marcos as he explained how Mexican women change after migrating. Why? "Because society allows it, because this country allows it, because we are in a country where morality matters are foreign. In other words, that famous so-called 'equality.' So, if the man is messing around with a prostitute, a woman feels that she has the same right. She feels she can fool around with a man in the same way." Marcos's opinion was echoed by many of the observations of the men in this study concerning the sexual behaviors and attitudes of immigrant women. As they responded to my questions about Mexican women's sexual behavior, they reported their personal observations of women's sexual experiences based on what they themselves had lived or witnessed within their immigrant communities. Consistently, all of the men articulated views of female sexuality within the context of heterosexual relationships. Some went beyond the erotic and reported their views of other relational issues such as domestic violence.

In our interview, Marcos emphasized that he was critical of both extreme submissiveness as well as aggressiveness in women. He then expressed his admiration for women who became success stories in the United States. He explained why he believed immigrant women took more sexual risks in the United States: "Because nobody knows them, and anonymity gives you courage, right? 'Who am I over here? [women say]. Just another stupid person in the crowd.' Then . . . 'Hey, let's go and have fun!' And over there, it is not that way." Of additional factors shaping the sex lives of Mexican women, he said:

> The big city gives you the power to be able to say, "Over there, I visit all these places," right? "Of course! Over there, I go to Chippendale's, I go to Tropicana!" And then, in the pueblo, [women say] "And you don't know what Chippendale's is all about? Do you know what the Tropicana is?" If you don't, you are ignorant. And women get so excited when the guy is dancing to them wearing that little underwear. They stick a buck into these men's underwear and they want to get some change back too, right? [Laughs]

Marcos's observations of how women developing social power in their rural communities of origin because of the sexual knowledge they acquire in the United States reflects the complex array of meanings and contradictions concerning female sexuality that exists in some rural areas of Jalisco. The views of rural women concerning this process of empowerment, and how it occurs, are yet to be explored.

Daniel also mentioned the concept of anonymity within a large geographical area weakening morality:

> Over here, you find more libertinaje and they can go wherever they want to go, to nightclubs. And since the city is kind of big, they have the opportunity to say, "Ay! Let's go to this place. They don't know me, anyway." And I don't know, they have a greater opportunity to go up and down, they are free, so they develop those ideas and all that. Their parents are far away.

Men like Marcos and Daniel, raised in rural areas, seemed to especially emphasize the social control of women's sexual behavior. After I listened to both of them, I thought of Eudoro Ibarra, one of Hondagneu-Sotelo's (1994) informants, who admitted that his extramarital affairs in the United States were facilitated by a sense of anonymity, and of Esperanza, one of the farm workers in Castañeda and Zavella's study (2003, 140), who reflected on how access to motels and cars in the United States — where "no one will notice" — could facilitate sexual encounters. A similarly feeling of anonymity offered Hirsch's (1999) female immigrants in Atlanta the freedom to wear comfortable clothes instead of dressing up in order to comply with their small town's social dress code. They had "the realization that *aquí nadie te conoce* (here no one knows you)," which becomes a part a migrant's sense of enhanced freedom and diminished social control of behavior (Hirsch 2003, 194–95). Thus, unlike in small towns, where *el chisme* (gossip) becomes a form of social control and moral surveillance (Amuchástegui 2001), the sexual freedom of many immigrants is enhanced after they move to and settle in large urban contexts.

A sense of anonymity — a part of everyday life in urban Mexico — was not present in the narratives of men from Mexico City or Guadalajara. In contrast, some urban men identified the family as a source of female control, as they offered their individual perspectives and emotions. For example, Diego exclaimed, "I love it! I like it when women express what they feel! And if she wants to describe it with her hands, let her say it!" He used the word *atrevidas* (risktakers) to elaborate on what he has observed among Mexican immigrant women he has met in Los Angeles, "The woman gives herself more permission over here. She is far from the family house, or from whatever, and she is here in this big party . . . she gives herself more permission to do things and to be inventive." As I listened to Diego, I remembered my interview with Idalia, who said that her sexual experimentation had been only possible because her parents were not close enough to have any control over her decision to experiment with premarital sex and, later on, to establish a cohabitation relationship.

Diego had more to say about women and sexuality. For him, geographical distance from the place of origin made another difference in women's lives:

> I have seen and heard women talking among themselves, the way I used to hear men talk. "Did you see the big butt that man has?" Or, "He did this to me, or he did that." And I'm like, "What?" Or, "We had a quickie!" "Really?" And they describe the whole thing! They appear much more alert and interested with regard to sexual matters. Their parents are far away.

In contrast to rural men like Marcos and Daniel, urban men like Diego seem to embrace an expression of masculine identity that promotes both gender equality and a more tolerant attitude toward women embracing sexually assertive expressions of feminine identities, expressions of femininity that may create social discomfort in rural social contexts.

Besides anonymity, isolation, weakened family control, and geographical distance, men reported that an additional dynamic was responsible not only for the changes in women's sex lives, but also for their loving relationships with men: networking with other immigrant women. Women and networking was the topic that provoked the most intense emotional reactions in the men. Eugenio, for example, began by exclaiming, "They become more rebellious, they create their groups." He saw a gender conspiracy that would unfold between women as they tried to cope with the tensions of a sexual and loving relationship:

> Some married women who do not have a good marital experience, or those who are abused by their husbands, cheat on them. Then, they like start feeling guilty, and they start having an accomplice, and so the other accomplice does not feel that she is alone in this situation. It's like they convince other married people so they do the same with their husbands, and a vicious circle is created.

Other men expressed similar views as they spoke on behalf of friends who had paid a high price for their loving relationships with immigrant women. This complaint was consistent for the men, regardless of their places of origin. Joaquín, from Guadalajara, shared what he had observed within his sisters' circle of immigrant friends.

> They always find those close friends, those friends who say, "I would cut my veins to help you, you are my friend." And then they start talking about their husbands, "How is your relationship with your husband? How are things with him?" I have heard it, and I have heard my sister talking to people who visit her, her neighbors, and I stay there to listen to them. So, it is based on that. "Money is first, you can dress and do whatever you want, you can do this and that with your husband." "My husband? No way. I would leave him if he does this or that. I can send him to hell if I want." So, people start waking up.

Joaquín used as an example the story of a close immigrant friend and his relationship with his wife. "My friend's wife came from her small town and she was exquisitely in good shape. You know, she was a woman who behaved according to the values and customs of small towns. But over here she changed in a matter of months! So I asked him the other day, 'Where is she?' 'She left me for another man.' So, look! What a dramatic change!" Daniel, who is also from a small town, recalled a similar story:

> I used to live with a friend of mine, and he brought his wife from over there, so he went there and became married and when they got here she seemed to be shy, she would not even raise her hand to say something, so whatever he

said, she would say that it was okay. And then she started to hang out with her neighbors here. He never treated her bad. But then, suddenly, she started to change with him, she started to . . . many say that *"se le sube el norte"*: the North went to her head. She started to be aggressive with him and, definitely, her life with him changed. In the end, they had to get divorced.

Hirsch's (1999) Atlanta informants also identified the United States as a place where women might become too independent, self-sufficient, and empowered. They used the expression, *"En el Norte la mujer manda"* (In the North, the woman gives the orders) to explain how U.S. law protects women. In my study, Alfredo angrily described how his friend's wife used the law in Los Angeles:

> A friend of mine used to control his wife like this [makes a fist with his hand]. So, his wife gets here, and everything was fine until she met women who told her, "Look, over here the government defends you. If your husband beats you, or if he is abusive, you can sue him." He ended up in jail just because he slapped her twice on the face! She called 911 and he went to prison. They gave him a restraining order, he broke it, and he again slapped her on the face twice. This time, he went to prison for four months and had to pay $7,000 to an attorney to get out.

Men perceive networking as a way for women to learn alternative ways of experiencing sex, but the women also to learn about legal and institutional support systems that can rescue them from abusive forms of power and control within a marriage. Some of the men expressed their exasperation at both the networks within their community and at the system that they said disrupted marital harmony and created moral decadence for migrant couples living in immigrant barrios.

> *Joaquín:* The libertinaje begins by all the laws that we have over here, and I have seen it in many couples who come from over there. Laws are guilty of it, the same laws. I don't know, all the support they get: "If your husband does not do this, leave him and we support you." "Did he do this to you? He showed you a bad gesture? Sue him!" "Did he do this or that to you?" They would even give them welfare support for the child who was born here. They get this kind of support they even get support from all these churches. "You are not going to starve. Your husband? Leave him! Or if he leaves you? We are going to take part of his check."
>
> *Diego:* Here, the woman has a lot of protection and some women use it to intimidate men. If the man in the past used to yell at her and threatened to hit her, now all that is decreasing, especially over here. Here, every woman knows that she can send a man to prison if he hits her,

or if their child sees it. Men are afraid of the consequences of going beyond these limits with their women.

It's striking that Joaquín, Diego, and other urban men who passionately promoted gender equality in many sexuality-related areas of women's lives were fearful and concerned as they talked about the reasons why Mexicanas change in the United States. While some of these urban men may promote ideals about a woman's right to sexual pleasure and autonomy, tensions emerge for these men when they expose their views of women within the context of heterosexual relationships. As I invited the men to discuss issues about women's sexual behaviors in the United States, they spoke about what they had observed within their own communities and among their circles of friends.

Here, Women Show Their Claws

Sebastián repeated the warning he had heard used among immigrant men who might be thinking about bringing their women from Mexico to the United States: *"¡Ni te traigas a tu esposa porque aquí las mujeres sacan las uñas!"* (Do not even bring your wife, because here women show their claws!) In the men's conversations, U.S. laws that protect women were a recurrent theme. Said Sebastián:

> *Se vuelven unas cabronas* [They become bitches]. Later on, they put their foot on top of you. They won't even wash the dishes; they make you do it. And since the government here defends the woman a lot, it is that way over here, unfortunately. Thank God, my wife is not that type of woman.

Ernesto, who is from Guadalajara, put it this way:

> *Se pasan de la raya* [They go over the line]. Here, the woman sees that there is more freedom for her and at times they abuse that freedom. I agree the woman has to be at the same level as us, but many abuse it and dominate the man when they see that over here. It's like they are like a horse that has been under control and then is set free. Some even abuse men, and hit them.

Sebastián and Ernesto were not the only men who claimed that Mexican women took their revenge in the United States for the injustices they might have lived before migrating:

> *Alfonso:* Women change much more than men. Over here, they are less oppressed, there is less sexual inequality, so women have more sup-

port. *Libertad* [freedom] becomes *libertinaje* [lack of moral restraint], and they abuse it.

Raúl: After they migrate, *se emborrachan de libertad* [they get drunk with freedom]. For us Hispanics, a Latina is even more dangerous than an Anglo-Saxon woman. The Anglo woman knows that laws are there to be when there is a real reason to use them. But the Latina woman comes from repression, so even when the reason is not a big one, they take it [the law] to extreme consequences. And that is when the man begins to experience that in this country you really have to respect women — though I don't see that as something negative.

Other men from Mexico City echoed the perception of Mexicanas as more threatening than white women. Said Emiliano:

You can't even ask the woman to keep the house clean. They always say "Ha! Over here, we are equal or nothing!" I have seen it a lot in my work, I visit a lot of homes, I visit different homes every day. I have become aware of how people live over here, and the truth is that it is scary, it makes me feel fear because they are that way, sexually speaking, but also in the cultural aspect.

I asked Emiliano if he believed that there was less moral restraint in the United States. He said no, that it was more true of Latinos. "I visit Anglo-Saxons and I have seen that the woman has a better moral behavior. I had a different concept of the American woman, I thought she was more liberal, but now I see that it is not that way." Emiliano explained that North American women were more faithful to their partners and more conservative than Mexican women. I asked him if he believed that Mexican women were more *libertinas* than white women, and he replied, "Yes, yes, Latina women, much much more!" I deliberately used the term *libertina*, which is a common expression used in Mexican society to identify a woman who exhibits immoral or indecent behavior. Its masculine equivalent — *libertino* — is rarely used to characterize men who display similar conduct. Emiliano explained the reasons behind the differences between Latina and white women:

Because they [Latina women] get here and they find out about freedom and the truth is that they [Latina women] have a lot of protection. And many take it like overprotection because . . . Let's say, for example, you and I are talking here today, and if in a given moment you say, "Hey! You tried to abuse me," by the time they do all the investigations and all that, I am screwed. Then, in that regard, I think they are overprotected. So I think it's okay they protect them when their husbands beat them up, that is okay. But the Latina woman does not see it from that point of view.

I interviewed Emiliano in the living room of his apartment. During our interview, only the two of us were there. After I left, I thought about how my own gender and ethnicity had transformed me from a researcher into a potential menace. This is fascinating because, in general, many Mexican women and men might perceive me as being vulnerable, by the fact of being a relatively young, never-married woman alone with a married adult man in his house. Migration, however, had inverted this image. I still wonder about what Emiliano's reaction would have been had I been a white woman.

The perceptions that men like Raúl and Emiliano develop in the United States have some parallels to research conducted by Yen Le Espiritu (2001). Espiritu found that Filipina mothers perceive Filipina girls as morally superior to white girls as they educate their daughters with regard to sex. By doing so, Espiritu concludes, mothers cope with the racism they themselves have experienced in the United States. Similarly, I would argue that men like Raúl and Emiliano may perceive white women as morally superior and "safer" than Mexicanas as a way of dealing with the gender relation instabilities and challenges they face as men after migrating. That is, some men may develop and embrace the idea of the moral supremacy of white women as a way to cope with Mexican women's active attacks on the patriarchal gender arrangements and inequalities by which they were raised — a process some male migrants may perceive as a threat. In short, some Mexicanos — and even my urban respondents, who generally promoted gender equality — may use racism against Mexicanas as a way to deal with a potential loss of gender privilege.

Talking about women's sexuality within the context of migration triggered broader fears and concerns from many of the men I interviewed. From their social positions as immigrants, the men see female gender and sexual identity being redefined in the United States by women's exposure to a sense of anonymity and isolation, by their geographical distance from family, by the empowerment and freedom they receive via networking, and by laws that promote women's rights within what is frequently perceived as a society suffused with moral decadence, or *libertinaje*. While a woman may migrate from Mexico in "exquisitely good shape," both her sex life and her views of heterosexual relationships are vulnerable as she is exposed to the combined effects of these multidimensional and mutually interacting factors. In the best case, she may become a sexually and emotionally assertive woman whose erotic experiences may be celebrated by some men. In the worst case, she may become a woman that other men perceive as over-empowered, that is, a legally overprotected female who instills fear and threatens the stability of previously established gender relations and norms within the local immigrant community and in the larger patriarchal system.

In Mexico, some men may resist and feel discomfort when women "change" and engage in emancipatory practices (Mummert 1994).[9] In the United States, men resent these changes, even as they themselves are exposed to racism and an anti-immigrant social climate, class-ism, segregation, and second-class-citizenship status in a society where white, middle- and upper-middle-class men define and control economic and political power. From their disadvantaged social position as immigrant men of color, they are coping with both their concerns within their immigrant communities and with inequalities in a larger socioeconomic context. Even though some have argued that immigrant men may rely upon hegemonic expressions of masculinity as a coping mechanism (see, e.g., Peña 1991), the personal lives of male immigrants are more complex. Hondagneu-Sotelo and Messner (1994), for example, have examined the weakening of patriarchal power in the experience of Mexican immigrant men by looking at spatial mobility, family decision-making, and household labor. They conclude that, "although they are oppressed by class, race, and/or sexual systems of power, they also commonly construct and display forms of masculinity as ways of resisting other men's power over them, as well as asserting power and privilege over women" (215). This chapter has offered examples of both the former and the latter. In the end, as these themes intermingle with gender relations and disparities, immigrant women and men continue deciphering their sex lives within the context of their loving relationships in the United States.

CHAPTER 8

Gendered Tapestries

Sexuality Threads of Migrant Sexualities

"As two people begin undressing to make love for the first time, they invite one another to share their life histories. The ways in which they begin kissing and caressing one another are only the prologue to what has not yet been revealed. Their lovemaking becomes the language they use to gradually tell one another their stories, without being aware of it. And as each one tells of a personal past in silence, as their sex stories are being written invisibly through the movement of their sexualized bodies, they are being slowly embroidered in their bedsheets." I originally wrote these lines in Spanish after attending a workshop offered by sex and marriage therapist David Schnarch at a sexuality conference in the late 1990s. When I walked out of the workshop, I reflected upon the disclosures of the Mexican women in this book, with whom I was then conducting my very first interviews. I kept thinking about the revealing nature of their bedsheets, the stories that they were telling their partners through the slow, fast, or painful movements of their bodies. Though I had not even finished collecting my data with the women, I was already thinking about what the men would have to say. Five years later, I have now finished the book I dreamed of writing back then, a book about the endless sexual stories Mexican immigrant women and men live in the United States, their private lives unfolding, invisible to mainstream society. This chapter condenses the social processes connected to the sexual stories of the forty women and twenty men in this study, all of them Mexicans living in Los Angeles. It summarizes my findings and discusses additional implications for other Mexican and Latin American immigrants, their partners, and their families.

Weaving the Erotic: Embroidering Inequality

Sex is the language through which we reveal our personal stories, but it is also the way many forms of social inequality are expressed. The stories of the women and men in this book not only reveal their sex lives and their erotic secrets. Their narratives also expose the ways in which injustice and privilege are negotiated through sexualized bodies before and after migrating. This book situates migrant sexualities within the context of different forms of social inequality. The many expressions of social inequality — at the macro and structural, and micro and relational and nuanced levels — have shaped the sex lives of these women and men throughout their life courses, from early experiences of the erotic in Mexico to migration to and settlement in Los Angeles. Even though women may seem to be more vulnerable as a social group, men are not necessarily privileged, even when they have been raised in a traditionally patriarchal society. And as my informants interpreted the social forces that had shaped their sex lives, they alternately explored desire and pleasure, reclaiming the possibility of sexual agency and satisfaction.

The immigrants I interviewed started their migration journeys with sex histories that were well rooted yet incomplete. As they shared their sex stories with me, they revealed how gender, class, and racialized ideologies and practices have regulated their sexualities in infinite ways between bedsheets and beyond borders. Their experiences of sexual initiation indicate how women are disadvantaged when compared to men. However, the latter do not enjoy sexual privileges without a social cost. These Mexicanos, like other men, tended to "pay a price for their power" (Messner 2000, 22).

Sexual Debut: She Said, He Said

Listening to women places men in the background, yet engages them in the women's sex stories.

Virginity has been socially constructed by both women and men as a life-enhancing resource. Premarital virginity becomes what I have called *capital femenino*. That is, virginity takes on a social exchange value that Mexican women — a subordinated social group in a patriarchal society — use to improve and maximize their life conditions and opportunities.

Premarital virginity is tied to socially constructed concepts of family and gender dynamics. First, the imposition of virginity on a woman is interwoven with a sophisticated ethic of *respeto a la familia* which links family honor with a daughter's virginity. Second, the ideal of preserving virginity until marriage stems from a woman's socially learned fear of sexism and men's expecting to marry virgins.

Premarital sex exposes women to risk. Women's heterosexual experiences occur along a dynamic continuum that runs from danger to pleasure. The overwhelming majority of the women in this study (70 percent) were not virgins when they got married. Their first sexual experiences reveal the many moral and social contradictions shaping Mexican women's sexualities, as well as the possibilities that exist for exploring sexual autonomy, agency, and pleasure.

The men's sexual initiation stories exposed the labyrinths of gender that they had to pick their way through with their peers and with their first heterosexual partners, from early puberty or early adolescence on into young adulthood.

The sexual initiation experiences of men are constructed as a collective rite of passage from boyhood into manhood. Young men begin to construct male heterosexual desire as they discuss, among their peer groups of male friends, the many erotic expectations, fantasies, and enchantments of the highly anticipated first sexual encounter. This becomes part of peer group acceptance and helps forge the masculine identity of a young man. Compulsory heterosexuality is essential for the construction of men's gender and sexual identities: sex with a woman (at times coercive) and sexual performance for peers become central in the construction of heterosexual masculinities and sexualities.

Multiple heterosexual experiences are represented along a pleasure–danger continuum that is constituted by the paradoxes and contradictions surrounding the men's first sexual encounters. These encounters reflect the identities of manhood and masculinity that selectively oppress women and men educated in a patriarchal society. The men's stories illustrate how men living in a patriarchal society may benefit from a "patriarchal dividend" (Connell 1995) but also may pay a "patriarchal cost."

Socioeconomic contexts shape the ways in which men interpret their first sexual experiences. The sexual initiation of a man is defined by the gender prescriptions existing in a particular socioeconomic context. Men educated in communities characterized by more accentuated gender inequalities (e.g., rural areas) are more likely to have their first sexual experience with a sex worker. Men who are exposed to more fluid gender identities in urban areas are more likely to report their first sexual experience was with a friend or an acquaintance. Regardless of the socioeconomic context, an ethic of *respeto a la mujer,* the fear of pregnancy out of wedlock and coercive marriage, and a fear of rejection and loss of a relationship influence a man's decision to avoid having his first sexual experience with a girlfriend, whether casual or steady.

Emotions are the threads that women and men use to weave their first sexual encounters, with anxiety and apprehension prominent among them. A culture of sexual fear shapes the sex lives of these women and men in multiple ways and varying degrees. Fear was at the core of their sex histories of dating and sexual initiation. Though reported individually, the fear was shared collectively. This culture of sexual fear that seems to exist in Mexican society is fluid, changing, and non-monolithic. It is influenced by regionally defined ideologies, socioeconomics, and patriarchal institutions, including the family.

Patriarchal Families: What Women and Men Said

The family is the primary institution that creates, organizes, and controls the gender politics that govern expressions of femininity, masculinity, and ideals of heterosexual love and sex. It is the original social channel through which these gender politics are put into practice in everyday life.

Premarital sexual activity occurs within family norms and regulations of heterosexual relations. Young people's premarital sexual activity unfolds within complex family mechanisms of control, especially when unexpected pregnancy becomes public. In some instances, parenting enforces coercive marriage.

Mothers are responsible for selectively safeguarding and mediating the sex education of both daughters and sons. Via motherhood, adult women shape the ways in which their daughters and sons (and at times, their children's partners) perceive and live their sexuality. They promote gendered beliefs and practices with regard to premarital sex, dating, courtship, and ideals of heterosexual relationships.

Virginity and sexual initiation are both private and public experiences. Both the preservation and the loss of premarital virginity, through socially constructed symbols (e.g., pregnancy out of wedlock, the white dress, orange blossoms, an embroidered wedding-night bedsheet, a white coffin) transform what is intimate and private into a public, family, collective, and social affair.

PELIGRO, WARNING: The United States May Be Hazardous to Your Sexual Health

Sex within the context of gender relations, socioeconomic marginality, and racial disparities produces similar yet new forms of inequality in the United States. After migrating to and settling in Los Angeles, inequality continued to shape the sex lives of the women and men in this study. The political economy of migration incorporated the women and men into the complex inequalities that permeate certain segregated sectors of U.S. society while offering them unequal paid employment opportunities within a highly industrialized and fast-paced capitalist economy. But labor migration is not only about economic forces, employment, or push-and-pull forces. Establishing a life in the United States revealed a "political economy of risk" that inevitably included risks to their sex lives.

Mexican immigrants' sex lives become vulnerable as they are exposed to some of the risks and hazards they encounter in the United States. As they settle and establish their permanent lives, they begin to identify such hazards as crime, violence, and illness. Thus, the culture of sexual fear migrates and begins to take new forms that are embedded in the new social and economic realities of immigrants. These risks not only cause fear. Child sexual abuse, alcohol and drug use, gang activity in the community, and the fear of sexually transmitted diseases (i.e., HIV/AIDS) permeate the daily lives of these women and men, and shape their perceptions, ideologies, and sex lives. Though most are aware of the risks, some find them potentially stimulating, as they explore sex within dangerous social contexts and circumstances.

These informants' sex lives are influenced by the world of work in a highly industrialized capitalist economy. The concept of the "Taylorization of sex" explains how survival needs and an intrusive work schedule invade their bedrooms. For these Mexican immigrants to the United States, the Taylorization of sex represents "sexual costs" or "sexual gains," depending on whether their sex lives deteriorate or improve.

Sexo en El Barrio: Networking and Sex

In both Mexico and the United States, socioeconomic and gender inequalities are played out sexually, and sex beliefs and practices in turn seem to reinforce them. In the midst of these processes, risks emerge. But women and men are active social actors, and they dynamically engage in sex-related conversations within their immigrant communities as they decipher the new fears they encounter, and examine the sex-related beliefs and values that have accompanied them since they left for California.

Women and men experience transformations in their sex lives as they exchange information about sexuality within different types of immigrant social networks. Expressions of feminine and masculine identities shape the nature of the networking activities women engage in when compared to men. Women more frequently than men reported engaging in one-on-one, sex-related conversations with other women and men; and men more frequently reported joking and mocking in their sex-related group conversations. Regardless of gender, these immigrants are active agents who scrutinize the information flowing through the networking exchanges that shape the sexual morality, ideology and behavior of their immigrant communities.

Networking within Latino/Mexican immigrant and multicultural communities has two central functions in the participants' sex lives. First, it represents a source of social support for coping with sexual difficulties and concerns. Second, it provides alternative sexual ideologies as the women and men educate each other while challenging, renegotiating, and redefining their previously established sexual moralities, ideologies, and behaviors.

Via networking, women and men share information and gain perspectives that alternatively enhance and challenge gender inequality. Women and men may share sexual information in order to promote sexually liberating methods and insights into equality in heterosexual relationships. But they may also create new ways to effectively discipline, stigmatize, and negatively label other Mexican women. Men less frequently than women reported the gender inequalities they may promote via networking. However, the voices of their male immigrant friends and coworkers confirm how men may either challenge or promote sexism within their immigrant communities.

The Political Economy of Migrant Bedrooms: Negotiating Pleasure

Paid employment, money, and sex all combine to expose the gender, class, and race relations that shape participants' renegotiation of power and control within the family as they become productive and essential components of the U.S. economy.

Women's sex lives are transformed as they gain full-time employment, receive an income, and become financially independent. I introduced the Gender Stratification Theory (Theory of Relative Resources) to examine how working outside the home, earning a salary, and enjoying control over her income may provide a Mexican immigrant woman with personal power. This in turn may transform her sex life and perceptions of sexuality within the contexts of marital and family relationships, including her stance as a mother.

Women's experiences of sexual objectification within the socioeconomic context reveal social mechanisms of gender inequality. I introduced a feminist perspective of gender as a relational process to examine the power of money and the objectification of sexual intercourse as part of the sex lives of immigrant women within the context of marital and family life. A larger picture of society complements this image by illustrating how some women and poor immigrant men are exposed to the commodification of their sexualized bodies within a context of socioeconomic marginality.

As men express their views of immigrant women's sexual attitudes and behaviors, they reveal the relational nature of sexuality and gender underlying the way they see Mexicanas and sexuality. The Mexican women experience changes in their sex lives after migrating because of anonymity, geographical distance, weakened family control, networking, and U.S. laws that protect women, while consistently incorporating their views of female sexuality within the context of women's heterosexual loving relationships. Men articulate their multiple masculine identities and sexualities as they alternately celebrate or resent women's postmigration experiences of emancipatory sexual and gender identities between two extremes: some of the men favor gender equality, others fear patriarchal disenfranchisement. Men's own sexual transformations in the United States reveal the multiplicity of Mexican masculinities and their respective expressions of heterosexuality.

The Sex Education of Children in the United States

For many of these women and men, establishing a stable marriage and family life, and educating a new generation of children about sex while living on the socioeconomic margins of Los Angeles was the last and most challenging chapter of their own sex lives. As they talked about the sex education they want to provide to their daughters and sons, they revisited their views of youth and sexuality, premarital sex, the role of the family in sex education and coercive marriage — the social forces that had shaped their sex lives in Mexico. Parenting their children with regard to sex was an opportunity to unpack their own sexuality luggage and to revise their views of sexuality.

In a book chapter entitled "De madres a hijas" (2003), I examine how these mothers reconstruct their meaning of virginity within their U.S. communities as part of their immigration experience. For these women, motherhood becomes a vehicle that leads them to revisit and reorganize the beliefs and practices they learned before migrating with regard to pre-marital sex. For them, mothering a daughter serves as an opportunity to resolve some of their unfinished issues as women: protecting their daughters from the gender inequality they experienced within the specific regional patriarchies of their regions shapes the sex education they teach to them. Rural women whose husbands reproached them for not being virgins at marriage promote pro-virginity values before marriage as a way to protect their daughters from a similar fate. Others, especially those from urban areas, want the new generation of women to be educated within more egalitarian values. Most want their daughters to climb the education ladder, develop professional careers, and obtain well-paid jobs. As they replace marriage goals with career goals for their daughters, their ideas about appropriate sexual behavior also change. Virginity depreciates as a form of social capital, to some extent replaced by new goods: education and employment opportunities.

The mothers' views of virginity are also shaped by the *pláticas* (sexuality workshops) some of them attend at clinics in their communities, as well as their exposure to the Spanish-language media, social networking, immigrant culture, and employment. In this way, they transform an ethic of sexual abstinence that once governed their own lives into an ethic of protection and care represented by sexual moderation. It is essential to protect their daughters from pregnancy out of wedlock, sexually trans-mitted diseases, HIV/AIDS, sexual violence, and promiscuity — sex-related dangers associated with modernity and urban life. As a group, these mothers invert the pleasure–danger continuum that controlled their first sexual experience. They hope their daughters will be able to avoid danger while embracing sexual autonomy and associating eroticism with pleasurable feelings and experiences.

As a group, the fathers have similar yet contrasting views. Some used the expression *"Nomás con que se cuide"* to explain that their main con-cern was to make sure a daughter would learn to "take care of herself." *Cuidarse,* or "to take care of oneself," has more than one meaning in

Mexico. For women of reproductive age, "taking care" also suggests the use of contraception to prevent pregnancy. Fathers consistently recited this notion as they revisited and expressed their views with regard to premarital sexual activity in their daughters' lives. I also learned that fathers encouraged sexual moderation within the same ethic of protection and care that mothers promoted for their daughters. Like the mothers, these fathers wished to improve their daughters' living conditions and opportunities while protecting them from the sexual dangers mentioned above. Across generations, fathers challenged the ethic of *respeto a la familia* and severely condemned coercive marriage due to a daughter's pregnancy. Fathers did not demand sexual abstinence from their daughters. However, some of them promoted the postponement of premarital sex as a strategy in their daughter's life; delaying sex would protect a young woman from getting pregnant. In this way, a young woman might develop the intellectual and emotional maturity necessary to accomplish the dream many of the men have for their daughters: obtaining a college degree.

Fathers also decided whether to advocate for premarital virginity for their daughters, based on the regional patriarchies they had been exposed to as young men and depending on their specific socioeconomic contexts before migrating. Rural men were more likely to say that they expected their daughters to refrain from premarital sex as a way of reproducing the traditions and social symbolism they had been taught in their own families, such as the bride's wearing of a white dress on her wedding day. In contrast, the men from Mexico City, and all the more educated men, saw premarital sex as a daughter's exclusive and personal decision, and claimed not to be concerned about the moral, religious, or family values traditionally associated with virginity. In addition, urban fathers were more likely to advocate for a daughter's sexual autonomy and for her right to actively seek out and experience desire and pleasure, before or after marriage. Regardless of their place of origin, however, some fathers preferred not to be aware of their daughters' sexual activity before marriage, due to their self-confessed feelings of jealousy as men.

Fathers perceived their immigrant barrios as sexually dangerous places for their daughters. Even for rural fathers who promoted premarital abstinence, virginity might be a secondary consideration within the context of socioeconomic segregation. Protecting a daughter from the high-risk living conditions of the neighborhood became a father's priority after migration. Most fathers were concerned about high rates of adolescent pregnancy and single motherhood, violence against women, and sexually transmitted diseases, including HIV/AIDS, and they would actively discourage a daughter's romantic involvement with men perceived as undesirable, such as criminals, drug dealers and addicts, gang members, the unemployed, or high school dropouts.

Even though fathers frequently claimed to lack the knowledge, self-confidence, or comfort level to talk with their daughters about sex, all said they wanted their daughters to be well informed with regard to reproductive health and contraceptive use, so that they could enjoy a responsible, healthy, and safe sex life if they decided to become sexually active before marriage. Regardless of their place of origin, some fathers used sex education to improve the quality of their daughters' relationships and to protect them from domestic violence or getting pregnant and being abandoned by a man. Virginity, for them, remained an asset that evoked both pleasure and danger. They taught their daughters to perceive virginity as a commodity (i.e., "a treasure") that she could exchange as a symbol of love, intimacy, and respect within a premarital loving relationship. In this way, these fathers hoped their daughters would learn to become highly selective in choosing a sexual partner who would be "worthy of" a daughter's virginity — that is, a non-abusive, good, and decent man who truly loved her. None of the fathers mentioned any religious values with regard to virginity (see González-López 2004).

To what extent were generational and regional patriarchies, on the one hand, and immigration and U.S. life, on the other, responsible for these transitions in female sexuality across generations? These seem to be mutually interlocking forces. A mother's individual gendered sexual history, experienced within a specific socioeconomic context and regional patriarchy, interacts with the particular changes she experiences in the United States. These might include learning more about sex through educational materials and workshops at community-based agencies, networking with other Latinas, employment, control over her income, financial independence, and exposure to the Spanish-language media within the immigrant community.

The migration- and gender-related transformations across generations experienced by the women in this study match up with the research findings from studies of Mexican immigrants, Mexican Americans, and other Latina groups across disciplines. Hirsch (1999) reported similar findings from her ethnographic work with migrants from Jalisco and Michoacán living in Atlanta. By comparing two generations of an extended family from both a receiving community in the United States and a sending community in Mexico, Hirsch found that younger women transform both the functions of sexuality within marriage (i.e., from an act of procreation to one of emotional intimacy and sexual pleasure) and the nature of their marital relationships across generations (i.e., "from an ideal of *respeto* [respect] to one of *confianza* [trust]") (Hirsch 1999, 1332). Williams concluded, from her qualitative research with Mexican American couples living in various locations in Texas, that the double standards of discipline for both genders, as well as past rigid patterns controlling a daughter's behavior, become less strict as parents educate a younger generation (1990, 134). She noted, however, that adolescent sons continued to enjoy more freedom than adolescent daughters. Prieto (1992) examined Cuban immigrant mothers living in New Jersey and observed that these women expected their daughters to be careful as they began to date. However, these women did not expect their daughters to preserve their virginity until marriage. For these mothers, communication with their daughters with regard to sex had improved across generations.

A father may be also influenced by the pre-migration socioeconomic conditions shaping his masculine identity, which ultimately influence his views of a daughter's sexuality. Racial and class segregation in the United States additionally reorganize a father's view of sexuality. Virginity may become an ideal of the past, but protecting a daughter from the dangers of the immigrant barrio is a reality of the present. For some, virginity is still an asset that will protect a daughter — not from a husband's recriminations but from premarital emotional involvement with an undesired partner. In the end, for these parents, feelings of love and concern; values of sexual moderation, protection, and care; and explorations of the best ways to improve the living conditions of their daughters may have originated from different gendered avenues, but they know no borders.

Bourdieu's (2001) economy of symbolic exchanges comes to mind within the context of migration. While virginity may still be perceived as a symbolic treasure by some parents, it may have lost its value as *capital femenino* in the United States. A family is not necessarily honored when a daughter or a son abstains from premarital sex; however, new expressions of symbolic capital may emerge for these families. For instance, many mothers and fathers said they would feel rewarded for their hard work by knowing that they had successfully parented a child who would eventually finish high school and attend college. For mothers and fathers, education was perceived as central as they sought out ways to help their children develop relatively stable and secure financial and personal lives in the United States. All of them wanted a better life for their children, compared to what they had had as young women and men.

As these mothers and fathers articulated their views of their daughters' sex lives, they revisited their own sexual experiences before migrating. And as I listened to each one of these immigrants describe her or his family life in the present and in the past, the importance of challenging mono-lithic, static, and stereotypical notions of families in general was confirmed (see Stacey 1998; Thorne and Yalom 1992), along with the importance of recognizing the changing nature and diversity of Mexican and Mexican immigrant families living in the United States (see Zambrana 1995; Gutmann 1996; Módena and Mendoza 2001; Escobar Latapí 2003).

There is no doubt that the family as an institution immersed in a patri-archal society has created, organized, and enforced the gender politics underlying the sex lives of these immigrants. Their families of origin became the social channels through which these gender politics were put into practice. Within these families, however, gender, socioeconomics, and parents' subjectivities intricately shaped the meanings of premarital sex, virginity, and pregnancy out of wedlock for each one of these women and men. Cultural beliefs and values simultaneously shaped my inform-ants' meanings and interpretations of their sexual experiences within heterosexual relationships. These processes, in addition, were neither uni-directional nor rigid. Informants were at times complicit, at times com-plaisant, at times exerting force, and at times cognizant of the delicate nuances surrounding them — for example, in a woman's decision to wear a white dress, or in a woman or man's acceptance of an unwanted mar-riage. My other respondents figured out the gender maze and defied fam-ily rules governing their sexuality, in subtle or explicit ways. Some of them described their parents as having practiced different levels of discipline and control, but many said they understood their parents' well-intentioned attempts to do their best as family moral authorities. Still others recalled with nostalgia the warm feelings of love and care either or both parents always expressed to them. What the overwhelming majority of these informants had in common was a deep sense of love and respect for their parents and their families.

Geographical distance, generational differences, and migration trans-formed these narratives through the years into something more than memories for all of my respondents. Many of the women and men I inter-viewed still seemed to be dealing with unresolved feelings from their youthful sexual experiences. And as they established the first generation of their Mexican American families in the United States, many of them, especially those who had experienced confusion and pain, reported their desire to avoid re-creating their parents' attitudes and behaviors with regard to sexuality. They embraced this hope for their daughters as well as for their sons.

Sons and Sexuality

Even though many respondents revealed their frustration, confusion, and interest in learning more about sexuality, these mothers and fathers said they believed in an equal sex education for their children, regardless of gender. The concerns these parents have for their children include threats of sexual abuse, promiscuity, unprotected sex, and sexually transmitted diseases such as HIV/AIDS, as well as the possibility that their children will combine sexual activity with drugs, alcohol, gang activity, and violence. In addition, all of these parents viewed the United States as a dangerous place for children, but especially for daughters. For example, even though most perceived a young son as equally responsible for a girl's pregnancy, many perceived him as less susceptible with regard to the negative consequences of pregnancy out of wedlock. For many parents, a daughter has a higher risk of being emotionally involved with an abusive partner. These patterns are closely associated with double standards of morality. The stories shared by these participants reveal how gender inequality is reproduced or disrupted via motherhood and fatherhood.

Many of the mothers used the expression *respeto a la mujer* when talking about the sex education they wanted to provide for their sons. Paradoxically, these women's attempts to promote *respeto a la mujer* did not prevent them from reproducing many forms of gender inequality and double morality in the sex education they offered to their sons. Amparo and Irasema, for example, talked about witnessing their adolescent sons' dating behaviors with their girlfriends, such as hugging, petting, kissing, or getting home late. When these mothers perceived these behaviors and attitudes as morally inappropriate, they were protective of their sons while making the young women responsible for the young man's sexual reaction. Fathers, in contrast, reported these patterns with regard to their sons less frequently. They observed, however, the same ethic of respect for women. And these values become more evident in the sex education they provide for their daughters. More frequently than mothers, fathers from all socioeconomic contexts used the expression *"El hombre llega hasta donde la mujer quiere"* (The man goes as far as the woman wants him to) to explain how they might teach their daughters to demand respect from men. A popular saying in Mexican society, men use it to either assert that women have sufficient power to stand up for their rights to demand respect and to challenge a man's sexual advances, or to argue that women are responsible for becoming pregnant out of wedlock and for provoking inappropriate sexual behavior on the man's part, such as sexual harassment.

Women used the same ethic of respect for women by actively facilitating social change as they educated their male children. Tomasita exclamation, "*¡Ay mujer!*" seems to voice the concerns of these mothers. "Some fathers teach their little boys to be *machistas* from the very beginning. Just because he is a man, many fathers tell their boys to screw all the women. No! I am against that mentality!" For Tomasita and many of the other mothers who are educating sons, teaching respect for women by promoting monogamy is a central issue in preventing potential sexist behavior in their sons. Sexism is also challenged by teaching a son to be gentle and non-aggressive in his personal and romantic relationships with women. In addition, some mothers questioned social practices that promote the sexual objectification of specific groups of women who have been marginalized in Mexican society throughout history. These mothers expressed strong opposition to their sons being sexually initiated by women who participate in commercial sex, or by domestic workers. Fathers echoed similar issues as they talked about the sex education they are providing for their sons. Some urban fathers further emphasized a son's need to learn to be gentle and kind with his romantic partners, and to learn about experiencing his own sexual pleasure as a man by sexually pleasing his partner or a future wife. Like mothers, some men objected to the coercive sexual initiation of young boys or to their sexual initiation with sex workers. This was especially relevant for fathers who had been exposed to this practice when they were adolescents.

Fathers raising both girls and boys expressed more concern and spent more time talking about their daughters when the topic of the sex education of children was first introduced in our interviews. Though a father might identify the risks to a son, he also saw him as a young man "who sooner or later will learn about sex and to take care of himself, anyway." Ernesto, the father of a girl and a boy, best articulated what many of these fathers thought: "You have to put much more emphasis on women, because the woman is more, she has the hardest job, the most difficult one with regard to sexuality, to have a child, and tolerate all that. That is why I say, 'Poor women!'" More research on how this gender pattern shapes the sex lives of Mexican and Mexican American young men is badly needed, especially with regard to teenage pregnancy and other reproductive health issues.

Thus, these mothers and fathers continue reproducing and actualizing a wide array of fluid and nuanced possibilities of feminine and masculine identities, experiences of heterosexuality, and gender inequality within the socioeconomics of their Mexican immigrant communities. How do these mothers and fathers put their beliefs into practice? How do young Mexican American women and men experience and continue to reproduce these gendered sexualities in flux? Aída Hurtado (2003) has recorded the sexual narratives of a group of 101 college-educated Chicanas who echo, sometimes verbatim, some of the same issues the women and men in this book illustrate. While reading these young women's sex narratives, I felt as if I were listening to the young daughters of some of the women and men I interviewed, especially those in their early forties. The sex lives of Hurtado's informants echo similar views of virginity, double standards of morality that favor young men over women, mothers playing the role of the mediator of sexual morality within the family, and new expressions of chaperonage, among other issues, including but not limited to parents' encouragement that children attend college. Research on how Mexican American men from the same cohort as Hurtado's informants is needed. It would be interesting to know how they perceive virginity, experience erotic desire within heterosexual relationships, and their opinions on other sex-related concerns. There is still much to know about the ways in which a new generation of young women and men are experiencing their sexualities within the social factors that influence their adaptation in the United States — racism, geographic location, and the structure of labor markets (see Portes and Rumbaut 1996).

With regard to virginity, the additional social and cultural meanings attached by other Mexicanas and Latina immigrants to an intact hymen need to be examined. Journalists have written about clinics in Southern California and New York that offer hymen reconstruction services to Latina immigrants.[1] And the sexualized Spanish-language media continue to capture the attention of audiences by inviting women with extensive sexual experience to speak about their concerns about "passing by" as virgins with their future partners. On her April 8, 2002, broadcast, Cristina Saralegui (who is sometimes called "the Hispanic Oprah") interviewed a group of women who reportedly used balloons, Chinese balls, vaginal creams, and herbal remedies to tighten their vaginas. Saralegui also introduced a commercial line of products designed to achieve the same results. Women's fears of sexism? Transnational gender inequalities? Pure sensationalism? Regardless, the fact that clinics exist for the repair of hymens in the United States and that the Spanish-language media presents sexualized discourses reflects some of the fascinating intricacies of female sexualities I have attempted to examine in this book. I hope my examinations may inform some of the as yet unheard narratives with regard to virginity and Latinas living in the United States.

The Catholic Church: Beyond Guilt and Shame

> *The peak of sexuality, orgasm, is characterized by a sense of*
> *timelessness, a loss of ego, completely natural — unless you are*
> *faking it — defenselessness, communion and surrender. These*
> *are saintly qualities.*
>
> Deepak Chopra, *Los Angeles Times Magazine*

The testimonies offered by the women in this study make orthodox Church-blaming discourses difficult to sustain as the exclusive or major source of social control over heterosexual Mexicanas. Within the field of the sociology of sexualities, Mexicana sexuality studies cannot afford to be decontextualized from the everyday social practices and experiences connected to women's sex lives. Among these socially constructed contexts we find the following: gender relations, family life, socioeconomic conditions and segregation, community life, social networks, media, and the ways in which organized religion is interpreted and experienced by women. It is essential to examine how women's experiences of sexuality are constructed within the power structure of society and its institutions, including but not limited to ecclesiastical organizations.

How do the women participating in this study perceive Catholic religious teachings on sexuality and morality? What do they say they do with these teachings in their actual sex lives? In order to explore how the women in this study themselves perceive and judge the influence of the Catholic Church on their sexuality as Catholic women, I read the sexuality section of the *Carta al Papa* (Letter to the Pope) to the women in Spanish as part of my interviews. The Letter to the Pope is a document written by a group of actively involved churchwomen (religious nuns, catechists, and secular women) and made public during the Pope's visit to Mexico in 1990.[2] The Mexican Catholic women who signed the letter used it to bring their progressive ideology with regard to the sexuality of women to the attention of the Pope. This is the text I read to my informants:

> It is about time that we, as a Church, recognize sexuality as holy and divine.
> It is about time that we assume sexuality as part of God's gratitude, and of
> those who mutually give themselves in freedom and generosity, not only to
> have children. It is about time to meditate and recognize that sexuality is holy

and divine. It is about time that we, as Catholic women, recognize that God has granted us with a body which we should love and rescue because it is a transcendent part of us as persons and of our unity with God. It is urgent for the Vatican, bishops, and priests to act and think in a radically different manner, by allowing themselves to be questioned by the experiential world of women so they act according to the Plan of God. It is urgent for all of you to consider us as adult persons, capable to possess our lives and our bodies so our options are trusted and respected, and the right to intimacy, to sexuality, in a responsible manner and in harmony with the values of the Kingdom: in truth, in justice, in love, and in equality. Only in mutual respect, and with a recognition in plenitude of everybody's rights as persons, will we be able to contribute to a humanity with no limits and a "life in abundance" (John 10: 10).

The overwhelming majority of the women in this study (80 percent) supported the request in the *Carta* for progressive changes within the Catholic Church. The minority who objected to the *Carta* were from rural Jalisco, women who had been exposed to more emphatic gender inequalities and who said they were afraid to challenge the status quo. What might be the reasons behind such great support for the idea of questioning and rebelling against traditional moralities with regard to women's sexuality? My women respondents had experienced the interconnection between their sex lives and religion, based on the following dynamics.

First, the women were not only aware of the patriarchal nature of the Catholic Church as an institution but they perceived it as morally incompetent to regulate women's sexuality. They perceived the ecclesiastical organization as morally fractured and in need of socially progressive change. They questioned and condemned the ethical contradictions and hypocrisies they had observed within the system, including priests sexually abusing children and priests being married or having lovers.

Second, the women who reported this type of awareness had not abandoned their faith or religious practices. They reconciled their Catholic faith and their own private sexual beliefs and practices by following two central patterns. Some established a division between "sex/sexuality/the body" and "religion/the Church/the spirit," framing each category as an autonomous dimension of experience. For them, sex is a private matter, and religion is a spiritual, not a public affair. These women compartmentalized sex and religion (see Mikawa et al. 1992). Others asserted personal agency and selectively embraced values compatible with their social reality as women. They discriminately selected and incorporated into their sex lives only specific morality teachings, based on their convenience or appropriateness to their own lifestyles. So what they reported doing in their sex lives with regard to Catholic sexual morality was based on each woman's critical adaptations of these moral principles. In this way, the women socially constructed emancipatory sexual moralities as they claimed their right to control their own sexuality, including their reproductive rights.

I suggest that Mexican women, as a subordinate social group, are neither submissive nor passive, but are active individuals who mediate Catholic teachings on sexual morality based on their personal subjectivities. Their individual judgments with regard to sexual morality are determined from "within," in connection with their everyday and real-life sexual, social, and economic situations and circumstances. For Dorothy Smith, the standpoint of women is defined as "a method that, at the outset of inquiry, creates the space for an absent subject, and an absent experience that is to be filled with the presence and spoken experience of actual women speaking of and in the actualities of their everyday worlds" (1987, 107).[3]

Did these women have these views before migrating? Many of them did. However, I conducted my interviews during the 1997–98 academic year. And as I reflect on this data in the year 2003, I would like to suggest that the current crisis in the Catholic Church with regard to the scandal of pedophile priests may further accentuate these and other immigrant women's perceptions of the Church as morally fragile. In addition, thirty-nine of the forty women I interviewed were raised in the Catholic faith while growing up and living in Mexico; only one (Diamantina) was raised Protestant in Mexico. Of the thirty-nine Catholic women, three had converted to a Protestant denomination in the United States. Even though the conversion incidence is low, it is important to mention that two out of the three women who became Protestants (Belén and Fernanda) became more fundamentalist in their attitudes with regard to sexual morality, especially with regard to educating their daughters. Based on their religious values, both hoped that their daughters would refrain from premarital sex. Interestingly, both women supported the socially progressive changes proposed in *La Carta al Papa*. Eréndira was the only single woman who became Protestant, and she reported a change in sexual morality (from conservative to liberal) after religious conversion, which was enhanced by her access to paid employment, as illustrated in a previous chapter. During our interviews, the women did not deny the punishing nature of Catholic morality. Some identified religion as a source of guilt, shame, and remorse about premarital sex, about having or imagining having an abortion, or in promoting socially progressive changes like those identified in *La Carta al Papa*.[4] However, women experience Catholic religious guilt and shame as a subjective, or internalized — personal or private — expression of control over their sex lives. In addition, shame and guilt followed the "sinful" act; they did not precede it. Eventually, a Catholic woman may confess her sins and be forgiven by a male figure who represents the Church. In addition, the externalized mechanisms shaping women's experiences of sexuality and heterosexual love include the following: family life, various types of socially constructed patriarchies, feminine and masculine identities shaped by socioeconomic contexts, a malleable culture of sexual fear, and women's and men's actual subjective experiences of the erotic. All combine in complex ways to reveal the actual nuanced social venues regulating multiple expressions of female sexuality. Thus, in theory, the Catholic Church may formulate a religious code of sexual and moral conduct for Mexican women. In practice, however, religious morality is neither an exclusive nor an isolated social force controlling a woman's sex life, especially in her everyday-life interactions and social contexts.

These Mexicanas are not alone in their critical views of Catholic sex ethics. "The Vatican's sexual morality is not accepted by large groups of Catholics, even though it is supported by Los Legionarios de Cristo and Opus Dei, which have great economic power and political influence," writes Edgar González Ruiz (1998, 58), a specialist in sexual morality research in Mexico. González Ruiz explains that a national survey conducted in 1991 showed that 74, 79, and 65 percent of the population (upper, middle, and working class, respectively) rejected the Church's position against AIDS prevention campaigns; another survey conducted in 1993 by GIRE and Gallup indicated that 82.7 percent of Mexicans believe that abortion is a woman's and/or a couple's decision (59). In July 2003, Católicas por el Derecho a Decidir and the Population Council of Mexico published the results of a major survey they conducted among 2,328 Catholic women and men from seventeen different states in Mexico. In this study, 82 and 81 percent of the informants, respectively, said that gays and lesbians should be legally protected against discrimination, and that women who abort should not be excommunicated. This pattern coincides with Zavella's reflections on religion and Mexicans, who "do not simply follow church doctrines when it comes to decisions about contraception, abortion, or submitting to sexual violence" (1997, 392), and the current academic debate in Latina and Latino sexuality research about whether religion shapes actual sexual beliefs and behaviors (Marín and Gómez 1997, 80). Finally, research on a variety of sex-related issues and concerns, such as reproductive health, virginity, and HIV/AIDS research, has shown either no association between religion and the actual sexual values and practices of Mexican women and men raised in the Catholic faith (Amaro 1988; Mikawa et al. 1992; Organista et al. 1996, 1997, 2000; Villarruel 1998; Castro-Vásquez 2000; Carrillo 2002), or only a minor influence of the former on the latter (Forrest et al. 1993).

These findings with regard to religion and sexuality led me to reflect on the notion in contemporary Mexican scholarship of "the secularization of sexuality." For example, Amuchástegui observes that her informants' views of virginity as "sacred" do not expose an "explicit" relationship with Catholicism, and she concludes that these individuals' views on virginity seem to be linked to their *costumbres* — the relatively uniform patterns of beliefs and practice developed in and adopted by a community (2001, 361). In addition, Amuchástegui describes Mexico as a "hybrid culture," where Catholicism coexists with modernity, and thus, religion is not always an influence on sexuality because of the gradual secularization of culture the country is experiencing. Amuchástegui and Rivas (1997) suggest that the family and the church have lost their power, as a proliferation of health institutions, schools, media, and publicity also create multiple discourses of sexuality.

I offer an alternative way of examining sexuality and religion within the context of gender relations and the history of Mexican society. The secularization of a society and its corresponding expressions of sexuality may lead to less religious influence on or control over sex, such as less religious guilt or no association between sex and religion — a sort of more "secular" view and experience of sex and the erotic. However, this process does not necessarily guarantee more gender equality for citizens. In this regard, historians who examine the gender–state interaction have indicated that, "It is often argued that the Catholic Church has always undermined gender equality. The conclusion scholars draw from this interpretation is that secularization has always modernized the gender order. Neither the former nor the latter propositions are entirely true in the case of Latin America. Secularization in Latin America had contradictory gendered effects over the course of the long nineteenth century" (Dore 2000, 22).

In the case of Mexico, the state has been predominantly patriarchal and traditionally (and officially) secular for more than one hundred years. However, women did not enjoy constitutional rights as citizens between 1916 and 1934, a period characterized by the emergence of the women's movement in the nation. Their status did not change after the Mexican Revolution (1910–1920); they were only granted full rights to vote in municipal, state, and federal elections in 1953 (see Rodríguez 2003).

As I write this conclusion, women political leaders in Mexico and human rights activists are celebrating the fiftieth anniversary of women's right to vote while still addressing many gender inequality issues with regard to reproductive health, abortion, women's political participation, and sexual and domestic violence, among other issues and concerns, including the unresolved murders of hundreds of women in Ciudad Juárez. At the same time, even though the Catholic Church's normative discourses of sexuality coming from the Vatican may dramatically disadvantage women, vibrant progressive women's rights groups in Latin America and the United States, such as Católicas por el Derecho a Decidir in Mexico and groups of Latina feminist theologians, struggle at the activist and intellectual levels within the Church.

It is my hope that future sexuality research will continue to examine the complexities linking Mexican women's and men's sexualities and the erotic to both macro structural and larger social, economic, and political forces, and micro everyday-life practices and interactions. We need to conduct in-depth explorations of the subjective and relational experiences of sexuality, as well as the actual beliefs and practices of religion and spirituality, beyond the overused Church-blaming paradigms that may obscure other forms of inequality in contemporary society. This may generate innovative and alternative paradigms for more comprehensive theoretical examinations and more effective strategies for justice and social change. As illustrated by the women and men in this study, experiences of sexuality and heterosexual relationships are constructed and controlled by and through complex gendered social mechanisms taking place within a socioeconomic structure — a social construction wherein fluidity and possibilities for contestation and change exist. While consistently promoting socially progressive changes within the Church, a comprehensive understanding and integration of each and every one of the social forces controlling Mexican women's and men's experiences of sexuality may highlight new avenues for social change, especially in the area of women's reproductive health.

The Expropriation of Sexualized Bodies: Some Reflections on Mexicanas and Their Reproductive Health

When many women in this study explained that condom use was their contraceptive method of choice, they used the expression *"Él me cuida"* (He takes care of me). A statement that some women may interpret as being loving and caring and as an expression of "companionate marriages" (Hirsch 2003, 261) may have additional meanings. I took this finding one step further and asked myself: If a Mexican woman learns to perceive a male partner as the one "who takes care" of her sexualized body, what are the social and psychological consequences for her reproductive and sexual health? If the feminine body of a woman is constructed in some cases as family and male property, what implications do these gender politics have on a woman's sense of ownership over both her sexualized body and her reproductive health?

According to CONAPO (the Consejo Nacional de Población, Mexico's National Population Council), "Twenty-five years since the inception of the National Plan of Family Planning, 48 percent of Mexican women have to ask for their husbands' permission in order to use a contraceptive method" (CIMAC 2002). In addition, academics at the Transborder Consortium for Research and Action on Gender and Reproductive Health on the Mexico–U.S. Border have indicated that cervical cancer (the second most common cancer among the world's women) jumped from twenty-fourth to second position as a cause of death among Mexican women within the last six decades (Méndez Brown de Galaz 1998).[5] The incidence of this disease is four times higher in Mexico than in the United States; disease rates for women of Mexican origin living in the United States are higher than for non-Mexicans (Giuliano 1998). The specific risk factors behind such a striking incidence have been identified, including malnutrition, vaginal infections, lack of medical services, and inappropriate testing, but we need to study the ways in which women learn to take care of their sexualized bodies and the implications for their reproductive health. The same dynamics need to be explored with regard to cervical cancer, HIV/AIDS and other sexually transmitted diseases, breast cancer, teenage pregnancy, family planning, abortion, and other sexuality-related health issues and concerns affecting Mexican women.

How does a patriarchal society express its property rights over a woman's sexualized body? Community educators working with immigrant women may have more than one of the answers. During an informal interview, a Latina sex educator currently working with Latina immigrant women at one of my research sites told me the strongest reason women gave for refusing to have a mammogram as part of their breast cancer prevention examination: *"No puede verme otra persona, sólo me ha visto mi esposo"* (Nobody else can see me; only my husband has seen me). Others have similarly addressed this pattern. At a conference in Mexico, Vicente Díaz, the Director of Family Planning at the Health Secretariat in Mexico, explained that both women and men are negatively affected by men's learned limited involvement in contraceptive methods and the prevention of cervical cancer, among other reproductive health-related issues. Díaz expressed his interest in advocating changes in public schools textbooks, with the purpose of challenging stereotypes of masculinity and promoting gender inequality (Magally 2002).

Linguistic taboos may be masking additional answers. The social uses of the terms *señorita* and *señora* are determined by specific social contexts which expose particular aspects of a woman's sexuality and reproductive health. Their use in social contexts reveals linguistic prohibitions that are prevalent in Mexican society. The term *señorita* possesses meaningful moral and sexual implications. A young girl becomes a *señorita* after she has her first period and her sexualized body leads her into adolescence. Later in life, she remains a *señorita* as a young single woman, and officially becomes a *señora* when she gets married. Being a *señorita* means being single and therefore being a virgin. It is always seen as offensive to use the term *señora* to refer to a woman who is still a *señorita,* because to do so implies that she has lost her virginity and is sexually active. Since sexual activity transforms a *señorita* into a *señora,* it is seen as morally and politically correct to use *señorita* to refer to a woman whose marital status is unknown.

I gained a personal insight into this dynamic in 1998 during a trip to my hometown of Monterrey. During my stay in Mexico, I underwent both my annual Pap smear and a mammogram. While trying to locate a doctor by telephone and in person, and later on while being examined, secretaries, nurses, medical assistants, and doctors consistently referred to me as Señora González, without asking me if I was single or married. I have never been married, but a *señorita* (a single and therefore a virgin woman) would never have requested a Pap smear. Only a *señora,* a married and sexually active woman, would have requested this type of medical service. A *señorita* socially disowns and does not possess control over either her sexualized body or her reproductive health.[6]

As a Mexicana gets older, how do patriarchal rights over her gradually declining sexualized body get expressed? How does a *señora* take care of her body when it is no longer socially controlled as a potentially productive body (i.e., not able to get pregnant) or when it is desexualized and socially devalued as a feminine body (i.e., not sexually attractive)? How do women who are no longer of reproductive age perceive their bodies and their reproductive health?

It is my hope that feminist paradigms like the ones I have presented here will be useful to analyze the many ways in which reproductive health and other health issues affecting Mexicanas at different life stages are bound up with social contexts promoting not one, but varying, relational and changeable patterns of female subordination. They may offer alternative avenues to explore ways in which women can reclaim and own control over their bodies and their sexuality, and improve the quality of their individual, couple, and family lives. The sexual health of men and their relationships with their own bodies deserves equally important attention as well.

Toward Future Sexual Explorations

In this book, I have attempted to explore potential answers to the research questions I presented in my introduction. I engaged in this process by revisiting the sex lives of a group of women and men, first in Mexico, and later on, after they had migrated to the United States. In this process, I hoped to create a bridge for myself and others to continue exploring our sociological sexual inquiry with those who have become the fastest-growing minority group in the United States. And as I think of this bridge, I realize I am the one who has been mentored by these women and men with regard to sexuality. The lessons I learned confirmed the theory I put forth in chapter 1, and offered additional reflections as well.

There is a normative variety of heterosexualities in Mexican society. As part of everyday life within a diversified variety of rural and urban socio-economic contexts, multiple patriarchal as well as non-hegemonic processes prompt the creation of different and regionally crafted femininities and masculinities and their respective discourses of heterosexual relationships. And while women, men, and their families actively participate in the reproduction of these gender expressions, their sexualities are being shaped by a structure, but there is also flexibility and the possibility to contest and change them. Rural communities, for instance, are plural and subject to modification and evolution. They are neither monolithic nor static patriarchal enclaves. This was confirmed by the women and men who clarified for me that their descriptions of their hometowns during their adolescent years would not be the same if they were adolescents living in their *pueblos* today. Globalization, media, satellite antennas, return migration, the relative economic growth in the region, local political change, cars and trucks with U.S. license plates, young people hugging and kissing in the dark, among other things, have made of some of these communities relatively different places these days. Virginity may still be important, but now girls wear miniskirts in the towns where Marcos, Felipe, and Fidel grew up. And while cantinas still exist in *el pueblo,* these men's hopes for boys is that they will be less likely to be forced to experience coercive sexual initiation like many of their old friends. Thus, while there is fluidity and change, there might be the same constant variable taking place: normative ideals of heterosexuality are continuously regulated and redefined by women, men, and their families as they decipher economic, social, and political change. "Mexico is also changing," most of these informants said.[7] But for those who continue to come and for those returning, migration will continue emphasizing the malleable nature of sex.

Heteronormative models of sexuality are fluid and vulnerable to forces such as migration and modes of social and economic incorporation. Socioeconomic inequalities structure the ways in which these women and men experience heterosexual desire after migrating. At times, within hazardous situations and circumstances, sex has become a danger to be avoided but also a risky pleasure that some find worth exploring. At the same time, a resourceful community and a vibrant and stimulating network of relationships emerging as part of everyday life in the United States offer the means not only to cope with the risks associated with sex, but to reconstruct new meanings attached to love, intimacy, sex, and relationships. And as time passes, parenting becomes another opportunity to revisit and reorganize new meanings of sexuality, virginity, and gender identities for daughters and sons. This process is linked to these women's and men's perceptions of the sexual as part of the immigration and settlement experience. In general, with or without children, either single or married, all of them identify, encounter, and cope with similar risks and dangers prompted by socioeconomic and other social forces that give life to their migration and settlement experiences. In the end, the reproduction of gender identities and new sexual possibilities offering new paths to reinvent heterosexual love and sex may become viable.

How do women use trust and reciprocity about sexual matters to strengthen their position in American society? Do they find ways to redefine what it means to be female and Mexican in a foreign environment? Or do they willingly surrender to the forces of assimilation? The people I interviewed do not surrender to those forces. As they experience a process of "segmented assimilation" (Portes 1995), however, those vulnerable to living in poverty and marginality are exposed to high-risk situations that affect their sex lives. And beyond strengthening their position in American society, women use their knowledge to take care of everyday life issues and concerns, such as the sex education of their children, protecting themselves and their children from all types of abuse, pregnancy out of wedlock, and sexually transmitted diseases, including HIV/AIDS. Their redefinition of what it means to be female and Mexican in the United States is contextualized also by their interaction with other Latina/o immigrants and their continuous exchange in everyday life interactions within their communities, as well as the promotion of a pan-Latino identity and *el sueño americano,* with very Latin American flavors and colors, by the ever-growing Spanish-language media. Through a new generation, mothers and fathers define new expressions of what it means to be a woman or a man, as they educate their children in the United States. For their daughters and sons, marriage should not be undertaken for economic reasons, and sex is not only for reproduction purposes, as it was in small-town Mexico for them. For a new generation, marriage and sex should involve marital sharing, intimacy, respect, and pleasure. Even though they may not know exactly how to accomplish these goals, these parents also dream of love, education, and financial stability in the lives of their children.

Gender and sexuality are unstable, and they are re-made through migration. Both women and men construct new expressions of femininity, masculinity, and heterosexuality as they migrate and settle in Los Angeles. As they engage in these processes, multiple expressions of patriarchy and hegemonic masculinity are still powerful yet vulnerable. Patriarchy has to be monitored and safeguarded, especially when women are perceived by men as over-empowered. Collectively, men may react with resentment and concern to changes that challenge their privileges. These dynamics take place as men themselves cope with race and class relations that create socioeconomic disadvantages, and in extreme cases, sexual objectification for some of them.

Hegemony does not necessarily mean absolute domination. Sexuality is multilayered; sex is not always about power. And gender identities are multidimensional; women and men alternately promote or challenge equality depending on the situations and contexts. In fact, some women and men may become "gender experts," as they strategically manipulate some of the social prescriptions that create gender identities in their communities. For instance, Marcos said that one of his girlfriends agreed to have sex with him, but that immediately afterward she asked him to start making plans to get married. When I asked him why he thought she reacted that way, he said, "Because el compromiso moral comes along.

She thinks: 'What are you going to think about me now?' Right? So, that is the path they follow." He said that women may use sex strategically, as a way to get married. Unfortunately, he said, "women have such bad experiences in their marriages because they get hooked up that way with just any asshole." When Joaquín went to talk to his future in-laws about his desire to marry their daughter, they objected to the marriage. So he told them that they "had been together" to pretend she might be pregnant. Then the parents had no choice but to accept the marital union of a daughter who had been sexually active, he said. Joaquín was lucky to have known how to successfully manipulate sexual morality to his advantage and marry the woman he loved.

As a group, the women I interviewed (as well as the female partners of the men I interviewed) may remain in a subordinate status when compared to the men, especially before migration. Except for extreme cases, however, adult women have avenues to explore, maneuver, and capitalize on the complex nature of their consensual heterosexual relationships in order to explore (from subtle to more emphatic) possibilities for renegotiation. And men — as the official social protagonists of hegemony — do not always enjoy privilege. Some have beliefs and practices imposed upon them, such as coercive sexual initiation and marriage. In extreme situations, as in the case of poor *jornaleros,* men are not only underpaid but at risk of being sexually objectified and abused. In the end, as some of the women and men map themselves onto their own heterosexual tensions and contradictions, both identify the many nuances and labyrinths leading them to explore possibilities for change. Women's access to equal education and paid employment opportunities is crucial in the attempt. The experiences of marginalized men deserves equal and special attention as well.

Migration does not necessarily mean sexual liberation or sexual modernity. Moving to the United States does not automatically translate into an improved or emancipatory sex lifestyle. Even though many of these immigrants were exposed to sex instructional materials in the United States, with regard to the sex education of children, adolescents, and adults alike, or because of a sense of anonymity that protected them to explore casual sex, those changes occurred surrounded by some concerns. Life in the United States may offer a shy woman a sense of anonymity in which to explore casual sex, but she must now worry about STDs and AIDS. Crowded housing may invite some men to explore adventures with other men, but these come with some dangers and risks. Some mothers may feel fortunate to have a good job, but worrying about a small child being sexually abused, kidnapped, or exposed to drugs, or a young adolescent daughter at risk of becoming pregnant, does not always give them peace during a lunch break. Even though these migration-related risks are more "de-gendered" (Gutmann 1996), and as such they represent a sexual danger for both genders, men said they were more exposed to risks associated with alcohol and drug use, and women were more concerned about sexual violence and rape, and being responsible for their children.

Enjoying a satisfying sex life is a social privilege for many of those who live in a fast-paced, highly industrialized capitalist society. In an advanced capitalist economy, time and money transform the multiple meanings and experiences of sexuality and intimacy. For many immigrants, sex and the erotic represent more than just pleasure or a basic need. Having the time just to have sex with a partner — let alone good sex — becomes a luxury. Survival and a busy routine become priorities, and individuals see themselves forced to reorganize the meanings of intimacy and erotic life. A woman may enhance the quality of her sexual encounters with her husband as a consequence of paid employment and the redefined gender politics unfolding in her bedroom. However, being on time at a new job or adjusting to a demanding schedule may continue to redefine some of her new sexual gains at unexpected sexual costs. Like the ideal of love, erotic journeys are continuous and fluid. They do not seem to end.

There is not an absolute, but a selective "sexual silence" in Mexican immigrant communities. The testimony I have presented here is an invitation to revisit an increasingly popular notion in the Latina and Latino sexuality studies literature, that of "sexual silence" (Alonso and Koreck 1993; Marín and Gómez 1997; Díaz 1998; Carrillo 2002). These informants revealed how their families were more likely to be silent with regard to issues of child sexual abuse and rape, men's extramarital affairs, and homosexuality. These three topics interestingly identify the three nondominant social groups at the core of these silences: children and girls, women, and gays and lesbians. Thus, I suggest that selective silence may at times have more to do with social inequality than with the "cultural traits" associated with a so-called "Latino culture." In addition, talking about sexuality-related issues and concerns was not a foreign activity within their immigrant communities. Why? These immigrants had sex-related conversations because of the following factors:

1. Gender. The normative patterns of mothering help women learn to develop emotional ties with other women (Chodorow 1978; Segura and Pierce 1993) as they explore ways to cope with their individual and collective concerns, in this case with regard to sexuality.

2. Heterosexuality. It is the dominant sexual identity, and as such, it normalizes and grants social permission to those who have the need to talk with someone else about their sexual issues and despairs.

3. Diversity. Within vibrant immigrant communities and cultures — especially the inner-city barrios of U.S. megacities — community-based agencies and clinics promote sex education programs, such as AIDS and reproductive health education.

4. Sexualized Spanish-language media. Television and radio capitalize on sexuality-related issues, which are discussed with the audience in news, advertising, and talk shows.

Sex research seems to be a lifelong, stimulating affair for those I interviewed and for myself. I have attempted to study the processes of social inequality as connected to heterosexuality in two countries. And as such, my research focuses more frequently on the pains of the erotic, the panics, the fears, the concerns. The reader might have wanted to learn more about the pleasures of sex. This book leaves many questions unasked, many issues unexplored. Yet to be disclosed are these informants' sexual secret desires, the pleasures of their actual sexual encounters, the fantasies they have put into practice, their unmet sexual needs, their new erotic fears and threats, and their same-sex desires and concerns, among many other sexual intricacies connected to various forms of social inequality and also privilege. This book is an attempt to articulate women's and men's voices with regard to their heterosexual experiences as migration and settlement unites both Mexico and the United States. In addition, by incorporating men's sexual vulnerabilities and their views of women, I hoped to do more than just validate what many men told me when I explained my interest in listening to them. As Diego put it:

> Some people have said that the man–woman relationship is like a war. Well, I think it's about time to have a pact. Men and women need to sit down in order to have a conversation, to come up with a treaty, just like in a war, to come out of our trenches and stop shooting at each other because this became an indiscriminate shooting. The woman has embraced her trenches and she is shooting against us and she uses whatever she has available at hand to do it. And we are not going to get anywhere that way.

I hope the coincidences, contradictions, and complexities that have emerged from these sexual narratives have highlighted some avenues for social change, as Diego and many others hope for the people in communities on both sides of the border. In addition, Diego's and the other men's stories reveal what Michael Burawoy (1991) has identified as "theoretical gaps or silences": "A given theory may fail to address an aspect of a particular empirical phenomenon that, once included, compels the reconstruction of theory" (10). Thus, may the gender tapestries and sexuality threads of these narratives offer us new possibilities for future sociology of gender and sexuality research, women's and men's studies theorizing, Latina and Latino studies inquiry, and activism for social justice beyond the bedsheets and intimacies of these sixty Mexicans' erotic journeys.

Appendixes

APPENDIX A. Study Participants

	Place of Origin	Age	Years in the United States	Marital Status	Children Female	Children Male	Education	Occupation
STATE OF JALISCO								
Women								
Amparo	ST	45	25	Married	2	3	Primaria, Academia	Homemaker
Beatriz	ST-50	33	10	Married	1	1	Primaria	Seamstress
Candelaria	ST	36	11	Married	1	3	Primaria, Academia	Homemaker
Deyanira	ST/G	41	11	Married	2	1	Primaria	Homemaker
Eréndira	G	32	11	Single	0	0	Secundaria, Academia	Health educator
Felicia	ST	37	10	Cohabiting*	2	2	Primaria	Homemaker
Graciela	ST-50	32	12	Divorced	0	0	Secundaria (2 years)	Artisan
Hortencia	ST-50	33	13	Married	2	1	Secundaria (1 year)	Homemaker
Idalia	ST	30	10	Cohabiting	1	1	Secundaria	Homemaker
Juanita	ST	30	8	Married	3	1	Primaria	Homemaker
Lorena	ST	34	10	Married	0	4	Primaria	Homemaker
Margarita	ST-50	39	14	Married	2	1	Primaria	Homemaker
Nora	ST	33	9	Cohabiting	1	0	Bachelor's degree	Physician's assistant
Oralia	ST-50	39	15	Married	1	1	Primaria, Academia	Health educator
Patricia	ST-50	34	6	Married	3	0	Primaria	Child care P/T

Name	Code	Age		Marital status			Education	Occupation
Romelia	G	32	7	Cohabiting	2	1	Primaria, Trade School	Sales P/T
Salomé	ST-G	43	20	Separated	3	2	Primaria (4 years)	Machine operator
Tomasita	ST	30	9	Separated	4	1	Secundaria	Homemaker
Victoria	ST-50	34	14	Married	1	2	Primaria (5 years)	Homemaker
Xóchitl	ST	34	9	Married	1	1	Secundaria, Academia	Sales P/T
Men								
Fidel	ST	37	13	Married	3	0	Preparatoria	Technician
Joaquín	G	44	5	Separated	1	2	Secundaria, Normal*	Construction worker
Marcos	ST, IR	43	14	Single	0	0	Preparatoria, College*	Lay parish minister
Felipe	ST	44	16	Married	3	1	Secundaria	Truck driver
Ernesto	G	43	20	Married	1	1	Preparatoria (2 years)	Technician
Gabriel	ST/G	42	12	Married	0	1	Master's degree	Machine operator
Nicolás	ST, IR	38	14	Married	0	3	Bachelor's degree	Administrative job
Vinicio	ST	33	18	Married	2	1	Secundaria, Academia*	Maintenance (janitor)
Jacobo	G	35	15	Married*	1	3	High school	Administrative job
Daniel	ST	28	8	Single	0	0	Secundaria (2 years)	Construction worker

(continued)

Study Participants *(continued)*

	Place of Origin	Age	Years in the United States	Marital Status	Children Female	Children Male	Education	Occupation
MEXICO CITY								
Women								
Azucena	MC	43	11	Married*	1	2	Secundaria, Normal	Community educator
Belén	MC	43	9	Married	2	2	Secundaria, Normal	Homemaker, volunteer
Cecilia	MC	32	8	Married	2	1	Secundaria, Academia (2 years)	Office clerk, student
Diamantina	MC	31	5	Married	2	0	Secundaria	Homemaker
Emilia	MC	32	7	Married	0	0	College (3 years)	Tax advisor, student
Fernanda	MC	31	8	Cohabiting*	2	0	Preparatoria (1 year), Normal	Factory assembler
Gabriela	MC	30	10	Married	1	1	Secundaria, Nursing school	Homemaker
Lolita	MC	26	5	Single	3	0	Secundaria, Preparatoria (1 year)	Apartment manager
Irene	MC	38	13	Married	1	2	Secundaria, Nursing school	Homemaker
Jimena	MC	40	8	Cohabiting*	2	3	Secundaria	Seamstress
Macaria	MC	37	9	Single	0	0	Preparatoria, Normal	Seamstress
Norma	MC	38	8	Married	1	0	Secundaria, Academia	Homemaker
Olga	MC	32	10	Married	0	0	Preparatoria, Trade school	Tax advisor
Irasema	MC	39	9	Married*	1	1	Secundaria, Academia	Seamstress
Rosalía	MC	40	10	Married*	3	3	Primaria	Seamstress

Name		Age		Marital status			Education	Occupation
Soledad	MC	27	6	Married	1	1	Secundaria, Trade school	Seamstress P/T
Trinidad	MC	40	10	Married*	1	1	Bachelor's degree	Public relations
Yadira	MC	41	14	Married	1	2	Primaria	Domestic worker
Zenaida	MC	33	5	Married	0	2	Preparatoria, College (1 year)	Secretary
Azalea	MC	43	12	Cohabiting*	2	3	Primaria	Apartment manager
Men								
Alejandro	MC	37	8	Married	1	1	College (1 year)	Small business owner
Mauricio	MC	26	5	Cohabiting[2]	2	0	Secundaria (2 years)	Construction worker
Eugenio	MC	43	11	Single	0	0	Preparatoria (0.5 years)	Construction worker
Alfredo	MC	36	11	Cohabiting[1]	1	1	Preparatoria (2.5 years)	Construction worker
Diego	MC	36	15	Separated	1	1	Preparatoria (1 year)	Schoolteacher P/T
Fermín	MC[a]	42	17	Married	3	0	Preparatoria (1.5 years)	Bus driver
Raúl	MC	34	12	Divorced	1	0	College (2.5 years)	Technician
Sebastián	MC	40	5	Married	2	1	College (2.5 years)	Technician
Alfonso	MC	33	10	Married	2	1	College (2 years)	Construction foreman
Emiliano	MC	43	7	Married	2	1	Secundaria	Technician

(continued)

[a]Fermín grew up in both urban Mexico City and a small town in the State of Mexico (see ch. 4).

Birthplace Codes

ST	Born and raised in a small town far from Guadalajara (at least 60 miles)
ST-50	Born and raised in a small town located within 50 miles of Guadalajara
G	Born and raised in Guadalajara
ST-G	Born in a small town and raised in Guadalajara
ST/G	Born and raised in a small town, migrated as an adolescent or a young adult to Guadalajara
IR	Intraregional migration from a rural to a mid-size (i.e., semi-industrial) town as an adolescent or a young adult
MC	Born and raised in Mexico City

Marital Status Codes

Married*	Married; previously married and divorced
Cohabiting*	Cohabiting; previously married and divorced
Cohabiting₁	Cohabiting for the first time
Cohabiting₂	Cohabiting for the second time

Marital Status: Married*, Cohabiting*, Cohabiting$_1$, Cohabiting$_2$

Education Codes

Primaria	Equivalent to elementary school; grades 1–6
Secundaria	Equivalent to middle school; grades 7–9
Preparatoria	Equivalent to high school
Academia	Trade school training to become a certified secretary
Academia*	Completed 2 years of Academia
Normal	Escuela Normal, equivalent to teachers college
Normal*	Completed 1 year of Escuela Normal
College*	Completed an Associate Degree

APPENDIX A. Averages

	Age	Years in the United States	Marital Status	Children		Education[a]	Occupation[b]
				Female	Male		
STATE OF JALISCO							
Women	35.0	11.68	Married: 12 out of 20	1.6	1.3	7.10 years	Women with paid employment: 9 out of 20
Men	38.7	13.50	Married: 7 out of 10	1.1	1.2	12.45 years	All men had paid employment
MEXICO CITY							
Women	35.8	8.85	Married: 15 out of 20	1.3	1.2	10.15 years	Women with paid employment: 15 out of 20
Men	37.0	10.1	Married: 5 out of 10	1.5	0.6	11.45 years	All men had paid employment

[a] With the exception of the women from the State of Jalisco, the average level of education for the women and men in this study is higher than the average educational level for all women and men in Mexico, where the national average for individuals fifteen years old and older is 7.1 years for women and 7.6 years for men (INEGI 2004).

[b] Men reported an average annual income that fluctuated between $12,000 and $24,000. Some women with paid employment reported that their jobs did not offer them a stable or easy-to-calculate income; therefore, I do not offer an average for them. These informants were mestizas and mestizos.

Methodological Considerations

The research with the women and men was conducted in accordance with a human subjects protocol approved by the Institutional Review Board at the University of Southern California, and the Committee for Protection of Human Subjects at the University of California at Berkeley, respectively.

As I was engaged in my analytical tasks, I became keenly aware of crucial methodological considerations. First, being an insider (Mexican, immigrant, woman, and heterosexual) might have influenced the ways in which I designed and conducted my interviews and coded and analyzed my data. From a positivist approach, my own biases might have given me some methodological disadvantages. For example, I came of age as a *señorita* while being afraid of premarital sex. I was exposed in my *grupos de amigas* to a particular fear: "Men talk among themselves about their sexual adventures and, during these conversations, men denigrate the women they have sex with." Thus, conducting qualitative research on Mexicans and heterosexuality — with the explicit objective of explaining the sexual behavior of other heterosexual Mexicans — automatically reflected back on me.

Alternatively, being an insider enhanced my strengths, as I am intimately familiar with the historical, social, and cultural background of many of the issues and concerns about Mexicans and heterosexuality. My own personal background made me particularly sensitive to exploring some specific issues with regard to my participants' need to preserve premarital virginity, in addition to many other sexuality-related themes. In other words, being an insider provided me with deep "insider understandings" (Lofland and Lofland 1995, 61).

Beyond this evident advantage, I was determined to be a tactful researcher who is eager to benefit from being an insider, but who is also sensitive enough to become an outsider throughout the entire research process. I constantly monitored myself with regard to my own biases and preconceptions about Mexicans and sexuality. Being an outsider meant learning to think critically about my own research as I received and examined the feedback generously offered to me by

Latino(a) and non-Latino(a) professors, colleagues, and friends who thoroughly read and critiqued my work on a frequent basis. In this way, I learned to be a researcher who "wishes not to be one or the other but to be both or either as the research demands" (Lofland and Lofland 1995, 23). Lastly, being an outsider-within (Collins 1991) provided me with a shared standpoint with my informants and a unique vision of their sexual histories, first, as an immigrant exposed to but excluded from North American mainstream academia and feminist ideas, and second, as a well-educated never-married Mexicana who belongs to, but who is usually perceived as "too unusual," within Mexican immigrant communities.

A second methodological consideration was the concepts of reliability and validity. This study was not designed to offer standardized and fixed responses that can be obtained or replicated by different researchers or by the same scientist on more than one intervention — the concept known as reliability (Silverman 1994, 145). Instead, my main purpose was to conduct in-depth examinations and analyses of the socially constructed meanings attached to what heterosexual Mexicans living in the United States report they believe (ideologies, beliefs) and put into practice (actual sexual behavior) with regard to central aspects of their sex lives. Thus, validity or the search for true testimonies that may accurately represent the social construction of Mexicans and heterosexuality, is emphasized in this study.

Data collection represented a third methodological challenge. I told my informants that I had been trained as a therapist, a strength that represented an invitation for them to freely open up about their intimate lives, and a learning experience for me to explore the best ways to deal with challenging methodological issues. In the case of the female participants who disclosed stories of sexual violence, I offered them the choice of having the tape recorder turned off and of stopping the interview. This intervention became necessary when the women's emotions became intense and did not allow them to continue talking. At that moment, I made use of my previous training as a therapist to make a brief clinical intervention. This intervention consisted of two or three sentences which I used to express my sensitivity and caring. While this intervention reportedly made the informants feel safe and comfortable, my interventions and self-identification as a *consejera* may represent a bias during the data collection phase. Such professional identity and clinical training facilitated the collection of a wide range of information from participants in general. However, my identity might have also invited some of them to expose their emotional difficulties and concerns. In the case of women survivors of sexual violence who shared their stories openly, they might have perceived the interview as a potential opportunity for healing and/or future therapy sessions with me. But as I explained both the research nature of my interviews and my genuine interest in listening to their pain, after our official interviews, if necessary, the interviews lasted longer than expected. In all cases, we were able to successfully complete our interviews. At the end of each interview, I offered each woman a list of professionals who specialized in the treatment of sexual violence against women.

I used a qualitative methodology to investigate sexuality because it is a complicated construct established, formulated, and transformed by, through, and within social practice (Gagnon and Simon 1973; Gagnon 1977; Weeks 1985; Plummer 1995; Seidman 1994). If I had used a quantitative methodology (i.e., a fixed design) in order to conduct a sociological study about the experiences of heterosexuality among Mexican immigrants, I would have disregarded the fluid nature underlying the social construction of human sexuality. For decades, the field of sociology of sexualities has emphasized this principle. Thus, positivist assumptions (objectivity, social reality as a static process that can be measured and replicated, and the belief that we can best know the social world through distance and detachment) are difficult to sustain for a sociological study of Mexicans and heterosexuality as part of the immigrant experience.

After finishing the study and critically examining my research work, I was able to identify some of the challenges of the present project. First, since all of my interviews were conducted in Spanish (only the quoted excerpts used in my analysis were translated into English), I was concerned about the extent to which the emotional meaning and tone of the participants' stories could be lost in the translation process. For my informants, Spanish remains the language of emotions because it was in Spanish that affective or emotional meanings were originally imprinted (Espín 1987, 1999). Thus, I attempt to save these processes by inserting expressions, in Spanish, in the quoted excerpts. Second, the nature of the present study did not allow me to assess how the specific age of a participant at time of immigration might have affected her/his sex life. Similarly, the impact of length of time in the United States on the sex life of these informants was impossible to assess with this small of a sample size. And third, my study consisted of "one-time interview" materials. A longitudinal technique might have allowed me to examine the changes informants experienced over a specific period of time (e.g., five or ten years).

Notes

Introduction

1. For research on Mexican men and gay and bisexual experiences, see Carrier 1976, 1977, 1985, 1995; Almaguer 1993; Liguori 1995; Prieur 1998; Díaz 1998; and Cantú 1999, 2000, 2002. Additional publications have also examined the homophobic experiences of Latina/Chicana lesbians (e.g., Moraga and Anzaldúa 1981; Moraga 1983; Argüelles and Rich 1984, 1985; Rosenberg 1993; Espín 1986; Anzaldúa 1987, 1993).

2. Elsewhere (2000, 2003), I have used the concept of regional patriarchies and *machismos regionales* as pseudonyms. I realize now, however, that the concept of *machismo* as a theoretical category to study gender inequality contributes to the reproduction of stereotypes commonly identified in gender studies in Latin America and the United States. Therefore, here, I only use the term *regional patriarchies* and I no longer adopt the term *regional machismos* as its pseudonym.

3. The Mexican migration literature has been dominated largely by economic concerns brought about by labor migration. The prolific and highly respected work produced by leading scholars of Mexican labor migration, including Frank Bean, Jorge Bustamante, Wayne Cornelius, Manuel García y Griego, Agustín Escobar Latapí, Rodolfo Tuirán, David Heer, Douglas Massey, Philip Martin, Michael Piore, Alejandro Portes, J. Edward Taylor, Roger Waldinger, Karen Woodrow-Lafield, and Sidney Weintraub, exemplify this tendency in the field of Mexican migration studies since the late 1970s.

4. For the interview guide, see González-López 2000.

5. Personal reactions to vignettes have been widely used by researchers conducting work on morality, moral reasoning, and gender (e.g., Gilligan 1982; Stack 1994).

Chapter 1. Twice Forgotten

1. The acculturation approach has become the dominant model or paradigm to study many aspects of the lives of Latinas and Latinos as they incorporate within the new country. The *Hispanic Journal of Behavioral Sciences* (the oldest academic publication in the United States examining the behavior of Latinas and Latinos) published, from 1979 to 1998, at least thirty articles that included the term "acculturation" in their titles. In June 1987, the journal dedicated an entire issue to acculturation research and Latinos. The May 1994 issue was dedicated to two specific areas: acculturation and women's studies.

2. Given the dramatic consequences of the AIDS epidemic on Latino communities, the sexual practices and attitudes of U.S. Latino/Hispanic cultural groups have become the main focus of many research projects conducted since the late 1980s. Analyses of the possible causes for the dramatic increase in the incidence of HIV/AIDS among U.S. Latinos have resulted in the publication of numerous articles in behavioral and epidemiological journals, as well as groundbreaking monographs (e.g., Díaz 1998) and edited volumes (e.g., Mishra, Conner, and Magaña 1996).

3. The fertility rate was 6.8 in 1970, 5.0 in 1980, and 3.4 in 1990 (CONAPO 2003).

4. For a discussion of *la casa chica,* see Gutmann 1996.

Chapter 2. Beyond the Hymen

1. Religion plays a role as a source of guilt for some of the women in the study who had premarital sexual relations. But "religious guilt" seems more likely to be experienced as a consequence rather than as an antecedent or prior factor. Interestingly, these women rarely referred to religion as an isolated or exclusive condition controlling a woman's sexuality. Instead, it is always examined in conjunction with other circumstances, such as the family's education in regard to sexuality in general and virginity in particular. In *De Madres a Hijas* (2003), I discuss the mother-daughter relationship with regard to promoting virginity. Of those mothers who expect their daughters to preserve virginity until marriage, only three of them do it based on their religious values. Interestingly, two of these three mothers promote virginity based on their Protestant religion, and only one does it based on her Catholic faith.

2. Historical examinations of archives on colonial social life have analyzed how male supremacy in both indigenous and Hispanic cultures reinforced women's subordinate position in colonial Mexican societies. For a discussion of Mexican women's social life during the colonial years, see Tostado Gutiérrez 1991; Stern 1995; and J. Tuñón Pablos 2000.

3. The Council of Trent (1545–63), or El Concilio de Trento, written by Fray Gabino Carta, explains the Catholic Church's teachings with regard to sexuality, and how this document served as the basis for indoctrinating the indigenous

population (Rubio 1997). In the Council of Trent, virginity was defined as an idealized condition. Accordingly, virginity was socially defined in Mexico as the best "certificate" a woman had to prove her decency and honorability: *"La virginidad era un estado más perfecto que el matrimonio"* (Virginity was a state more perfect than marriage) (Tostado Gutiérrez 1991, 197).

4. Brianda Domecq (1992) examines how the Aztecs advised women against the loss of virginity. The Tzotzil (a Mayan group) used lack of virginity, if the husband was not aware of it, as a good reason to invalidate marriage. And the Zapotecs expected the just-married husband to show his mother, during the wedding night, a white silk handkerchief with spots of blood to prove his wife's virginity. Domecq cites Fray Diego de Landa (1959) as saying that, among Mayans, "little girls were asked to be 'honest' and *la falta de recato y pudor* [lack of modesty/honesty and chastity/shyness] was punished by rubbing them with black pepper [because of the sensitive nature of the subject it cannot be said where] which caused a lot of pain" (Domecq 1992, 17–21).

5. See chapter 8 and González-López 2000 for general examinations of sexuality and religion in the lives of the women in this study.

6. Leading researchers in sexuality studies in Mexico, Ivonne Szasz and Juan Guillermo Figueroa, have found that, on average, premarital intercourse is experienced by women for the first time immediately before their first marriage. According to Szasz and Figueroa (1997), this dynamic has not changed over four generations. Even though the reasons for this pattern of sexual behavior in Mexican women have not been examined in depth, it is important to mention the following evidence. In his professional work as a premarital counselor with 446 young, working-class, heterosexual couples living in Mexico City, Miguel Padilla Pimentel found that 95 percent had practiced premarital sex. Based on the testimony of male partners, for many of them, premarital sex was a way to "make sure" their future wives were virgins. According to Padilla Pimentel, after the men ascertained that the women were in fact virgins, they felt a moral commitment to marry them, as a way to comply with the traditional sexual morality (1972, 84–85). De la Peña and Toledo, in a major study of 613 women and men living in Mexico City, indicated that about 40 percent of them (about the same percent for both genders) identified as "very important" a woman's preservation of her virginity until the day of her marriage. An additional 25 percent defined premarital virginity as "somewhat important." In contrast, only 25 percent of the respondents identified premarital virginity as something that had "absolutely no importance" (1991, 19). In another study, of adults living in Baja California, De la Peña and Toledo (1992) found that 54 percent of females had experienced premarital intercourse. The only two women in the present study who are virgins by virtue of never having cohabited with a man or been married are preserving their virginity for reasons other than religion.

7. Ann Twinam (1989) offers an analysis of the historical and elitist roots of the link between a woman's virginity and family honor, respect, and decency in colonial Latin America. Mexican researchers conducting research with Mexican women on their sexuality have identified the concept of *casarse bien*. Mexican

anthropologist Rosío Córdova Plaza (1998) explains that young Mexican women living in Tuzamapán, Veracruz, "dream of 'getting married the right way' because the prestige it involves accompanies their marriage throughout the years and it will be remembered even when partners separate and each one establishes a new relationship with another person."

8. In her research with women and men living in three Mexican communities (Guanajuato, Oaxaca, and Mexico City), Ana Amuchástegui conceptualizes premarital virginity as an asset or a transaction commodity for Mexican women. Amuchástegui writes, "The importance of female virginity seems to depend on the idea of its nature as an asset which is exchanged for marriage, and as a consequence, for the future economic security of the woman" (1998, 108). Amuchástegui also found that informants living in areas where gender inequalities may be less rigid (e.g., urban areas) are more likely to recognize a woman's right to experience sexual desire in comparison to other social contexts (e.g., rural areas). Patricia Zavella examines the sexual story of a heterosexual Chicana and concludes that "the strategy of saving her virginity for marriage and eventual motherhood would provide her with the expectation of economic stability, for the assumption was that a young man would support her in exchange of her unsullied reputation" (1997, 395). And Córdova Plaza concludes, in her anthropological study of a community in Tuzamapán, Veracruz: "There is a normative discourse in the community which overvalues the possession of an intact hymen as a type of symbolic capital which is at risk because there is only one card to play, a condition which supposedly provides the woman with benefits later on in her marital union" (1998, 8). The concept of *capital femenino* is inspired by sociological conceptualizations of *cultural capital* as defined by Pierre Bourdieu (1973).

9. Ann Twinam examines the connections between women's sexuality, socioeconomic status, honor, and birth out of wedlock in colonial Latin America. She writes: "Illegitimate women not only found their pool of potential marriage partners restricted, but their illegitimacy could adversely affect the occupational choices of their sons and the marriage potential of their daughters. Absence of honor could thus limit the social mobility of both sexes, as well as the future of succeeding generations" (1989, 124). Marcela Tostado Gutiérrez also describes the experiences of Mexican women in colonial society with respect to virginity and its social exchange value: "In this way, the law recognized for the woman the importance of the preservation of her sexual virtue, a condition upon which her possibilities to get married, to maintain family honor and social status, depended" (1991, 200).

10. This evidence resonates with the previously discussed conceptualization of virginity as *capital femenino* which acquires a higher or lower exchange value depending on the gender inequalities the woman is exposed to in a given social context. Sexuality studies conducted in Mexico identify parallel patterns. Barrios and Pons (1994) have found that Mexican women living in rural areas are subjected to more severe gender inequalities than women living in more complex social contexts. And Szasz and Figueroa (1997) suggest more relaxed sexuality regulations for women living in large cities, indicating a correlation between

access to education, employment opportunities, social spaces, and sexuality. As they state: "Women who live in less socially restrictive contexts or social groups, where they enjoy greater spatial mobility, and alternatives regarding their place of residence, life styles, and access to education and paid work outside the home experience other standards regarding sexuality" (13). Consistent with this assumption, my analysis of gender inequality and the ways in which mothers from Jalisco educate their daughters with regard to virginity (see González-López 2003) illustrates sexism as more frequently perceived to be a potential danger by women born and raised in Jalisco than by women from Mexico City. The concept of regional patriarchies explains this and other social dynamics.

11. The term *señorita* refers to a woman who has never been married. The social use of this term implies that the woman is a virgin. A *señorita* becomes a *señora* when she gets married. In my conclusion, I discuss some of the socially constructed linguistic taboos and gender traps associated with both terms.

12. In her academic and clinical examinations of Latina sexuality, Oliva M. Espín has identified a similar paradigm: "To enjoy sexual pleasure, even in marriage, may indicate lack of virtue" (Espín 1986, 279).

13. My use of this paradigm is inspired by Carole S. Vance's (1984) examinations of women's sexuality.

14. Amuchástegui (2001), Hirsch (2003), Prieur (1998), Szasz (1997), and others doing sex research in various regions of Mexico have found similar patterns. The terms *fracaso* or *mujer fracasada* were used by many of the women and men to describe the experiences of women who have had sexual relations before marriage and also those of *madres solteras,* that is, single women who get pregnant out of wedlock and do not get married. This commonly used expression is quite revealing: being a *fracaso* means failing to comply with the social and moral expectation of being a virgin before marriage and therefore having the risk of being socially and morally devalued. Juana Armanda Alegría (1974) examines the social and moral burden placed on women who are described as a *fracaso:* society places an existential *fracaso* on them.

15. Women who had intercourse for the first time after getting married did not have an easier experience. Most reported feeling discomfort, shame, embarrassment, fear, anxiety, or confusion about what "they were supposed to do" before, during, and after their first sexual encounter. Two women from Jalisco had extreme reactions. Salomé did not visit her family for two months after she was married. She was ashamed to see her parents because "they would know she was sexually active." And Beatriz experienced a panic attack on her wedding night. She and her husband sought the professional services of a psychotherapist during their honeymoon on the Pacific Coast.

Chapter 3. Pleasurable Dangers, Dangerous Pleasures

1. Other sex researchers have identified similar concerns to those Fermín articulated. Amuchástegui found that some rural men may not want to have sex

with a sex worker, but having sex with a girlfriend may lead to the moral obligation to marry her (2001, 386). Similarly, young men from Mexico City may feel the obligation to marry a virgin woman after they have had sex with her (Padilla 1972, 85).

2. According to Casa Alianza, a non-governmental organization, "40 Million Children Live or Work on the Streets in Latin America" ("En la pobreza, más de la mitad de la población de América Latina," *La Jornada*, June 1, 2004 [http://www.jornada.unam.mx]).

3. Leading sociologists studying gender have identified the following challenges with regard to sex role theory: (1) it assumes gender as a prescribed static "role" by negating its fluidity; (2) it ignores non-universal and multiple notions of masculinity and femininity; (3) it overlooks the relational nature of gender; (4) it neglects the situational and contextualized character of gender; (5) it depoliticizes gender by overlooking structural forces driving power, social life, and everyday life interactions; and (6) it offers no light with regard to social justice and change (see Kimmel 2000, 89–91).

4. See Ayala, Carrier, and Magaña 1996 for an examination of the experiences of a group of immigrant women (many were mothers of children and heads of households) who became sex workers after migrating to the United States. For many of these women, a cantina owner in the United States covered the smuggling fees to bring them across the border. Most had never visited a cantina or worked as sex workers before migrating; many were from rural areas and had low education levels and no employment history.

5. For an examination of the romantic and sexual relationships within families in some rural areas of Western Mexico, see Chávez Torres 1998, 153. For similar marriage practices in other countries, including Middle Eastern cultures, see Korotayev 2000.

6. None of the men I interviewed reported experiences of sexual initiation with domestic workers. This is no surprise, especially for men who were from working-class backgrounds whose families could not afford the services of *domésticas*. However, some of the men from middle-class backgrounds explained that either they or some of their friends had sexually harassed and/or experienced sexual adventures with *"la muchacha"* — the young woman working as a domestic at their parents' or relatives' home. For a discussion of the sexual objectification of domestic workers as the sexual initiators of young men in the family, see Romero 1992. This process of sexual objectification of domestic workers is reproduced through media, mainly television and movies. See Le Vine (1993, 91) for a discussion of young married men who have extramarital affairs with older women.

7. For contemporary urban societies, see Gutmann 1996; for women's construction of "the pluralization of patriarchs" as a maneuver to protect themselves in late colonial Mexico, see Stern 1995.

8. The original letters, in Spanish, from "Amelia" and "Matías" (and Dr. Ochoa's responses to both of them) were published in *Desnudarse: Revista de Cultura y Educación Sexual*, December 1999, p. 12; and May 2000, p. 21, respec-

tively. Dr. Ochoa offered a feminist-informed response to both Amelia and Matías. Dr. Ochoa also broadcasts a radio show entitled *Desnudo Total*. The show has been aired since 1996, late at night, Monday through Friday, on the XEW 900 AM radio dial, one of the oldest and most respected radio stations in Mexico and Latin America. In addition, the doctor gives sex advice on her TV show, *El Buen Sexo*, every night at 9 P.M. Central Time, broadcast on TV Azteca in Mexico (Azteca America in the United States).

Chapter 4. Sex Is a Family Affair

1. When my informants recalled their childhood and adolescent years, many described their parents (their mothers, in particular) as shy, evasive, and at times aggressive when they were asked questions with regard to menstruation, pregnancy, and rape. With some exceptions, conversations with older friends or teachers' lectures about biology were the first sources of information about reproductive health and sex for many of them. In many instances, the women learned about menstruation from their friends, older sisters, aunts, and neighbors, and from mothers as well — but only after they had already begun menstruating. Many men sought answers and advice about sex in conversations with peers, older brothers, cousins, or uncles. Men, more frequently than women, reported reading pornographic magazines, alone or in groups, as they sought for answers about sex. Some of these findings have been reported by others who have conducted research with Mexican populations (e.g., LeVine 1993; Gutmann 1996; Rafallei and Ontai 2001; Amuchástegui 2001; Carrillo 2002; Hirsch 2003; Hurtado 2003; Stern et al. 2003).

2. As I began my interviews in 1997, coercive marriage as a measure "to repair the moral damage done to a woman and her family" was still a legal practice in many Latin American countries. One journal reported: "Laws that exonerate rapists who marry their victims exist in Argentina, Brazil, Chile, Colombia, Ecuador, Guatemala, Honduras, Nicaragua, Panama, Paraguay, the Dominican Republic and Venezuela, according to an attorney for the Center for Reproductive Law and Policy. In Costa Rica, a rapist is exonerated if he only expresses a desire to marry his victim, regardless of whether or not she accepts his offer. Only a quarter of rapes are reported in Peru, where an estimated 25,000 women are believed to be raped each year. Particularly, in poor areas, families pressure rape victims to marry their assailants because they believe a marriage offer restores honor to both the victim and her family. If the victims are reluctant to go through with their marriages, families will often tell them that law says they must marry their assailants or withdraw the charges" (*Contemporary Sexuality* 31, no. 4 [April 1997]: 11). In Turkey, "sexual assaults against women are classified by law 'as felonies against public decency and family order,' not felonies against individual women." Nearly half of forensic physicians conduct virginity tests for many reasons, including issuing a certification of virginity before marriage, or after, if there has been no vaginal bleeding following first marital inter-

course (Frank et al. 1999). See Gruenbaum (1982, 1996) and Boddy (1982) for compelling anthropological studies of the social and cultural dynamics connecting family honor, virginity, and clitoridectomy in Sudan and other parts of the Muslim world.

3. Between the 1930s and 1990s, the rates for marriage as a result of out-of-wedlock pregnancies have decreased from 59.6 to 19.3 percent for whites, and from 21.8 to 6.7 percent for African Americans (Bachu 1999, 5). Even though cohabitation has not become an alternative to marriage in contemporary society, it is becoming a more socially acceptable arrangement in general, and "singles are increasingly cohabiting in response to pregnancy" (Raley 2001, 66). In contemporary society, however, some men expect sexual abstinence before marriage for their daughters, and accordingly, some women may be exposed to their fathers' punishment for engaging in premarital sex (Secunda 1992, 151–52). Research with a group of white college women also identified fear of parental disapproval as one of the reasons they remained virgins until marriage (Sprecher and Reagan 1996).

4. Twinam (1989) examines the interconnections between honor, female sexuality, virginity, and birth out of wedlock (*hijos naturales*) as parts of a code of morality during the colonial period of Latin America history (1630–1820). Her findings show the historical roots of coercive marriage as experienced by women like Irasema and Trinidad in contemporary Mexican society. Amuchástegui offers additional explanations for coercive marriage. She states, "In the three communities where [her] study was conducted, loss of a young woman's virginity was considered a man's responsibility, who remained with the obligation to marry her in order to repair the 'damage.' In case he did not comply with this obligation, the young woman would remain contaminated and stigmatized, and she would lose the opportunity to have a legitimate husband. In that regard, the man would be considered a coward, abusive, and lacking honor" (2001, 382).

5. In Mexico, the law does not prohibit abortion in case of rape or when the mother's health is at risk (Rubio 1997). However, the process is complicated and excruciating for those who request it legally. For current debates on abortion and women's reproductive rights in Mexico and other Latin American countries, see Lucía Rayas 1998; Elena Poniatowska 2000; and Marta Lamas 1998, 2001.

6. Amuchástegui reports how Mexican women similarly use the term *defraudar* to associate moral disobedience toward the paternal figure and morally inappropriate sexual behavior (2001, 216).

7. In 1995 González Montes studied indigenous communities where *el robo* and *la huida* had been adopted and had come to replace the traditional marriage ritual, partly because of economic factors: running away was less expensive (as reported in Amuchástegui 2001, 390, 392). Similarly, Brandes examined parents' preferences that a daughter elope rather than have a traditional wedding because elopement would save the family a lot of money (cited in Prieur 1998, 213).

8. See Ramos Lira, Koss, and Russo 1999; Wilson 1990; Hirsch 2003.

9. The men reported having had more sexual partners in their adult life compared to the women. Other researchers among Mexicans living in Mexico indicates a similar pattern: men have had more sexual partners in any given period of time (Szasz 1998).

10. "In Mexico City, marriage is the majority's response to an undesired pregnancy, according to the study 'Más vale prevenir que lamentar: Percepciones sobre el embarazo en la adolescencia' [Prevention is better than regret, perceptions of pregnancy in adolescence]" (Godínez 2002). Godínez describes a study, conducted among youth living in the sixteen delegations that compose Mexico City, that found that up to 45 percent of young women and men facing an out-of-wedlock pregnancy decided to marry, whereas 17 percent decided to have an abortion. Virginity was not considered important by the men participating in the study; they perceived premarital sex as a step toward strengthening future relationships.

11. In Spanish, the verb *fallar* goes beyond "letting someone down." *Fallar* also means: (1) *malograrse* [to turn out badly]; (2) *faltar* [to not comply with a mandate or obligation]; (3) *frustrarse* [to frustrate]; and (4) *fracasar* [to be a failure] (Spanish synonyms are from the *Diccionario Larousse Sinónimos/Antónimos,* 1986 ed.). Thus, for a woman who associates premarital sexual relations with the expression *"Le fallé a mamá,"* the phrase means much more than just "letting her mother down." *Fallar* also has multiple sexual and moral connotations that define a young daughter's sex life within the family and within social contexts.

12. Consistent with these gender dynamics, in her anthropological research in a Michoacán community, Annelou Ypeij (1998) has identified the maternal figure as the one who is to blame for her daughter's immoral behavior, or *conducta indecorosa*. Ypeij examines three central aspects of the maternal figure for a better understanding of the mother–daughter relationship. First, the mother is *la figura de confianza,* that is, she inspires intimacy, sensibility, and trust in her daughter. Second, the mother, responsible for the education of her daughter, becomes *la mediadora,* or the mediator, in the father–daughter relationship. That is, gender arrangements within the family context make the mother responsible for the education of her children, while the absent father works outside the home to comply with his obligations as the family provider. As part of this dynamic, the maternal figure may protect the daughter from her father. And third, the mother is in charge of protecting *"el honor y la reputación de la hija"* (her daughter's honor and reputation) while controlling her daughter's behavior. In their clinical research with women from Latin America living in the United States, Boyd-Franklin and García-Preto (1994) have similarly identified the mother's learned pattern as the family's conflict mediator. And Raffaelli and Ontai (2001) have examined instances in which mothers would intervene in order to facilitate their daughter's going out with the men they were dating without the father's knowledge.

13. Ypeij examines how young *michoacanas* working in the *congeladoras* (refrigeration warehouses/plants) in Zamora learned to obey and accept the masculine figure's authority within both domestic (family) and public (work) con-

texts. This dynamic would be reproduced in future generations within the context of marital life, as *michoacanas* are trained, as working daughters and future wives, not to question the authority of the male figure in the family (1998, 207).

14. In Marcos's town, integrity and decency seem to be symbolized by the *rebozo* that some single women wear. See Hirsch (2003) for an anthropological examinations of the meaning of the *rebozo* for married women.

15. In this study, men from Mexico City were more likely than rural men to report their mother's intervention with regard to the sex education they received at various stages in their lives. Some potential explanations include urban mothers' concerns about the undesired traits of the women their sons might get involved with in a city where anonymity, and thus a more relaxed social surveillance of morality, is part of everyday life. In addition, women educating sons in urban contexts may have more access to information on sex education, including the risks of sexually transmitted diseases and commercial sex. When compared to their rural counterparts, these mothers may feel more comfortable talking with their sons about sex-related topics, as they simultaneously try to protect them from the dangers of the big city and promote ideals of feminine identity in a potential wife.

16. Hurtado examines how, for example, young siblings become the chaperones for a generation of Mexican Americans dating in contemporary society (2003, 301).

17. See Gutmann's reflections on Steve Stern's (1995) "myth of complicity," with regard to women becoming "complicit" while reproducing and promoting social beliefs and practices promoting gender inequality (1996, 102–3). Gutmann notes, for example, the cultural prohibition little boys receive from their mothers, familiar to many who have been raised in Mexico: *"¡No llores como una niña!"* [Don't cry like a girl!] Gutmann reflects on the emotional price adult men may pay for such a social prescription. Even though this message is not exclusively Mexican (and it is received by many men from their fathers as well), it appears to be connected with the difficulty some men have in expressing their feelings (pain in particular), something I have observed in my clinical and personal experiences with Mexican men and with men from other Latin American countries.

18. Tostado Gutiérrez explains why, in practice, this law was more rigidly enforced among the dominant classes — the white upper classes and the indigenous nobility. In this way, the law served a socioeconomic purpose, as it helped elite families to preserve and reproduce their status in Mexican society. As I indicated in chapter 1, the state-building process that followed Mexican independence in 1821 further reinforced patriarchal beliefs and values.

19. Varley's work is a historical examination of how some mothers-in-law became "accomplices" to domestic violence against their daughters-in-law, by promoting values of female subordination within the context of their sons' marital relationship. Among other things, the mothers-in-law managed the income of their married sons. Varley similarly shows how daughters-in-law would adapt to or contest these practices as twentieth-century Mexican society evolved amid

social transformations that included the introduction of mass media (i.e., television), as well as urbanization, education, and economic growth.

20. Zhou (1989) explains how some Chinese women who are no longer virgins may fake fear during the wedding night in order to postpone sexual intercourse so that it will coincide with their period and thus show blood as evidence of their virginity.

Chapter 5. Sex and the Immigrant Communities

1. Portes and Rumbaut use the term "epidemiological paradox" to describe the contradictions immigrants encounter (1996, 182). For example, they discuss the findings of the Hispanic Health and Nutrition Examination Survey, conducted in 1982–84, to explain why second-generation Mexican American women give birth to babies with lower weight compared to Mexican immigrant mothers. When compared to the former, the latter live in lower socioeconomic conditions, give birth at an older age, and receive insufficient prenatal medical attention (1996, 181). Public health scholars such as Richard Scribner (1996) have been similarly intrigued by these same "contradictions," which he calls the "paradox of Hispanic health." And Rumbaut (1997) offers the most comprehensive sociological examination of public health research into immigrants' physical and mental health, which deteriorates as they and their progeny establish permanent lives in the United States. Other research reports that family stress among Latina girls with higher "acculturation levels" may prompt substance abuse. Latina girls also engage in increased sexual activity resulting in an increased risk of pregnancy, display a lower desire for educational achievement, and exhibit higher risks for dropping out of school, as well as for depression and suicide (National Alliance for Hispanic Health 2000, 59). For additional research on the inadequate health care immigrants receive, see Berk et al. 2000; Macías and Morales 2000; De la Torre et al. 1996; and Hubbell et al. 1991.

2. Marcelo M. Suárez-Orozco and Mariela M. Páez have edited a collection of essays about Mexican immigrants to the United States (*Latinos: Remaking America*, 2002). Among the more interesting essays in the book, for our purposes, Celia Jaes Falicov offers a compelling examination of immigrants' emotional experiences of loss, grief, and mourning; Jacqueline Hagan and Nestor Rodriguez write about INS detentions and deportations of undocumented Latinos; and Diego Vigil discusses gang activity and urban violence in a socioeconomic context. See also Ainslie 1998 for more on anomie, isolation, loneliness, mourning, and loss within the context of immigration.

3. In an informal conversation, a Mexican immigrant friend of a study participant told me about the death of one of her children. She blamed her inability to speak English for the death of her son: she could not describe his symptoms to the paramedics and her child died in the ambulance on the way to the hospital.

4. Low and Organista address some of the complexities of this issue. Socio-

economic and racial segregation in the United States may make Mexican American women vulnerable not only to sexual violence but other problems. On the other hand, over time, women may develop the social capital (e.g., language fluency and knowledge about legal rights, among others) necessary to be able to report violent attacks (Low and Organista 2000, 134).

5. In both countries, men report higher alcohol consumption rates than women. Alcoholism is the leading cause of death among men between the ages of thirty-five and sixty-five in Mexico (Brandes 2002, 111). For alcoholism among Mexicans living in the United States, see *Alcohol Use among U.S. Ethnic Minorities* 1985.

6. Gutmann similarly reports on the experiences of alcoholic men living in the *colonia* Santo Domingo in Mexico City. These men reported being *jurado* — a person who makes a pledge not to drink, to God or to another religious entity, as a way to cope with alcoholism (1996, 186). In a project-in-progress I examine my informants' reevaluations of their Catholic values as part of their migration experiences. These analyses include the stories of Eugenio and Fermín. For an anthropological study of how and why Catholic beliefs and practices influence Alcoholics Anonymous in Mexico, see Stanley Brandes 2002.

7. Arlene Stein's research with a group of mostly white lesbians similarly illustrates how some of these women may engage in casual sexual encounters with men without compromising their lesbian identities (1997, 160, 161, 190, 191). See also Laumann et al. 1994 for a sociological examination of sexual behavior, desire, and identity as interconnected yet independent dimensions of same-gender sexualities.

8. Liguori relates that the consensus of some sociologists is that the level of bisexual practice among men in Mexico is very high, "possibly, one of the highest in Latin America and no doubt higher than in the United States" (1995, 140).

9. Szasz (1998) reports similar findings on alcohol and substance abuse and men's sexual practices in her review of sex and masculinity research in Mexico.

10. For examinations and examples of *"el juego de los albures,"* see Prieur 1998 and Carrillo 2002.

11. Women rarely reported erotic desire, sexual fantasies, or actual sex practices with other women. Most of the women reported feeling an emotional closeness with many of their women acquaintances and friends. However, same-sex desire was not reported as fluidly or as frequently as with the men. As part of the interview, I read a vignette about a lesbian relationship. Some women were defensive and disapproved of the main character's behavior, describing her as "dirty." The vignette at times prompted anxiety. Deyanira, for example, used the expression *"fantasías macabras"* to indirectly suggest that she had had lesbian fantasies in the past which provoked feelings of consternation. The women's reactions are no surprise, given that, compared to men, in general, Mexican women are socialized to repress sexual exploration.

12. See Ayala, Carrier, and Magaña (1996) for an examination of how and why both immigrant women and men participate in the creation of local commercial sex cultures in the United States.

13. According to Scott, Jorgensen, and Suarez, "Each year, thousands of Spanish-speaking Hispanics call the Center for Disease Control and Prevention National AIDS Hotline to ask questions about HIV. During 1995 alone, Spanish line staff answered more than 29,000 calls" (1998, 501).

14. For an examination of immigrant women's and men's association of "being dirty" with being infected with sexually transmitted diseases, including AIDS, see Ayala, Carrier, and Magaña 1996; Carrillo 2002; and Stern et al. 2003.

15. For an examination of Mexican men, extramarital relationships, and HIV/AIDS risk, see Pulerwitz et al. 2001.

16. Mexican labor migration to the United States, Los Angeles in particular, is rooted in the early 1900s (Portes and Rumbaut 1996, 9). Since then, migration patterns have followed social and political processes, and economic restructuring, that takes place on both sides of the border. The effects of these processes have been felt in particular ways during different periods throughout the twentieth century, a dynamic that has been examined extensively.

17. In the 1970s and early 1980s migration from "low-wage countries" such as Mexico has occurred in tandem with the economic restructuring of global cities such as Los Angeles, which has experienced a shift toward a service economy that depends on low-wage jobs (Sassen-Koob 1984). For an examination of globalization, world economic restructuring, and transnational and international market relations, see Sassen 1991.

Chapter 6. Sexual Discourses and Cultures in the Barrio

1. Networking is just one of the social avenues that shaped the participants' sex lives. Spanish-language TV and radio talk shows, as well as the sexuality workshops that some of them attended at community-based agencies, clinics, and schools, also affected their sex lives (see González-López 2000).

2. Ainslie (1998) offers a culturally and socially contextualized psychological analysis of the cultural loss and grief experienced by Mexican immigrants and their corresponding psychological survival mechanisms. He argues that "immigrants make use of linking objects and linking processes to help sustain the sense of connection to the lost worlds, a connections that is essential to the maintenance of one's psychological equilibrium" (297). For the women in this study, networking seems, in part, to provide this linking role with regard to their sex lives.

3. For a discussion of how some mothers promote sexual autonomy in their constructions of virginity as they educate a new generation of women, see González-López 2003.

4. I have examined fathers' views of their daughters' sex lives with respect to how the men feel they should educate their daughters who are growing up in Los Angeles (see González-López 2004).

5. In my research on the Spanish-language media and women's sex lives (see González-López 2000), I learned that, as with networking, women and men

undergo transitions in their sex lives as they are exposed to discussions of sexuality in the media. Even though these discussions take place in contrasting social situations — networking usually happens outside in the community and talk shows are viewed in the privacy of one's home — they involve similar dynamics. First, talk shows represent a meaningful source of information, and, at their best, they have the potential to provide powerful means for sexual liberation in the community. Second, they offer a way for women and mothers to become "sexually literate" with regard to the sex education they are providing for their children. Third, they have a potential influence on the sexual morality, ideology, and behavior of Mexican immigrant women and men. And fourth, they prompt women and men to become proactive, in that social networking and talk shows encourage group discussion. It should be mentioned, also, that "Spanish-language radio stations in the United States are airing programs with increasingly crude sexual content and jokes, creating a genre known as: *radiopornografía*" (quote is from "Group Assails Spanish Stations for Obscenities," *San Francisco Chronicle*, August 16, 2001, D2).

6. The concept of internalization has been used by feminist scholars across disciplines. Chicana lesbian writer and activist Cherríe Moraga talks about the ways she personally experienced "internalized racism and classism" as a half-white individual who could "pass" (because of her skin color) when she was a college student attending a private college in Los Angeles. She reflects on her own oppression as a process coming not only from *outside* but also from *inside* herself (1983, 54). Feminist sociologist Patricia Hill Collins explains the many ways in which African American women have internalized the oppressive and devalued images that society has created about them. Collins looks at Toni Morrison's novel *The Bluest Eye* (1970) to analyze how an "'ugly' eleven-year-old Black girl . . . internalizes the denigrated images of African-American women and believes that the absence of blue eyes is central to her 'ugliness'" (1991, 83). Similarly, feminist psychologist Beverly Greene (1994) uses the term "internalized racism" to examine African American women's lives. Greene argues that internalized racism "is observed in African American women when they internalize both the negative stereotypes about African Americans and their cultural origins and the idealization of white persons and their cultural imperatives, negatively affecting their sense of self" (20). As illustrated in this chapter, internalized sexism may be contested and challenged, in part, as women find safe spaces through their networking with other Latina immigrant and non-immigrant women. See Gutmann (1996) for an examination of the ways by which women may participate in reproducing patriarchy and gender inequality.

7. For an examination of the tensions, animosities, and discrimination that exists between inhabitants of Mexico City and people from other regions of Mexico, especially those from rural areas, see Gutmann 1996, 59–64.

8. I use the terms "sexually literate" and "sexual literacy" to refer to well-informed or research-based information and education on human sexuality. I have adopted these term from Reinisch and Beasley 1990.

Chapter 7. Sexual Bargains

1. In *American Couples,* Philip Blumstein and Pepper Schwartz explored the dynamics between money, work, and sex in a sample of more than six thousand North American couples. They concluded that in heterosexual marriages where women work and bring money into the household, women have the possibility to win more power, influence, and control over their personal lives. Blumstein and Schwartz proposed five reasons for this dynamic: (1) men show more respect for paid work outside the home than for housework (men's sense of self-respect comes to some extent from the world of work); (2) women explore and develop a sense of self-worth that emerges from their decision-making abilities, required as part of their job responsibilities and interactions with coworkers; (3) women who are employed outside the home may discover unknown personal abilities and qualities; (4) women may not want to give up the self-confidence that emerges from their interactions at work; and (5) men show more respect for their wives as result of their success at work.

2. Men used the term *chantaje* (blackmail) to explain that their wives or sexual partners have strategically used intercourse as a way to negotiate not only material goods (e.g., shoes, clothing, home repairs, money, financial security) but to resolve tensions and conflicts in their respective premarital, extramarital, and marital bedrooms.

3. Benería and Roldán (1987) illustrate the clear understanding of the marriage contract held by a group of 140 women living in fifteen *colonias* in Mexico City. They write: "It is important to stress that all wives thought that their behavior — in the domestic and public spheres — should not transgress the limits imposed by the 'respect' owed to their 'masters' (their *señores*), respect being defined as obedience and deference, although the exact definition and limits of respect varied according to each individual's marital experience. The elements mentioned as constituents of wives' duties under the marriage contract: unpaid domestic work; child bearing and rearing; and sexuality in particular, their articulation, may be differently defined and enacted according to women's conception of 'proper' wifedom-motherhood and gender-related worlds and values" (139).

4. The stories of Victoria and Candelaria are not isolated or unique cases. Fiona Wilson offers an anthropological perspective on *el rapto,* or *el robo* (the kidnapping of women) and *la violación* (rape) as recurring forms of sexual violence against Mexican women living in the rural areas of western Mexico. According to Wilson, these forms of sexual brutality were prevalent in this particular geographical area in the 1950s and 1960s, where families and husbands were especially protective of their daughters and wives, respectively (1990, 78–80). Wilson argues that education and women's increased participation in paid labor have been responsible for a decrease in these types of sexual crimes.

5. See Skerry and Rockwell 1998 for a discussion of the experience of twenty-three Mexican immigrant women (including a thirteen-year-old) from the state of Veracruz, who became prostitution slaves in Florida in order to pay off their smuggling fees to their *coyotes.*

6. A study of 481 day laborers (Valenzuela 1999) found that they were over-whelmingly Latino, male, and undocumented, and that they were usually paid daily and in cash "under the table." Seventy-seven percent of them were of Mexican origin. For a further examination of the *jornaleros'* experiences, see Valenzuela 1999, 2002, 2003; and Malpica 1996.

7. The women in my study resembled those studied by Hondagneu-Sotelo (1994, 131). This finding is not true for all Latina immigrant women. Engagement in commercial sex has been found to be exploitative and dangerous for Latina immigrant women living in conditions of marginality, segregation, and poverty (see Ayala, Carrier, Magaña 1996).

8. In the new country, immigrant mothers continued to educate their daughters with regard to sex, relationships, and marriage (see González-López 2003).

9. In her anthropological work with women working at packing plants in Michoacán, Mummert (1994) observed some adult men's feelings of resistance and discomfort as women challenged traditional beliefs and practices with regard to gender relations within family and community contexts.

Chapter 8. Gendered Tapestries

1. Schoenkopf (2001) found that hymen reconstruction clinical services were being offered in Southern California; Paternostro identified a lucrative clinic catering to Latinos in Queens and Brooklyn, New York, that charged between $1,800 and $2,000 for hymen reconstruction services (1998, 270–89).

2. The *Carta al Papa* was published by Teresita de Barbieri in the Mexican journal *Debate Feminista* (Year 1, vol. 2 [September 1990]: 357–61). In my study, women gave their opinions and reactions to the letter and to the role of the Catholic Church in shaping women's sexuality and their own sex lives.

3. In a work in progress, I examine additional processes behind these women's reactions, such as Smith's (1987) notion of the bifurcation of consciousness.

4. Abortion remains a controversial issue for the women in this study. About half of the women objected to abortion practices; eight supported abortion or pro-choice ideologies; eight expressed ambivalent opinions about this issue; and four did not give an opinion about abortion. Even though the majority of the women in this study were more likely to promote and support progressive changes within the Church, a substantial number of them express an anti-abortion ideology. Why? Two groups within the anti-abortion category reveal an interesting paradox. First, women who simultaneously support progressive changes within the Catholic Church at times perceive abortion as a socially regressive alternative for women. For them, a woman should be able to take contraceptive pills or to have access to other forms of contraception, such as the rhythm method, or "natural family planning" and condom use instead of choosing abortion. And second, women who support progressive changes may perceive abortion as a crime for reasons not having to do with religion. For

them, a woman's personal decision to have an abortion transforms her publicly into a socially regressive woman who is living in the Dark Ages: an ignorant woman who does not know about contraceptive methods. Ultimately, the decision to have an abortion or not becomes a public affair subjected to the corresponding moral control of social institutions. As stated by Lucía Rayas (1998): "The feelings of guilt and indecency that surround abortion arise because the very fact of pregnancy attests to having exercised sexuality—a tremendous affront to institutions like the state, law, and religion which seek to control women's sexual lives" (22). For additional information on the forty women's views of abortion, see González-López 2000.

5. The Transborder Consortium for Research and Action on Gender and Reproductive Health on the Mexico-U.S. Border is constituted of academic institutions located in Mexico (El Colegio de la Frontera Norte and El Colegio de Sonora) and in the United States (the Southwest Institute for Research on Women–University of Arizona).

6. For an examination of the social dynamics linked to the use of the term *señorita,* see Marcela Lagarde 1997.

7. For research on changes in gender relations and sexual morality values and practices across generations of families in Mexico, see Rivas Zivy 1997, Módena and Mendoza 2001, and Escobar Latapí 2003.

References

Accad, Evelyne. 1991. Sexuality and Sexual Politics: Conflicts and Contradictions for Contemporary Women in the Middle East. In *Third World Women and the Politics of Feminism*, edited by Chandra T. Mohanty, Ann Russo, and Lourdes Torres, 237–50. Bloomington: Indiana University Press.

Ainslie, Ricardo C. 1998. Cultural Mourning, Immigration, and Engagement: Vignettes from the Mexican Experience. In *Crossings: Mexican Immigration in Interdisciplinary Perspectives*, edited by Marcelo M. Suárez-Orozco, 283–300. Cambridge, Mass.: Harvard University, David Rockefeller Center for Latin American Studies.

———. 2002. The Plasticity of Culture and Psychodynamic and Psychosocial Processes in Latino Immigrant Families. In *Latinos: Remaking America*, edited by Marcelo M. Suárez-Orozco and Mariela M. Páez, 289–301. Berkeley: University of California Press; Cambridge, Mass.: Harvard University, David Rockefeller Center for Latin American Studies.

Alcohol Use among U.S. Ethnic Minorities: Proceedings of a Conference on the Epidemiology of Alcohol Use and Abuse among Ethnic Minority Groups, September 1985. Edited by Danielle Spiegler et al. Research monograph, no. 18. Rockville, Md.: U.S. Department of Health and Human Services, Public Health Service, Alcohol, Drug Abuse, and Mental Health Administration, National Institute on Alcohol Abuse and Alcoholism.

Alegría, Juana A. 1974. *Psicología de las mexicanas*. Mexico City: Editorial Samo, S.A.

Almaguer, Tomás. 1993. Chicano Men: A Cartography of Homosexual Identity and Behavior. In *The Lesbian and Gay Studies Reader*, edited by Henry Abelove, Michele A. Barale, and David M. Halperin, 255–73. New York: Routledge.

Alonso, Ana María, and María Teresa Koreck. 1993. Silences: "Hispanics," AIDS, and Sexual Practices. In *The Lesbian and Gay Studies Reader*, edited by

Henry Abelove, Michele A. Barale, and David M. Halperin, 110–26. New York: Routledge.

Altman, Dennis. 2001. *Global Sex*. Chicago: University of Chicago Press.

Amaro, Hortensia. 1988. Women in the Mexican-American Community: Religion, Culture, and Reproductive Attitudes and Experiences. *Journal of Community Psychology* 16: 6–20.

Amuchástegui, Ana. 1994. La primera vez: El significado de la virginidad y la iniciación sexual para jóvenes mexicanos. Research Report. Mexico City: Population Council.

———. 1998. La dimensión moral de la sexualidad y de la virginidad en las culturas híbridas mexicanas. *Relaciones* 19, no. 74 (Spring 1998): 101–33.

———. 2001. *Virginidad e iniciación sexual en México: Experiencias y significados*. Mexico City: EDAMEX and Population Council.

Amuchástegui, Ana, and Marta Rivas Z. 1997. La modernización de la sexualidad de las jóvenes. *La Jornada*, Letra S, sida cultura y vida cotidiana, March 6, 1997. http://www.jornada.unam.mx/1997/mar97/970307/ls-calidad.html.

Anzaldúa, Gloria. 1987. *Borderlands: La Frontera*. San Francisco: Aunt Lute Books.

———. 1993. La historia de una marimacho. In *The Sexuality of Latinas*, edited by Norma Alarcón, Ana Castillo, and Cherríe Moraga, 64–68. Berkeley: Third Woman Press.

Argüelles, Lourdes, and B. Ruby Rich. 1984. Homosexuality, Homophobia, and Revolution: Notes toward an Understanding of the Cuban Lesbian and Gay Male Experience. Pt. 1. *Signs* 9, no. 4 (Summer): 683–99.

———. 1985. Homosexuality, Homophobia, and Revolution: Notes toward an Understanding of the Cuban Lesbian and Gay Male Experience. Pt. 2. *Signs* 11, no. 1 (Autumn): 120–36.

Argüelles, Lourdes, and Anne M. Rivero. 1993. Gender/Sexual Orientation Violence and Transnational Migration: Conversations with Some Latinas We Think We Know. *Urban Anthropology* 22, no. 3–4: 259–75.

Ayala, Armida, Joseph Carrier, and J. Raúl Magaña. 1996. The Underground World of Latina Sex Workers in Cantinas. In *AIDS Crossing Borders: The Spread of HIV among Migrant Latinos*, edited by Shiraz I. Mishra, Ross F. Conner, and J. Raúl Magaña, 95–112. Boulder, Colo.: Westview Press.

Baca Zinn, Maxine. 1982. Mexican American Women in the Social Sciences. *Signs* 8, no. 2: 259–72.

Bachu, Amara. 1999. *Trends in Premarital Childbearing, 1930–1994*. Current population reports, series P-23; Special studies, no. 197. Washington, D.C.: U.S. Department of Commerce, Economics and Statistics Administration, Bureau of the Census.

Baird, Traci L. 1993. Mexican Adolescent Sexuality: Attitudes, Knowledge, and Sources of Information. *Hispanic Journal of Behavioral Sciences* 15, no. 3 (August): 402–17.

Barrios, W., and L. Pons. 1994. Sexualidad y religión en Los Altos de Chiapas. Cited in Sexuality, Gender Relations, and Female Empowerment, a conference presentation delivered by Ivonne Szasz and Juan Guillermo Figueroa at the seminar on Female Empowerment and Demographic Processes: Moving Beyond Cairo, Lund, Sweden, April 21–24, 1997.

Basnayake, Sriani. 1990. The Virginity Test — A Bridal Nightmare. *Journal of Family Welfare* 36, no. 2: 50–59.

Béjar Navarro, Raúl. 1986. *El mexicano: Aspectos culturales y psicosociales.* Mexico City: Universidad Nacional Autónoma de México.

Benería, Lourdes, and Martha Roldán. 1987. *The Crossroads of Class and Gender: Industrial Homework, Subcontracting, and Household Dynamics in Mexico City.* Chicago: University of Chicago Press.

Berk, Marc L., Claudia L. Schur, Leo R. Chávez, and Martin Frankel. 2000. Health Care Use among Undocumented Latino Immigrants. *Health Affairs* 19, no. 4: 51–64.

Bernard, Jessie S. 1972. *The Future of Marriage.* New York: Bantam Books.

Besserer, Federico. 1999. *Moisés Cruz: Historia de un transmigrante.* Culiacán: Universidad Autónoma de Sinaloa; Mexico City: Universidad Autónoma Metropolitana, Iztapalapa.

Blumberg, Rae Lesser. 1991. Income under Female versus Male Control. In *Gender, Family, and Economy: The Triple Overlap,* edited by Rae Lesser Blumberg, 97–127. Newbury Park, Calif.: Sage.

Blumstein, Philip, and Pepper Schwartz. 1983. *American Couples: Money, Work, and Sex.* New York: William Morrow.

Boddy, Janice. 1982. Womb as Oasis: The Symbolic Context of Pharaonic Circumcision in Rural Northern Sudan. *American Ethnologist* 9, no. 4: 682–98.

Bourdieu, Pierre. 1973. Cultural Reproduction and Social Reproduction. In *Knowledge, Education, and Cultural Change,* edited by Richard Brown, 71–112. London: Tavistock Publications.

———. 2001. *Masculine Domination.* Stanford, Calif.: Stanford University Press.

Boyd-Franklin, Nancy, and Nydia García-Preto. 1994. Family Therapy: The Cases of African American and Hispanic Women. In *Women of Color: Integrating Ethnic and Gender Identities in Psychotherapy,* edited by Lillian Comas-Díaz and Beverly Greene, 239–64. New York: Guilford Press.

Bozzoli, Belinda. 1983. Marxism, Feminism, and South African Studies. *Journal of Southern African Studies* 9, no. 2: 139–71.

Bracho de Carpio, America, Felix F. Carpio-Cedraro, and Lise Anderson. 1990. Hispanic Families Learning and Teaching about AIDS: A Participatory Approach at the Community Level. *Hispanic Journal of Behavioral Sciences* 12, no. 2: 165–76.

Brandes, Stanley. 2002. *Staying Sober in Mexico City.* Austin: University of Texas Press.

Bronfman, Mario, Sergio Camposortega, and Hortencia Medina. 1989. La migración internacional y el SIDA: El caso de México y Estados Unidos. In *SIDA: Ciencia y Sociedad en México,* edited by Jaime Sepúlveda-Amor, Mario Bronfman, Guillermo Ruiz Palacios, Estanislao Stanislawski, and José Valdes-pino, 435–56. Mexico City: Secretaría de Salud, Instituto Nacional de Salud Pública, and Fondo de Cultura Económica.

Bronfman, Mario, and Sergio López Moreno. 1996. Perspectives on HIV/AIDS Prevention among Immigrants on the U.S.–Mexico Border. In *AIDS Crossing Borders,* edited by Shiraz I. Mishra, Ross F. Conner, and J. Raúl Magaña, 49–76. Boulder, Colo.: Westview Press.

Brown, E. Richard, and Hongjian Yu. 2002. Latinos' Access to Employment-based Health Insurance. In *Latinos: Remaking America,* edited by Marcelo M. Suárez-Orozco and Mariela M. Páez, 236–53. Berkeley: University of California Press.

Buitelaar, M. W. 2002. Negotiating the Rules of Chaste Behaviour: Reinterpretations of the Symbolic Complex of Virginity by Young Women of Moroccan Descent in the Netherlands. *Ethnic and Racial Studies* 25, no. 3: 462–89.

Burawoy, Michael. 1991. Reconstructing Social Theories. In *Ethnography Unbound: Power and Resistance in the Modern Metropolis,* edited by Michael Burawoy et al., 8–27. Berkeley: University of California Press.

Burgos, Nilsa M., and Yolanda I. Díaz Perez. 1986. An Exploration of Human Sexuality in the Puerto Rican Culture. *Journal of Social Work and Human Sexuality* 4, no. 3: 135–50.

Butler, Judith. 1990. *Gender Trouble: Feminism and the Subversion of Identity.* New York: Routledge.

Canak, William, and Laura Swanson. 1998. *Modern Mexico.* Boston: McGraw-Hill.

Cantú, Lionel. 1999. Border Crossings: Mexican Men and the Sexuality of Migration. Ph.D. diss., University of California at Irvine.

———. 2000. Entre Hombres/Between Men: Latino Masculinities and Homosexualities. In *Gay Masculinities,* edited by Peter Nardi, 224–46. Thousand Oaks, Calif.: Sage.

———. 2002. A Place Called Home: A Queer Political Economy: Mexican Immigrant Men's Family Experiences. In *Sexuality and Gender,* edited by Christine L. Williams and Arlene Stein, 382–94. Malden, Mass.: Blackwell.

Carrier, Joseph M. 1976. Cultural Factors Affecting Urban Mexican Male Homosexual Behavior. *Archives of Sexual Behavior* 5, no. 2: 103–24.

———. 1977. "Sex-Role Preference" as an Explanatory Variable in Homosexual Behavior. *Archives of Sexual Behavior* 6, no. 1: 53–65.

———. 1985. Mexican Male Bisexuality. In *Bisexualities: Theory and Research,* edited by Fritz Klein and Timothy J. Wolf, 75–85. New York: Haworth Press.

———. 1995. *De Los Otros: Intimacy and Homosexuality among Mexican Men.* New York: Columbia University Press.

Carrillo, Héctor. 1999. Cultural Change, Hybridity, and Male Homosexuality in Mexico. *Culture, Health, and Sexuality* 1, no. 3: 223–38.

———. 2002. *The Night Is Young: Sexuality in Mexico in the Time of AIDS.* Chicago: University of Chicago Press.

Castañeda, Carmen. 1989. *Violación, estupro y sexualidad: Nueva Galicia, 1790–1821.* Guadalajara: Editorial Hexágono.

Castañeda, Xóchitl, and Patricia Zavella. 2003. Changing Constructions of Sexuality and Risk: Migrant Mexican Women Farmworkers in California. *Journal of Latin American Anthropology* 8, no. 2: 126–51.

Castro-Vázquez, Genaro. 2000. Masculinity and Condom Use among Mexican Teenagers: The Escuela Nacional Preparatoria No. 1's Case. *Gender and Education* 12, no. 4: 479–92.

Cazés, Daniel. 1993. Normas del "hombre verdadero" en Kafka y Sartre: Pasos de una metodología y elementos para asumir una masculinidad crítica. Cited in Fernando Huerta Rojas, *El juego del hombre: Deporte y masculinidad entre obreros*. Mexico City: Plaza y Valdés Editores.

Chávez, Eda. 1999. Domestic Violence and HIV/AIDS in Mexico. In *AIDS and Men: Taking Risks or Taking Responsibility?* edited by Martin Foreman, 51–63. London: Panos Institute and Zed Books.

Chávez, Leo R. 1992. *Shadowed Lives: Undocumented Immigrants in American Society*. Fort Worth, Texas: Harcourt Brace.

Chávez, Leo R., F. Allan Hubbell, Shiraz I. Mishra, and R. Burciaga Valdez. 1997. Undocumented Latina Immigrants in Orange County, California: A Comparative Analysis. *International Migration Review* 31, no. 1: 88–107.

Chávez Torres, Martha. 1998. *Mujeres de rancho, de metate y de corral*. Zamora: El Colegio de Michoacán.

Chodorow, Nancy J. 1978. *The Reproduction of Mothering: Psychoanalysis and the Sociology of Gender*. Berkeley: University of California Press.

———. 1995. Gender as a Personal and Cultural Construction. *Signs* 20, no. 3: 516–44.

CIMAC. 2002. Casi la mitad de la población femenina en Mexico "pide permiso" para usar métodos anticonceptivos: Conapo [Almost half of the female population in Mexico "asks for permission" to use contraceptives: Conapo]. CIMAC: Comunicación e Información de la Mujer, March 28, 2002. http://www.cimacnoticias.com/noticias/02mar/02032804.html.

———. 2003. Fue presentado el libro *Infancia sin amparo*, de Judith Calderón — Casi dos millones de niños se encuentran en situación de calle [The book *Childhood Without Protection* by Judith Calderón was presented — Almost two million children work on the streets]. CIMAC: Comunicación e Información de la Mujer, December 10, 2003. http://www.cimac.org.mx.

Cindoglu, Dilek. 1997. Virginity Tests and Artificial Virginity in Modern Turkish Medicine. *Women's Studies International Forum* 20, no. 2: 253–61.

Collins, Patricia Hill. 1991. *Black Feminist Thought*. New York: Routledge.

CONAPO 2003. Consejo Nacional de Población. http://www.conapo.gob.mx.

Connell, R. W. 1987. *Gender and Power: Society, the Person, and Sexual Politics*. Stanford, Calif.: Stanford University Press.

———. 1995. *Masculinities*. Berkeley: University of California Press.

———. 2000. *The Men and the Boys*. Berkeley: University of California Press.

———. 2002. *Gender*. Cambridge: Polity Press.

Córdova Plaza, Rosío. 1998. Sexualidad y orden moral: De las concepciones corporales al control social en una comunidad campesina en Mexico. Paper presented at the annual meeting of the Latin American Studies Association, Chicago.

Cornelius, Wayne A. 1998. The Structural Embeddedness of Demand for Mexican Immigrant Labor: New Evidence from California. In *Crossings: Mexican*

Immigration in Interdisciplinary Perspectives, edited by Marcelo M. Suárez-Orozco, 113–44. Cambridge, Mass.: Harvard University, David Rockefeller Center for Latin American Studies.

D'Emilio, John, and Estelle B. Freedman. 1988. *Intimate Matters: A History of Sexuality in America.* New York: Harper and Row.

De Beauvior, Simone. 1949. *The Second Sex.* Repr., New York: Vintage Books, 1989.

De la Peña, Ricardo, and Rosario Toledo. 1991. *El sexo en Mexico* (pt. 1 of 4). *El Nacional Dominical,* May 26.

———. 1992. Cited by Eusebio Rubio, s.v. "Mexico (Estados Unidos Mexicanos)," in *The International Encyclopedia of Sexuality,* edited by Robert T. Francoeur, 869–94. New York: Continuum.

———. 1996. Sexo, pudor y gráficas. In *Entre las sábanas,* edited by José Carlos Castañeda et al., 131–76. Mexico City: Cal y Arena.

De la Torre, Adela, Robert Friis, Harold R. Hunter, and Lorena Garcia. 1996. The Health Insurance Status of U.S. Latino Women: A Profile from the 1982–1984 HHANES. *American Journal of Public Health* 86, no. 4: 533–37.

De la Vega, Ernesto. 1990. Considerations for Reaching the Latino Population with Sexuality and HIV/AIDS Information and Education. *SIECUS Report* 18, no. 3.

Del Río Zolezzi, Aurora, Ana Luisa Liguori, Carlos Magis-Rodríguez, José Luis Valdespino-Gómez, María de Lourdes García-García, and Jaime Sepúlveda Amor. 1995. La epidemia de VIH/SIDA y la mujer en México. *Salud Pública de México* 37, no. 6: 581–91.

Díaz, Esperanza, Holly Prigerson, Rani Desai, and Robert Rosenheck. 2001. Perceived Needs and Service Use of Spanish Speaking Monolingual Patients Followed at a Hispanic Clinic. *Community Mental Health Journal* 37, no. 4: 335–46.

Díaz, Rafael M. 1998. *Latino Gay Men and HIV: Culture, Sexuality, and Risk Behavior.* New York: Routledge.

di Leonardo, Micaela, and Roger N. Lancaster. 1997. Embodied Meanings, Carnal Practices. In *The Gender Sexuality Reader,* edited by Roger N. Lancaster and Micaela di Leonardo, 1–10. New York: Routledge.

Domecq, Brianda. 1992. *Acechando al unicornio: La virginidad en la literatura mexicana.* Mexico City: Fondo de Cultura Económica.

Dore, Elizabeth. 2000. One Step Forward, Two Steps Back: Gender and the State in the Long Nineteenth Century. In *Hidden Histories of Gender and the State in Latin America,* edited by Elizabeth Dore and Maxine Molyneux, 3–32. Durham, N.C.: Duke University Press.

Dore, Elizabeth, and Maxine Molyneux. 2000. *Hidden Histories of Gender and the State in Latin America.* Durham, N.C.: Duke University Press.

Duncombe, Jean, and Dennis Marsden. 1996. Whose Orgasm Is This Anyway? "Sex Work" in Long-Term Heterosexual Couple Relationships. In *Sexual Cultures: Communities, Values, and Intimacy,* edited by Jeffrey Weeks and Janet Holland, 220–38. New York: St. Martin's Press.

Durand, Jorge. 1998. Migration and Integration: Intermarriages among Mexicans and Non-Mexicans in the United States. In *Crossings: Mexican Immigration in Interdisciplinary Perspectives,* edited by Marcelo M. Suárez-Orozco, 207–21. Cambridge, Mass.: Harvard University, David Rockefeller Center for Latin American Studies.

Dworkin, Andrea. 1987. *Intercourse.* New York: Free Press Paperbacks.

El Saadawi, Nawal. 1997. *The Hidden Face of Eve: Women in the Arab World.* London: Zed Books Ltd.

Escobar Latapí, Agustín. 2003. Men and Their Histories: Restructuring, Gender Inequality, and Life Transitions in Urban Mexico. In *Changing Men and Masculinities in Latin America,* edited by Matthew C. Gutmann, 84–114. Durham, N.C.: Duke University Press.

Espín, Oliva M. 1986. Cultural and Historical Influences on Sexuality in Hispanic/Latin Women. In *All American Women: Lines that Divide, Ties that Bind,* edited by Johnnetta B. Cole, 272–84. New York: Free Press.

———. 1987. Psychological Impact of Migration on Latinas: Implications for Psychotherapeutic Practice. *Psychology of Women Quarterly* 11, no. 4: 489–503.

———. 1999. *Women Crossing Boundaries: A Psychology of Immigration and Transformations of Sexuality.* New York: Routledge.

Espiritu, Yen Le. 2001. We Don't Sleep Around Like White Girls Do: Family, Culture, and Gender in Filipina American Lives. *Signs* 26, no. 2: 415–40.

Falicov, Celia J. 1982. Mexican Families. In *Ethnicity and Family Therapy,* edited by Monica McGoldrick, John K. Pearce, and Joseph Giordano, 134–63. New York: Guilford.

Fernández-Kelly, María Patricia. 1983. *For we are sold, I and my people: Women and industry in Mexico's Frontier.* Albany: State University of New York Press.

Figueroa Perea, Juan Guillermo. 1997. Algunas reflexiones sobre el enfoque de género y la representación de la sexualiad. *Estudios Demográficos y Urbanos* 12, no. 1–2: 201–44.

Flaskerud, Jacquelyn H., Gwen Uman, Rosa Lara, Lillian Romero, and Karen Taka. 1996. Sexual Practices, Attitudes, and Knowledge Related to HIV Transmission in Low Income Los Angeles Hispanic Women. *Journal of Sex Research* 33, no. 4: 343–53.

Forrest, Katherine A., David M. Austin, M. Isabel Valdes, Efrain G. Fuentes, and Sandra R. Wilson. 1993. Exploring Norms and Beliefs Related to AIDS Prevention among California Hispanic Men. *Family Planning Perspectives* 25, no. 3: 111–17.

Foucault, Michel. 1979. *Discipline and Punish: The Birth of the Prison.* New York: Vintage Books.

Frank, Martina W., Heidi M. Bauer, Nadir Arican, Sebnem K. Fincanci, and Vincent Iacopino. 1999. Virginity Examinations in Turkey: Role of Forensic Physicians in Controlling Female Sexuality. *Journal of American Medical Association* 282, no. 5: 485–90.

Fraser, Deborah, John Piacentini, Ronan Van Rossem, Denise Hien, and Mary Jane Rotheram-Borus. 1998. Effects of Acculturation and Psychopathology on Sexual Behavior and Substance Use of Suicidal Hispanic Adolescents. *Hispanic Journal of Behavioral Sciences* 20, no. 1: 83–101.

Freire, Gloria M. 2002. Hispanics and the Politics of Health Care. *Journal of Health and Social Policy* 14, no. 4: 21–35.

Gagnon, John H. 1977. *Human Sexualities*. Glenview, Ill.: Scott, Foresman.

Gagnon, John H., and William Simon. 1973. *Sexual Conduct: The Social Sources of Human Sexuality*. Chicago: Aldine Publishing.

Gilligan, Carol. 1982. *In A Different Voice: Psychological Theory and Women's Development*. Cambridge, Mass.: Harvard University Press.

Giuliano, Anna. 1998. Cervical Cancer and the Human Papilloma Virus (HPV) in the Hispanic Population of the U.S. Working paper presented at a seminar organized by the Transborder Consortium for Research and Action on Gender and Reproductive Health at the Mexico–U.S. Border. The Southwest Institute for Research on Women–University of Arizona, El Colegio de Sonora, and El Colegio de la Frontera Norte constitute the Transborder Consortium.

Glassner, Barry. 1999. *The Culture of Fear: Why Americans Are Afraid of the Wrong Things*. New York: Basic Books.

Godínez, Lourdes. 2002. "Mas vale prevenir que lamentar," analiza la problemática del embarazo en la adolescencia. CIMAC: Comunicación e Información de la Mujer, Noticias, March 12, 2002. http://www.cimacnoticias.com/noticias/02mar/02031208.html.

Gómez Mena, Carolina. 2001. Califican como "bastante pobre" la calidad erótica del mexicano. *La Jornada*, March 26, 2001. http://www.jornada.unam.mx.

González-López, Gloria. 2000. Beyond the Bed Sheets, Beyond the Borders: Mexican Immigrant Women and Their Sex Lives. PhD diss., University of Southern California.

——. 2003. De madres a hijas: Gendered Lessons on Virginity across Generations of Mexican Immigrant Women. In *Gender and U.S. Migration: Contemporary Trends*, edited by Pierrette Hondagneu-Sotelo, 217–40. Berkeley: University of California Press.

——. 2004. Fathering Latina Sexualities: Mexican Men and the Virginity of Their Daughters. *Journal of Marriage and Family* 66, no. 5: 1118–30.

——. Forthcoming. Nunca he dejado de tener terror: Sexual Violence in the Lives of Mexican Immigrant Women. In *Mexican Women in Transnational Context: The Politics of Everyday Life*, edited by D. Segura and P. Zavella.

González Ruiz, Edgar. 1998. *La sexualidad prohibida: Intolerancia, sexismo y represión*. Mexico City: Grupo Interdisciplinario de Sexología.

González Salazar, Gloria. 1980. Participation of Women in the Mexican Labor Force. In *Sex and Class in Latin America: Women's Perspectives on Politics, Economics, and the Family in the Third World*, edited by June Nash and Helen Icken Safa, 183–201. South Hadley, Mass.: J. F. Bergin.

Grant, David M. 2000. A Demographic Portrait of Los Angeles County, 1970 to 1990. In *Prismatic Metropolis: Inequality in Los Angeles*, edited by Lawrence D. Bobo, Melvin L. Oliver, James H. Johnson Jr., and Abel Valenzuela Jr., 51–80. New York: Russell Sage Foundation.

Greene, Beverly. 1994. African American Women. In *Women of Color: Integrating Ethnic and Gender Identities in Psychotherapy,* edited by Lillian Comas-Díaz and Beverly Greene, 10–29. New York: Guilford Press.

Gruenbaum, Ellen. 1982. The Movement against Clitoridectomy and Infibulation in Sudan: Public Health Policy and the Women's Movement. *Medical Anthropology Newsletter* 13, no. 2: 4–12.

———. 1996. The Cultural Debate over Female Circumcision: The Sudanese Are Arguing This One Out for Themselves. *Medical Anthropology Quarterly* 10, no. 4: 455–75.

Guerrero Pavich, Emma. 1986. A Chicana Perspective on Mexican Culture and Sexuality. *Journal of Social Work and Human Sexuality* 4, no. 3: 47–65.

Gutiérrez, Ramón A. 1991. *When Jesus Came, the Corn Mothers Went Away.* Stanford, Calif.: Stanford University Press.

Gutmann, Matthew C. 1996. *The Meanings of Macho: Being a Man in Mexico City.* Berkeley: University of California Press.

———. 2003. Machismo (macho). In *Men and Masculinities: A Social, Cultural, and Historical Encyclopedia,* edited by Michael Kimmel and Amy Aronson. Santa Barbara: ABC-CLIO.

Halley, Janet E. 1993. The Construction of Heterosexuality. In *Fear of a Queer Planet: Queer Politics and Social Theory,* edited by Michael Warner, 82–104. Minneapolis: University of Minnesota Press.

Harvey, S. Marie, Linda J. Beckman, and Sheryl T. Bird. 2003. Feeling Powerful in Heterosexual Relationships: Cultural Beliefs among Couples of Mexican Origin. *Culture, Health, and Sexuality* 5, no. 4: 321–37.

Harvey, S. Marie, Linda J. Beckman, Carole H. Browner, and Christy A. Sherman. 2002. Relationship Power, Decision Making, and Sexual Relations: An Exploratory Study with Couples of Mexican Origin. *Journal of Sex Research* 39, no. 4: 284–91.

Hayes-Bautista, David E. 2002. The Latino Health Research Agenda for the Twenty-first Century. In *Latinos: Remaking America,* edited by Marcelo M. Suárez-Orozco and Mariela M. Páez, 215–35. Berkeley: University of California Press; Cambridge, Mass.: Harvard University, David Rockefeller Center for Latin American Studies.

Hennessy, Rosemary. 2000. *Profit and Pleasure: Sexual Identities in Late Capitalism.* New York: Routledge.

Hines, Alice M., and Raúl Caetano. 1998. Alcohol and AIDS-related Sexual Behavior among Hispanics: Acculturation and Gender Differences. *AIDS Education and Prevention* 10, no. 6: 533–47.

Hirsch, Jennifer S. 1999. En el norte la mujer manda: Gender, Generation, and Geography in a Mexican Transnational Community. *American Behavioral Scientist* 42, no. 9: 1332–49.

———. 2000. "Because he misses his normal life back home": Masculinity, Sexuality, and AIDS Risk Behavior in a Mexican Migrant Community. *Migration World Magazine* 28, no. 4: 30–32.

———. 2003. *A Courtship after Marriage: Sexuality and Love in Mexican Transnational Families.* Berkeley: University of California Press.

Hirsch, Jennifer S., Jennifer Higgins, Margaret E. Bentley, and Constance A. Nathanson. 2002. The Social Constructions of Sexuality: Marital Infidelity and Sexually Transmitted Disease — HIV Risk in a Mexican Migrant Community. *American Journal of Public Health* 92, no. 8: 1227–37.

Hochschild, Arlie R. 1997. *The Time Bind: When Work Becomes Home and Home Becomes Work.* New York : Metropolitan Books.

Hodge, G. Derrick. 2001. Colonization of the Cuban Body: The Growth of Male Sex Work in Havana. *Report on Gender, NACLA Report on the Americas* 34, no. 5: 20–28.

Hondagneu-Sotelo, Pierrette. 1992. Overcoming Patriarchal Constraints: The Reconstruction of Gender Relations among Mexican Immigrant Women and Men. *Gender and Society* 6, no. 3: 393–415.

———. 1994. *Gendered Transitions: Mexican Experiences of Immigration.* Berkeley: University of California Press

———. 2001. *Doméstica: Immigrant Workers Cleaning and Caring in the Shadows of Affluence.* Berkeley: University of California Press.

———. 2002. Families on the Frontier: From Braceros in the Fields, to Braceras in the Home. In *Latinos: Remaking America,* edited by Marcelo M. Suárez-Orozco and Mariela M. Páez, 259–73. Berkeley: University of California Press; Cambridge, Mass.: Harvard University, David Rockefeller Center for Latin American Studies.

Hondagneu-Sotelo, Pierrette, and Michael A. Messner. 1994. Gender Displays and Men's Power: The "New Man" and the Mexican Immigrant Man. In *Theorizing Masculinities,* edited by Harry Brod and Michael Kaufman, 200–218. Thousand Oaks, Calif.: Sage.

Hubbell, F. Allan, Howard Waitzkin, Shiraz I. Mishra, John Dombrink, and Leo R. Chávez. 1991. Access to Medical Care for Documented and Undocumented Latinos in a Southern California County. *Western Journal of Medicine* 154, no. 4: 414–17.

Hurtado, Aída. 2003. *Voicing Chicana Feminisms: Young Women Speak Out on Sexuality and Identity.* New York: New York University Press.

INEGI. 2004. Instituto Nacional de Estadística, Geografía e Informática. http://www.inegi.gob.mx.

Ingraham, Chrys. 1994. The Heterosexual Imaginary: Feminist Sociology and Theories of Gender. *Sociological Theory* 12, no. 2: 203–19.

———. 1999. *White Weddings: Romancing Heterosexuality in Popular Culture.* New York: Routledge.

Juárez, Ana María, and Stella Beatriz Kerl. 2003. What Is the Right (White) Way to be Sexual?: Reconceptualizing Latina Sexuality. *Aztlán* 28, no. 1: 7–37.

Katz, Jonathan Ned. 1995. *The Invention of Heterosexuality.* New York: Dutton.

Kimmel, Michael S. 2000. *The Gendered Society.* New York: Oxford University Press.

Korotayev, Andrey. 2000. Parallel–Cousin (FBD) Marriage, Islamization, and Arabization. *Ethnology* 39, no. 4: 395–407.

Lagarde, Marcela. 1997. *Los cautiverios de las mujeres: Madresposas, monjas, putas, presas y locas.* Mexico City: Universidad Nacional Autónoma de México.

Lamas, Marta. 1998. Scenes from a Mexican Battlefield. Report on Sexual Politics. *NACLA Report on the Americas* 31, no. 4: 17–21.

——. 2001. *Política y reproducción. Aborto: La frontera del derecho a decidir.* Mexico City: Plaza & Janés Editores.

Laumann, Edward O., and John H. Gagnon. 1995. A Sociological Perspective on Sexual Action. In *Conceiving Sexuality: Approaches to Sex Research in a Postmodern World,* edited by Richard G. Parker and John H. Gagnon, 183–213. Routledge: New York.

Laumann, Edward O., John H. Gagnon, Robert T. Michael, and Stuart Michaels. 1994. *The Social Organization of Sexuality: Sexual Practices in the United States.* Chicago: University of Chicago Press.

Lavrin, Asunción. 1989. *Sexuality and Marriage in Colonial Latin America.* Nebraska: University of Nebraska Press.

LeVine, Sarah. 1993. *Dolor y Alegría: Women and Social Change in Urban Mexico.* Madison: University of Wisconsin Press.

Liguori, Ana Luisa. 1995. Las investigaciones sobre bisexualidad en México. *Debate Feminista* 6, no. 11: 132–56.

Lofland, John, and Lyn H. Lofland. 1995. *Analyzing Social Settings: A Guide To Qualitative Observation and Analysis.* 3rd ed. Belmont, Calif.: Wadsworth.

Low, Georgiana, and Kurt C. Organista. 2000. Latinas and Sexual Assault: Towards Culturally Sensitive Assessment and Intervention. In *Violence: Diverse Populations and Communities,* edited by Diane de Anda and Rosina M. Becerra, 131–57. Binghamton, N.Y.: Haworth Press.

Macías, Eduardo P., and Leo S. Morales. 2000. Utilization of Health Care Services among Adults Attending a Health Fair in South Los Angeles County. *Journal of Community Health* 25, no. 1: 35–46.

Magally, Silvia. 2002. Anuncia SS modificaciones a libros de texto para acabar con estereotipos — El machismo es nocivo para la salud [Health Department announces changes to textbooks in order to eliminate stereotypes — Machismo is a health risk]. *Cimac: Comunicación e información de la mujer,* May 30, 2002. http://www.cimac.org.mx.

Magis-Rodríguez, Carlos, Aurora Del Río Zolezzi, José Luis Valdespino-Gómez, and María de Lourdes García-García. 1995. Casos de sida en el área rural de México. *Salud Pública de México* 37, no. 6: 615–23.

Malpica, Daniel M. 1996. The Social Organization of Day-Laborers in Los Angeles. In *Immigration and Ethnic Communities: A Focus on Latinos,* edited by Refugio I. Rochín, 81–92. East Lansing, Mich.: Julian Samora Research Institute.

Marcelli, Enrico, and Wayne Cornelius. 2001. The Changing Profile of Mexican Migrants to the United States: New Evidence from California and Mexico. *Latin American Research Review* 36, no. 3: 105–31.

Marcos, Sylvia. 1989. Curas, diosas y erotismo: El catolicismo frente a los indios. In *Mujeres e iglesia: Sexualidad y aborto en América Latina,* edited by Ana María Portugal, 11–34. Mexico City: Distribuciones Fontamara, S.A.

Marín, Barbara V., and Cynthia A. Gómez. 1997. Latino Culture and Sex: Implications for HIV Prevention. In *Psychological Interventions and Research with*

Latino Populations, edited by Jorge G. García and María Cecilia Zea, 73–93. Boston: Allyn and Bacon.

Marín, Barbara Van Oss, Cynthia A. Gómez, and Norman Hearst. 1993. Multiple Heterosexual Partners and Condom Use among Hispanics and Non-Hispanic Whites. *Family Planning Perspectives* 25, no. 4: 170–174.

Marín, Barbara V., Jeanne M. Tschann, Cynthia A. Gómez, and Steve Gregorich. 1998. Self-Efficacy to Use Condoms in Unmarried Latino Adults. *American Journal of Community Psychology* 26, no. 1: 53–71.

Massey, Douglas S. 1987. Understanding Mexican Migration to the United States. *American Journal of Sociology* 92, no. 6: 1372–1403.

Massey, Douglas S., Rafael Alarcón, Jorge Durand, and Humberto González. 1987. *Return to Aztlán: The Social Process of International Migration from Western Mexico.* Berkeley: University of California Press.

McCoy, Terry L. 1974. A Paradigmatic Analysis of Mexican Population Policy. In *The Dynamics of Population Policy in Latin America,* edited by Terry L. McCoy, 377–408. Cambridge: Ballinger.

Méndez Brown de Galaz, Elena. 1998. Cervical Cancer in Mexico and Sonora: Its Prevention and Risk Factors. Working paper presented at a seminar organized by the Transborder Consortium for Research and Action on Gender and Reproductive Health at the Mexico–U.S. Border. The Southwest Institute for Research on Women–University of Arizona, El Colegio de Sonora, and El Colegio de la Frontera Norte represent the Transborder Consortium.

Mernissi, Fatima. 1982. Virginity and Patriarchy. *Women's Studies International Forum* 5, no. 2: 183–91.

Messner, Michael A. 1992. *Power at Play: Sports and the Problem of Masculinity.* Boston: Beacon Press.

———. 1996. Studying Up on Sex. *Sociology of Sport Journal* 13, no. 3: 221–37.

———. 2000. *Politics of Masculinities: Men in Movements.* Walnut Creek, Calif.: AltaMira Press.

Mikawa, James K., Pete A. Morones, Antonio Gomez, Hillary L. Case, Dan Olsen, and Mary Jane Gonzalez-Huss. 1992. Cultural Practices of Hispanics: Implications for the Prevention of AIDS. *Hispanic Journal of Behavioral Sciences* 14, no. 4: 421–33.

Mirrer, Louise. 1996. *Women, Jews, and Muslims in the Texts of Reconquest Castile.* Ann Arbor: University of Michigan Press.

Mishra, Shiraz I., Ross F. Conner, and J. Raúl Magaña. 1996. *AIDS Crossing Borders: The Spread of HIV among Migrant Latinos.* Boulder, Colo.: Westview Press.

Módena, María Eugenia, and Zuanilda Mendoza. 2001. *Géneros y generaciones: Etnografía de las relaciones entre hombres y mujeres de la ciudad de México.* Mexico City: EDAMEX, S.A. de C.V. y Population Council.

Mohanty, Chandra Talpade. 1991. Under Western Eyes: Feminist Scholarship and Colonial Discourses. In *Third World Women and the Politics of Feminism,* edited by Chandra Talpade Mohanty, Ann Russo, and Lourdes Torres, 51–80. Bloomington: Indiana University Press.

Moraga, Cherríe. 1983. *Loving in the War Years: Lo que nunca pasó por sus labios.* Boston: South End Press.

Moraga, Cherríe, and Gloria Anzaldúa. 1981. *This Bridge Called My Back: Writings by Radical Women of Color.* New York: Kitchen Table, Women of Color Press.

Mummert, Gail. 1992. Changing Family Structure and Organization in a Setting of Male Emigration, Female Salaried Work, and the Commercialization of Agriculture: Case Study from Michoacán, Mexico. Lecture delivered on March 11, 1992, in the Research Seminar on Mexico and U.S.–Mexican Relations, Center for U.S.–Mexican Studies, University of California, San Diego.

———. 1994. From Metate to Despate: Rural Mexican Women's Salaried Labor and the Redefinition of Gendered Spaces and Roles. In *Women of the Mexican Countryside, 1850–1990,* edited by Heather Fowler-Salamini and Mary Kay Vaughan, 192–209. Tucson: University of Arizona Press.

Murphy, Peter F. 2001. *Studs, Tools, and the Family Jewels: Metaphors Men Live By.* Madison: University of Wisconsin Press.

Nathanson, Constance A. 1991. *Dangerous Passage.* Philadelphia: Temple University Press.

National Alliance for Hispanic Health. 2000. *The State of Hispanic Girls.* Washington, D.C.: Estrella Press.

Olivera, María Elena. 1995. Educación. *Revista Fem* 19, no. 152: 44.

Organista, Kurt C., Pamela Balls Organista, John R. Bola, Javier E. García de Alba G., and Marco Antonio Castillo Morán. 2000. Predictors of Condom Use in Mexican Migrant Laborers. *American Journal of Community Psychology* 28, no. 2: 245–65.

Organista, Kurt C., Pamela Balls Organista, Javier E. García de Alba G., Marco Antonio Castillo Morán, and Héctor Carrillo. 1996. AIDS and Condom-Related Knowledge, Beliefs, and Behaviors in Mexican Migrant Laborers. *Hispanic Journal of Behavioral Sciences* 18, no. 3: 392–406.

Organista, Kurt C., Pamela Balls Organista, Javier E. García de Alba, Marco Antonio Castillo Morán, and Luz Elena Ureta Carrillo. 1997. Survey of Condom-Related Beliefs, Behaviors, and Perceived Social Norms in Mexican Migrant Laborers. *Journal of Community Health* 22, no. 3: 185–98.

Ortiz, Vilma. 1996. The Mexican-Origin Population: Permanent Working Class or Emerging Middle Class? In *Ethnic Los Angeles,* edited by Roger Waldinger and Mehdi Bozorgmehr, 247–77. New York: Russell Sage Foundation.

Padilla, Amado M. 1980. *Acculturation: Theory, Models, and Some New Findings.* Boulder, Colo.: Westview Press.

Padilla Pimentel, Miguel. 1972. *La moral sexual en México.* Mexico City: Editorial Novaro, S.A.

Pagnini, Deanna L., and S. Philip Morgan. 1996. Racial Differences in Marriage and Childbearing: Oral History Evidence from the South in the Early Twentieth Century. *American Journal of Sociology* 101, no. 6: 1694–1718.

Paternostro, Silvana. 1998. *In the Land of God and Man: Confronting Our Sexual Culture.* New York: Dutton.

Paz, Octavio. 1950. *El laberinto de la soledad: Vida y pensamiento de México.* Repr., Mexico City: Fondo de Cultura Económica, 1987.

Peña, Manuel. 1991. Class, Gender, and Machismo: The "Treacherous Woman" Folklore of Mexican Male Workers. *Gender and Society* 5, no. 1: 30–46.

Pérez, Miguel A., and Helda L. Pinzón. 1997. Latino Perspectives on Sexuality. In vol. 3 of *The International Encyclopedia of Sexuality,* edited by Robert T. Francoeur, 1423–36. New York: Continuum.

Plummer, Ken. 1995. *Telling Sexual Stories: Power, Change, and Social Worlds.* London: Routledge.

Ponce, Dolores, Ana I. Solórzano, and Antonio Alonso. 1990. Lentas olas de sensualidad. In *El nuevo arte de amar: Usos y costumbres sexuales en México,* by Hermann Bellinghausen (Coordinador), 13–35. Mexico City: Cal y Arena.

Poniatowska, Elena. 2000. *Las mil y una . . . (la herida de Paulina).* Mexico City: Plaza & Janés Editores.

Portes, Alejandro. 1995. Children of Immigrants: Segmented Assimilation and Its Determinants. In *The Economic Sociology of Immigration: Essays on Networks, Ethnicity, and Entrepreneurship,* edited by Alejandro Portes, 248–79. New York: Russell Sage Foundation.

Portes, Alejandro, and Robert L. Bach. 1985. *Latin Journey: Cuban and Mexican Immigrants in the United States.* Berkeley: University of California Press.

Portes, Alejandro, and Rubén G. Rumbaut. 1996. *Immigrant America.* Berkeley: University of California Press.

Prieto, Yolanda. 1992. Cuban Women in New Jersey: Gender Relations and Change. In *Seeking Common Ground: Multidisciplinary Studies of Immigrant Women in the United States,* edited by Donna Gabaccia, 185–201. Westport, Conn.: Greenwood Press.

Prieur, Annick. 1998. *Mema's House, Mexico City: On Transvestites, Queens, and Machos.* Chicago: University of Chicago Press.

Pulerwitz, Julie, Jose Antonio Izazola-Licea, and Steven L. Gortmaker. 2001. Extrarelational Sex among Mexican Men and Their Partners' Risk of HIV and Other Sexually Transmitted Diseases. *American Journal of Public Health* 91, no. 10: 1650–52.

Raffaelli, Marcela, and Lenna L. Ontai. 2001. "She's sixteen years old and there's boys calling over to the house": An Exploratory Study of Sexual Socialization in Latino Families." *Culture, Health, and Sexuality* 3, no. 3: 295–310.

Raley, R. Kelly. 2001. Increasing Fertility in Cohabiting Unions: Evidence for the Second Demographic Transition in the United States? *Demography* 38, no. 1: 59–66.

Ramos Lira, Luciana, Mary P. Koss, and Nancy Felipe Russo. 1999. Mexican American Women's Definitions of Rape and Sexual Abuse. *Hispanic Journal of Behavioral Sciences* 21, no. 3: 236–65.

Rapp, Rayna. 1999. *Testing Women, Testing the Fetus: The Social Impact of Amniocentesis in America.* New York: Routledge.

Rayas, Lucía. 1998. Criminalizing Abortion: A Crime against Women. Report on Sexual Politics. *NACLA Report on the Americas* 31, no. 4: 22–26.

Reid, Pamela T., and Vanessa M. Bing. 2000. Sexual Roles of Girls and Women: An Ethnocultural Lifespan Perspective. In *Sexuality, Society, and Feminism,* edited by Cheryl B. Travis and Jacquelyn W. White, 141–66. Washington, D.C.: American Psychological Association.

Reinisch, June M., and Ruth Beasley. 1990. *The Kinsey Institute New Report on Sex.* New York: St. Martin's Press.

Rich, Adrienne. 1980. Compulsory Heterosexuality and Lesbian Existence. *Signs* 5, no. 4: 631–60.

Rivas Zivy, Marta. 1996. La entrevista a profundidad: Un abordaje en el campo de la sexualidad. In *Para comprender la subjetividad: Investigación cualitativa en salud reproductiva y sexualidad,* edited by Ivonne Szasz and Susana Lerner, 199–223. Mexico City: El Colegio de México.

———. 1997. La diversidad en la norma: Algunas diferencias en las significaciones de la sexualidad femenina. *Estudios Demográficos y Urbanos* 12, no. 1–2: 129–51.

———. 1998. Valores, creencias y significaciones de la sexualidad femenina: Una reflexión indispensable para la comprensión de las prácticas sexuales. In *Sexualidades en Mexico: Algunas aproximaciones desde la perspectiva de las ciencias sociales,* edited by Ivonne Szasz and Susana Lerner, with the collaboration of Lía Rojas Mira, 137–54. Mexico City: El Colegio de Mexico.

Rocha, Martha Eva. 1991. *El álbum de la mujer: Antología ilustrada de las mexicanas.* Vol. 4. Mexico City: Instituto Nacional de Antropología e Historia.

Rodríguez, Gabriela, Esther Corona, and Susan Pick. 1996. Educación para la sexualidad y la salud reproductiva. In *Mujer: Sexualidad y salud reproductiva en Mexico,* edited by Ana Langer and Kathryn Tolbert, 343–76. Mexico City: Population Council and EDAMEX.

Rodríguez, Victoria E. 2003. *Women in Contemporary Mexican Politics.* Austin: University of Texas Press.

Romero, Mary. 1992. *Maid in the U.S.A.* New York: Routledge.

Rosenberg, Lou. 1993. The House of Difference: Gender, Culture, and the Subject-in-Process on the American Stage. Special Issue — Critical Essays: Gay and Lesbian Writers of Color. *Journal of Homosexuality* 26, no. 2–3: 97–110.

Rosenthal-Urey, Ina. 1984. Church Records as a Source of Data on Mexican Migrant Networks: A Methodological Note. *International Migration Review* 18, no. 3: 767–81.

Ross, Ellen, and Rayna Rapp. 1997. Sex and Society: A Research Note from Social History and Anthropology. In *The Gender Sexuality Reader: Culture, History, Political Economy,* edited by Roger N. Lancaster and Micaela di Leonardo, 153–68. New York: Routledge.

Rouse, Roger. 1996. Mexican Migration and the Social Space of Postmodernism. In *Between Two Worlds: Mexican Immigrants in the United States,* edited by David G. Gutiérrez, 247–63. Jaguar Books on Latin America, no. 15. Wilmington, Del.: Scholarly Resources.

Rubin, Gayle. 1976. The Traffic in Women: Notes on the "Political Economy" of Sex. In *Toward an Anthology of Women,* edited by Rayna R. Reiter, 157–210. New York: Monthly Review Press.

Rubin, Jeffrey W. 1996. Decentering the Regime: Culture and Regional Politics in Mexico. *Latin American Research Review* 31, no. 3: 85–126.

Rubin, Lillian B. 1979. *Women of a Certain Age: The Midlife Search for Self.* New York: Harper and Row.

———. 1983. *Intimate Strangers: Men and Women Together.* New York: Harper and Row.

Rubio, Eusebio. 1997. Mexico (Estados Unidos Mexicanos). In *The International Encyclopedia of Sexuality,* edited by Robert T. Francoeur, 869–94. New York: Continuum.

Ruiz, Vicki L. 1992. The Flapper and the Chaperone: Historical Memory among Mexican-American Women. In *Seeking Common Ground: Multidisciplinary Studies of Immigrant Women in the United States,* edited by Donna Gabaccia, 141–57. Westport, Conn.: Greenwood Press.

———. 1993. "Star Struck": Acculturation, Adolescence, and the Mexican American Woman, 1920–1950. In *Building With Our Hands: New Directions in Chicana Studies,* edited by Adela de la Torre and Beatríz M. Pesquera, 109–29. Berkeley: University of California Press.

Rumbaut, Rubén G. 1997. Assimilation and Its Discontents: Between Rhetoric and Reality. *International Migration Review* 31, no. 4: 923–60.

Salgado de Snyder, V. Nelly, Andrea Acevedo, María de Jesús Díaz-Pérez, and Alicia Saldívar-Garduño. 2000. Understanding the Sexuality of Mexican-born Women and Their Risk for HIV/AIDS. *Psychology of Women Quarterly* 24, no. 1: 100–109.

Salgado de Snyder, V. Nelly, María de Jesús Díaz-Pérez, and Margarita Maldonado. 1996. AIDS: Risk Behaviors among Rural Mexican Women Married to Migrant Workers in the United States. *AIDS Education and Prevention* 8, no. 2: 134–42.

Sassen, Saskia. 1991. *The Global City: New York, London, Tokyo.* Princeton, N.J.: Princeton University Press.

Sassen-Koob, Saskia. 1984. The New Labor Demand in Global Cities. In *Cities in Transformation: Class, Capital and the State,* edited by Michael Peter Smith, 139–71. Beverly Hills, Calif.: Sage.

Schoenkopf, Rebecca. 2001. Like a Virgin: Tight for the Very First Time. *OC Weekly,* April 3, 2001. http://www.ocweekly.com/ink/archives/97/lede-2.13.98–3.shtml.

Scott, Sheryl A., Cynthia M. Jorgensen, and Lourdes Suarez. 1998. Concerns and Dilemmas of Hispanics AIDS Information Seekers: Spanish-speaking Callers to the CDC National AIDS Hotline. *Health Education and Behavior* 25, no. 4: 501–16.

Scribner, Richard. 1996. Paradox as Paradigm: The Health Outcomes of Mexican Americans (editorial). *American Journal of Public Health* 86, no. 3: 303–5.

Secunda, Victoria. 1992. Women and Their Fathers: The Sexual and Romantic Impact of the First Man in Your Life. New York: Delta.

Segal, Lynne. 1994. *Straight Sex: Rethinking the Politics of Pleasure.* Berkeley: University of California Press.

Segura, Denise A., and Jennifer L. Pierce. 1993. Chicana/o Family Structure and Gender Personality: Chodorow, Familism, and Psychoanalytic Sociology Revisited. *Signs* 19, no. 1: 62–91.

Seidman, Steven. 1994. *Contested Knowledge: Social Theory in the Postmodern Era.* Oxford: Blackwell.

Shahidian, Hammed. 1999. Gender and Sexuality among Immigrant Iranians in Canada. *Sexualities* 2, no. 2: 189–222.

Silverman, David. 1994. *Interpreting Qualitative Data: Methods for Analysing Talk, Text, and Interaction.* London: Sage.

Skerry, Peter, and Stephen J. Rockwell. 1998. The Cost of a Tighter Border: People-Smuggling Networks. *Los Angeles Times,* Opinion Section, May 3, 1998.

Smith, Dorothy. 1987. *The Everyday World as Problematic: A Feminist Sociology.* Boston: Northeastern University Press.

Solís, Guadalupe Irma. 1998. Personal interview with Dr. Guadalupe I. Solís in Ciudad Valles, San Luis Potosí, Mexico, January 3.

Sprecher, Susan, and Pamela C. Reagan. 1996. College Virgins: How Men and Women Perceive Their Sexual Status. *Journal of Sex Research* 33, no. 1: 3–15.

Stacey, Judith. 1998. *Brave New Families: Stories of Domestic Upheaval in Late-Twentieth-Century America.* Berkeley: University of California Press.

Stack, Carol B. 1994. Different Voices, Different Visions: Gender, Culture, and Moral Reasoning. In *Women of Color in U.S. Society,* edited by Maxine Baca Zinn and Bonnie Thornton Dill, 291–301. Philadelphia: Temple University Press.

Stavans, Ilán. 1996. The Latin Phallus. In *Muy Macho: Latino Men Confront Their Manhood,* edited by Ray González, 143–64. New York: Anchor Books.

Stein, Arlene. 1997. *Sex and Sensibility: Stories of a Lesbian Generation.* Berkeley: University of California Press.

Stephen, Lynn. 2002. Sexualities and Genders in Zapotec Oaxaca. *Latin American Perspectives* 29, no. 2: 41–59.

Stern, Claudio, Cristina Fuentes-Zurita, Laura Ruth Lozano-Treviño, and Fenneke Reysoo. 2003. Masculinidad y salud sexual y reproductiva: Un estudio de caso con adolescentes de la Ciudad de México. *Salud Pública de México* 45, no. 1: 34–43.

Stern, Steve J. 1995. *The Secret History of Gender: Women, Men, and Power in Late Colonial Mexico.* Chapel Hill: University of North Carolina Press.

Suárez-Orozco, Marcelo, and Mariela M. Páez. 2002. *Latinos: Remaking America.* Berkeley: University of California Press; Cambridge, Mass.: Harvard University, David Rockefeller Center for Latin American Studies.

Szasz, Ivonne. 1997. Género y valores sexuales: Un estudio de caso entre un grupo de mujeres mexicanas. *Estudios Demográficos y Urbanos* 12, no. 1–2: 155–75.

———. 1998. Masculine Identity and Meanings of Sexuality: A Review of Research in Mexico. *Reproductive Health Matters* 6, no. 12: 97–104.

Szasz, Ivonne, and Juan Guillermo Figueroa. 1997. Sexuality, Gender Relations, and Female Empowerment. Conference presentation at the seminar on

Female Empowerment and Demographic Processes: Moving Beyond Cairo, Lund, Sweden, April 21–24.

Thompson, E. P. 1991. *Customs in Common.* New York: New Press.

Thorne, Barrie, and Marilyn Yalom. 1992. *Rethinking the Family: Some Feminist Questions.* Rev. ed. Boston: Northeastern University Press.

Tostado Gutiérrez, Marcela. 1991. *El álbum de la mujer: Antología ilustrada de las mexicanas.* Vol. 2. Mexico City: Instituto Nacional de Antropología e Historia.

Tuñón, Julia. 1991. *El álbum de la mujer: Antología ilustrada de las mexicanas.* Vol. 3. Mexico City: Instituto Nacional de Antropología e Historia.

Tuñón Pablos, Enriqueta. 1991. *El álbum de la mujer: Antología ilustrada de las mexicanas,* Vol. 1. Mexico City: Instituto Nacional de Antropología e Historia.

Tuñón Pablos, Julia. 2000. *Women in Mexico: A Past Unveiled.* Austin: University of Texas Press.

Twinam, Ann. 1989. Honor, Sexuality, and Illegitimacy in Colonial Spanish America. In *Sexuality and Marriage in Colonial Latin America,* edited by Asunción Lavrin, 118–55. Lincoln: University of Nebraska Press.

U.S.–Mexico Migration Panel. 2001. *Mexico–U.S. Migration: A Shared Responsibility.* Report of the Panel, convened by the Carnegie Endowment for International Peace (International Migration Policy Program) and the Instituto Tecnológico Autónomo de México (Faculty of International Relations). Washington, D.C.: Carnegie Endowment for International Peace. http://www.migrationpolicy.org/pubs/2001.php.

Valenzuela, Abel, Jr. 1999. Day Laborers in Southern California: Preliminary Findings from the Day Labor Survey. Working Paper, no. 99–04. Center for the Study of Urban Poverty, Institute for Social Science Research, University of California, Los Angeles.

———. 2002. Working on the Margins in Metropolitan Los Angeles: Immigrants in Day Labor Work. *Migraciones Internacionales* 1, no. 2: 5–28.

———. 2003. Day Labor Work. *Annual Review of Sociology* 29, no. 1: 307–33.

Valenzuela, Abel, Jr., and Elizabeth Gonzalez. 2000. Latino Earnings Inequality: Immigrant and Native-Born Differences. In *Prismatic Metropolis: Inequality in Los Angeles,* edited by Lawrence D. Bobo, Melvin L. Oliver, James H. Johnson Jr., and Abel Valenzuela Jr., 249–78. New York: Russell Sage Foundation.

Valle, Victor M., and Rodolfo D. Torres. 2000. *Latino Metropolis.* Minneapolis: University of Minnesota Press.

Vance, Carole S. 1984. *Pleasure and Danger: Exploring Female Sexuality.* Boston: Routledge and Kegan Paul.

Varley, Ann. 2000. Women and the Home in Mexican Family Law. In *Hidden Histories of Gender and the State in Latin America,* edited by Elizabeth Dore and Maxine Molyneux, 238–61. Durham, N.C.: Duke University Press.

Vigil, Diego. 2002. Community Dynamics and the Rise of Street Gangs. In *Latinos: Remaking America,* edited by Marcelo M. Suárez-Orozco and Mariela M.

Páez, 97–109. Berkeley: University of California Press; Cambridge, Mass.: Harvard University, David Rockefeller Center for Latin American Studies.

Villarruel, Antonia M. 1998. Cultural Influences on the Sexual Attitudes, Beliefs, and Norms of Young Latina Adolescents. *Journal of the Society of Pediatric Nurses* 3, no. 2: 69–79.

Waldinger, Roger, and Michael I. Lichter. 2003. *How the Other Half Works: Immigration and the Social Organization of Labor.* Berkeley: University of California Press.

Weeks, Jeffrey. 1985. *Sexuality and Its Discontents.* London: Routledge.

West, Candace, and Don H. Zimmerman. 1987. Doing Gender. *Gender and Society* 1, no. 2: 125–51.

Williams, Norma. 1990. *The Mexican American Family: Tradition and Change.* Dix Hills, N.Y.: General Hall.

Wilson, Fiona. 1990. *De la casa al taller: Mujeres, trabajo y clase social en la industria textil y del vestido. Santiago Tangamandapio.* Zamora: El Colegio de Michoacán.

Woo Morales, Ofelia. 1995. Las mujeres mexicanas indocumentadas en la migración internacional y la movilidad transfronteriza. In *Mujeres, migración y maquila en la frontera,* edited by Soledad González, Olivia Ruiz, Laura Velasco, and Ofelia Woo Morales, 65–87. Tijuana: El Colegio de la Frontera Norte.

———. 1997. *La migración de las mujeres mexicanas hacia Estados Unidos.* Ph.D. diss., Universidad de Guadalajara.

Youssef, Nadia. 1973. Cultural Ideals, Feminine Behavior, and Family Control. *Comparative Studies in Society and History* 15, no. 3: 326–47.

Ypeij, Annelou. 1998. Las hijas "buenas" y las empacadoras zamoranas. In *Rehaciendo las diferencias: Identidades de género en Michoacán y Yucatán,* edited by Gail Mummert and Luis Alfonso Ramírez Carrillo, 179–209. Zamora: El Colegio de Michoacán y la Universidad Autónoma de Yucatán.

Zambrana, Ruth E. 1995. *Understanding Latino Families: Scholarship, Policy, and Practice.* Thousand Oaks, Calif.: Sage.

Zavella, Patricia. 1997. Playing with Fire: The Gendered Construction of Chicana/Mexicana Sexuality. In *The Gender Sexuality Reader: Culture, History, Political Economy,* edited by Roger N. Lancaster and Micaela di Leonardo, 392–408. New York: Routledge.

Zhou, Xiao. 1989. Virginity and Premarital Sex in Contemporary China. *Feminist Studies* 15, no. 2: 279–88.

Index

Text:	10/13 Galliard
Display:	Galliard
Indexer:	Sharon Sweeney
Compositor:	BookMatters, Berkeley
Printer and binder:	Sheridan Books, Inc.